ORIGINAL LETTERS

RELATIVE TO

THE ENGLISH REFORMATION.

The Parker Society.

Instituted A.D. M.DCCC.XL.

MVNDVS TRANSIT

For the Publication of the Works of the Fathers and Early Writers of the Reformed English Church.

ORIGINAL LETTERS

RELATIVE TO

THE ENGLISH REFORMATION,

WRITTEN DURING THE REIGNS OF

KING HENRY VIII., KING EDWARD VI.,

AND QUEEN MARY:

CHIEFLY FROM THE ARCHIVES OF ZURICH.

TRANSLATED FROM AUTHENTICATED COPIES OF THE AUTOGRAPHS,

AND EDITED FOR

The Parker Society,

BY THE

REV. HASTINGS ROBINSON, D.D. F.A.S

RECTOR OF GREAT WARLEY, ESSEX;
AND FORMERLY FELLOW OF ST JOHN'S COLLEGE, CAMBRIDGE.

THE FIRST PORTION.

CAMBRIDGE:

PRINTED AT

THE UNIVERSITY PRESS.

M.DCCC.XLVI.

ADVERTISEMENT.

IN the preface to the Second Series of letters from the Archives of Zurich and other repositories in Switzerland, published by the Parker Society, it was stated that the Council had procured from the same collections more than three hundred other letters, written during the reigns of Henry VIII., Edward VI., and queen Mary, also having reference to ecclesiastical affairs and the progress of the Reformation. The translation of these letters will form the present and a subsequent publication : for as the printing proceeded, it was found that the entire series could not be conveniently contained in one volume : but as the first portion is now completed, the Council have issued it as one of the earliest books in return for the subscriptions of the present year, various though unavoidable circumstances having de-layed the publication of another work originally intended to be issued at this time.

The question respecting the chronological or other ar-rangement of the letters now published was long and maturely considered : in the result it appeared best to print those of each writer together. As the present correspondence does not, like the letters written in the reign of Queen Elizabeth, involve that regular view of the history of the times, which made the chronological arrangement in that case desirable, the plan now adopted has been considered, on the whole, the least liable to objection. A table of contents will how-ever be given with the succeeding portion, which will em-brace the entire series of ante-Elizabethan correspondence, in the chronological order of the respective letters. The Indices, and a fuller preface, will also be given with the remaining portion, which will form another of the volumes of the present or following year, whichever may be found most expedient, and according to the progress made with the other works now in course of publication; the Council not being unmindful of the general desire of the members, frequently expressed, that the books should be issued as speedily as possible in return for the subscriptions of each year. It is however hardly necessary to state, that the uncertainties attendant upon all literary proceedings will often prevent the adoption of that course which would be most in accordance with the wishes of those concerned in them. The plan of publication adopted by the Society, it will also be remembered, is not that of works printed for ordinary circulation; and while its volumes involve far more than the usual difficulties of preparing for and passing through the press, the precise time of the appearance of any particular book is not a matter of so much importance as in publications for common sale.

The greater part of these letters are now printed for the first time: they will be found to contain many details of interest, relative to various proceedings of that period, and occasionally to give much information respecting the customs and manners of the times, as well as the private history of the writers and other individuals to whom they refer.

October 1, 1846.

CONTENTS.

viii

ERRATA.

p. 25, l. 11, *for* you *read* your.
p. 80, l. 17, *for* the sixth Sunday before Easter, *read* Good Friday.
p. 113, l. penult. *for* Jenkins *read* Tomkins.

LETTER I.

EDWARD VI. TO THE SENATE OF ZURICH.

Dated at WESTMINSTER, *Oct.* 20, 1549.

EDWARD the sixth, by the grace of God, of England, France, and Ireland, king, defender of the Faith, and of the church of England and Ireland supreme head upon earth, &c. To the honourable and valiant Lords of Zurich, our right entirely beloved friends, greeting. After we had taken upon ourselves, by ancient and hereditary right, the government of our kingdoms, nothing was more ardently desired by us than to conciliate, and most firmly retain, the friendship of those sovereigns who had been especially esteemed by our most serene father of most happy memory : and as in the number of these he always regarded, as long as he lived, your most noble and valiant nation; so we likewise cannot but regard you with especial esteem, and exceedingly value your friendship; and the rather, because we have understood by the frequent letters of our faithful and beloved servant, Christopher Mont, both your favourable disposition towards us, and ready inclination to deserve well of us. In addition to which, there is also a mutual agreement between us concerning the christian religion and true godliness, which ought to render this friendship of ours, by God's blessing, yet more intimate. We therefore return you our warmest thanks for your singular and favourable disposition towards us, which you shall always find to be reciprocal on our part, whenever an opportunity shall present itself. We have therefore commanded this our servant to salute you most cordially, to inform you more fully of our affection and good-will, and to lay before you, in our name, some other things which we have thought fit should at this time be made known to you. We therefore earnestly request you to place assured and undoubting reliance upon what he shall communicate. So farewell. From our palace at Westminster, Oct. 20, A.D. 1549, and of our reign the third.

Your good friend,

EDWARD.

LETTER II.

LADY JANE SEYMOUR[1] TO BUCER AND FAGIUS.

Dated at SION, *June* 12, 1549.

I HAVE perused your letter, most reverend fathers, which has not only pleased, but highly delighted me. For I easily perceived therein your singular good-will towards me, a grace and eloquence equal to that of Cicero, together with a most abiding remembrance of me, which, as it is in most persons of very rare occurrence, I cannot sufficiently admire in you. But when I consider in what way I can recompense the sincerity of your friendship, I plainly perceive that this is quite out of my power; and that I can only offer you, as I shall do as long as I live, my warmest acknowledgments. I dare not presume to write to you how very acceptable were the books that you presented to my sister and myself, for fear lest my ineloquent commendation of them may appear impertinent. From your exceeding praise of the addresses of myself and my sister, which we might more truly be said to babble than to recite before you, I perceive your incomparable benevolence and friendship, abounding in such kind exaggeration respecting us. For neither my sister nor myself assume to ourselves a single atom of this commendation, nor have we any right to do so. My mother, thank God, is in good health: she desires her best respects to you both, and also thanks you for your salutations to her grace. Farewell, both of you, and may your life long be preserved! Dated at Sion[2], June 12, 1549.

Your attached well wisher,

JANE SEYMOUR.

[1 This lady was the third daughter of the protector Somerset, and intended by him to become the wife of Edward VI. She afterwards became one of the maids of honour to queen Elizabeth, and died unmarried in 1561. Strype, Mem. II. ii. 7, and Ann. I. i. 399.]

[2 Sion House was built on the site of the dissolved monastery of that name at Isleworth, by the protector Somerset, to whom the site

LETTER III.

HENRY[3], DUKE OF SUFFOLK, TO HENRY BULLINGER.

Dated at LONDON, *Dec.* 21, 1551.

THAT you have not received, my very dear Bullinger, any letter from me before now, by which I might testify towards you that good-will which you have on so many accounts deserved, and also thank you most heartily for your exceeding courtesy to me, which I most entirely appreciate, has been solely attributable to those affairs of state, upon which I had to bestow all my zeal, labour, and diligence, unless I would fail in satisfying my duty to God, my own dignity, and the expectation of the public. You will therefore, I know, easily pardon my delay, especially as I would have you assured that my regard for you can be diminished by no circumstances, and much less by time. For the book[4] which you have published under the auspices of my name, I return you, not only for my own sake, but for that of the whole church of Christ, the thanks I ought; and I acknowledge the divine goodness towards his church, and, as Paul expresses it, *the love of God to man*[5], that he has chosen to adorn and illuminate his church with such lights, as that we who are less enlightened, may follow those guides in the beaten path of true religion, who may both be able, by reason of the gifts they have received from God, and willing, by reason of their affection to their brethren, diligently to point out the way in which we ought to walk. It would indeed have been all

was granted by Edward VI., who, on the duke's execution, bestowed it upon John Dudley, duke of Northumberland. It was afterwards given by James I. to Henry Percy, the ninth earl of Northumberland, in which family it now remains.]

[3 Henry Grey, third marquis of Dorset, having married Frances, daughter of Charles first duke of Suffolk, by whom he had lady Jane Grey, was created duke of Suffolk, Oct. 10, 1551. He was beheaded in 1554.]

[4 Bullinger had dedicated a volume of his Decades to the duke of Suffolk in March, 1551. See Strype, Mem. II. i. 397.]

[5 φιλανθρωπίαν. Tit. iii. 4.]

over with us, had not he provided pillars of this kind to support his church, which otherwise would beyond all doubt have been overthrown.

I acknowledge myself also to be much indebted to you on my daughter's account, for having always exhorted her in your godly letters to a true faith in Christ, the study of the scriptures, purity of manners, and innocence of life; and I earnestly request you to continue these exhortations as frequently as possible. Farewell, most accomplished Bullinger, and may Almighty God prosper your endeavours in the church, and evermore defend you! From my house in London. Dec. 21, 1551.

HENRY, DUKE OF SUFFOLK.

LETTER IV.

LADY JANE GREY TO HENRY BULLINGER.

Dated at [BRADGATE, *July* 12, 1551[1].]

I GIVE you, most learned sir, unceasing thanks, and shall do so as long as I live, for I cannot engage to requite the obligation; as I seem to myself quite unable to make a suitable return for such exceeding courtesy, unless indeed you should be of opinion that I return a favour while I retain it in my remembrance. Nor are these professions made without reason. For I have received from you a most weighty and eloquent epistle, which was indeed very gratifying to me, not only because, to the neglect of more important engagements, you have condescended to write from so distant a country, and in your declining age, to me, who am unworthy of the correspondence of so distinguished a personage; but also because your writings are of such a character, as that they contain, not mere ordinary topics for amusement, but pious and divine thoughts for instruction, admonition and counsel, on such points especially, as are suited to my age and sex and the

[1 This letter was sent to Zurich inclosed in one bearing the same date from John ab Ulmis.]

dignity of my family. In this epistle, as in every thing else
that you have published to the great edification of the christian
commonwealth, you have shewn yourself not only a man of
exquisite learning and singular acquirement, but also a skilful, prudent, and godly counsellor; one who can relish nothing
that is not excellent, think nothing that is not divine, enjoin
nothing that is not profitable, and produce nothing that is not
virtuous, pious, and worthy of so reverend a father. Oh!
happy me, to be possessed of such a friend and so wise a
counsellor! (for, as Solomon says, "in the multitude of coun-
sellors there is safety[2];") and to be connected by the ties of
friendship and intimacy with so learned a man, so pious a
divine, and so intrepid a champion of true religion! On
many accounts I consider myself beholden to Almighty God;
but especially for having, after I was bereaved of the pious
Bucer[3], that most learned man and holy father, who unweari-
edly did not cease, day and night, and to the utmost of his
ability, to supply me with all necessary instructions and direc-
tions for my conduct in life; and who by his excellent advice
promoted and encouraged my progress and advancement in all
virtue, godliness, and learning; for having, I say, afforded me
in his place a man so worthy to be reverenced as yourself, and
who, I hope, will continue, as you have begun, to spur me on,
when I loiter and am inclined to delay. For no better fortune
can await me than to be thought worthy of the correspondence
and most wholesome admonitions of men so renowned, whose
virtues cannot be sufficiently eulogized; and to experience
the same happiness as was enjoyed by Blesilla[4], Paula, and
Eustochium, to whom, as it is recorded, Saint Jerome imparted instruction, and brought them by his discourses to the
knowledge of divine truths; or, the happiness of that venerable matron[5], to whom St John addressed an exhortatory

[2 Prov. xi. 14. In the original, written in Latin, Lady Jane quotes
the Hebrew.]

[3 Bucer died at Cambridge, Feb. 27, 1551.]

[4 Blesilla was the eldest, and Eustochium the third, daughter of
Paula, who was descended from the Roman family of that name.
They were instructed in the christian religion by Jerome. Paula
followed him to Bethlehem, where she died, after having lived there
twenty years in a monastery erected by herself.]

[5 Called in the English version *the elect lady.* 2 John, 1.]

and evangelical epistle; or that, lastly, of the mother[1] of Severus, who profited by the counsels of Origen, and was obedient to his precepts. All which personages were less indebted for their renown and celebrity to their beauty of person, nobility of birth, and large possessions, than to the glory and happiness they derived from the instructions of wise men, who, though singularly eminent for erudition and piety, did not disdain to lead them, as it were, by the hand to every thing excellent, and to suggest to them such thoughts as might especially conduce to their eternal salvation and happiness in the life to come. And I request again and again, that as you cannot be deemed inferior to any of these in understanding, or learning, or godliness, you will condescend to manifest a like kindness to myself. My unreserved requests may carry with them an appearance of boldness; but if you will consider the motive by which I am actuated, namely, that I may draw forth from the storehouse of your piety such instruction as may tend both to direct my conduct, and confirm my faith in Christ my Saviour, your goodness cannot, and your wisdom will not, allow you to censure them.

From that little volume[2] of pure and unsophisticated religion, which you lately sent to my father and myself, I gather daily, as out of a most beautiful garden, the sweetest flowers. My father also, as far as his weighty engagements permit, is diligently occupied in the perusal of it: but whatever advantage either of us may derive from thence, we are bound to render thanks to you for it, and to God on your account; for we cannot think it right to receive with ungrateful minds such and so many truly divine benefits, conferred by Almighty God through the instrumentality of yourself and those like you, not a few of whom Germany is now in this respect so happy as to possess. If it be customary with mankind, as indeed it ought to be, to return favour for favour, and to shew ourselves mindful of benefits bestowed; how much rather should we endeavour to embrace with joyfulness the benefits conferred by divine goodness, and

[1 Mammæa, mother of the emperor Alexander Severus, caused Origen to come from Alexandria to Antioch, that she might hear him preach, A.D. 229.]

[2 This was a treatise on Christian Perfection, dedicated in 1551 to Henry II. of France.]

at least to acknowledge them with our gratitude, though we may be unable to make an adequate return!

I now come to that part of your letter which contains a commendation of myself, which as I cannot claim, so also I ought not to allow: but whatever the divine goodness may have bestowed upon me, I ascribe solely to himself, as the chief and sole author of any thing in me that bears any semblance of what is good; and to whom I entreat you, most accomplished sir, to offer your constant prayers on my behalf, that he may so direct me and all my actions, that I may not be found unworthy of his so great goodness. My most noble father would have written to you, to thank you both for the important labours in which you are engaged, and also for the singular courtesy you have manifested by inscribing with his name and publishing under his auspices your fifth Decade, had he not been summoned by most weighty business in his majesty's service to the remotest parts of Britain; but as soon as public affairs shall afford him leisure, he is determined, he says, to write to you with all diligence[3]. To conclude, as I am now beginning to learn Hebrew, if you will point out some way and method of pursuing this study to the greatest advantage, you will confer on me a very great obligation.

Farewell, brightest ornament and support of the whole church of Christ; and may Almighty God long preserve you to us and to his church!

Your most devoted,
JANE GREY.

LETTER V.

LADY JANE GREY TO HENRY BULLINGER.
Dated at [BRADGATE, July 7, 1552.]

I SHOULD seem altogether ungrateful, unmindful of my duty, and unworthy of your favours, could I do otherwise than thank you, most accomplished sir, for your many acts of

[3 See the preceding Letter written subsequently to this.]

kindness to myself. I do this however with diffidence, inasmuch as the great friendship which you desire to exist between us, and the many favours you have conferred upon one who is so entirely undeserving of them, seem to demand something more than mere thanks; and I cannot satisfactorily repay by my poor and worthless correspondence the debt of gratitude I owe you. The consideration also of my unfitness to address a letter to a person of your eminence, greatly adds to my uncomfortable feelings; nor indeed should I either desire or presume to disturb your important labours with my trifles and puerilities, or interrupt your eloquence by my so great rudeness of speech, only that I know I have no other means of testifying my gratitude, and that I have no doubt of your accustomed and long experienced indulgence.

With respect to the letter I lately received from you, you must know, that after having read it twice over, (for one perusal did not satisfy me,) I seemed to have derived as much benefit from your excellent and truly divine precepts, as I have scarcely obtained from the daily perusal of the best authors. You exhort me to embrace a genuine and sincere faith in Christ my Saviour. I will endeavour to satisfy you in this respect, as far as God shall enable me to do; but as I acknowledge faith to be his gift, I ought therefore only to promise so far as he may see fit to bestow it upon me. I shall not however cease to pray, with the apostles, that he may of his goodness daily increase it in me. And to this I will add, as you exhort me, and with the divine blessing, such holiness of life, as my (alas!) too feeble powers may enable me to practise. Do you, meanwhile, with your wonted kindness, make daily mention of me in your prayers. In the study of Hebrew I shall pursue that method which you so clearly point out. Farewell, and may God protect you in the task you have undertaken, and prosper you for evermore!

Your most religiously obedient,

JANE GREY.

LETTER VI.

LADY JANE GREY TO HENRY BULLINGER.

Before *June* 1553.

THE tardy performance of a duty, most learned sir, ought not to be censured, especially if it has not been omitted through neglect. The truth is, I am at a great distance from you, the couriers are few, and news reaches me slowly : but as I can now avail myself of the messenger, by whom my letters to you, and yours to me, have usually been conveyed, I must not be wanting in my duty of writing to you, but as diligently as possible, by word and deed, discharge the obligation. For so great is your authority with all men, so great, as I hear, is the solidity of your preaching, so great too is the integrity of your conduct, according to the report of those who know you, that foreign and remote nations, as well as your own countrymen, are excited not only by your words, but by your actions, to follow after a good and happy life. For you are not only, as St James[1] says, a diligent herald and preacher of the gospel, and of the holy commands of God, but also a true observer and doer of them ; and you manifest in your own life the practice that your precepts enjoin, not deceiving yourself. Neither, indeed, do you resemble those who behold their natural face in a glass, and, as soon as they have gone away, forget the form of it ; but you preach true and sound doctrine, and by your manner of life afford an example and pattern for others to follow what you both enjoin and practise. But why do I thus address your gravity, when my ignorance is such that I can neither adequately praise your piety, nor sufficiently eulogise your integrity of life, nor set forth your profound and admirable learning in a becoming manner? Were I indeed to extol you as truth requires, I should need either the oratorical powers of Demosthenes, or the eloquence of Cicero ; for your merits are so great, as to demand not only length of time, but an acuteness of intellect and elegance of expression far beyond that of my age to set them forth. For God, it seems, has looked upon you with

[1 See James i. 22—24.]

such complacency, as to have fitted you both for his kingdom
and for this world : for in this earthly prison you pass your
days, as though you were dead; whereas you live, and this
not only to Christ in the first place, without whom there can
be no life, and in the next place to yourself; but also to
others without number, whom you strenuously labour and
assiduously endeavour to bring, by God's blessing, to that
immortality which, when you shall have departed this life,
you will obtain yourself.   And that your piety may accomplish what you desire, I will not cease to implore of God, the
supreme ruler of the universe, nor constantly to importune
the divine ears for your long continuance in this life.

In writing to you in this manner I have exhibited more
boldness than prudence : but so great has been your kindness
towards me, in condescending to write to me, a stranger, and
in supplying the necessary instruction for the adornment of
my understanding and the improvement of my mind, that I
should justly appear chargeable with neglect and forgetfulness
of duty, were I not to shew myself mindful of you and of
your deservings in every possible way.   Besides, I entertain
the hope that you will excuse the more than feminine boldness of me, who, girlish and unlearned as I am, presume to
write to a man who is the father of learning; and that you
will pardon that rudeness which has made me not hesitate
to interrupt your more important occupations with my vain
trifles and puerile correspondence.   Let me but obtain your
indulgence, and I shall consider myself on every account exceedingly indebted to your kindness.   For if I have been to
blame in this matter, you must ascribe it rather to the ex-
cess of my regard for you and for your virtues, than either
to a boldness which ought not at all to exist in our sex, or
a temerity which is for the most part adverse to our better
judgment; inasmuch as the splendour of your endowments is
so dazzling to my mental perception, whenever I read your
works or meditate upon yourself, that I do not consider what
is becoming to my condition, but what is due to your worth
and excellence.   My mind, moreover, is fluctuating and un-
decided : for while I consider my age, sex, and mediocrity, or
rather infancy in learning, each of these things, much more
all of them, deter me from writing ; but when I call to mind
the eminence of your virtues, the celebrity of your character,

and the magnitude of your favours towards me, the higher consideration yields to the inferior; a sense of what is becoming me gives way to your worth, and the respect which your merits demand usually prevails over all other considerations.

It now only remains for me, most illustrious sir, earnestly to entreat you cordially to salute in my name, though I am personally unacquainted with him, the excellent Bibliander[1], that pattern of erudition, godliness, and authority. For so great is the reputation of his learning in our country, and so renowned his name among all people, by reason of the singular endowments which God has bestowed upon him, that though I have acquired but little learning myself, I cannot resist my inclination to pay respect to the piety and integrity of such a man, who, if I am not mistaken, has been sent to us from heaven. And I pray God that such pillars of the church as you both are, may long enjoy good health. As long as I shall be permitted to live, I shall not cease to offer you my good wishes, to thank you for the kindness you have shewed me, and to pray for your welfare. Farewell, learned sir.

Your piety's most devoted,

JANE GREY.

LETTER VII.[2]

ARCHBISHOP CRANMER TO JOACHIM VADIAN[3].

Dated [1537.]

HAVING obtained a release, or rather a respite, from public affairs and deliberations, and beginning, illustrious and most learned Vadian, at the turn of the year, to reply to you among my other learned correspondents, to whose letters I had long been owing an answer, (to you, I say, as having

[1 Theodore Bibliander, or Buchman, was born in 1504, at Bischoffzel near St Gall. He was professor of theology at Zurich, where he died in 1564.]

[2 The original of this letter is published by Colomesius and others: (see Strype, Cranmer, 94, 740) also in Jenkyns's Remains of Cranmer, Vol. I. p. 193.]

[3 Joachim Vadian was born at St Gall in Switzerland, in 1484. He was distinguished as a scholar and mathematician.]

received your letter last winter, together with a literary present, which kind of presents I always regard as of the greatest value,) I first begin to consider with myself, and entertain some apprehension, lest by my so long protracted silence I may have given occasion in your mind to some suspicion or opinion not altogether favourable to me. For I know that it is usual among the generality of mankind, that when one person sends his commendations to another, he anxiously expects an acknowledgment of them by the very first opportunity : and if this be delayed, he will suspect that it has been owing to pride, or neglect, or at least forgetfulness; and will conclude beforehand that the party will continue such through the whole of his life, as he has been found to be upon a first introduction. Whereas the person who sends a speedy reply, is judged to have done so from kind and friendly motives, and is therefore regarded as courteous, accessible, and grateful ; he on the other hand, who is tardy in his acknowledgments, is considered hard of access, and a person of rude and disagreeable manners. So true it is, that whatever a man does quickly and without delay, he may be said to do twice over. But I promise myself a far better reception from your more than ordinary discretion and courtesy, and am confident that you will take in good part this my involuntary tardiness or delay, and not ascribe it so much to my manners as to my engagements. The nature and importance of these has, I think, long since been made known to you by report; and I have written something respecting them to our common friend Grynæus, who will, I doubt not, as the rights of friendship require, make you acquainted with every circumstance. To him therefore I refer you, in case you are offended with me in this matter, as to one who will render me more excusable in your eyes.

I perceive in your letter, and readily accept and embrace, your good-will towards me, and inclination to cultivate a more intimate friendship with me. For I consider you as one who, by reason of your extraordinary erudition, (by which I shall not scruple to acknowledge that I have myself derived benefit,) and of your probity of morals, confirmed by the testimony of many most excellent persons, is worthy of being regarded by me with all love, favour, and respect. Nevertheless, if I may candidly express my sentiments, (as ought to be the case between good men,) the subject you treat of in those six books[1] which you sent me as a present, is altogether displeasing to me; and I could wish you had bestowed your labours to better purpose, and commenced an agreeable friendship with myself under better, or at least more approved auspices. For, unless I see stronger evidence brought forward than I have yet been able to see, I desire neither to be the patron nor the approver of the opinion maintained by you. And I am plainly convinced, and from this circumstance especially, that the cause is not a good one, because you who are so shrewd, so eloquent, and so perfectly accomplished in all arts and learning, do not seem to defend and support it with sufficient vigour. I have seen almost every thing that has been written and published either by Œcolampadius or Zuinglius, and I have come to the conclusion that the writings of every man must be read with discrimination. And perhaps one might apply to these men, and not without reason, the remark of Jerome respecting Origen, that where they wrote well, nobody wrote better, &c.: you know what follows. As far indeed as they have endeavoured to point out, confute, and correct papistical and sophistical errors and abuses, I commend and approve them. And I wish that they had confined themselves within those limits, and not trodden down the wheat together with the tares; that is, had not at the same time done violence to the authority of the ancient doctors and chief writers in the church of Christ. For how much soever you may exercise your ingenuity, you will certainly never convince me, nor, I think, any unprejudiced reader, that those ancient authors are on your side in this controversy. You have been, in fact, more than enough inquisitive in your investigation of errors; and while you are endeavouring to purify every thing, you have fancied error to lurk in places where none existed. And this error most certainly, if error it be, has been handed down to us by the fathers themselves,

[1 Namely, Aphorisms upon the consideration of the Eucharist, intended to disprove the corporal presence, which tenet was held by Abp. Cranmer up to the year 1546; when by more mature and calm deliberation, and considering the point with less prejudice, and the sense of the fathers more closely, in conference with Dr Ridley, afterwards bishop of Rochester, and his fellow-martyr, he at last quitted and freed himself from the fetters of that unsound doctrine. Strype, Cranmer, 94, 97; see also Cranmer's works on the Lord's supper, published by the Parker Society.]

and men of apostolical character, from the very beginning of the church. And what godly man could endure to hear this, much less to believe it? Not to mention in the mean time, that our gracious Lord would never have left his beloved spouse in such lamentable blindness for so long a period.

Wherefore, since this catholic faith which we hold respecting the real presence has been declared to the church from the beginning by such evident and manifest passages of scripture, and the same has also been subsequently commended to the ears of the faithful with so much clearness and diligence by the first ecclesiastical writers; do not, I pray, persist in wishing any longer to carp at or subvert a doctrine so well grounded and supported. You have sufficiently made the attempt already. And unless it had been firmly founded upon a solid rock, it would long since have fallen with the crash of a mighty ruin. It cannot be told, how greatly this so bloody controversy has impeded the full course of the gospel both throughout the whole christian world, and especially among ourselves. It brings very great danger to yourselves, and occasions to all others a stumbling-block greater than I can express. Wherefore, if you will listen to me, I exhort and advise you, yea, I beg, beseech, and implore and adjure you in the bowels of Jesus Christ, to agree and unite in a christian concord, to exert your whole strength in establishing it, and at length to afford to the churches the peace of God which passeth all understanding, so that we may, with united strength, extend as widely as possible one sound, pure, evangelical doctrine, conformable to the discipline of the primitive church. We should easily convert even the Turks to the obedience of our gospel, if only we would agree among ourselves, and unite together in some holy confederacy. But if we go on in this way to "bite and devour each other," there will be reason to fear, lest (what I abhor the mention of), according to the warning of the apostle, we "be consumed one of another."

You have, worthy Vadian, my true and genuine opinion respecting that entire controversy, together with a free and faithful admonition. To which if you will pay attention, I shall enrol your name not only among my friends, but among my best friends. Farewell. [1537.]

T. CANTUAR.

LETTER VIII.

ARCHBISHOP CRANMER TO WOLFGANG CAPITO.

Without place or date[1].

THE treatise[2], my friend Capito, which you had dedicated to the king's majesty, I presented to him with my own hand. He received it, as I thought, with pleasure and satisfaction. I also hinted to him that he should recompense your labours, and he promised to see to it. Not long after, when the bishop[3] of Hereford and I were together in company with the Lord Crumwell, the keeper of the privy seal, who is one of the privy councillors, and who has himself done more than all others together in whatever has hitherto been effected respecting the reformation of religion and of the clergy; we united in requesting him to put his majesty again in mind of you, which he has done, and a hundred crowns are assigned to you as a present, which he has ordered the bearer of this letter to take with him. Do you still desire to know whether your offering was acceptable? Well, I will state, not what I myself know to be the fact, but what I have heard from others who have been at court more recently than myself. The king, who is a most acute and vigilant observer, is wont to hand over books of this kind that have been presented to him, and those especially which he has not the patience to read himself, to one of his lords in waiting for perusal, from whom he may afterwards learn their contents. He then takes them back, and presently gives them to be examined by some one else, of an entirely opposite way of thinking to the former party. When he has thus made himself master of their opinions, and sufficiently ascertained both what they commend and what they find fault with, he at length openly declares his own judgment respecting the same points. And this, I understand,

[1 Dr Jenkyns, who has published the Latin original of this letter from the archives of Zurich, assigns the date of 1537.]

[2 This treatise is entitled, Responsum de Missa, Matrimonio, et jure magistratus in religione, 11 Martii, 1537, Henrico VIII. inscriptum. Jenkyns, Cranmer, I. 192.]

[3 Edward Foxe, bishop of Hereford, 1535, died in 1538.]

he has done with respect to your book; and while he was much pleased with many things in it, there were also some things which he could by no means digest or approve. I suspect they were the statements you made concerning the mass. You now have every thing respecting that book which I have been able either to hear and see in person, or to gather and collect, when absent, from the report of others. As to myself, be assured of this, that I love and reverence you from my heart, and regard you as one who, by reason of your remarkable erudition united to an equal integrity of manners, is deserving of the friendly offices of all good men. And I wish that my ability corresponded with my inclination to serve you; for you should then perceive, my Capito, how greatly I esteem you. I request you in the mean time to take in good part from me this trifling present, small indeed, if your deserts are taken into account, but yet not to be despised, if you duly consider, either the feelings of the giver, or the necessary and manifold expenses with which I am burdened almost beyond my strength. In fine, I request you to favour and assist for my sake, as far as you can, this my friend Thomas Tybald[1], who is the bearer of this letter. Farewell.

T. CANTUAR.

LETTER IX[2].

ARCHBISHOP CRANMER TO JOHN A LASCO.

Dated at LONDON, *July* 4, 1548.

I AM sorry that your coming to us has been prevented by the unlooked for intervention of some other engagement; for I have no doubt but that I should easily have satisfied

[1 Cranmer wrote a letter to Crumwell, dated 22d July, [1537], especially to recommend Tybald as "a very honest man, and both loved and trusted of the learned men in those parties," namely, Germany and Switzerland. See Jenkyns's Cranmer, I. 191.]

[2 The original of this letter is published in Jenkyns's Cranmer, and also in Gabbema Epp. Clar. Virorum.]

you as to your invitation[3], if I had had an opportunity of conversing with you upon the subject. But as you are not able to come at present, but write word that you intend to come at some future time, if you shall have previously been informed by a letter from me as to the nature of your vocation amongst us; I will converse with you by letter, and briefly explain in writing, what I shall perhaps state somewhat more copiously to you in person. We[4] are desirous of setting forth in our churches the true doctrine of God, and have no wish to adapt it to all tastes, or to deal in ambiguities; but, laying aside all carnal considerations, to transmit to posterity a true and explicit form of doctrine agreeable to the rule of the sacred writings; so that there may not only be set forth among all nations an illustrious testimony respecting our doctrine, delivered by the grave authority of learned and godly men, but that all posterity may have a pattern to imitate. For the purpose of carrying this important design into execution we have thought it necessary to have the assistance of learned men, who, having compared their opinions together with us, may do away with all doctrinal controversies, and build up an entire system of true doctrine. We have therefore invited both yourself and some other learned men; and as they have come over to us without any reluctance, so that we scarcely have to regret the absence of any of them, with the exception of yourself and Melancthon, we earnestly request you, both to come yourself, and, if possible, to bring Melancthon along with you. I am now sending a third letter to Melancthon[5], in which I exhort him to come to us; and if your exhortation be added to my letter, I have no doubt but that he will be persuaded to accept an invitation so often repeated[6]. He need not, I think, be under any fear of the attacks of enemies, or the dangers of the roads, which, if

[3 Dr Jenkyns is of opinion, from a letter of John a Lasco to Hardenberg, in Gerdes, Scrin. Antiq., that this invitation had been given in the preceding year. Jenkyns, Cranmer, I. 329.]

[4 For an account of Cranmer's design to unite all the protestant churches, see Strype, Cranmer, 584.]

[5 See Strype, Cranmer, 574, and Latimer's Sermons, Parker Society Edition, Vol. I. p. 141.]

[6 John a Lasco, Jenkyns states, (Remains of Cranmer, I. 331) forwarded Cranmer's letter to Melancthon by Æpinus, as appears from a letter to Hardenberg, July 28, 1548, given in Gerdes.]

they exist at all, are however far less than where he now is[1]. You may add too, that by undergoing a little inconvenience for a short time, he will procure to himself ease for many years, and to the state everlasting benefit. If I anticipated that his visit to us would be either useless or unpleasant, no one would dissuade him from it more earnestly than myself. But now, when I perceive that he can in nowise act more advantageously either for himself or for the state, than by coming over to us at this juncture, I am the more urgent upon the subject, and exhort you to exert all your diligence and consideration to this one end, namely, to make our friend Philip ours in reality. I explained to you, a short time since, what will be the situation of you both; but I so explained it, as desiring that you should learn to be pleased with England from your own experience rather than by my commendation of it. Farewell and happily. London, July 4, 1548.

I am exceedingly desirous of your presence.

T. CANTUAR.

LETTER X[2].

ARCHBISHOP CRANMER TO ALBERT HARDENBERG.

Dated at CAMBRIDGE, *July* 28, 1548.

BUT if our friend Philip will consider for what purpose he is invited, and also by what persons, those, assuredly, who are most friendly both to himself and to true religion; and also with how great anxiety he is both invited and expected; truly I know not whether he can neglect this summons, especially as he must perceive that he has no certain vocation yonder which he can properly place in opposition to it. If

[1 Cranmer alludes to the attempt of Charles V. in 1548, to force the Interim on the German protestants.]

[2 A fragment only of this letter has been preserved, a portion of which will be found in the preceding one, from the words "We are desirous," &c. p. 17, to "my commendation of it," p. 18. Cranmer then proceeds as is here given. The Latin original is published in Jenkyns's Cranmer, and in the Parker Society edition of the archbishop's works.]

he felt unwilling to refuse the venerable elector of Cologne upon a like invitation, he cannot certainly decline the present one, upon an occasion of much greater importance and necessity. His friends perhaps will be unwilling to let him go, and he too will be unwilling to part with his friends at this particular juncture: but I fear in the mean time that all parties yonder do not attend to him from such motives as we could wish; and even if they do, I know not whether he can now remain there with as much advantage as can now be derived from his presence in our England, and which nevertheless ought not to be disregarded by us, inasmuch as we think it our duty to seek truly and heartily the glory of Christ our Lord. I wish he would once make up his mind, and acquaint us with his intention, or that he would come over to us immediately, and anticipate every messenger. We will provide for the expense, either through you, or elsewhere, as soon as we know to what extent, and in what place, he wishes provision to be made. Cambridge, July 28, 1548.

LETTER XI[3].

ARCHBISHOP CRANMER TO MARTIN BUCER.

Dated at LONDON, Oct. 2, 1548.

GRACE and peace of God in Christ. I have read your letter to John Hales[4], in which you relate the miserable condition of Germany, and inform us that you can scarcely preside in the ministry of the word in your city. With groanings therefore I call out with the prophet, "Shew thy marvellous loving-kindness, O thou that savest them which trust in thee from those that rise up against thy right hand."

[3 The original of this letter is printed in Strype, Cranmer, 844; Jenkyns, I. 335, Bucer, Script. Angl. p. 190, and in the Parker Society edition of the archbishop's works.]

[4 John Hales was a learned and good man, and clerk of the hanaper to Edward VI. and queen Elizabeth. In queen Mary's time he was an exile at Frankfort. See Strype, Mem. II. i. 47; III. i. 405; Cranmer, 280.]

(Ps. xvii. 7, marg. ver.) Nor do I doubt but that God will regard both this and the like lamentations of godly men; and that he will preserve and defend the true doctrine, which has hitherto been sincerely set forth in your churches, against all the rage of the devil and of the world. Those, in the mean time, who are unable amidst the raging storm to launch out into the deep, must take refuge in harbour. To you, therefore, my Bucer, our kingdom will be a most safe harbour, in which, by the blessing of God, the seeds of true doctrine have happily begun to be sown. Come over therefore to us, and become a labourer with us in the harvest of the Lord. You will not be of less benefit to the universal church of God while you are with us, than if you retain your former position. In addition to this, you will be better able to heal the wounds of your distressed country in your absence, than you are now able to do in person. Laying aside therefore all delay, come over to us as soon as possible. We will make it manifest that nothing can be more gratifying or agreeable to us than the presence of Bucer. But take care that you suffer no inconvenience from the journey. You are aware of those who pursue your life : do not therefore commit yourself into their hands. There is an English merchant yonder, Richard Hilles, a godly and most trustworthy man, with whom I would have you confer respecting all the arrangements for your journey. Moreover, I pray God, the eternal Father of our Lord Jesus Christ, with my whole heart, that in the midst of wrath he may remember mercy, and look upon the calamities of his afflicted church, and kindle the light of true doctrine increasingly among us, and not suffer it to be extinguished, after having now shone with so much splendour for many years among yourselves. May he likewise, my Bucer, guide and preserve you, and bring you over to us in safety. Farewell and happily. London, Oct. 2, 1548. Most anxious for your arrival,

THOMAS CRANMER, archbishop of Canterbury.

LETTER XII.

ARCHBISHOP CRANMER TO PHILIP MELANCTHON[1].

Dated at LONDON, *Feb.* 10, 1549.

WE are experiencing, most learned Melancthon, the truth of all that our Lord Jesus Christ has foretold respecting the trials of his church. "But God is faithful, who will not suffer his people to be tempted above that they are able, but will also with the temptation make a way to escape, that we may be able to bear it." For though from his hatred to the Son of God the devil exercises a horrible tyranny over the members of Christ, yet God has promised that his church shall never perish; nay, of these last times he expressly declares, "To hoar hairs will I carry her; I will bear, I will deliver her[2]." And God has always willed some civil societies to be the refuge of his churches, and that their rulers should support the friends of heavenly doctrine; just as Obadiah befriended the hearers of Elias, whom the kings of Israel were persecuting on every side. Wherefore, eternal Father of our Lord Jesus Christ, I give thee thanks for having rescued our island from the waves, like the ark of Noah, and for having granted us such rulers as seek thy glory, and who devote their houses and possessions to the church and its service, as in old time the cottage of the widow of Sarepta afforded a home to Elias. And I pray God to direct us, and to gather unto himself a perpetual church amongst us, not only out of our own countrymen, but also from among those of foreign nations, as according to his infinite mercy he has already begun to do. For many pious and learned men have come over to us, some from Italy, some from Germany, and we are daily expecting more; which society of the church if you will vouchsafe to increase and adorn with your presence, I know not by what means you will be able more effectually to set forth the glory of God.

I am aware that you have often desired that wise and godly men should take counsel together, and, having com-

---

[1 The original letter is printed by Jenkyns, and in the Parker Society edition of Cranmer.]

[2 See Isaiah xlvi. 4.]

pared their opinions, send forth under the sanction of their authority some work, that should embrace the chief subjects of ecclesiastical doctrine, and transmit the truth uncorrupted to posterity. This object we are anxiously endeavouring to accomplish to the utmost of our power. We therefore request you to communicate your counsel and opinions with us in person, and not so to shut up your mind as to seem wanting even to your own wishes, or acting in opposition to so manifest a calling of God. I could relate many things upon this subject, which would bring you over to our opinion; but the brevity of a letter will not contain them all. I would rather, therefore, that you should learn them from the bearer, John a Lasco, a most excellent man. For he has resided with me upon the most intimate and friendly terms for some months past; and I pray you to give credit to whatever he may relate to you in my name. May our Lord Jesus Christ, the guardian of his church, who has said, None shall pluck my sheep out of my hands, preserve and defend the ministry of his gospel, and bring you in safety to the harbour of our church! Farewell. London, Feb. 10, 1549.

Most anxious for your arrival,

THOMAS CANTUAR.

Our German friends who are with us, request you to bring with you doctor Albert Hardenberg, as Jonas[1] will tell you in my name.

LETTER XIII.

ARCHBISHOP CRANMER TO HENRY BULLINGER[2].
Dated at LAMBETH, *March* 20, 1552.

MUCH health. That I reply, after a year's interval, to your letter dated at Zurich on the 24th of February, you must impute partly to my want of leisure, and partly to a

[1 This was Justus Jonas the younger, who came over with letters commendatory from Melancthon. Strype, Cranmer, 581.]

[2 The original letter is printed by Jenkyns, and in the Parker Society edition of Cranmer.]

kind of dislike to a duty of this nature, and which I must candidly admit myself to entertain. But as it is better to perform a duty tardily than not at all, you shall now receive a reply to the whole of your letter.

You write to me upon two subjects, one of a public, the other of a private nature. With respect to that which is public, namely, that I would advise the king's majesty not to send any delegate to the council of Trent[3], there was no need of any advice of mine to dissuade him from a measure which never came into his mind: but I considered it better, forasmuch as our adversaries are now holding their councils at Trent to confirm their errors, to recommend his majesty to grant his assistance, that in England, or elsewhere, there might be convoked a synod of the most learned and excellent persons, in which provision might be made for the purity of ecclesiastical doctrine, and especially for an agreement upon the sacramentarian controversy. To which plan (as considering it most useful to the christian commonwealth) I perceived that the mind of his majesty was very favourably disposed. We must not therefore suffer ourselves to be wanting to the church of God in a matter of such importance. I have written upon the subject[4] to masters Philip [Melancthon] and Calvin; and I pray you to devise the means by which this synod may be assembled with the greatest convenience, either in England or elsewhere.

The private affair upon which you wrote to me, was, that I should put an end to the controversy between the bishop of London and Hooper, bishop of Gloucester, respecting which it is now too late to reply. For I am aware that you have been informed long since[5], that this controversy has been entirely settled. And master Hooper is in such great esteem among us, that he is now appointed bishop of Worcester[6], and

[3 The first session of this year was held on the first of May. For an account of its proceedings, see Burnet, II. 299.]

[4 See the next and following letters.]

[5 Namely, by Hooper, whose letter to Bullinger, dated Aug. 1, 1551, is given in a subsequent part of this volume. Peter Martyr also wrote to Bullinger upon the same subject in the April of the same year. Strype, Cranmer, 309.]

[6 Hooper was appointed to the see of Worcester in October 1551, and held it in commendam with that of Gloucester, to which he had been consecrated in the preceding March.]

is at this time living in my house upon the most intimate terms, during the sitting of parliament. May the Lord Jesus guide and defend you by his holy Spirit! Farewell. Lambeth, March 20, 1552.

Your reverence's most attached,

THOMAS CANTUAR.

LETTER XIV.

ARCHBISHOP CRANMER TO JOHN CALVIN[1].

Dated at LAMBETH, *March* 20, 1552.

MUCH health. As nothing tends more injuriously to the separation of the churches than heresies and disputes respecting the doctrines of religion, so nothing tends more effectually to unite the churches of God, and more powerfully to defend the fold of Christ, than the pure teaching of the gospel, and harmony of doctrine. Wherefore I have often wished, and still continue to do so, that learned and godly men, who are eminent for erudition and judgment, might meet together in some place of safety, where by taking counsel together, and comparing their respective opinions, they might handle all the heads of ecclesiastical doctrine, and hand down to posterity, under the weight of their authority, some work not only upon the subjects themselves, but upon the forms of expressing them. Our adversaries are now holding their councils at Trent for the establishment of their errors; and shall we neglect to call together a godly synod, for the refutation of error, and for restoring and propagating the truth? They are, as I am informed, making decrees respecting the worship of the host[2]: wherefore we ought to leave no stone unturned, not only that we may guard others against this idolatry, but also that we may ourselves come to an agreement upon the doctrine of this sacrament. It cannot

[1 The original of this letter is published by Jenkyns, and in the Parker Society edition of Cranmer.]

[2 περὶ τῆς ἀρτολατρείας. The decree of the council of Trent on the Lord's Supper was passed on the 11th of October, 1551. Sleidan, de Stat. Rel. Lib. XXIII; Jenkyns, Cranmer, I. 346.]

escape your prudence, how exceedingly the church of God has been injured by dissensions and varieties of opinion respecting this sacrament of unity ; and though they are now in some measure removed, yet I could wish for an agreement in this doctrine, not only as regards the subject itself, but also with respect to the words and forms of expression. You have now my wish, about which I have also written to masters Philip [Melancthon] and Bullinger; and I pray you to deliberate among yourselves as to the means by which this synod can be assembled with the greatest convenience. Farewell. Lambeth, March 20, 1552.

You very dear brother in Christ,

THOMAS CANTUAR[3].

LETTER XV.

ARCHBISHOP CRANMER TO PHILIP MELANCTHON[4].

Dated at LAMBETH, *March* 27, 1552.

WE read in the Acts of the Apostles, that when a dispute had arisen, as to whether those who from among the Gentiles had been turned to God, should be compelled to be circumcised, and keep the law of Moses, the apostles and elders came together to consider of this matter ; and having compared their opinions, delivered the judgment of their council in a written epistle. This example I wish we ourselves could imitate, in whose churches the doctrine of the gospel has been restored and purified. But although all controversies cannot be removed in this world, (because the party which is hostile to the truth, will not assent to the judgment of the church,) it is nevertheless to be desired that the members of the true church should agree among themselves upon the chief heads of ecclesiastical doctrine. But it cannot escape your notice, how greatly religious dissensions, especially in the matter of the Lord's supper, have rent the churches asunder : had they

[3 Calvin's reply to the above proposals will be given in the Appendix.]

[4 The original of this letter is printed by Jenkyns, and in the Parker Society edition of Cranmer.]

been settled before, the emperor, I think, would never have made war against you. And it is truly grievous that the sacrament of unity is made by the malice of the devil food for disagreement, and (as it were) the apple of contention. I could wish therefore, that those who excel others in erudition and judgment, should be assembled together, after the example of the apostles, and declare their judgment as well respecting other subjects of dispute, as likewise especially respecting this controversy, and attest their agreement by some published document. But you will perhaps say, " And I also have often expressed the same wish; but this matter cannot be effected without the aid of princes." I have therefore [consulted with][1] the king's majesty, who places his kingdom of England at your disposal, and most graciously promises not only a place of security and quiet, but also his aid and assistance towards these godly endeavours. I have written likewise to masters Calvin and Bullinger, and exhorted them not to be wanting to a work so necessary, and so useful to the commonwealth of Christendom. You wrote me word in your last letter that the Areopagites of the council of Trent are making decrees respecting the worship of the host. Wherefore, since the adversaries of the gospel meet together with so much zeal for the establishment of error, we must not allow them to be more diligent in confirming ungodliness, than we are in propagating and setting forth the doctrine of godliness. Your commendation of master George Major[2] has greatly increased that regard for him, which his merits have produced in me; and if I can be of service to him in any way, he shall find my ability will fail sooner than my inclination. Farewell and happily. Lambeth, March 27, 1552.

Very desirous of seeing you some time,

THOMAS CANTUAR.

[1 One or more words are wanting in the original.]
[2 George Major was a zealous disciple of Luther, and minister at Eisleben. He died in 1574.]

LETTER XVI.

ARCHBISHOP CRANMER TO THE WIDOW OF MARTIN BUCER.

Dated at LAMBETH, *April* 20, 1552.

GREETING. The especial favour with which I regarded your husband during his lifetime, is by no means diminished now that he is no more. His remarkable piety indeed, and profound learning, has produced not a transient but an everlasting benefit to the church; whereby he has not only bound all godly persons, but myself more than all of them, under perpetual obligations to him. You must not therefore on any account allow yourself to be deterred from writing to me, should there be any thing in which I can be of use to you or to your affairs. For stirred up by your letters, I shall not only recal to myself, and not without satisfaction, the agreeable remembrance of a very dear friend; but will also most readily perform to you, his widow, those offices of kindness, which the word of God commands to be paid, and which shall be afforded you as occasion shall offer. With respect to what you have lately informed me, that it is necessary for the expediting of your affairs that it should be certified and attested by some formal document that the sum of a hundred marks which you received as a present from the king's majesty, when you left this country, belongs especially and exclusively to yourself, I have written a letter to the guardians[3] of Bucer's children, whereby they may clearly ascertain what was the intention of our most serene king upon the matter in question. I send you a copy of the letter of the lords of the council to master John Hales, his majesty's treasurer, (who is now, I think, at Strasburgh,) or to his deputy in his absence, written in English, which clearly testifies that a hundred marks were presented you by his majesty, and that too, after the death of your husband, inasmuch as that letter was written on the last day of March, and your husband departed this life at the end of February. May God, who is

[3 These were, Conrad Hubert, Quinter Andernach, and Huldric Chelius, to all of whom Cranmer addressed the following letter.]

the fountain and father of all comfort, vouchsafe to comfort you, and preserve you with all your family! Farewell. Lambeth, April 20, 1552.

Yours to the utmost of his power,

THOMAS CANTUAR.

LETTER XVII.

ARCHBISHOP CRANMER TO CONRAD HUBERT, AND OTHERS.

Dated at LAMBETH, *April* 20, 1552.

GREETING. As I have lately understood, from a letter written to this place by the widow[1] of master Bucer of pious memory, that for the purpose of dividing the property of her deceased husband amongst his children, a certain declaration or certificate is necessary respecting the sum of a hundred marks, presented by his majesty, as to whether it belongs to the widow or to the children; whereby the fact may be ascertained, and all doubt entirely removed; I affirm and attest that the said sum of a hundred marks was especially bestowed by his most serene majesty upon master Bucer's widow, after his death, and intended for her especial use; as is clearly manifest from the letter which the lords of the council wrote to the treasurer, a copy of which I have sent to master Bucer's widow. May God direct you by his holy Spirit, and grant you success in the labours of your calling! Farewell. Lambeth, April 20, 1552.

Yours heartily,

T. CANT.

[1 The name of Bucer's widow was Wibrand Bucerin. The university gave her an hundred crowns on the death of her husband; the king an hundred marks more, besides her husband's half yearly pension, though he died before Lady-day, when it became due. Strype, Cranmer, 358.]

LETTER XVIII.

ARCHBISHOP CRANMER TO PETER MARTYR[2].

Dated [from prison, 1555.]

AFTER much health in Christ our Saviour. As letters are then only necessary, when the messenger is either not sufficiently discreet, or is unacquainted with the circumstances we wish to communicate, or not thought worthy to be entrusted with secrets; and since by the goodness of God the bearer of this has fallen in my way, a man, as you know, of signal discretion, most faithful in all matters entrusted to him, exceedingly attached to us both, and possessing an entire acquaintance with the circumstances of our country, from whose mouth you may learn all that has taken place here; I have not thought it needful to write to you more at length, especially as letters are wont to occasion so much danger and mischief. Yet I have not deemed it right to pass over this one thing, which I have learned by experience, namely, that God never shines forth more brightly, and pours out the beams of his mercy and consolation, or of strength and firmness of spirit, more clearly or impressively upon the minds of his people, than when they are under the most extreme pain and distress, both of mind and body, that he may then more especially shew himself to be the God of his people, when he seems to have altogether forsaken them; then raising them up when they think he is bringing them down, and laying them low; then glorifying them, when he is thought to be confounding them; then quickening them, when he is thought to be destroying them. So that we may say with Paul, "When I am weak, then am I strong; and if I must needs glory, I will glory in my infirmities, in prisons, in revilings, in distresses, in persecutions, in sufferings for Christ." I pray God to grant that I may endure to the end! Nothing is at this time more distressing to me, than that no answer

[2 This letter is printed for the first time by the Parker Society. It was discovered at Zurich by the Rev. Steuart A. Pears, in 1843. The Latin original is subjoined.]

has as yet been given to M.A.[1], to whose subtilties, and
juggling tricks, and ravings, a reply would not have been
wanting long since, had not books and liberty been wanting
to myself. I have written to no one but you, nor do I wish
any one to know that I have written to you: wherefore
salute no one in my name.

THOMAS CRANMER.

Thomæ Cranmeri Epistola ad P. Martyrem.

POST plurimam in Christo Servatore nostro salutem. Quando
tum demum necessariæ sunt literæ, quum aut non satis prudens est
nuncius, aut rerum quas significare volumus ignarus, aut non fidus
cui arcana credas; quumque mihi Dei benignitate sese obtulisset hic
tabellarius, vir et prudentia (ut nosti) insigni, et qui rebus in cre-
dendis fidissimus sit, et nostrum utriusque amantissimus, et rerum
nostratium scientissimus, e cujus ore quæ hic acta fuerint intelligas
omnia; non necessarium existimavi ut prolixius ad te scriberem,
præsertim quum scripturæ tot pericula damnaque afferre soleant.
Illud tamen unum prætermittendum non censui, quod expertus didici,
nunquam Deum splendidius illucescere, et clementiæ suæ, consola-
tionis, aut roboris ac fortitudinis animi radios suorum mentibus clarius
aut pressius infundere, quam in summis animi corporisque angoribus
atque pressuris; ut tum vel maxime sese declaret suorum esse Deum,
quum illos deseruisse prorsus videtur; tum erigere quum dejicere
atque prosternere, tum glorificare quum confundere, tum denique vivi-
ficare quum occidere putetur. Ut cum Paulo dicere liceat, Quando
infirmor tunc fortior sum, et si gloriari oportet, in infirmitatibus meis
gloriabor, in carceribus, in contumeliis, in necessitatibus, in persecuti-
onibus, in augustiis pro Christo. Faxit obsecro Deus, ut in finem
perseveremus. Hodie nihil magis animum angit meum, quam quod
hactenus M. A. nihil est responsum; ad cujus astutias, præstigias, et
insanias jamdudum non defuisset responsum, nisi mihi defuissent et
libri et libertas. Præterquam tibi scripsi nemini, nec scire velim

[1 M.A. signifies Marcus Antonius, under which name Gardiner,
bishop of Winchester, replied to Cranmer's "Answer to a crafty and
sophistical cavillation, &c." which see in Cranmer's writings, published
by the Parker Society. The above letter confirms the statement of
Strype, that the archbishop was very desirous to prepare another book
in confutation of Marcus Antonius, and in vindication of his own
writing. Strype says, "He lived long enough to finish three parts;
whereof two unhappily perished in Oxford, and the third fell into
John Foxe's hands, and for ought I know, that by this time is perished
also." Strype, Cranmer, I. 371.]

quenquam quod ad te scripserim: proinde nomine meo salutabis
neminem.

THOMAS CRAMMERUS[2].

Hæc in manu Archiepiscopi Cantuarensis.
  Scripsit hæc ex carcere ad D. Pet.
Martyrem. M. A. significant Marc.
Antonium, nimirum Wintoniensem.
1555.

LETTER XIX.

MILES COVERDALE TO JOHN CALVIN.
Dated at FRANKFORT, *March* 26, 1548.

I CANNOT but avail myself, most illustrious sir, of the
offered opportunity of saluting your worthiness. There was
brought hither three days since, during the time of the fair,
a certain little book in English, containing that Order of
Holy Communion which the king's majesty has set forth, as
suitable to the present time[3]. And as I perceived many
persons were desirous of obtaining it, I forthwith translated
it both into German and Latin. And therefore, when I
understood the godly bearer of this letter to be a townsman
of yours, I thought I should gratify your reverence by sending you this trifling present. One of the translations I intended for the Germans; the other, namely the Latin one, I
am exceedingly anxious should be forwarded to your reverence. And should you feel inclined to make known to

[2 The signature is added by another hand, and the subjoined note
is in that of Bullinger. Cranmer was burned at Oxford, March 21,
1556: this letter, which appears undoubtedly to be his autograph, was
written only a few months previously.]

[3 The English work, the Order of the Communion, is printed in
the volume containing the Liturgies of King Edward VI., published
by the Parker Society. The translation into Latin by Coverdale, here
mentioned, does not seem to have been printed; but there is a Latin
translation extant, printed apparently in 1548, with the initials A. A.
S. D. Th, probably indicating Alexander Alesse, who also translated
into Latin the first Liturgy of King Edward VI. A.D. 1549. It is a
very rare small volume, bearing the title of "Ordo distributionis sacra-
menti altaris sub utraque specie, et formula confessionis faciendæ in
regno Angliæ. Hæc Londini evulgata sunt octavo die Martii Anni
MDXLVIII." See "The ancient Liturgy of the Church of England," by
Rev. W. Maskell, p. xlv; also Burnet II. 247, and Strype, Mem. II. i. 96.]

others this cause for congratulation, and first-fruits of godliness, (according as the Lord now wills his religion to revive in England,) you will be able to commit this token of my affection for you to the press more easily than I can. I am now on my return to England, having been invited thither after an exile of eight years. Farewell, most excellent master, and affectionately salute your wife, who deserved so well from me and mine, when we went up to Strasburgh. Frankfort, March 26, 1548.

MICHAEL (*alias* MILO) COVERDALE, *Anglus.*

LETTER XX.

MILES COVERDALE TO PAUL FAGIUS.
Dated at WINDSOR CASTLE, *Oct.* 21, 1548.

PEACE and joy in the Holy Ghost! Your letter, most excellent sir, dated on the 22nd of August, I received from my wife on the 8th of this present month, with exceeding compassion for those individuals whom this dreadful tyranny[1] so greatly distresses. I also shewed your letter yesterday to the most reverend the archbishop of Canterbury; who, as he has undertaken to educate your dear son (whom he has just sent away to Canterbury, by reason of the plague that is raging at this place), both in religion and learning, at his own expense ; in like manner, reflecting upon the lamentable condition of your churches, he truly sympathises in your misfortune : wherefore he desired you most especially to come over to us, rather than to go away either into Turkey or Hungary. Oh! my master, if you should seek a refuge any where else than with us, since the faithlessness of mankind is every where so great, how will that most excellent gift, which the good and gracious God has bestowed upon you, grow cool! If the most reverend archbishop, whose answer I inclosed in my letter to you, had foreseen so much danger to the church, truly what I wrote to you would have been no impediment. You must think therefore that we are both of us sorry for what we did, although there was nothing

[1 Namely, the persecutions in Germany by Charles V., to enforce compliance with the Interim.]

stated in those letters but what the occasion then called for. For myself, indeed, my master, I am in no little apprehension both for yourself and for our churches and schools deprived of your most happy ministrations. Wherefore, although our rulers may not invite you by name, eminent as you are among the best scholars of Germany, and this probably, as I have before hinted to you, from secret motives; yet we, who know you well, entreat you most solemnly to come over to us, where you need not doubt but that you will be most acceptable, and therefore treated with the greatest kindness. Farewell. From the king's castle, which we call Windsor. Oct. 21, 1548.

Yours from my heart,

M. COVERDALE.

LETTER XXI.

JOHN HOOPER TO HENRY BULLINGER.

Dated at STRASBURGH, *Jan.* 27, [probably in 1546].

NOT many years since, most honoured master, and much loved brother in Christ, when I was a courtier, and living too much of a court life in the palace of our king[2], there most happily and auspiciously came under my notice certain writings of master Huldrich Zuinglius[3], a most excellent man, of pious memory; and also some commentaries upon the epistles of St Paul, which your reverence had published for the general benefit, and which will prove a lasting monument of your renown.

These singular gifts of God exhibited by you to the world

[2 Hooper probably refers to the period, when he was retained as chaplain and steward in the house of Sir Thomas Arundel, who was executed in 1552, as a partisan of the duke of Somerset. See Strype.]

[3 The collected writings of Zuinglius were published by Rodolph Gualter, in four volumes, folio, in 1544. He was slain in a battle between the five Roman Catholic cantons of Switzerland, and those of Zurich and Berne, Oct. 11, 1531; having attended the troops as one of their ministers.]

at large, I was unwilling to neglect, especially as I perceived them seriously to affect the eternal salvation and happiness of my soul; so that I thought it well worth my while, night and day, with earnest study, and an almost superstitious diligence, to devote my entire attention to your writings. Nor was my labour in this respect ever wearisome to me : for after I had arrived at manhood, and by the kindness of my father enjoyed the means of living more unrestrainedly, I had begun to blaspheme God by impious worship and all manner of idolatry, following the evil ways of my forefathers, before I rightly understood what God was. But being at length delivered by the goodness of God, for which I am solely indebted to him and to yourselves, nothing now remains for me in reference to the remainder of my life and my last hour, but to worship God with a pure heart, and know my defects while living in this body, since indeed the tenure of life is deceitful, and every man is altogether as nothing; and to serve my godly brethren *in* Christ, and the ungodly *for* Christ : for I do not think that a Christian is born for himself, or that he ought to live to himself; but that, whatever he has or is, he ought altogether to ascribe, not to himself, but to refer it to God as the author, and regard every thing that he possesses as common to all, according as the necessities and wants of his brethren may require. I am indeed ashamed beyond measure, that I have not performed these duties heretofore ; but that like a brute beast, as the greater part of mankind are wont to do, I have been a slave to my own lusts : but it is better to be wise late, than not at all.

By reason of my love and respect towards you, I had often proposed to visit you, though I have always been prevented hitherto, partly by my ill-health, and partly because I am mistrustful of the favour of fortune; for my father, of whom I am the only son and heir, is so opposed to me on account of Christ's religion, that should I refuse to act according to his wishes, I shall be sure to find him for the future, not a father, but a cruel tyrant. Shortly however, in about a month's time, I mean to go down to my native place[1] to bid farewell to the honours, pleasures, and friends of this world; and I will then endeavour, if possible, by the assist-

[1 Hooper was a native of Somersetshire. Godwin de Præsul. 552.]

ance of my friends, to obtain at least some portion of what I am entitled to, wherewith I may be able to subsist upon my slender means among you at Zurich : and should God order it otherwise, and see fit to visit me with poverty and want, or in any other way, I will bear it with an undisturbed mind, and choose rather, as an exile, to suffer affliction with the people of God, than to enjoy the pleasures of sin for a season; esteeming the reproach of Christ (I use the words of St Paul) greater riches than the treasures in Egypt; for I have respect unto the recompence of the reward, and hope for eternal life, obtained, not by my merits, but by the blood of Christ.   I entreat you, therefore, O man of God, by our Lord Jesus Christ, that you aid me in this journey by your prayers to God for me.   For I am in fear, and not without reason, of those perfidious bishops, to whom nothing is more acceptable than the spilling of the blood of the godly, and whose temper and disposition I have often experienced to the great peril of my life[2].   I desire therefore, to defend myself against their treachery and tyranny with the remedies that God has given me ; and I seek the aid of your church, that by the help of her prayers I may derive some comfort, according to the promise of God, who is ever present with all who call upon him in truth, and from whom alone assistance is to be sought for in every kind of danger.   For there cannot be a more powerful safeguard than believing prayer : by this Hezekiah overcame the king of the Assyrians, Elijah called down fire from heaven, and Jehoshaphat obtained a signal victory.   But I will dilate no longer upon this subject, for fear of offending your pious and learned ears by so rude and unpolished a letter.

[2 While Hooper was Sir Thomas Arundel's steward, "his master, having intelligence of his opinions and religion, which he in no case did favour, found the means to send him on a message to the bishop of Winchester [Gardiner], writing his letter privily to the bishop, by conference of learning to do some good upon him. Winchester, after long conference with master Hooper four or five days together, sent him home again, right well commending his learning and wit, *but yet bearing in his breast a grudging stomach against master Hooper still.*" See Foxe, Acts and Monuments, VI. 637; and Soames, Hist. Ref. III. 559.   Shortly after this occurrence took place, Hooper found himself obliged to flee for his life, to avoid the operation of the act of the Six Articles.]

Accept, my very dear master, in few words, the news from England. As far as true religion is concerned, idolatry is no where in greater vigour. Our king has destroyed the pope, but not popery; he has expelled all the monks and nuns, and pulled down their monasteries; he has caused all their possessions to be transferred into his exchequer, and yet they are bound, even the frail female sex, by the king's command, to perpetual chastity. England has at this time at least ten thousand nuns, not one of whom is allowed to marry. The impious mass, the most shameful celibacy of the clergy, the invocation of saints, auricular confession, superstitious abstinence from meats, and purgatory, were never before held by the people in greater esteem than at the present moment.

I have just been informed by letter, that the treaty[1], which was concluded two years since between the emperor and our king, is renewed: may God direct every thing to the glory of his name! There is no hope of peace between France and England, but we are in daily expectation of a bloody war.

The chief supporters of the gospel in England are dying every hour: many very illustrious personages have departed within these two years; the lord chancellor Audley[2], the duke of Suffolk[3], [Sir Edward] Baynton, the queen's first lord of the bedchamber; Poinings[4], the king's deputy at Boulogne; Sir Thomas Wyat[5], known throughout the whole world for his noble qualities, and a most zealous defender of

[1 The alliance here referred to was concluded between the emperor Charles V. and Henry VIII., on Feb. 11, 1543, for an account of which see Robertson's Charles V., III. 246, Soames, II. 535.]

[2 Thomas Audley, Lord Chancellor, 1532, created baron Audley of Walden, co. Essex, 29 Nov. 1538, died 1544, when the barony became extinct.]

[3 Charles Brandon, created duke of Suffolk, Feb. 1, 1514, married to his third wife, Mary Tudor, daughter of Henry VII., and queen dowager of France. He died Aug. 24, 1545, and was buried in St George's chapel, Windsor. His epitaph, written by Parkhurst, is printed in Strype, Annals, II. ii. 496.]

[4 Sir Thomas Poinings died in August, 1545. See Hollingshed, Chron. II. 969.]

[5 Sir Thomas Wyat died in 1542, aged 38. He was the first that put into English verse the "seven penitential Psalms."]

yours and Christ's religion; Dr Butts[6], a physician who had
the charge of the king's person: all these were of the privy
council, and real favourers of the gospel, and promoted the
glory of God to the utmost of their power. They all died of
the plague and fever; so that the country is now left altogether to the bishops, and those who despise God and all
true religion.

The bishops of Winchester and Westminster[7] are now on
an embassy from our king to the emperor in Brabant.
Another bishop, namely, of Durham, who was sent into
Picardy to treat there with the ambassadors of the king of
France respecting a peace between the French and English,
has lately returned to England without the accomplishment
of that object. The state of affairs between the Scots and
English is still very doubtful and uncertain: the English however
have sacked their principal cities and villages; but I shudder
to mention the devastation of that country, which was effected
last summer by the earl of Hertford[8]. The queen of Scotland, together with the cardinal [Beaton], is lying in con-
cealment in the mountains, where they possess fortresses
beyond the reach of attack.

The conference at Ratisbon, as far as I understand by a
letter from master Bucer, is suspended: I am more inclined
to believe this, because Philip Melancthon is neither yet come
to them, nor does he intend it. And Bucer, as I hear, is
about to come to us sooner than I expected: but as yet we
have nothing certain; as soon as this shall be the case, I will
inform your reverence forthwith, and you may expect a more
copious letter whenever any new tidings shall require it. The
count Palatine has lately provided for the preaching of the
gospel throughout his dominions: but as far as relates to the
eucharist he has descended, as the proverb has it, from the

[6 Dr William Butts died Nov. 17, 1545. An interesting letter
written to him by Sir John Cheke, during his last illness, is given in
Strype, Cheke, 27.]

[7 Namely, Stephen Gardiner and Thomas Thirlby. The bishop
of Durham here mentioned was Cuthbert Tonstal.]

[8 Edward Seymour, earl of Hertford, landed 10,000 men near
Leith, in May, 1544, which, with Edinburgh, was abandoned to pillage,
and then set on fire. See Hall's Chronicles, p. 860, ed. 1809; also
Robertson's Hist. Scotland.]

horse to the ass; for he has fallen from popery into the
doctrine of Luther, who is in that particular more erroneous
than all the papists; and those who deny the substance of
bread to remain in the sacrament, and substitute the body of
Christ in its place, come more closely to the truth than those
who affirm that the natural body of Christ is with the bread,
in the bread, and under the form of bread, and yet occupies
no place. God I hope will at length give him a better mind.

Master Richard [Hilles] the Englishman, and his godly
wife, salute you affectionately in Christ. He has now in his
house two sisters of noble family, the younger of whom,
named Anna, is exceedingly favourable to true religion. She
prays for your continued happiness, and commends herself,
whom I hope you will see shortly, to the prayers of your
church. Salute affectionately in my name those excellent men
masters Bibliander and Pellican, with the other godly brethren.
Farewell, most learned and godly sir, and suffer me, I pray
you, to be numbered amongst those who truly and from the
heart admire the majesty of your religion. Strasburgh, Jan.
27, [1546].

Yours entirely,

JOHN HOOPER, *Anglus*.

LETTER XXII.

JOHN HOOPER TO [HENRY BULLINGER.]

Without place or date [1].

If your engagements would permit, I should much wish
to ascertain your judgment and opinion. I certainly do not
consider it lawful for a godly man to be present at the mass
and impious observances of the like kind among the papists;
but yet there are some arguments which in some measure
press my mind, and for a time keep me in suspense. Master
Calvin has written much upon that subject; but, as it appears

[1 This letter is without date or address, but appears from the
subsequent letter to have been written to Bullinger, and probably
from Strasburgh, in 1546.]

XXII.] JOHN HOOPER TO HENRY BULLINGER.

to me, he hardly satisfies the arguments which may be alleged against him, one or two of which I will propose to your erudition.

Concerning Naaman the Syrian, though it is not allowable to bring forward a private individual by way of general example, yet it very much bears upon the subject before us; for the prophet said, "Go in peace." Persons, who are unacquainted with the Hebrew, understand this expression as though the prophet had said, "If you choose to return, it will be at your peril, but I do not sanction your doing so :" in my opinion, however, the Hebrew words will not bear this interpretation; for לֵךְ לְשָׁלוֹם, *go in peace*, is an expression of command and confirmation, and therefore the prophet permitted Naaman to worship the true God in the house of Rimmon, with the hope of gaining over the king of Syria and others to the true God: and, if I rightly interpret this passage, as the prophet gave this permission to a godly man, so we ought also to make the same allowance ourselves.

In the time of Elijah, when he complained before God that he was the only worshipper of the true religion then remaining, he was informed by the divine voice that there were left seven thousand. Now certainly, if this great number of men had kept themselves aloof from the idolatrous worship, there must have been at least some few of them known to the prophet of God; nor do I see how any one can deny that though these pious men, by the mention of whom God comforts his afflicted servant, were often openly and publicly in the idol-temples together with a yet more numerous assemblage of the ungodly, they nevertheless retained in their hearts a pure and holy reverence for the one true God. No argument moves me more than this.

In the same way as God forbids idolatry, does he also prohibit adultery, fornication, and other kinds of wickedness; nor does he condemn one more than another : but no one is bound to leave his country, as they say, by reason of either one or the other.

I do not write these things, my accomplished friend, merely for the sake of learning your opinion[2]; but when I have once ascertained it, I shall, by God's blessing, most diligently follow

[2 It appears by the following letter that Hooper's objections were satisfied by the arguments of Bullinger in his reply.]

it without any deceit or dissimulation: not that I am in any doubt upon the subject myself; but I desire to satisfy some godly men who are not yet sufficiently instructed in the faith. May the Lord Jesus long preserve you in safety! Salute, I pray you, your wife in my name, and my English brother and friend in Christ, master Burcher, who resides with you at Zurich.

Yours to serve,

JOHN HOOPER, *Anglus*

LETTER XXIII.

JOHN HOOPER TO HENRY BULLINGER.

Without place or date[1].

MUCH health. I received, most excellent and revered friend in Christ, at Strasburgh, almost a year ago, your equally learned and godly letter, in which you desired altogether to convince me that the true worship of God could have nothing in common with outward idolatry: you therefore considered it more advisable and consistent with godliness, that I should rather endure the loss of home and fortune for Christ's sake, than participate in the ungodly worship of the mass. I reverence and cherish this advice, and willingly come into the same opinion. I cannot repay to your excellence the thanks you deserve; but I pray that he who worketh all in all, and who, when called upon in true faith through his Son Jesus Christ, will do far more than we can believe, may be, according to his mercy and loving-kindness, your exceeding great reward and recompence. Of this I have no doubt, that you will be, when this frail tabernacle is dissolved, the everlasting friend of God. Meanwhile, as long as you continue in this life, defend your churches, deliver them from wolves and hirelings, gather together the people of God, and bring back his flock, now miserably scattered, to Christ the true and only shep-

[1 This letter was probably written from Basle, and shortly after Dec. 12, 1546. See p. 42, note 1.]

herd: fight the good fight; there is laid up for you a crown
of righteousness, which you shall receive from the righteous
Judge in that day.

I will relate to your excellence in person the events of
my long and most dangerous journey to England. I suffered
many things by land; twice I suffered bonds and imprisonment; whence being marvellously delivered by the mercy
of God, though with the heavy loss of my fortune, I was
wretchedly harassed by sea for three months both by
enemies and storms. But the end is not yet; and I
pray God that whatever may yet remain to me of this
wretched life, may be for the glory of his name, and for the
edification of his church. Having been delivered from fire
and water, I came upon war : I see nothing but the death of
all godliness and religion; the enemy of God will destroy (if
it be possible that the faith of Peter can perish) every mouth
that speaks of Christ, and the mother with her children, that
is, the universal church : but the Lord, I doubt not, will look
down upon his people, and not suffer the tyranny of this cruel
enemy to rage at pleasure. In the mean time let us be
heartily and truly turned unto the Lord, and he will undoubtedly look upon our tears. But alas! gracious Lord, we
are sleeping in the greatest security, while in the greatest
danger; and it is therefore no wonder if we terribly experience the wrath of God, and the heavy consequences of our
ungodliness. Let us amend therefore, lest he inflict upon us
yet greater severities, namely, to become after this life the
everlasting enemies of God : let us patiently bear, as the time
requires, the chastisement that our sins have deserved; for he
punishes the children of men for their iniquities.

The bearer will inform your excellence of the good news
we received yesterday from Strasburgh. There will be a
change of religion in England, and the king will take up
the gospel of Christ, in case the emperor should be defeated
in this most destructive war : should the gospel sustain a loss,
he will then retain his impious mass, for which he has this last
summer committed four respectable and godly persons[2] to the

[2 These were, Ann Askew, John Lacels, John Adams, and Nicholas
Belenian. They were burned at the stake about the month of June,
1546, according to Foxe's account (v. 550.) or on July 16th, according
to Stowe.]

flames. Our king has now confined in the tower of London the duke of Norfolk[1], together with his eldest son and heir: they say that both father and son had conspired the death of the king and of our prince,—a horrible deed, if my account is correct.

My wife most dutifully salutes your excellence, with the other learned and godly persons among you. We hope to visit you shortly, God willing. Master de Valys, together with his wife and all his family, wish for you every happiness. There is in his house a certain godly and learned youth, whom I intend to bring down with me to Zurich: I request you, for Christ's sake, if it be possible, to procure him a teachership in some class in your school. He is studious and diligent, and will not shrink from the severest labours; and if he can but meet with some moderate means of subsistence, he will be of service to the church of God : remember him for Christ's sake, and let your excellence, if possible, write me an answer. Nothing can come to me more acceptably than a letter from you. May the Lord Jesus long preserve you in safety, to the glory of his name, and the benefit of his church! Amen. Salute in my name masters Bibliander, Pellican, Gualter, and all the rest. I earnestly commend myself to the prayers of your church. Excuse, I pray you, my pen running on too fast. I request your excellence to salute in my name, and that of my wife, the godly matron Falkner, who came with us to Basle from Strasburgh, which place she left unmarried, but I have now, with the consent of her parents, bestowed her in marriage.

Your excellence's most attached,

JOHN HOOPER.

[1 The duke of Norfolk, and his son, the earl of Surrey, were committed to the Tower of London, Dec. 12, 1546 ; the latter was executed on Tower Hill on the 19th of the January following.]

LETTER XXIV.

JOHN HOOPER TO [HENRY BULLINGER.]

After *Sept.* 10, 1547.

THE order of battle[2] between the Scots and English in Scotland on the 10th of September, four miles from Edinburgh.

Lord Grey, the king of England's deputy at Boulogne, and the commander in chief of the English cavalry in this battle, after the artillery was silenced, made a charge upon the Scottish front, with a view of throwing them into confusion; but disappointed of his expectation, he was forced to retreat with the loss of forty-eight of his cavalry. The earl of Warwick, who commanded the archers, perceiving the cavalry to give way, immediately and suddenly advanced with 4000 archers, and attacked that part of the Scottish army where the artillery and baggage were stationed. He so pressed the Scots by the discharge of his arrows, that they were unable any longer to stand to their guns, which having gained possession of, by his cannon-balls and volleys of arrows he compelled the whole Scottish army to fall back from their former position into one where they had not only the enemy both in front and rear, but also the sun shining full in their eyes. Which when lord Grey perceived, he made a second attack with his cavalry on their flank with much noise and clamour, shouting, " The Scots are running away, the Scots are running away." The Scots, being inferior in cavalry, were quite unable to keep their ranks, which being thrown into disorder, they betook themselves to flight; in the which there fell 15,000 men, and 2,000 were taken prisoners, among whom was lord Huntley, the chancellor of Scotland. On the same day the English ships sailed into the various Scottish harbours, and took possession of all their vessels which were adapted either for trade or naval warfare; the rest they burned. The queen, upon the

[2 For a full account of this battle, called the battle of Pinkey, in which the Scots sustained a signal defeat, see Hollingshed's Chronicles, Vol. III. p. 984, &c., or the other histories of the period.]

receipt of this unfortunate intelligence, gave herself up to the
protector upon his own terms.   Taking with him six of the
nobility as hostages for the fidelity of the queen, and leaving
troops in five places of the kingdom of Scotland, for fear lest
any rebellion should take place during his absence, he returned to London, where parliament is daily expected to meet,
in which, if it please God, this quarrel will be settled.   This
is a true statement; for my informant was present at the
battle, and witnessed the close of it.

Your excellence's ever devoted,

JOHN HOOPER.

The number of soldiers belonging to each army were,
of the English seventeen thousand, of the Scots thirty
thousand.

LETTER XXV.

JOHN HOOPER TO MARTIN BUCER.

Dated at ZURICH, *June* 19, 1548.

MUCH health.   The day before I wrote this letter, I met
master Pellican, whom I saluted in your name, and at your
request.   He has received into his family the widow of master
Matthias, a godly and upright woman : I understood from
him that you had sent me a letter by her ; and he requested
me that, if I had any thing to write in reply, I would do it by
the morrow, for on that day the widow was about to leave us.
I was unwilling therefore that she should return to you without a letter from me, lest you should think me undeserving of
your godly epistle, which I read with the greatest possible
affection and delight.   You say well, that in this shall all men
know that we are Christ's disciples, " if we have love one to
another :" let us love therefore, " not in word, neither in
tongue, but in deed and in truth."   For love is the most certain evidence of our justification, and the heavenly seal of our
acceptance in Christ Jesus ; as John saith, " Every one that

loveth is born of God, and knoweth God ; he that loveth not, knoweth not God, for God is love." If indeed we have tasted that the Lord is gracious, " let us cast off the works of darkness, and let us put on the armour of light, walking honestly, as in the day, not in strife and envying, but putting on the Lord Jesus Christ;" that we may restore the infirmities of our brethren in the spirit of meekness, or patiently bear with them. Let all malice, and all guile, and hypocrisies, and envyings be put away, for we are new-born babes, to the end that we may desire the sincere milk of the word, and grow thereby.

My master, I pray you in Christ Jesus, not to pay too much regard to envious and slanderous calumniators. You are not ignorant that the malevolence of envy is ever wont to tear most persons in pieces ; that detractors invent many falsehoods, and that brotherly love is disturbed by envy and detraction. Away with the persons who would sow dissension between yourself and those men. This I promise you, that they very frequently make mention of you in friendly and honourable terms. And although they may dissent from your opinion in the matter of the eucharist, as I do myself, yet they do not make any breach in christian love, much less regard you with hostility, but are anxious to aid by their prayers both yourself and those whom the Lord has entrusted to you in his church ; and they earnestly hope that, on your part, you will do the same for them. For Christ's sake therefore, who by his own blood hath triumphed on the cross over all enemies, hell, and sin, be ye not at variance through strife and emulation, that ye may neither quarrel any more with your tongue, nor give ear to those persons who are deficient in nothing but religion and virtue. Let controversy be settled by the authority of the word. Let no one defend his opinion with obstinacy ; but let us rather return unto the way of truth, and humbly acknowledge our errors, than continue always to go on in error without repentance, lest we should seem to have been in the wrong. Let us bear in mind that we were made for friendship and concord, that in this most miserable age we may, by our mutual kindness, relieve the distresses of each other, and at last reign together with Christ in everlasting happiness. For what frenzy is it, what folly or madness, to pursue with hostility here on earth that in-

dividual, who, should he die in Christ, will pass from death
unto life, (whither I also, Christ being my guide, hope to
flee away after this darkness,) and with whom we shall be
united in perpetual love and everlasting joy! I entreat you,
my master, not to say or write any thing against charity or
godliness for the sake of Luther, or burden the consciences of
men with his words on the holy supper. Although I readily
acknowledge with thankfulness the gifts of God in him who
is now no more[1], yet he was not without his faults. I do not
say this by way of reproach of the departed individual, because I know that no living man is without blame, and that
we all stand in need of the grace of God. After the dispute
with Zuinglius and Œcolampadius respecting the [Lord's]
supper had begun to grow warm, he did violence to many
passages of scripture, such for instance as the following, "He
ascended that he might fill all things[2];" "I am with you
alway even unto the end of the world[3];" and "we are flesh
of his flesh, and bone of his bones[4];" that he might establish
the corporal presence of the body of Christ in the bread; but
how mistakenly, is declared by the very nature of the passages. Did we not at this present time stand in need of consolation rather than of controversy, I could easily prove to the
satisfaction of every one, that these places cannot properly
be brought forward in confirmation of his opinion. Every
one too is aware, with what calumnies and reproaches he
attacked even the dead. Christ taught his disciples another
doctrine. He rebuked James and John, who wished that fire
might fall from heaven to consume the people of Samaria.
And he has commanded us to do good to our enemies, and
bless them that curse us. He, my good sir, who knoweth the
secrets of the heart, may judge what spirit occasioned so much
wrath to be kindled among the ministers of the word of God.
Nevertheless all the ministers of this church[5] were grieved at
his death, not as if they had lost an adversary or a detractor,
but rather an ally and partner in their glorious work. These
things are, in my mind, great and real evidences of kindness
and charity. I do not write thus by way of reproach of a
most learned man, but that no one may swear by his opinions,

[1 Luther died Feb. 18, 1546.]   [2 Eph. iv. 10.]
[3 Matt. xxviii. 20.]   [4 Ephes. v. 30.]
[5 Namely, of Zurich, whence this letter is dated.]

as if whatever he wrote were an oracle of Apollo, or a leaf of the Sibyl.

You write word, reverend sir, that you cannot believe the sacraments to be bare signs.   Far be such a belief from the most unlearned Christian !   The holy supper is not a bare sign, neither in it is the true and natural body of Christ corporally exhibited to me in any supernatural or heavenly manner : nevertheless, I religiously and with all honour venerate and reverence the institution of Christ upon other grounds, because it is a sign of the good-will of God towards me, and an outward testimony added to the promise of grace.   Not that this promise is applied to me by means of any sacrament, but because the promise previously applied to me by faith is thereby confirmed.   In like manner the church of God publicly receives him in baptism, who had been previously received by grace.   Thus Abraham, saith Paul, "received the sign of circumcision, a seal of the righteousness of the faith which he had yet being uncircumcised[6];" that is, a testimony by which God bare witness that he was received into grace, not that he was to be *received* by the sacrament, but rather *confirmed* in it.   Thus the holy supper is a testimony of grace, and a mystery of our redemption, in which God bears witness to the benefits bestowed upon us by Christ: not that the remission of sins, which in believers ought to precede all use of sacraments, is there applied; nor that the true body of Christ, which is in heaven and not on earth, is exhibited together with the bread; but that it may confirm that faith which I have in the death and passion of that body which was alive, died, and rose again.   And the minister gives what is in his power, namely, the bread and wine, and not the body of Christ; nor is it exhibited by the minister, and eaten by the communicant, otherwise than in the word preached, read, or meditated upon.   And to eat the body of Christ is nothing else than to believe, as he himself teaches in the sixth of John.   It is necessary therefore to bring Christ to the sacraments by faith, and not to look for him there. And thus the promise of grace is received by faith, as are also the sacraments, of which faith they are the testimonies and the seals.   There are many other ends, but this is the chief; and those who thus use the sacraments do not make them

[6 Rom. iv. 11.]

bare signs. Thus John the Baptist said, that he baptized with water, but that there was one to come after him who should baptize with the Holy Ghost. He had water in his hand, by which remission of sins was confirmed in those who believed; but he had not in his hand the Holy Ghost, that he might give remission of sins to all that were baptized; for he baptized many hypocrites. From these sensible objects therefore faith teaches us to recognise things insensible and invisible. Regard these things, I pray you, in a godly spirit. I do not write for the sake of dispute, but that I may testify to you, that the sacraments with us are not bare signs. For if faith shine forth in the mind of the recipient, the bridegroom is thereby joined[1] to the bride, so that none may put asunder what God hath joined together.

I do not rightly understand what you write respecting Calvin. I had never any intention of using my pen either against him or Farell, although his commentaries on the first epistle to the Corinthians displeased me exceedingly. I should have written my thoughts upon the Interim, had I not been told for certain that you were about to do so; which I earnestly entreat you to do, as you possess great and peculiar gifts of God, and in a thousand ways are far more fitted for this undertaking than I am, who have but lately, and as yet only in a cursory way, studied the Greek language. May the Lord Jesus ever preserve you both in body and soul, to the glory of his name! My wife salutes you. Zurich, June 19, 1548.

Your very loving,

JOHN HOOPER.

LETTER XXVI.

JOHN HOOPER TO HENRY BULLINGER.

Dated at BASLE, [*March* 28,] 1549.

MUCH health. By the mercy of God, most reverend master and gossip, we arrived at Basle about 10 o'clock on

[1 The word is illegible in the MS.]

the 27th of March, safe and sound; and if the sailors are to
be relied upon, we shall sail from hence to-morrow morning.
To spare expense therefore, I send away the driver with the
carriage and horses, and hope your worthy citizen will receive
all his property safe and uninjured by to-morrow evening.
That I have been longer delayed upon my journey than he
expected, to his inconvenience and my great expense, must
be attributed to the roughness of the journey, and not to any
loitering on my part or fatigue of the horses. I entreat you
to offer my warmest thanks to this excellent man; or else
impose this duty of courtesy in my name and at my request
upon our very loving friend, master Gualter, who, if I mistake
not, is related either by consanguinity or affinity to the owner
of the horses.

Nothing new is as yet reported to us at this place, excepting only that some persons who have just arrived from
Strasburgh, affirm for certain that the mass is not yet admitted by the citizens. For this reason the bishop of that
city is not merely angry, but rages as it were with madness
and fury, and has appointed a conference in his own territory
about two [German] miles from Strasburgh[2]; and all those
who have visited me here in a way of friendship, tell me
that he is bringing forth some horrible monstrosity; but it
will, I hope, prove abortive.

You will receive from the bearer one sheet, a blanket,
and a pillow, with many thanks; all the other things that I
borrowed to make use of upon my journey I shall send back
as far as Basle. In haste. Basle, 1549.

You shall hear more, God willing, in the course of three
days. I send back a flask; to whom it belongs, I know not.
Inquire, I pray you, of my landlord, and do not grudge to
undertake this office for my sake, who so boldly presume to
impose all my burdens upon your shoulders.

Your most devoted,

JOHN HOOPER.

P. S. We salute most respectfully your dear wife with
all your family, masters Theodore [Bibliander], Pellican,
Gualter, Butler, and all the rest[3].

[2 Namely at Saverne, about 20 miles W. N. W. of Strasburgh.]
[3 Foxe gives an interesting account of Hooper's parting interview
with his friends at Zurich. Acts and Mon. VI. 638.]

LETTER XXVII.

JOHN HOOPER TO HENRY BULLINGER.

Dated at STRASBURGH, *March* 31, 1549.

MUCH health. Grace and peace from the Lord. I obey your command, my very dear friend and gossip[1], that I should acquaint you with the progress of our journey. We arrived at Strasburgh on the 29th instant, all of us, by the blessing and favour of God, safe and sound. We think of remaining here till the third of April, that we may join some worthy and excellent companions who are now on their way to the fair. The fretfulness too of our little daughter Rachel in some measure prevents our journey; for she is cutting her teeth, and exposure to the air aggravates the painfulness of incipient illness.

I believe there is no truth in the reports respecting Hedio[2]. On the 30th of this month I was present at his lecture, which was upon the 10th chapter of the epistle to the Romans. He spoke very clearly and openly upon the excellency of the word of God, and warned his hearers most carefully to beware of the beguiling snares of the Interim. What he said however, I think, proceeded rather from excessive terror and alarm, than from actual dislike. He is not wanting in godliness, but he has too great a dread of offending the emperor. On the same day I was present at his evening sermon, where, among other things that he said, and which I heard with pain, he absurdly inveighed with great bitterness against the Suvermerians[3]. May the Lord forgive him, and bring him to a better mind!

Paul Fagius left this place before my arrival. Bucer, I believe, will depart this evening, but I do not yet know

[1 Bullinger was God-father to Hooper's daughter Rachel.]

[2 Caspar Hedio was professor of theology at Strasburgh, where he died in 1552, and was succeeded by Hierome Zanchius.]

[3 The Saxon divines were exceeding hot against the Swiss divines, on account of their rejecting the doctrine of consubstantiation held by the Lutherans. In their ordinary discourses, Strype says, "they styled them heretics, false prophets, Suvermeros, Sacramentiperdas." Strype, Cranmer, 508.]

whither he is going. He is invited into England, Poland, and Saxony. He received me at dinner yesterday, where I met John Sturmius, Sapidus, and Christopher Mont. They were very much delighted at the concord of the people of Switzerland, which I pray the Lord to continue and confirm. I myself, my wife, Rachel, and Joanna, diligently commend to our good and gracious God in our prayers the well being of yourself and all your family, and that of the other most godly ministers of your church, all of whom we sincerely and cordially salute. Farewell, most excellent and ever esteemed sir. Strasburgh, March 31.

Your most devoted,

JOHN HOOPER.

LETTER XXVIII.

JOHN HOOPER TO HENRY BULLINGER.
Dated at MAYENCE, *April* 8, 1549.

MUCH health. I hope, my worthy friend and gossip, that the letter which I wrote to you on my journey was safely delivered; by which you would ascertain our route and progress as far as Strasburgh. We sailed from thence on the second of April, all of us by the goodness and favour of God in good health. The first day of our voyage from Strasburgh was a prosperous one, with the wind and stream in our favour: on the second day also God was not less gracious to us. We passed the night of this day in a village near Spires, where on the same day there had been dining sixty-four Spaniards, all cavalry, who were going up towards the duchy of Wurtemberg, so sharpened by hunger, that they left the landlords neither flesh nor fish for us. We fared very sparingly, satisfying ourselves with their broken victuals. There is no distinction of meat among them, nor any observance of days, for which such abundance of christian blood is shed by the madness of the papists. The third day of our voyage passed most comfortably; the fourth was somewhat dangerous. We met with a contrary wind, high waves, ignorant and careless sailors, so that we were twice exposed to great peril; and unless we had reached the land, which we effected with great difficulty, we should all of us have been lost. This happened about half a mile from Mayence: we all entered the city on foot, safe and sound. The other vessel which accompanied us suffered far more than we did; much of the cargo was spoiled by the water, and the master of the vessel, knocked about by the violence of the storm, just as he was about to cast anchor, got his leg entangled in the cable which sustained the whole weight of the anchor, and was hurt very severely. At Mayence we sojourned at the Golden Swan, where we found six merchants who had come from the city of Liege. They told us that the emperor was now at Brussels with his son Philip in great triumph and magnificence. They say that the wily and bad landgrave is detained prisoner near Ghent. I inquired whether the emperor was preparing a second expedition into upper Germany. They replied that no rumours of that kind had been spread amongst them. I asked too concerning the people of the lake territories. They told me that the emperor would lead all his forces against them this summer. May the victory be on their side, who most desire the safety of the church of Christ! Let us pray God, and he will deliver his people out of temptations. I have great hope that this will be the case, provided only they are cemented by a holy concord, which alone can destroy the power of the emperor. The affairs of Saxony are fluctuating and uncertain, and, as it is reported here, are placed in the greatest danger by reason of intestine discords, by which, if they are not healed, they will mutually destroy each other.

I have nothing to write respecting England, except that she is miserably and dangerously exposed to a bloody war, and is safe on no side. The French and Scots are open enemies; there is a third in secret, more powerful than either of them; and I fear that he will take advantage of the present juncture. I have often earnestly besought you and your people to interpose your mediation between France and England; and I now again and again suppliantly entreat and beseech you the same thing, for the sake of Christ, who is the restorer of peace. Bear in mind that reward which is promised you by him who cannot lie: "Blessed are the peace-makers, for they shall be called the

XXVIII.] JOHN HOOPER TO HENRY BULLINGER. 53

children of God." Let not the majesty of the royal name or
the vapouring of any other title deter you. Moreover, the
state and condition of the king and the realm of England is
now very different from what it was formerly: he is your
brother, he worships the same God with yourselves, and, I
hope, in the same manner. But if they will go on as they
are doing, and will admit of no equitable terms, one or the
other of them must necessarily yield before long.

A new gold coinage is now being struck in England
of a purer standard than that which was coined under the
late king; but what is increased in one way is diminished in
another, for the standard weight of the crowns is diminished
by nearly a fourth part. I will not be unmindful of the
cloth which I promised you, but will send it as soon as I
possibly can.

While I was writing the above, the letter, my most reverend
master and gossip, was delivered to me, which you wrote on
the 26th of March. In truth I receive nothing with greater
pleasure than this evidence of your good health, which may
the Lord, the Almighty Maker of heaven and earth, long
preserve to you safe and sound! I wish you had written one
word respecting that pious matron, my good friend, the wife
of master Bibliander. I hope in the Lord Jesus that she has
had a happy delivery: were it otherwise, I should be much
concerned. I should now write to my worthy gossip, master
Bibliander, if there were any subject to supply me with an
occasion for writing. When I have proceeded lower down on
my journey, I will write to you more at length. Meanwhile
farewell, and may our most merciful heavenly Father grant
that you may be always well, through the blood of his Son
Jesus Christ our Saviour: and remember, my dear friend, to
persevere with energy, as you do, in your holy and dangerous warfare. If but the least doubt of your perseverance
disturbed my thoughts, I would add spurs to a running
horse. But I know you well and intimately, and doubt not
but that you will in many ways surpass my expectation. This
at least I can assuredly promise myself concerning you, that,
like a good shepherd, you will lay down your life for your
sheep. And I have the same persuasion respecting our learned and vigilant brother, master Gualter. Let others talk, and
extenuate, and make what excuses they please, who, when the
wolf is coming, have left their sheep to be torn in pieces by

thieves and robbers : unless they repent, they will wretchedly suffer the punishment of hirelings in that day when the true Shepherd shall come to separate the sheep from the goats.

According to your singular kindness and benevolence towards me, when my amanuensis shall come to you for the purpose of writing out for me the heads of your sermons, urge him, I pray you, carefully to copy out not only your remarks on the epistle to the Romans, but also those on Isaiah and the other prophets; that I, though distant, may benefit others by the gifts of God bestowed upon you. Will you also make the same request in my name to my masters and brethren; master Gualter and the most learned Theodore [Bibliander], men most truly esteemed by me? I left sufficient money at Zurich, and will liberally recompense their labour if they will but comply with my entreaties. I have desired them to forward my wishes in this respect, and to use all diligence in copying out the sermons and lectures at my expense. Do you only, my kind friend, exhort them to this; I do not ask you to do it yourself; sufficient burdens are imposed upon your shoulders from other quarters.

I shall say nothing as to the civility of the innkeepers from Strasburgh to this city ; they are barbarous Scythians, and harsh and uncivilized Getæ. Once more farewell. My wife and daughter, Stumphius, Joanna, and Martin, salute you, as I do myself, with your dear wife and all your family; likewise masters Bibliander, Gualter, Pellican, excellent and most deserving men, with their families. Moreover, I commend to Almighty God your holy church, and commonwealth, and most worthy magistrate Lavater, that he may defend you against the enemies of his name. Mayence. In haste. April 8, 1549.

Yours in body and soul,

JOHN HOOPER.

P. S. Sleidan[1] of Strasburgh has written a book of history for our king. Doctor Andernach too, a physician of

[1 In March 1551, archbishop Cranmer procured for John Sleidan, from king Edward, an honorary pension of 200 crowns a year, as some aid for the carrying on his commentaries, which he was then busy about; and, as it seems, encouraged by Cranmer to take in hand and prosecute. See Strype, Cranmer, 595.]

Strasburgh, has translated a work upon medicine from the
Greek into Latin, and dedicated it to the archbishop of Canterbury. You see how active all persons are in running after
gain. Beyond doubt, if there were no danger hanging over
them, both our king and his kingdom would be without their
favour and support. I hear that Bernardine's wife exhibits
herself in England both in dress and appearance as a French
lady of rank. But I shall soon know more about her, and
so shall you. Respectfully salute, I pray you, the preacher
from Memmingen, and also my host and hostess Zinchia.

LETTER XXIX.

JOHN HOOPER TO HENRY BULLINGER.

Dated at COLOGNE, *April* 14, 1549.

GRACE and innocency of life from the Lord. If you are
well, my most esteemed master and gossip, with your dear
wife and family, it is well; and we are all of us by the divine
mercy in good health. I hope you have received all my
letters, which gave you full information respecting the success
of our journey as far as Mayence. We arrived at Cologne
on the 11th of April without any thing untoward in our
voyage, except a contrary wind and rough weather. We had
however a favourable landing. On the 8th of April two other
ships suffered much more than we did, namely, shipwreck,
with the total loss of their respective crews. Two other
vessels here at Cologne sustained the same misfortune during
the late carnival: in one there were twenty-eight men, and
twelve in the other, not one of whom, with the exception of
two sailors, escaped with life.

I have nothing to write respecting the affairs of England,
except that the gospel of Christ our Lord is daily striking
root more deeply. The admiral[2] is dead. He was beheaded,
and divided into four quarters; with how much unwillingness

[2 Lord Seymour was beheaded on Tower Hill, March 20, 1549.
See Latimer's Sermons, Parker Society Edition, p. 161.]

he suffered death, master John Utenhovius[1], who is the bearer of this letter, will fully explain to you by word of mouth. When he comes to you, receive him with that ancient kindness, which the country of Switzerland has ever manifested of her own accord towards all strangers. He is a man illustrious both by his birth and virtues, most sincere in the true religion, and entirely opposed to all the mischiefs of sectarianism: he is very dear both to myself and my wife, and by long habits of familiarity and intercourse exceedingly attached to us; and he is moreover exceedingly intimate with master John à Lasco. There is no occasion for me to commend him to you more at length. His noble qualities and remarkable learning will sufficiently recommend him to all pious and learned men. He is coming to you on my recommendation, that he may hear your godly sermons and theological lectures, and observe the mode of administering the Lord's supper, which as it is most simple among you, so is it most pure. He will board with his old friend master Butler, an Englishman. It would be foreign to my present purpose to inform you how much he has suffered from the emperor for the sake of the gospel of Christ.

May the Lord preserve you all, your church and commonwealth! My wife, my little daughter, Stumphius, Martin, and Joanna dutifully salute your excellency, your whole family, and all the other godly members of your church. Cologne, April 14, 1549.

Your excellency's most attached,

JOHN HOOPER.

P. S. I send you a compendium of the doctrine of the eucharist, which I know will much please you. See that he [Utenhovius] be introduced to and form a friendship with masters Gualter, Pellican, Gesner and the rest. I would write a general letter to the whole assembly of the learned men at Zurich in favour of this good brother, if I had time.

[1 Bullinger thus writes of Utenhovius in a letter to Burcher, dated June 28, 1549. "The nobleman, Utenhovius, of Ghent, has far exceeded your commendation of him; and I thank you, that through the instrumentality of yourself and Hooper I have contracted a friendship with a man every way so worthy."]

LETTER XXX.

JOHN HOOPER TO HENRY BULLINGER.

Dated at [ANTWERP, *April 26, 1549.*]

MUCH health.   Grace and innocency of life from the Lord.
How mercifully God has hitherto been present with us, and
made our journey prosperous, we hope, most honoured friend
and gossip, you have learned from the letters written at
Dietikon, Basle, Strasburgh, Mayence, and Cologne.   That
which I wrote from Cologne you will receive by master John
Utenhovius, an excellent and worthy man, born of an honourable family at Ghent.   We earnestly pray you to receive him
with kindness.   Moreover, should there occur any mention of
the holy supper of the Lord, diligently admonish and instruct
him upon the subject; you will find no one more tractable,
or more ready to learn.

We left Cologne on the 14th of April, and directed our
course through the barren and sandy plains of Brabant to
Antwerp, where we all of us arrived, by God's blessing, safe
and sound, on the 18th of the same month.   Compelled by
the entreaties of the commissioner[2] of our king, who is now
attending upon the emperor, I went over to Brussels with
John Stumphius, that he might see the effeminacy and
wretchedness of the court, and also the bondage of the good
citizens of Brussels, who are now forced to endure the im-
periousness of the Spaniards, their depredation and robbery,
the violation of their daughters, the corruption of their wives,
and lastly, threatenings and blows from that most profligate
nation[3]; to the end that he might more feelingly consider the
state and condition of his own country, pray for it more
ardently, and more earnestly warn his countrymen, and
by letting them know the misfortunes of others render them
more cautious.   We did not see the emperor, who very
seldom leaves his chamber, nor yet his son, who was keeping
Easter in some monastery out of the city.   John Stumphius
saw the duke of Saxony at a window.   I was twice at his
house, and very courteously entertained by his German at-

[2 Namely, Sir Philip Hobby.   See Burnet, III. 289.]

[3 The particulars mentioned in this letter are confirmed by Sleidan and Brandt.]

tendants, who are about thirty in number. The duke wished
two or three times to admit me to an interview, but the
presence of the Spanish general always prevented him. He
abides stedfast in the faith, and is in a very good state of
health. There is no hope whatever of his deliverance, unless,
which will not I trust be the case, he should change his religion : he does not despair of the word of God. The Landgrave[1] of Hesse is in confinement at Oudenarde, seven miles
from Ghent: he is a man thoroughly wretched and vacillating;
at one time he promises all obedience and fidelity to the emperor, receives the mass and other impious idolatries with
open arms ; at another time he execrates and abominates the
emperor, with his Interim. May the Lord have compassion
upon him! he is in a state of great wretchedness, and is
now paying the just penalty of his perfidiousness. We saw
likewise that traitor Lazarus Schuendi[2], with whom you are
acquainted. There is no need for me to write about
Brandenburg and the other Germans who are in bondage to
the Spaniards.

The pope's legate has been preaching in his palace
during the whole of Lent, with what impiety I shall not
write. This however I know for certain, that there is not
a friendly feeling between the pope and the emperor, neither between the king of France and the emperor. Both
of them are greatly afraid of him, and he, in his turn, is in
the greatest fear of the fulminations of the pope. It is now
seriously disputed between them, whether the general council
shall be held at Trent or Bologna. The pope urges, bids,
entreats, commands the emperor to consent to Bologna. He
resists, refuses, opposes in every possible way, and says that
he would rather break off all alliance with the pope, than allow
of that locality, namely, Bologna. It is easy to conjecture
what mischief lies hid in this proposal on the part of the
pope. He is in great apprehension for his kingdom; for I am
informed by our ambassador, that if the emperor's confessor[3]

[1 The Elector of Saxony and the Landgrave of Hesse became
prisoners of the emperor after the battle of Muhlberg in 1547.]

[2 Lazarus Schuendi is mentioned by Sleidan as having been sent
by the emperor with a party of soldiers to raze the castle of Gothen,
and set at liberty marquess Albert of Brandenburg, who was there kept
prisoner.]

[3 Peter de Soto, a Dominican, was confessor to Charles V. He

were but moderately religious, there would be the greatest
hope of shortly bringing him into the knowledge of Christ;
for he openly told me that both the emperor and all his
councillors were guided, persuaded, led and dragged about by
their confessor, who acts in every respect at the bidding and
advice of the pope. And I easily believe this; for when the
emperor was in upper Germany seven months since, he was
deserted by his confessor, because he would not act with
severity against some godly persons, and restore popery altogether. The emperor offered him a bishoprick in Spain
worth twenty thousand crowns per annum. He put a slight
upon the liberality of the emperor, and upon the emperor himself, in these terms: "I owe myself entirely to the church of
Christ, but neither to you nor to your gifts, unless you choose
to serve the church more zealously than you have done."

And now as to the emperor's views in regard to Switzerland.
All parties agree in this, that he is enviously opposed to your
liberty, and will therefore leave no stone unturned to destroy
your union. Should he not succeed in this way, he will
attempt every thing by promises. Beware therefore, lest he
deceive you with vain expectations. Last of all, he will without doubt attack you with an hostile army, not with a view
of overcoming you in this way, or exposing many of his troops
to danger, but merely to strike terror into you. I pray you
therefore to preserve your mutual regard and unanimity:
fear God, live holily, fight bravely, and expect the victory
from God, who will without doubt stand by and defend you.
People think that you are not in imminent danger at present;
but still you should always be prepared against a feeling of
security, lest he should overwhelm you when you little think
of it. The emperor is hitherto well aware that he cannot
manage the affairs of Germany as he desires. He has been
more troubled, as I have been informed upon good authority,
that he has made any alteration in religion, than if he had
promised the Germans the utmost liberty in that respect. They

afterwards accompanied Philip into England, where he was employed
at Oxford to lecture, and as much as possible to undo all that Peter
Martyr had done. He was afterwards accused for heretical opinions
to the Inquisition at Valladolid, but died at Trent in 1563 before the
preliminary proceedings had been completed. See Zurich Letters, 1st
Series, p. 33, and Llorente Hist. Crit. de l'Inquisition, III. 88.]

say that the emperor will shortly proceed to Ghent, and from
thence return to Brussels, or go up towards Spires.   He
has troops stationed near Bremen and the towns upon the
coast, but they are inactive; they neither make any progress,
nor are they much feared by the citizens, who are daily
adding to the strength of their cities, and have provisions for
five years, and do not any longer court the favour of the
emperor. You are, I think, aware of the severity of the
exactions the emperor now demands from his subjects: I will
relate, however, an affecting and lamentable statement which
a godly matron, my landlady, made to me in Brabant. " If,"
she said, "I could carry in my arms my large and troublesome
family of children, I would flee away, and obtain my livelihood by begging. For the tax-gatherers of the emperor and
the queen exhaust all the fruit of our labours." The English
too, are now sadly oppressed in this respect. A fifth of all
property has been granted to the king. But I must tell you
one more thing respecting Switzerland. Yesterday, April
25th, I was invited to dinner by a citizen of Antwerp, who is
well acquainted with Switzerland from having frequently exposed his goods to sale in all their cities. He told me that since
the emperor had left upper Germany, he had often seen in
his palace the public officers of the canton of Lucerne; for he
knew them well by the colour of their dress. It is to be
feared that the secret affairs of that country may be revealed
by this means, or that some yet greater evil may be latent.

On the first of May there will be fresh rejoicings at
Brussels in honour of the prince of Spain. You have, I suppose, heard of the former ones from master John Utenhovius;
but as he did not see the new gates and columns erected
in the city, you must know that at the first gate there is
a column on which is inscribed, " Happy are his subjects!"

> Quis genus Austriadum, quis stirpem Cæsaris altam
>   Herculei vere generis esse negat?

On the other side is written,

> Alcidem jactant nugæ et fictitia monstra;
>   Caroleos ausus fortia gesta probant.

On the second gate:

> Sancta fides merito collaudat vosque patresque,
>   Auxilio quorum cæpit et aucta fides.

On the other side :

> Se ter felicem hoc fausto tempore clamat,
> Prole quod Augusta vindice tuta manet.

The third gate bears the representation of Hercules sailing with his pillars, on each of which is placed a statue of a man. The first says, " go," the other, " come." The verses are these,

> Adsit Caroleo cœlestis palma labori,
> Et maneat soli gloria prima Deo.

Also,

> Fida lacessiti cunctatio restituit rem,
> Christicolamque fidem provehat ulterius.

At Antwerp there is represented an eagle with expanded wings, beneath whose feet is written this impious application of scripture, " Protect us under the shadow of thy wings."

On the first of May, at the rejoicings at Brussels, the prince of Spain, and the son of the duke d'Arschot, a native of Brabant, engaged with spears on horseback. Whether by chance or carelessness I know not, but the prince's helmet was badly fastened on, and could not withstand the force of the lance of d'Arschot's son; so that the prince was twice wounded in the face, once in the chin, the second time in the forehead, but the wounds are not dangerous. The emperor however, in alarm, put off the tournament till the following week.

I hear that east Friesland has received the Interim. If this be the case, master à Lasco will soon return into England. I greatly regret his absence, especially as Peter Martyr and Bernardine so stoutly defend Lutheranism, and there is now arrived a third, (I mean Bucer,) who will leave no stone unturned to obtain a footing. The people of England, as I hear, all of them entertain right notions upon that subject. Should not master à Lasco come to us in a short time, I will send him your letter with the writing. But, if it please God, I could wish to meet the parties in person. We have remained here a fortnight for the sake of passing over from hence into England more conveniently, with a well-informed and skilful English captain who is staying here, and waiting for a cargo. But I am afraid lest the wind should turn against us, in which case we shall lose both our time and money.

[JOHN HOOPER.]

LETTER XXXI.

JOHN HOOPER TO HENRY BULLINGER.

Dated at ANTWERP, *May* 3, 1549.

I HAVE desired for some days to take care of the health of my wife and our little girl, who, though they were entirely exhausted by the fatigue of the journey, have now by resting tolerably recovered their strength. You will receive with this letter a piece of cloth for hose, of a better quality than that which you bought of me before, but yet at the same or a lower price. It contains, I suppose, at least 20 Zurich ells: should it contain more or less, let me know in your next letter, which I pray you to send to our old friend Richard Hilles. It will then, I hope, be faithfully delivered to me. Let this cloth be divided between master Mayor and yourself: I would have sent you another piece, could I have met with any upon sale at this place. As soon as I arrive in London I will send you some, God willing, not inferior to this, nor more expensive. All those persons in this place who import cloth from England, sell it at a profit, and it is with difficulty that I have met with that which I now send. They have many thousand [pieces], but they will not sell except to those who will buy ten or twenty whole pieces together, for fear of mixing the different qualities of the cloth; as the best, the middling, and the inferior, mutually help each other both in the price and the sale. If you or the Mayor will, either of you, keep the cloth now sent, I will send a second piece to the one who shall be without it. I bought this for forty shillings, that is, six ducats, before it was dyed. A ducat is equivalent to forty stivers of Brabant, and forty stivers of Brabant make twenty-four batzen of Constance. I paid for the dyeing eight shillings of Brabant, which make twenty-eight batzen of Constance, and a little over: I do not know what I am to pay for the carriage to Strasburgh, but, exclusive of all expenses, you will have a Zurich ell for ten Zurich batzen. If there are twenty ells, this will amount to two hundred batzen, which make eight French solar crowns, which is the price of the entire piece. When I reach London, I may probably send you some at a less price; meanwhile take in good part my services, which I owe and shall owe you, as a father and a most esteemed master, as long as I live. I wish this cloth to be divided between master Mayor and yourself, that when I send you another piece you may be upon an equal footing both with respect to the quality of the cloth and the price. And if in future you should wish to wear English cloth for your coats or hose, (and state this also in my name to our brother Gualter,) I will always most willingly use my endeavours in your behalf. And you, as you love me, see that those who are taking copies at my expense, are most carefully supplied with the notes of your sermons. If they are not sparing in their labours, I will not be sparing of my money. Keep in your possession the money for this cloth, until I shall let you know by letter to what use I wish it to be applied.

My wife and all who are with me salute your reverence, your wife and all your family; and you will salute in all our names masters Gualter, Pellican, the Israelite indeed, and all the other learned and most loving brethren. Do not moreover omit to salute with the greatest respect and honour most dutifully in my name master Mayor, to whom and to the commonwealth of Zurich I most ardently wish every happiness. May the Lord long preserve you by his Spirit safe, pious, and sound; and may you defend the fold of Christ from wolves and hirelings until the coming of the glory of God! Antwerp, May 3, 1549.

Yours always in mind and body,

JOHN HOOPER.

P. S. Take care, I pray you, that the other letters which I send, may be delivered to those to whom they are directed. After Easter my wife wrote to her mother, who lives about fifteen miles from Antwerp. The messenger found her father dead. Her mother received the letter and gave it my wife's brother to read, who immediately threw it into the fire without reading it. You see the words of Christ are true, that the brother shall persecute the brother for the sake of the word of God.

LETTER XXXII.

JOHN HOOPER TO HENRY BULLINGER,

Dated at LONDON, *May* 31, 1549.

MUCH health. Pardon, most loving master and father, the shortness of my letter. You will learn from our brother, master Butler, by what circumstances I am hindered, and with whom I have to contend within these two days on the subject of divorce. In the commentaries[1] which I lately wrote on the decalogue, I allowed both to the man and his wife an equal liberty of divorce on account of adultery, if they are disposed to use that liberty which Christ has permitted in the gospel of his church, where the marriage contract is dissolved by adultery. My opponents allow the husband to divorce his wife by reason of adultery, and to marry another; but they do not allow the same liberty to the wife. In your next letter, as you love me, either confirm my opinion, or correct my error.

We are all well; I have sent John Stumphius to Oxford, recommended by many honourable men, and especially by Treherne, who is much attached to you. When I gave your letter to the archbishop of Canterbury, he did not vouchsafe a single word respecting either yourself, or your most godly church. Bucer has very great influence with him, and the bishop will appoint him to the regius professorship [of divinity] at Cambridge. Master à Lasco is absent, which is a great grief to all godly persons. I shall send your letter to him to-morrow by a good and trusty friend, together with the book and writing. You may expect, God willing, a longer letter within the next fortnight, with which you will also receive the cloth. My wife always makes mention of you in her prayers; she salutes you with your dear wife and all your family. Our little daughter Rachel with Martin and Joanna do the same in spirit. Do you, most esteemed master, salute in our names masters Gualter, Pellican, Gesner, and all the rest. London, May 31, 1549.

Your ever most affectionate, JOHN HOOPER.

[1 See a Declaration of the ten holy Commandments of Almighty God, in Hooper's early writings, Parker Society edition. The passage here referred to will be found in pp. 378, 379, where Hooper complains of the uncharitable construction put upon it.]

LETTER XXXIII.

JOHN HOOPER TO HENRY BULLINGER.

Dated at LONDON, *June* 25, [1549].

MUCH health.   I cannot express, my much honoured master and gossip, the delight afforded me by your letter, a most certain token as it was of your exceeding love to me.   I earnestly entreat you to act always thus; for nothing can be more agreeable to me than to hear often of your welfare, and of the safety of your church and commonwealth.   You shall always in return receive every intelligence from me respecting my own circumstances and those of our church.   Great, great I say, my beloved master and gossip, is the harvest, but the labourers are few.   May our most indulgent Father send forth labourers into the harvest!   Such is the maliciousness and wickedness of the bishops, that the godly and learned men who would willingly labour in the Lord's harvest are hindered by them; and they neither preach themselves, nor allow the liberty of preaching to others.   For this reason there are some persons here who read and expound the holy scriptures at a public lecture, two of whom read in St Paul's cathedral four times a week.   I myself too, as my slender abilities will allow me, having compassion upon the ignorance of my brethren, read a public lecture twice in the day to so numerous an audience, that the church cannot contain them. The anabaptists[2] flock to the place, and give me much trouble with their opinions respecting the incarnation of the Lord; for they deny altogether that Christ was born of the virgin Mary according to the flesh.   They contend that a man who is reconciled to God is without sin, and free from all stain of concupiscence, and that nothing of the old Adam remains in his nature; and a man, they say, who is thus regenerate cannot sin.   They add that all hope of pardon is taken away from those who, after having received the Holy Ghost, fall into sin.   They maintain a fatal necessity, and that beyond and besides that will of his which he has revealed to us in

---

[2 For an account of the opinions of the anabaptists of this period, see Strype, Mem. I. i. 552.]

5

the scriptures, God hath another will by which he altogether acts under some kind of necessity. Although I am unable to satisfy their obstinacy, yet the Lord by his word shuts their mouths, and their heresies are more and more detested by the people. How dangerously our England is afflicted by heresies of this kind, God only knows; I am unable indeed from sorrow of heart to express to your piety. There are some who deny that man is endued with a soul different from that of a beast, and subject to decay. Alas! not only are those heresies reviving among us which were formerly dead and buried, but new ones are springing up every day. There are such libertines and wretches, who are daring enough in their conventicles not only to deny that Christ is the Messiah and Saviour of the world, but also to call that blessed Seed a mischievous fellow and deceiver of the world. On the other hand, a great portion of the kingdom so adheres to the popish faction, as altogether to set at nought God and the lawful authority of the magistrates; so that I am greatly afraid of a rebellion and civil discord. May the Lord restrain restless spirits, and destroy the counsels of Achitophel! Do you, my venerable father, commend our king and the council of the nation, together with our church, to God in your prayers.

I have not yet seen my parents, but hope to do so shortly, if the Lord permit. It has hitherto been out of my power, both because I am daily expecting my baggage with books and other necessaries, which were detained at Antwerp by an unfavourable wind; and also because through the instigation of the devil and wickedness of man there has lately arisen in my part of the country[1] a commotion of the people against the government, not unattended with danger, and as yet hardly composed. Tumults of this kind are taking place not only in my country, but almost throughout the whole kingdom. The people are sorely oppressed by the marvellous tyranny of the nobility. Let us pray that all occasions of discord may be piously removed, and that the people may be kept in order to the glory of God's name. The state of our country is indeed most deplorable: we are however in expectation of a happy issue, when we shall feel pleasure in the recollection of what is past. When I visit my friends, I

[1 Namely, Devonshire and Somersetshire. See Strype, Mem. II. i. 259.]

will purchase for yourself and master Mayor the other cloth that I promised, and also another piece for master John Butler; I could not buy it here at your price.

Bucer is with the archbishop of Canterbury like another Scipio, and an inseparable companion. Paulus Fagius too, and Peter Alexander, formerly chaplain to queen Mary, the emperor's sister, are also there. Within a fortnight, God willing, you shall know more. Salute very much in all our names your wife with all your family, masters Gualter and Pellican with their wives, and all the other members of your church. I wish you were acquainted with our language, and that master Gualter also knew it for six months: I doubt not but that God would convert many hearts to the knowledge of himself. Farewell. London, June 25.

I send herewith a pattern of the cloth of this kind which is manufactured either in your neighbourhood or in Suabia. You will ascertain this from the wife of master Musculus. Ask master Butler to send me four or five florins worth, and send word how much it costs per ell. I have often grieved over my departure from you; for the Lord has opened my eyes to perceive the sad and dangerous situation of the clergy. I will endure it however, God willing, as long as I can do so with a pure conscience.

Yours ever most attached,

JOHN HOOPER.

P. S. My friend Martin, an excellent young man, affectionately salutes your excellency. You will deign to salute in my name my master, your most worthy Mayor, who is on every account so respectable. I hope you have received one piece of cloth. You shall receive the second in a short time.

LETTER XXXIV.

JOHN HOOPER TO JOHN STUMPHIUS.

Dated at LONDON, *Aug.* 1, [1549].

MUCH health. You will receive, my very dear brother, by the bearer of this letter all your books, which I doubt

5—2

not you have been long and anxiously expecting. The party to whom I gave in charge my luggage at Strasburgh anwered my expectation in this respect negligently enough. You need not be troubled about the carriage, as I have paid both the waggoners and sailors. Should you be in want of money, you can let me know by letter every week ; I will never be wanting to your necessities. I am obliged to remain here in London and in the family of the lord protector, till things become more settled : I tell you this, that you may know for certain where to direct your letters. Since you left me, I have received two letters from master Bullinger, from which I learn that the affairs of Switzerland are as safe and flourishing as ever. A letter, however, has lately reached me from Germany, which states that five cantons have lately entered upon a solemn treaty with the king of France against the English, but that the evangelical states had piously and boldly rejected it. Do you, my brother, as your love to your country requires, aid them together with me in your diligent and persevering prayers unto the Lord ; and he who has begun a godly work in the people of Zurich, will perform it even unto the end. Farewell, and respectfully salute in my name the wife of Peter Martyr, together with his attendant[1]; and also John ab Ulmis, with the Hessian who lately came over to you. I would salute my old friend master Garbrand[2], only that I have so often done so without any greeting in return, that I know not whether he can bear with patience to be saluted by me. London, August 1. In haste.

Yours ever to serve in any way,

JOHN HOOPER.

You will also receive three shirts. The fourth is still packed up among my baggage, which I have not yet unpacked. I will send it you next week.

[1 This was Julius Santerentianus, so often mentioned in the preceding series.]
[2 One of this name is mentioned by Strype, as a prebendary of Salisbury, and friend of bishop Jewel. Strype, Ann. II. i. 146.]

LETTER XXXV.

JOHN HOOPER TO HENRY BULLINGER.
Dated at LONDON, *Nov.* 7, 1549.

MUCH health.   The favour and blessing of God be with you! If you have not yet received my letter, with two entire pieces of cloth, one for yourself, and the other for master Butler, you will receive them, my much esteemed master and father, in a short time.   They are detained a longer time at Antwerp on account of the dyeing; but by the blessing of God they will all safely reach you.   You must not wonder at your not having yet received the cloth; for I have been so overwhelmed by difficult and constant business since my arrival in England, that I have not yet been able either to visit my native place or my parents.

The face of things is now changed, and the state of English affairs in some respects altered.   My patron[3], who was first minister and protector, is now imprisoned with many others in the Tower of London, as you will better learn from a letter which is now on the road to you.   We are greatly apprehensive of a change in religion; but as yet no alteration has taken place.   Help us in Christ by your prayers.   The young king by the mercy of God is alive and well, and is a prince of great learning and wisdom.   The papists are hoping and earnestly struggling for their kingdom.   The bishop[4] of London, the most bitter enemy of the gospel, is now living in confinement, and deposed from his bishoprick.   This was done when the affairs and fortunes of the duke of Somerset were more prosperous than they are at present.   I had a sharp and dangerous contest with that bishop, both publicly from the

[3 Namely, the duke of Somerset, who was sent to the Tower, Oct. 14, 1549.]

[4 Bishop Bonner, against whom a commission was issued out from the king to archbishop Cranmer, bishop Ridley, the secretaries Petre and Smith, and Dr May, dean of St Paul's. Strype, Cranmer, 269. A full account of the proceedings is given in Foxe, Acts and Mon. v. 741, &c. See also Collier's Eccles. Hist. of Great Britain.]

pulpit, in my turns at Paul's cross, and also before the king's council. Should he be again restored to his office and episcopal function, I shall, I doubt not, be restored to my country and my Father which is in heaven. Fourteen days since silence was imposed and enjoined upon all lecturers and preachers. But this only lasted seven days; and liberty of teaching is again allowed them. I read in public every day to a most crowded audience at London, and take John and Daniel by turns. I lectured upon the Psalms at the king's court as long as the situation of the duke permitted me to do so; but that lecture is now laid aside.

Will you kindly undertake, most reverend sir, out of your love to Christ and to myself, to have your notes on Isaiah copied out and forwarded to me with all fidelity, (for I am greatly in need of your assistance;) and also all the other comments which you have written on the other prophets, or upon the New Testament? I know that they are all pure in doctrine, and learned, and holy. I will satisfy the writer or copyist for his pains. I make, too, the same request from master Gualter, and from our gossip, master Bibliander, with respect to his lectures, which are doubtless holy, pious, and full of learning. You will receive with the cloth the disputation[1] of Peter Martyr with the papists at Oxford on the subject of the eucharist.

John Stumphius is well, and conducts himself with much credit: tell his parents, that should he stand in need of any assistance in any way, I will never be wanting to him. John ab Ulmis is also in good health. You will do well if you will admonish him by letter to pursue his studies with diligence, and remain at home. I am afraid that by his so frequently going backwards and forwards between Oxford and London, he will incur a loss not only of time, but of money. Use your own discretion in this matter. In haste. Salute all my good masters and instructors, together with all our friends and their godly wives in the name of us all.

I entreat you most kindly to salute that excellent man, master Butler, to whom I am not now able to write a letter; and request him to give two florins in my name to the widow of the deceased Zinkius. You will also tell this afflicted

[1 For an account of this disputation, which was afterwards published by Peter Martyr, see Strype, Cranmer, 283.]

widow, that we shall all of us bear in mind, as long as we live, the kindness with which she treated us.

Your excellence's most attached,

JOHN HOOPER.

LETTER XXXVI.

JOHN HOOPER TO HENRY BULLINGER.
Dated at LONDON, *Dec.* 27, 1549.

THAT you so seldom receive any letter from me, my very reverend master and gossip, I pray you to ascribe to the calamity of our time, and the alteration in my circumstances, rather than to any forgetfulness of your signal courtesy and kindness, which both reason and affection entirely forbid on my part.

We were in much alarm, and very great fear possessed the minds of the godly, as to the success that the religion of Christ just now budding forth in England would meet with upon the fall of the duke of Somerset, who is still confined in the Tower of London. We have as yet no certain information as to what will become of him. We hope that his life will be spared. May God grant this for the glory of his name, and the benefit of his church! although we see many dangers hanging over him, yet we hope and expect a favourable issue. We easily indeed give credit to what we wish.

No change in religion has taken place among us, and we hope that no alteration will be made hereafter. Although our vessel is dangerously tossed about on all sides, yet God in his providence holds the helm, and raises up more favourers of his word in his majesty's councils, who with activity and courage defend the cause of Christ. The archbishop of Canterbury entertains right views as to the nature of Christ's presence in the supper, and is now very friendly towards myself. He has some articles of religion, to which all preachers and lecturers in divinity are required to subscribe, or else a licence for teaching is not granted them; and in these his sentiments respecting the eucharist are pure, and religious, and similar to yours in Switzerland. We desire nothing more for him than a firm and manly spirit. Like all the other bishops in this country, he is too fearful about what may happen to him. There are here six[1] or seven bishops who comprehend the doctrine of Christ as far as relates to the Lord's supper, with as much clearness and piety as one could desire; and it is only the fear for their property that prevents them from reforming their churches according to the rule of God's word. The altars are here in many churches changed into tables. The public celebration of the Lord's supper is very far from the order and institution of our Lord. Although it is administered in both kinds, yet in some places the supper is celebrated three times a day. Where they used heretofore to celebrate in the morning the *mass* of the apostles, they now have the *communion* of the apostles; where they had the *mass* of the blessed virgin, they now have the communion which they call the *communion* of the virgin; where they had the principal, or high mass, they now have, as they call it, the high communion. They still retain their vestments and the candles before the altars; in the churches they always chant the *hours* and other hymns relating to the Lord's supper, but in our own language. And that popery may not be lost, the mass-priests, although they are compelled to discontinue the use of the Latin language, yet most carefully observe the same tone and manner of chanting to which they were heretofore accustomed in the papacy. God knows to what perils and anxieties we are exposed by reason of men of this kind.

You will apologize for me to master Mayor, and also to master Butler, respecting the pieces of cloth. Three months have elapsed since I sent them off, but they are detained at Antwerp; they will shortly, however, be delivered to you, God willing, and possibly before the receipt of this letter. I have just come from my lecture; I pray you therefore to interpret with kindness the shortness of my letter. I am obliged to lecture in public twice a day both to-morrow and the day following. May it be for the glory of God!

[1] It appears by the following letter that the bishops here referred to were Cranmer of Canterbury, Ridley of Rochester, Goodrich of Ely, Farrar of St David's, Holbeach of Lincoln, and Barlow of Bath.]

I shall finish the sixth chapter of John, and have proceeded thus far upon that evangelist. For my other lecture I expound Daniel, as affording a subject well-suited to our times; and I am now engaged in considering the third beast in the seventh chapter, towards the elucidation of which subject your remarks and annotations upon Daniel have contributed no small assistance.

I pray you, most reverend sir, by your great regard for me, to take care that all your annotations, especially those on Isaiah, be copied out with all speed, and sent to me with the greatest care. I will pay every expense: you know not how wonderfully they promote the glory of God. If I am able to effect anything, and my slender powers are of any benefit to the church of Christ, I confess, and by the blessing of God will confess, as long as I live, that I owe it to yourself and my masters and brethren at Zurich; whom I pray the Lord ever to preserve in safety for his name's sake. Moreover, if you have any thing which you purpose soon to send to the press, you should dedicate it to our most excellent sovereign, king Edward the sixth. On this subject I wish you would advise those learned men, namely, master Bibliander, our co-sponsor, and master Gualter. If you will comply with my wishes in this respect, you will advance the glory of God in no small degree. Believe me, all the English, who are free from popish tyranny and Romish craftiness, entertain correct views respecting the [Lord's] supper.

There are various other reasons which induce me to make this request to you; but I cannot at present state them by reason of the danger of the journey. Be alive, fight with that old serpent. Behold, your reward is great in heaven.

Salute masters Bibliander, Gualter, Pellican, with their wives, my most faithful master Butler with his wife, and all my other Zurich friends so much esteemed by me. Tell my excellent friend, master Gessner, that there is on the road for him a Welsh dictionary, and some writings in the language of Cornubia, commonly called Cornwall.

Yours now and for evermore,

JOHN HOOPER.

P.S.   My wife and your little god-daughter, Rachel, together with Martin and Joanna, salute your excellence with the good lady our gossip, your wife, and master Bibliander with his wife, our very dear gossips, and all the rest.

Rachel is endued with a most happy memory, and retains with the greatest facility every thing that is said to her, and of all other languages she best understands the Latin.

LETTER XXXVII.

JOHN HOOPER TO HENRY BULLINGER.

Dated at LONDON, *Feb.* 5, 1550.

GREETING. I much regret, most esteemed master and gossip, that the two letters which I sent you at the feast of St John the Baptist, are, as I understand from your letter, either intercepted or lost. Had they reached your excellency, you would neither have been ignorant of my present circumstances, nor of my affection towards you. I am, however, entirely persuaded of this, that we are united in such bonds of friendship as neither the miscarriage, nor even the intermission, of our correspondence will ever be able to break. But henceforth, God willing, I will make amends for my blameable silence by my diligence in writing. As far as I know, the letters of my wife to our very dear gossips, the wives of yourself and of our gossip master Bibliander, have not been delivered; or you would at least have learned from them the situation both of myself and of this kingdom. But as I now promise in this respect greater zeal and diligence than I have hitherto used, I trust to your kindness to forgive me. I will not now allege the just excuse, that the difficult and dangerous nature of my labours, very reverend sir, would call for at your hands; but proceed at once to comply with your injunctions. First of all, then, receive in a few words what relates to myself. Since my return to England, I have neither seen my native place nor my parents, by reason of the frequent and dangerous commotions stirred up in those parts on account of religion, and which indeed are not yet calmly and quietly settled. May God send a better state of things! My father is yet living in ignorance of the true religion, but I hope that the grace of God will at length teach him better. I have been explaining the holy scriptures here at London, and sometimes at court, by order of the duke of Somerset. In the city I have finished the epistle to Titus and about seven chapters of John. At court I have been lecturing upon the Psalms, and God knows at what risk I interpreted the sixth chapter of St John. I am also occupied at this time with the latter part of the seventh chapter of Daniel. I thought it best to explain the sixth of John and the seventh of Daniel by turns, that the people might rightly discern Christ from the one, and antichrist from the other. Thus much, then, respecting myself. My wife always remembers you in her prayers, that she may repay what she owes to your kindness: her health is not what it formerly was at Zurich, but is affected by the air of England and the relaxing nature of our climate. Our little Rachel is making progress both in body and mind. She understands the English, German, French and Latin languages very tolerably, and especially the Latin.

While I was writing this, namely on the fifth of February, on which day I received your last, the archbishop of Canterbury sent for me, and ordered me in the name of the king and council to preach before his majesty (who is now at London, and will not go anywhere else before Easter) once a week during the ensuing Lent. May the Lord open my heart and mouth, that I may think and speak those things which may advance his kingdom! I shall make choice, I think, of a very suitable subject, namely, the prophet Jonas[1]; which will enable me freely to touch upon the duties of individuals[2]. Do you, my reverend friend, write back as soon as possible, and diligently instruct me as to what you think may conveniently be said in so crowded an auditory. It must necessarily be great when before the king; for even in the city there is such a concourse of people at my lectures, that very often the church will not hold them.

[1 These sermons on Jonas, of which there are seven in all, were preached on the Wednesdays during Lent, in the year 1550, before the king and council. They are published among the Early Writings of Bishop Hooper, edited by the Parker Society, p. 435.]

[2 Additional reasons for making choice of this prophet are given in the Early Writings of Bishop Hooper, p. 445.]

Now as to what is doing in England. The bishops of Canterbury, Rochester, Ely, St David's, Lincoln, and Bath, are all favourable to the cause of Christ; and, as far as I know, entertain right opinions in the matter of the eucharist I have freely conversed with all of them upon this subject, and have discovered nothing but what is pure and holy. The archbishop of Canterbury, who is at the head of the king's council, gives to all lecturers and preachers their licence to read and preach: every one of them, however, must previously subscribe to certain articles, which, if possible, I will send you; one of which, respecting the eucharist, is plainly the true one, and that which you maintain in Switzerland. The marquis of Dorset, the earl of Warwick, and the greater part of the king's council favour the cause of Christ as much as they can. Our king is such an one for his age as the world has never seen. May the Lord preserve him! His sister, the daughter of the late king by queen Ann, is inflamed with the same zeal for the religion of Christ. She not only knows what the true religion is, but has acquired such proficiency in Greek and Latin, that she is able to defend it by the most ust arguments and the most happy talent; so that she encounters few adversaries whom she does not overcome. The people however, that many-headed monster, is still wincing; partly through ignorance, and partly fascinated by the inveiglements of the bishops, and the malice and impiety of the mass-priests.

Such then is the present state of things in England. Receive thus much concerning the affairs of government. On the sixth of October the king, together with the protector[1], fled from the palace, which we commonly call Hampton-court, to another castle, called in our language Windsor, for this reason, that the other members of the council in London had determined, as it was right they should, to make inquiry into the protector's conduct. Large numbers were collected by each party. As to myself, I determined not to interfere, because I had great enemies on both sides. The king was accompanied in his flight by his uncle the duke of Somerset, the arch-

[1 For an account of the conspiracy against Somerset, see Hollingshed, III. 1014, Tytler's Reign of Edward VI. Vol. I. 204, &c., Turner's Edward VI. i. 281, &c.]

bishop of Canterbury, the comptroller[2] of the household, and some of the lords of the bedchamber. All the other nobility and men of rank had lent their influence to the council, who conducted this affair in London: however, by the mercy of God, the business was at length settled without bloodshed. On the 14th of October the duke of Somerset with some others[3] was sent to the Tower of London, from whence he is not yet come out; but by the blessing of God he will be set at liberty, either this evening[4] or to-morrow. Be not alarmed at Dryander's returning to you; he consults his own interests, and cares but little for ours when gain is out of the question. Master Cox has received with the greatest respect your letter and present: I suppose you have received an answer from him before this time.

The archbishop of Canterbury, to say the truth, neither took much notice of your letter, nor of your learned present. But now, as I hope, master Bullinger and Canterbury entertain the same opinions. Should it be otherwise, you shall shortly hear.

With respect to what you write about the marquis of Dorset, if you have anything suitable in the press, contrive, I entreat you, to dedicate it to him. He is pious, good, and brave, and distinguished in the cause of Christ. You will not a little advance the glory of God by giving encouragement to him and others by your writings. Your reputation, believe me, is most honourably spoken of, as you well deserve, by all the learned and godly of this country. Take in good part the unpolished style of my letter. After some days you shall hear more. London. February 5, 1550.

Yours ever,

JOHN HOOPER.

[2 Namely, Sir William Paget, who was appointed to that office in 1547. The other persons here referred to were Sir William Petre, Sir Thomas Smith, and Mr William Cecil, master of Requests, and private secretary to Somerset. Tytler, I. 206.]

[3 At the same time that Somerset was secured and shut up in Beauchamp's tower, [Sir Thomas] Smith, Cecil, [Sir John] Thynne, [Sir Michael] Stanhope, and some others of his servants, were confined in their own apartments. MS. privy council books, quoted by Tytler, I. 243.]

[4 The duke was restored to liberty on the 6th of February. Grafton. Hollingshed. Stow.]

P. S.   You will remind masters Gualter, Bibliander and my other Zurich friends, that if they are about to print any religious work, they should dedicate it either to our king, a most excellent and learned youth, or to some one or other of the nobility.   I charge and enjoin you, my most learned gossip, and every way most esteemed master, to send me something of yours in print for our king.   I will take care that the work shall come to his hands, and that the offering shall not want a commendation from myself.

I entreat you not to mention this letter to any one.   I would write, as I ought to do, to masters Bibliander and Butler; but God knows I have no time.   I wish you all every happiness.   In three days time I will write again.   You shall hear in a few days respecting the Interim and other matters. The duke of Somerset will now come out of the Tower, and many other persons will be sent thither, whom I am not now at liberty to mention.

LETTER XXXVIII.

JOHN HOOPER TO HENRY BULLINGER.
Dated at London, *March* 27, 1550.

GRACE and innocence of life from the Lord! That I may in some measure extenuate, if I cannot entirely excuse, my blameable neglect of correspondence, (touching which, my much esteemed master and most loving gossip, you so deservedly and severely expostulated with me in your last letter,) this is the third letter that I have taken care should be sent you by the post since the end of January. I hope that you have received the others, and that you will receive this with all possible speed. I have already informed your excellence both as to my individual circumstances, and the news of this kingdom; but lest my letters should have been lost on the road, as has very often happened heretofore on both sides through the carelessness, or rather the dishonesty, of the courier, I think it worth my while to repeat the leading particulars in a few words.

Concerning me and mine, with whom you are acquainted,

I wrote that we are all of us in good health.   My wife however is weak and valetudinarian as usual, but, by the blessing
of God, in no danger of her life.   Rachel, by the mercy of
God, is in the enjoyment of excellent health : she grows both
in stature and in talent, and holds out the best promise of a
most happy memory.   She understands no language so well
as she does Latin.   I have not yet visited my native place;
being prevented, partly by the danger of the rebellion and
tumult in those quarters, and partly by the command of the
king that I should advance the kingdom of Christ here at
London : nor indeed am I yet able to stir even a single mile
from the city without a numerous attendance.   I comfort myself however in this, that the employment on which I had
entered under [un]promising and difficult auspices is blessed by
God every day more and more ; and he has given a sufficiently large and glorious increase to the seed sown by Peter
and Paul.   We do not water and plant in vain.   May the
name of the Lord be for ever blessed !   But there has lately
been appointed a new bishop[1] of London, a pious and learned
man, if only his new dignity do not change his conduct.
He will, I hope, destroy the altars[2] of Baal, as he did heretofore in his church when he was bishop of Rochester.   I can
scarcely express to you, my very dear friend, under what
difficulties and dangers we are labouring and struggling, that
the idol of the mass may be thrown out.   It is no small
hindrance to our exertions, that the form which our senate
or parliament, as we commonly call it, has prescribed for the
whole realm, is so very defective and of doubtful construction,
and in some respects indeed manifestly impious.   I sent it to
our friend, master Butler, about four months since.   I am so
much offended with that book, and that not without abundant
reason, that if it be not corrected, I neither can nor will communicate with the church in the administration of the [Lord's]
supper.   Many altars have been destroyed in this city since I
arrived here.   I commenced with the epistle to Titus, having

[1 Namely, Ridley, bishop of Rochester, who was translated to the
see of London on the deprivation of Bonner.]

[2 On this subject see Ridley's Injunctions to the diocese of London, and Reasons why the Lord's board should be in the form of a
table.   Parker Society edition of Ridley's works, pp. 319, 321.   See
also Soames, Hist. Ref. III. 571, and Burnet, II. 252.]

finished which, I lectured on the gospel of St John, and am
now engaged upon the eighth chapter.   I freely held forth
upon the sixth chapter to my audience, as God enabled me,
respecting the Lord's supper, for the space of three months,
and lectured once or twice every day ; and it pleased God to
bless my exertions.   A wonderful and most numerous concourse of people attended me, and God was with them; for
he opened their hearts to understand the things that were
spoken by me.   But I incurred great odium and not less
danger from the sixth chapter.   The better cause however
prevails; and during this Lent I have plainly and openly
handled the same subject before the king and the nobility of
the realm.   In this city an individual of the name of Crome[1],
a man of excellent erudition and holiness of life, a doctor in
divinity, and well known to master Butler, is combating my
opinions in a public discourse.

The bishop of Westchester will preach on the sixth Sunday before Easter, and will deliver his sentiments upon the
[Lord's] supper, the invocation of the saints, and the authority of the scriptures.   God grant that he may teach the
truth! We all piously agreed in the same opinion respecting
all the articles, in the presence of the king, this Lent; I will
let you know the result immediately after Easter.

The bishops of Winchester, London, and Worcester[2] are
still in confinement, and maintain the popish doctrines with
all their might.   The bishop of Winchester, who is a prisoner
in the Tower of London, came forward and challenged me to
a disputation about a month since : he doubtless assured himself of a glorious victory ; should he fail in obtaining which, he
would submit himself to the laws and to the king for punishment.   The keeper of the prison had at first accepted the
conditions.   The day was fixed.   But when the bishop knew
for certain that I would not shrink from that duty, but that
I would firmly maintain the best of causes even at the peril
of my life, he changed his mind, and said, that if the king
would set him at liberty, he would take his part in a disputation, in full reliance on the help of God, that he should
obtain the victory.   What will at length be done I know not.

[1 Dr Edward Crome was Rector of St Mary's Aldermanbury.   A
full account is given of him in Strype, Mem. III. i. 157, &c.]
[2 These were Gardiner, Bonner, and Heath.]

Meantime let us pray that God may be present with us, and that we may fearlessly advance his glory.

A book has lately been published here by the bishops, touching the ordination and consecration of the bishops and ministers of the church. I have sent it to master Butler, that you may know their fraud and artifices, by which they promote the kingdom of antichrist, especially in the form of the oath[3]; against which form I brought forward many objections in my public lecture before the king and the nobility of the realm: on which account I have incurred no small hostility. On the fourth day after the lecture an accusation was brought against me before the council by the archbishop of Canterbury. I appeared before them. The archbishop spoke against me with great severity on account of my having censured the form of the oath. I entreated the judges to hear with impartiality upon what authority I had done so. The question was long and sharply agitated between the bishops and myself; but at length the end and issue was for the glory of God.

If the ensuing summer should be free from disturbances, we hope for much good to our church; for peace is arranged between us and the French, but I am not yet informed upon what terms. I only pray our great and gracious God, that war may not lie hid under the name of peace. The day before I wrote this letter to your excellence, the emperor sent two most beautiful Spanish horses as a present to our king. On the same day a German Lutheran sent to [Sir John] Cheke, the king's tutor, a book which has lately come forth against the anabaptists and sacramentaries: he gave the book to the king to read, but it nowise pleased either the king, or his tutors, namely, Cook and Cheke, both of whom, as well as the king, have a pious understanding of the doctrine of the eucharist. Master Bucer is now lying dangerously ill at Cambridge. The subject of his lecture is the epistle to the Ephesians, and of his sermon, on holy-days, the sixth chapter of St John.

[3 Hooper's objection to the oath was the "swearing by God, the saints, and the holy gospels," when none but God himself ought to be appealed to in an oath. This clause was afterwards omitted. See the Parker Society edition of Hooper's Early Writings, p. 479, and compare the Liturgies of Edward VI. pp. 169, 339. Also Keeling's Liturgiæ Britannicæ, pp. 373, 390, and Burnet, Hist. Ref. II. 246.]

Master Valerandus[1] has recommended him by letter not to raise any controversy on the matter of the eucharist. He replied that he should teach nothing contrary to the opinion of Peter Martyr, which I sent you in manuscript about the middle of January.

Touching the *Interim,* (you know what I mean) I have not hitherto been able by any entreaties to obtain permission for committing it to the press; but I shall probably in a few days meet the king upon business, and I will give it him for his perusal. Believe me, my much esteemed friend, you have never seen in the world for these thousand years so much erudition united with piety and sweetness of disposition. Should he live and grow up with these virtues, he will be a terror to all the sovereigns of the earth. He receives with his own hand a copy of every sermon that he hears, and most diligently requires an account of them after dinner from those who study with him. Many of the boys and youths who are his companions in study are well and faithfully instructed in the fear of God, and in good learning. Master Cox is no longer the king's tutor. He still remains almoner, is much attached to you, and (as I have often told you before) most warmly thanked you for your present. You know how it was received by the archbishop of Canterbury. Now however, as far as I know, he has become my friend. The marquis of Dorset sends his best regards to your reverence. I could wish that you would dedicate either to the king or to him[2] the work you are shortly about to publish. Moreover, if our excellent and most learned friend, master Bibliander, or that learned and most faithful minister of Christ, master Gualter, are about to publish any thing, let them also dedicate it either to the king, or to the duke of Somerset, the king's uncle, my patron, (who is now living at Sion, eight miles from London, and in good health, but not at present one of the king's council, though I doubt not but that he will be shortly,) or to the marquis of Dorset, or to that most faithful and intrepid soldier of Christ, the earl of Warwick. He is ill at this time, but I hope in no imminent danger: unless

[1 Valerandus Pollanus was the preacher and superintendent of the French and Walloon church at Glastonbury.]

[2 Bullinger dedicated the remainder of his Decades to the marquis of Dorset, in March 1551.]

he had been on my side in the cause of Christ, it would have
been all over with me five months since, when the duke of
Somerset was in such difficulties.   Traheron is well; I think
you have received a letter from him not long since.   Your
dictations on Isaiah, which you gave in charge to Christopher
Hales, have not been delivered to me.   I must make allowance for the misfortune of the man; for when he was sailing
from Calais to England he was in so much danger from the
French, that they threw all the ship's cargo overboard.   I
entreat you to have a new copy made with all speed, not
only of [your notes] on Isaiah, but also of those upon the
books of Kings; and I will satisfy both by prayers and payment the labours of the copyist.   Do not send me any
thing for the cloth, which I hear you have received; but,
as you love me, pay for what I am now asking from
you out of the price of the cloth, and also for what I
may request from you in future, until you shall hear further
from me.   But I wish to inform you upon this point, that
when you write to me in future, you may inclose your letter
to me either in the letters of Richard Hilles or John Stumphius, or else they will scarcely ever come to my hands; such
is the envy and hatred of some parties, that if they see a
letter addressed to me they will retain it.   Unless therefore
you should meet with a trustworthy courier, it will be necessary to suppress what otherwise ought not to be concealed.
Such is now-a-days the perverseness of men's temper, that
they can interpret nothing with an upright and unprejudiced
mind.   Let me know how many letters you have received
from me since the first of January.   I do not ask this, as
though there would arise any danger either to your reverence or myself from the loss of the letters.   I value it not
a rush, into whosesoever hands they may have fallen; but I
wish to know, that I may learn to estimate the trustiness of
the bearer in future.   If you would sometime, as is befitting
your erudition and piety, send a letter of encouragement to
our king, take care to do so as soon as possible, and also to
the earl of Warwick and the marquis of Dorset: believe me,
they would receive it most gratefully; send it to me, and I
will place it in their hands with all fidelity.

The worshipful the Mayor will soon, I hope, receive
another good piece of cloth at the usual price, namely, ten

Zurich batzen the ell. Master Butler will also receive one, partly white, and partly black. We thank you very much for the present which you sent to your [god-daughter] Rachel. In return, I faithfully promise you in Christ that, as long as I live, your children shall be to me as my own, if I can in any respect be of use to them. John Stumphius is residing very creditably and studiously at Oxford. You may, if you please, in your letters apply a stimulus by way of exciting him to persevere honourably in what he has undertaken. Should he be in need of any thing, I shall always be ready to assist him. There is no occasion for his parents to be anxious about him in any way. Salute them in my name and in that of my wife. John Stumphius is a great favourite with her. John ab Ulmis is also well, and, as I hear, very diligent in his studies. He has been munificently and honourably presented, by the marquis of Dorset, with a yearly stipend of thirty crowns. Salute most dutifully in all our names the lady your wife with all your family, and masters Bibliander, Gualter, Pellican, Otto, Frisius, and Sebastian, with their respective wives. Martin Micronius wishes dutifully to salute your excellence and all his other friends at Zurich. I heartily salute master Haller, the most faithful minister of the church at Berne, and master Musculus. When you write to master Ambrose Blauer, and master Thomas his brother, salute each of them in my name. May the Lord Jesus preserve your church and commonwealth, that you may live in peace, fear, and holiness all the days of your life! Day and night do I remember you in my prayers, that God may guide, strengthen, and defend you by his holy Spirit against the snares of the devil and of the world. Do you also remember me and my labours in the Lord's vineyard: by the help of your prayers I shall raise a more glorious trophy in the church of God over our adversaries. With the exception of the church of Zurich, and those which agree with it in religion, the word is in no part of the world preached more purely than in England.

Write back, I pray you, immediately, if only one or two lines; for until I hear from you, I shall think that this letter also has been lost on the road. If you will always ask master Burcher to send your letters by the post, I will pay the expense. I desire to salute master Mayor, who is a man of God, most dutifully and affectionately in the bowels of Jesus Christ.

A certain native of Zurich, by name Valentine Wormulus, is detained here in prison : he is, if I mistake not, related to master Otho, the minister of the church at Zurich.   I do not yet know for certain the cause of his imprisonment: whether he offered violence to a woman, or obtained her consent, I am not informed, but some offence of this sort is alleged against him; besides which, he is charged with having stolen a small sum of money.   I shall send to-day to the prison, that I may learn more by means of master Utenhovius.   I wish you would shortly let me know whether he is a native of Zurich or not.   If the law can be satisfied by a pecuniary penalty, I will willingly pay it, as soon as your reverence shall authorise me to do so, provided the money be repaid me at Zurich.   Farewell, most honoured master, and continue to love me.   London, March 27, 1550.

On Wednesday next, God willing, I shall finish my exposition of the prophet Jonas before the king.

Yours ever,

JOHN HOOPER.

P. S.   Master Utenhovius dutifully salutes your worship, and doubtless aids you all in his diligent prayers to God. You would be quite astonished, did you know how many times he has thanked me for having sent him to Zurich. There is one request I have to make of you, my most faithful friend, that when you have read this, you will write to master Cœlius the younger, who resides at Basle, and apologize to him for my not writing to him at present.   I wrote some time since, and gave him intelligence respecting all the things that he had entrusted to my confidence; nor have I ever been unmindful of him, as he will know from me next Easter.   I have exerted myself in his favour, as you shall hereafter know. Entreat him to persevere in his purpose, and not to be afraid.   God liveth, from whom he will successfully obtain what he desires.   Salute the widow, my landlady, in my name; and should she be in need of any thing, I shall not be unmindful of the kindness with which she treated me during my sojourn with you.

LETTER XXXIX.

BISHOP HOOPER TO HENRY BULLINGER.

Dated at LONDON, *June* 29, 1550.

GREETING.   The letter which you wrote on the 13th
of March, I received at London on the last day of April,
by which I fully understood your ancient and fatherly affection towards me.   I rejoiced much [to learn] that you and
your church are regaining your former influence and reputation; but am much grieved to hear that my letters written
so frequently and with so much pains have been lost on the
road.   I will in future inquire more carefully as to the trust-
worthiness of the messenger.   I cannot too sufficiently wonder
that master Butler has so seldom heard from me.   I have
frequently written to him respecting his brother-in-law, who
not only holds an honourable employment at court, but most
honourably defends the cause of Christ in the palace; nor is
there any individual who is more fervent in this cause, or
more ardent in imparting to others the word of God.   He
is one of the four stewards of the royal household.   His
deceased wife, who was master Butler's sister, went to heaven
a year ago; and he has now married another pious and
godly virgin, of honourable rank and lineage.   He dutifully
salutes master Butler, and promises to exert himself to the
utmost of his power, if he should any way require his services.
Let master Butler know this.

I now return to the course and tenour of your former
letter, that I may reply to each head in its turn.   First
of all, receive this intelligence concerning me and mine.
We are all of us in good health.   I had an opportunity
of visiting my native place and my parents for a fortnight
at the Whitsun holidays.   I found my father still alive, and
though not a friend to the gospel, yet not an enemy to it.
My uncle also I found still living, and a favourer of the
cause of God; and my native country, considering the extent of its population, apt and docile.   We must pray God
to send forth labourers into his harvest.   Having returned
to London on the fourteenth day, I am going, by the king's
command, to-morrow or the next day into Kent and Essex, to

the lord chancellor of the realm, who is now, for various reasons, residing in the country. That district is troubled with the frenzy of the anabaptists more than any other part of the kingdom. May the Lord assist me, that my efforts there may be attended with success! At Easter, after the sermons were ended which master Ponet and myself preached before the king and council, he on the Friday, and I on the Wednesday, during Lent, it pleased his majesty and the council to offer the bishoprick of Rochester to Ponet[1], and that of Gloucester to myself. On many accounts I declined mine[2], both by reason of the shameful and impious form of the oath, which all who choose to undertake the function of a bishop are compelled to put up with, and also on account of those Aaronic habits which they still retain in that calling, and are used to wear, not only at the administration of the sacraments, but also at public prayers. All these things came to the ears of the king, and he wished to know the reason of my having refused to serve God in so pious and holy a calling. He understood that the causes which I have mentioned above altogether withdrew me from it. On last Ascension-day I was summoned before the whole council to state my reasons, that it might be seen whether I could justly and lawfully decline the royal favour. The matter was seriously agitated in the way of interrogatory. At last, for the glory of God, the discussion ended to the satisfaction of myself and that of all godly persons, not through my instrumentality alone, but by the grace of God, and the favourable inclinations of the council, and their love for God and for the purity and comeliness of the rising church. But you will say, I do not yet know the result. It was such as to set me clear from all defilement of superstition and from the imposition of the oath[3]. On these terms I took upon myself the charge committed to me. Aid wretched me with your prayers, that I may diligently and truly seek the glory of God, lest that little flock should perish, for which Christ died.

[1 Ponet was declared bishop of Rochester on June 26, 1550.]

[2 For an account of Hooper's troubles on his nomination to a bishopric, see Strype, Cranmer, I. 302 ; Burnet, II. 243 ; III. 304 ; and Soames, III. 560.]

[3 See a letter from Micronius to Bullinger, dated Aug. 28, 1550, which will be given in a subsequent part of this volume.]

I will not at present write much respecting myself, except only to inform your excellency, that I am now occupied upon the tenth chapter of St John, for my lecture in the New Testament, and upon the fourth chapter of Zechariah for my lecture in the Old Testament. I have finished Daniel, and also Jonah and his interpreter Nahum. I shall proceed as I can; and *I can do all things through Christ who strengtheneth me.* Unless his lovingkindness had assisted me, I should very often have looked back from the plough, since I begun. I could not have imagined that the office of preaching was exposed to so many and such painful anxieties. The agreement of Calvin and yourself touching the [Lord's] supper, and the letter in which the new-year's gift was inclosed for your little daughter Rachel, (for I so call her, as your sons and daughters are mine,) I have received, and replied to each. The marquis of Northampton, a man active in the cause of Christ, laid before the king's majesty, in my presence, your book that was intended for him, together with your letter. I should have presented it myself, had it not been forbidden by our laws for any one to lay before the king either a letter or anything else brought from foreign parts, without previously making it known to the council; and this law no one may dare to violate, until the king shall have arrived at the steadiness of mature age. But as far as relates to your letter and your book, he received them with the greatest courtesy and kindness, and not without many thanks; for he most earnestly inquired both respecting yourself and the welfare of your church. He moreover ordered the marquis to send you a royal present in token of his good-will. As soon as I understood this, I desired the marquis to thank his majesty in your name, and that you would esteem it a sufficient token of his gratitude, if he would himself actively and piously bestow his exertions on the vineyard of Christ; besides, that you were not in the habit of receiving presents from any one; and lastly, that it was forbidden by your municipal laws to receive gifts from princes or any other persons whatsoever: but if he wished to testify his approbation either by a letter from himself or through me, that an act of this kind would be most gratifying to you. The king then ordered me to salute you on every account in his name, and present his thanks, entreating you to remember him in your prayers, and to commend to God both himself and his kingdom. Master Cox also, whom, having been engaged in other matters of importance, I have not been able to call upon for many weeks, received your present in the same spirit. I have dutifully saluted all the earls and marquises in your name. They all salute you in return. The earl of Warwick has had a long illness, but by the blessing of God is now recovered, and will be present at the council on Wednesday next. To tell the truth, England cannot do without him. He is a most holy and fearless instrument of the word of God. May the Lord strengthen him! We have many other excellent councillors, the duke of Somerset, the marquises of Northampton and Dorset. [The archbishop of] Canterbury has relaxed much of his Lutheranism, (whether all of it, I cannot say;) he is not so decided as I could wish, and dares not, I fear, assert his opinion in all respects. As to your advice in your letter, that I should make friends of the bishops, I should be much to blame, if I did not endeavour by all means to do so, provided it can be done with a safe and pure conscience; and to speak the truth, there are six or seven who altogether desire and wish to promote the glory of God. These I venerate and reverence from my heart.

Now I most earnestly entreat you kindly to comply with the following request. If you can procure from master Froschover at the trade price, that is, the price at which he sells them to the booksellers in sheets, all the works of Zuinglius, your own, those of Bibliander, Pellican, Gualter, Œcolampadius, Gesner, both his Bibliotheca and the treatise on Birds, which he is now reported to be writing, you will exceedingly oblige me; and as soon as I know that he has agreed to this, I will take care that he shall have the money at the next Frankfort fair, nor will I require the books till the amount is previously paid. I request you also to salute dutifully in my name master Cœlius Secundus[1], whom I have constantly borne in mind since my arrival here, although I have not told him as much by letter; and let me know, when you write next, what are his present circumstances at Basle: I know him to be a man of profound learning, and one of whose services I

[1 Cœlius Secundus Curio was of a noble Piedmontese family. He abjured popery, and embraced Lutheranism, and was professor at Basle from 1547 till 1569, in which year he died, aged 67.]

would gladly avail myself, when I come to know the state of my bishoprick. As primitive antiquity employed the revenues arising from this office to the edification of the church and the education of the young, I could wish each of these objects to be restored by me, which can in no way be effected unless I shall be aided by the assistance of pious and learned men. On this subject I would gladly hear and follow your advice. Send me therefore by letter, as soon as possible, an answer to my inquiries. For I know you to be discreet and attached to me, and besides this, one who is well able to look forward to the future.

I doubt not but that the cloth sent to master Mayor and master Butler has reached you long since. I request that your notes on Isaiah, on the books of Kings, and on the epistle to the Romans, from the beginning of the thirteenth chapter to the end, may be copied out for me as soon as possible. I will recompense the copyist, and will not be un-mindful of the kindness of master Haller, for his having taken so much trouble for me before with respect to Isaiah. You here have the proper form of dedication of your book to the marquis of Dorset : when I return from the lord chancellor a fortnight hence, I will send the style of the earl of Warwick and the marquis of Northampton; you shall then receive farther and more certain intelligence. Meanwhile I pray the Lord to preserve you in prosperity, together with your whole family and the church ; and I congratulate you and your daughters on so happy and, I hope, so holy a marriage. My wife and Rachel pray for you all happiness in Christ. Make my apologies to masters Butler, Bibliander, and Gualter, for not now writing to them. The trustworthy bearer will assign weighty reasons for this. Do you, my most honoured master and most loving friend, take in good part what I have now written with a hasty pen. I will write more in a few days. Your most wished for and delightful letter of the seventeenth of May I received on the 25th of June, and will reply to it in my next letter. Live and fare well in Christ long and holily. London, June 29, 1550.

Your reverence's most devoted,

JOHN HOOPER.

LETTER XL.

BISHOP HOOPER TO HENRY BULLINGER.
Dated at GLOUCESTER, *Aug.* 1, 1551.

GRACE and peace from the Lord! I am not only aware, my much honoured gossip, that this long silence of mine is displeasing to your kindness, but I am also greatly displeased with myself for that very reason. But when you are acquainted with the arduous and important nature of my engagements, you will easily be induced to excuse me, and I shall free myself from the reproach of ingratitude to so dear a friend. But although, as your letter states, as well as that of my brother and singular good friend, master John Butler, I have suffered all those who have visited you from England to quit this country without any letters from myself, I have, nevertheless, written them to you very frequently; but for their having either been intercepted or lost on the road, I must blame the carelessness of the couriers, who have not only disappointed my labours, but also deceived the expectation of my best friend. And yet, if I have written to you less frequently than your exceeding kindness to me has deserved, it has not, my most learned gossip, arisen from forgetfulness of you, but from the difficulty and magnitude of my engagements. I was occupied during the past year with constant and important business, as you have doubtless heard from others. The question respecting the habits, which was always exceedingly displeasing to me, was gravely discussed between the bishop of London and myself. For my part, I very properly, if I am not mistaken, found fault with the use of them in the church, and contended for their entire removal. He, on the other hand, most urgently and pertinaciously defended their use[1]. But as the Lord has put an end to this controversy, I do not think it worth while to violate the

[1] A copy of bishop Ridley's "Conference by writing with M. Hoper exhibited up to the council in the time of King Edward the sixth," was in the possession of archbishop Whitgift. See his Defence of the answer to the Admonition, A.D. 1574, p. 25, but its existence was unknown (see Ridley's life of bishop Ridley) in later years, till a copy, slightly imperfect, was discovered in 1844, in the extensive collection of MSS. belonging to sir Thomas Phillips, Bart.]

sepulchre of this unhappy tragedy. In future, even if my
engagements should not admit of any cessation, I will perform
my duty in writing to you, and will not suffer any person to
go from me to you without a letter. As I now rely upon
the readiness to forgive, which is a part of your character, I
shall desist from offering any further apology for my silence.

My whole family is well, as I hope also that yours is,
and I daily pray God that they may both long continue
so. You must know however, that I have had no addition
to my family since the time that I quitted your godly society.
If the Lord will preserve my little daughter Rachel, so that
she may embrace his Son Jesus Christ, and promote his cause,
I shall think my desires abundantly accomplished in my old
age, even though I should have no more family. She very
frequently hears from her mother the great commendation of
the country and place where she was born; and she is with
great care and diligence instructed in the promises which she
formerly made to the church by means of your kindness and
that of the wife of master Bibliander. She sorely complains
of my not more frequently saluting by letter so holy a church
and such faithful ministers of Christ. She now sends an
entire piece of cloth as a token of her reverence and respect,
one half to yourself, the other to the wife of master Bibliander; and she heartily thanks her heavenly Father, that by
you as her sponsors she has been received into the society of
his holy church. Should it seem good to you that your sons
should visit England for their education, you need not feel
much anxiety as to what it would cost them to live here. I
will take the charge of them upon myself, and that too, faithfully and cheerfully.

I have never been able to procure the printing of those
writings of yours (you know what I mean) which I brought
away with me from Zurich: not that they are unacceptable
to godly and learned men, for they are exceedingly acceptable to all to whom I have given them for perusal;
but it has been prevented by the calamity of the time, or
rather by the timidity of men who prefer their own counsels to the glory of God. Many persons of learning and
rank desired to read that book, and I allowed them to do so,
as it was right I should; and it is now in the hands of master
Cecil, his majesty's principal secretary, a man endowed with
very great learning and piety, and a great favourer of the

gospel. Your other books, which you sent to the king's majesty, I delivered most carefully to the marquis of Northampton[1], the lord high chamberlain of England, to lay before the king in your name, which he did carefully and readily, and the king ordered him to salute you in return with many thanks; nor do I doubt but that the king will always remember you in future. I request that you will in your turn commend him for his godly procedure, and always in your letters exhort him to perseverance in it. For the king reads your letters with attention, and takes a most lively interest in the perusal. You must not therefore think your labour ill-bestowed, although you do not receive an answer. My lord of Canterbury, who is in truth a great admirer of you, when I received your last letter in his palace, and acquainted him with its contents, could hardly refrain from tears, when he understood your feelings in regard to the king and to the kingdom, and also the perseverance of your church in these most lamentable times. He made most honourable mention both of yourself and of your profound erudition. You have no one, I am sure, among all your dearest friends, who is more interested about you, and who loves you in Christ more ardently than he does. I know of a truth that he loves you from his heart. In my conversation with him I requested his kind offices with the king on behalf of the Italian of whom you wrote: he promised to use all his endeavours, and you need not doubt him. If our gracious and most merciful God would once deliver us from this harsh and cruel tyranny of the enemies of Christ, by which we are so dangerously [surrounded[2]] on all sides, all the godly and learned men will be as well provided for as our poor circumstances will admit of.

You asked me to settle with master a Lasco about those eighteen crowns, which you lent to some Italian; I have done as you requested, but know not whether you have yet been repaid. I know that you will not, with your own consent, be a burden to any one, (although what you may call a burden, your friends would consider an honour;) but your most splendid gifts, received from God, have so greatly benefited the commonwealth, and the church of Christ more especially, that we owe our all to you, and you may make what trial you please.

[1 William Parr, marquis of Northampton, was brother to King Henry the eighth's last wife.]

[2 A word is wanting in the original Latin.]

After I had begun this letter, my wife and five others of my chaplains and domestics were attacked by a new kind of sweating sickness, and were in great danger for twenty-four hours; I myself have but very recently recovered from the same disease. Pray the Lord that he may have compassion on us, and that we may always be waiting in the fear of God for the day of death. The infection of this disease is in England most severe, and, what is a most remarkable token of divine vengeance, persons are suddenly taken off by it[1]. You shall know more fully respecting my affairs next Michaelmas, when I shall have some little intermission of my engagements. My wife and the other invalids have, through the favour of God, escaped the danger of the disease.

I commend your whole church and commonwealth to God, and especially the most reverend father, master Pellican. For master Rodolph Gualter, your two sons-in-law, master Gesner, with their respective wives; for all others who embrace with you the religion of Christ; for our sister your wife, and all your family, and master Bibliander, and his wife and family, we sincerely and heartily wish salvation in Christ. May the Lord also preserve master Mayor. When you write to master Cœlius Secundus, salute him, I entreat you, in my name as much as you can, and you can as much as you please. Persuade our friend master John Butler to return to England; he may be useful in many respects both to the church and commonwealth. You know that we are born for our country, and not for ourselves: were it not so, I should not now be discharging the office of a bishop. At least ask him to visit us once in England, and he shall learn from me in what way and by what means he may best provide for himself and his family. May the Lord Jesus long preserve you to the glory of his name!

Gloucester, Aug. 1, 1551.

As heretofore and for so long a time,
your most loving brother and gossip,

JOHN HOOPER,
Bishop of the church of Gloucester.

[1 The sweating sickness was very fatal this year, especially in London, where eight hundred persons died of it within the first week. Seven householders supped together, six of whom were dead before morning. Stowe's Annals, A.D. 1551.]

P. S.   I have lent to the student who is the bearer of this letter to you, and to his companion, both natives of Zurich, forty-five English crowns.   You will oblige me much by sending me books printed at Zurich, those especially which contain your works, to an equal amount.   If the young men of Zurich who come over here for the sake of study, should stand in need of my assistance, I will aid them as far as my slender means will allow.   I return you my warmest thanks for your books and letter to me.   When I shall have emerged from the waves of danger, most reverend and learned friend, I will send a messenger of my own, from whom you shall learn all my affairs.   Do not, I pray you, be surprised, that I make no mention of your letters, which I very frequently kiss; for I can never forget either yourself or your kindness towards me.   You shall hear in a future letter, on what subject and on what occasion so fierce and quarrelsome a dispute arose between the bishops and myself.   I agree that the contest should be set at rest by the arbitration of godly men. I will explain in a few words the cause and ground of the dispute.   The use of vestments peculiar to popery in the ministry of the church has been the occasion here of great disturbance.   Master a Lasco alone, of all the foreigners who have any influence, stood on my side.   Farewell.   I pray God that you may live long and happily, and may all the people of Zurich fare well in Christ.   Amen.   I have written what I can; you know what I mean.   Altogether yours, and deservedly so, if I am my own.

LETTER XLI.

BISHOP HOOPER TO HENRY BULLINGER.
Dated at GLOUCESTER, *Oct.* 27, 1551.

GREETING.   If, my much honoured gossip, you had received the letters which I wrote to you towards the end of August and in the month of September, yours dated at Zurich on the 29th of August, which I received at Gloucester on the 22nd of October, would not have been so full of complaint.   I hope that you are by this time fully aware of the feelings and spirit which I entertain towards you.   I will make no answer by way of apology, although I have many weighty and allowable excuses which would avail with you, yourself being the judge. But you shall learn at another time, what it is still necessary for me to keep silent. You and all that belongs to you are not displeasing either to God or our king, but quite the contrary, and on that account you are acceptable to both. You say that they are displeasing to me, but I know you only say so: far be it that your writings should be lightly esteemed by me. Of all the learned men under heaven, I have none more dear to me than yourself, and deservedly so. In many ways I have received benefit, as I still do, from you and from your writings. Should it please God that I can in any respect be of service to you, you will find me most ready, and mindful, and grateful, both to you and yours. I return you my warmest thanks for your kindness in sending to me, together with your letter, your godly and learned meditations, which you are preparing by way of popular discourses: since, however, I left Zurich, I have received no manuscript besides your very useful and excellent Decades, except your commentary on Isaiah as far as the 40th chapter, and on the epistle to the Romans. I much wish for your other writings, and will amply recompense the copyist. I have not yet seen the remainder of your commentary on Isaiah; and I mourn over the faithlessness of the men to whom I from time to time entrust grave and honourable duties. But I would have you to be especially assured, that should I from henceforth fail to write to you every month, either sickness or death will be the occasion of my silence. You are altogether unconscious how deeply your complaints affect my mind. You have, I am sure, no one who loves you more in Christ than myself. Moreover, when I go to London, I will undertake, as I may be able, that a letter shall be sent you from the king, by which he may testify his good-will towards you; and I will endeavour too to relieve, if I can, by means of his royal majesty, the distress of that godly Italian, who is now suffering under the painful necessity of exile: I without doubt am entirely his debtor to serve him. You need not be anxious about the expense of sending letters from Strasburgh; I will willingly bear it. I wish that all the letters would reach me which you have sent already or shall send in future. I am greatly grieved at my letters having been lost on the road. But they always regarded, as they ought, both God and man, and therefore make me somewhat less anxious.

The report concerning the death of Peter Martyr, I thank God, was false and groundless; he is alive and well, and boldly stands forth as a brave and godly soldier in the army of the Lord. If he has any thing which he intends to print, I am sure that he will send it you. He has not yet determined to publish his annotations on Genesis; he is meditating something upon the epistle to the Romans. I will take care, to the utmost of my power, that none of his writings shall be lost. Meanwhile, do you always act, as you now do, for the glory of God. Your writings are exceedingly delightful to me, and to all who have the true worship of God at heart. I doubt not but that, while you are actively labouring in these endeavours, you incur the hatred and envy of the accomplices of the devil and of antichrist; but happy are those dangers, which are so much connected with the glory of God. You will receive an account of my labours, which are but small and slight in the vineyard of Christ, through John Rodolph, a worthy and godly youth, whom I entreat you to receive on his return with paternal kindness, and honour him, thus recommended to you by me, with your favour: he has conducted himself here modestly, piously, and studiously, as you will afterwards learn, if you please, from the letters of all the learned and godly students at Oxford; and, to tell the truth, I do not easily bear his going away. Let him return to us, if it please the Zurich authorities and yourself, for a year or two, and I will take a portion of his expenses upon myself. When the two young men from Zurich left this country, I gave them forty-five English crowns; if they will repay me in books printed at Zurich, I shall be quite satisfied. Among other books I wish for the Bible in one large volume.

You will learn from the messenger who is travelling between us and Zurich, by what important and perpetual engagements I am overwhelmed. Excuse, I pray you, my unpolished and too hasty pen. Salute the lady your wife, with all your family, masters Bibliander, Gualter, Pellican, with their wives; my countryman master Butler with his wife, and pray tell him from me, that he is not born for himself and his friends alone, but that his country also has a claim upon him. I wish he would at least come over to us

once, and perhaps he would not repent the journey. May
the Lord Jesus be always present with the Mayor, your whole
senate and commonwealth, and protect his church! In haste,
as you see, at Gloucester, Oct. 27, 1551.

Your ever most attached, as I ought to be,

JOHN HOOPER, bishop of Gloucester.

P. S.   I request you will salute in my name those most
excellent and learned men, masters Gesner and Otto, whom I
dearly love in Christ.   And should master Gesner wish at
any time to come over to us, I will provide him with suitable
companions who will shew him the rivers, and fishes, and ani-
mals of this country.   I defer, for the present, any further
communication.   Again farewell, and pray that I may long
fare well in Christ.

LETTER XLII.

BISHOP HOOPER TO JOHN STUMPHIUS.

Dated at GLOUCESTER, *Oct.* 27, 1551.

GREETING.   Your son[1] will, I hope, return from his travels as safe and prosperous as you sent him forth.   Receive
him on his return, I pray you, as a father should do.   I have
been endeavouring to prevent his going away, by reason of
the lateness of the season; but he has altogether made up
his mind to undertake the journey in company with some
other Germans, who flock over to us for the sake of study.
He has conducted himself soberly, piously, and studiously;
and should he happen to return, he will find me his friend.

[1 John Stumphius the younger, afterwards Antistes, studied at
Oxford with John ab Ulmis.   In his letters to Bullinger he mentions
evil reports which had been spread about him, and his father's anger
in consequence.   Hence Hooper's request that he would receive his
son *paterne*.   His father did not wish him to be a pensioner on royal
bounty at Oxford.   Note by Rev. S. A. Pears.]

Make him evermore to fear God, to whom I commend you; and salute your wife in my name.   Gloucester, Oct. 27, 1551.

Of yourself, and all the people of Zurich,

I am the most loving friend,

JOHN HOOPER, bishop of Gloucester.

LETTER XLIII.

BISHOP HOOPER TO HENRY BULLINGER.

Dated at LONDON, *Feb.* 28, 1553.

GREETING. The Englishman, Richard Hilles, promised me a month since that he would faithfully forward you my letter. If you have received it, it is well: if not, I hope that you will receive it. I request you not to impute the inter-mission of my letters either to ingratitude or forgetfulness, but to the weighty and important engagements by which I am continually distracted, and to other reasons which I suppress, until the time shall arrive, when I may be able to correspond with you more freely. I know that you are expecting an answer to the petitions which you have chiefly preferred by letter: wait a little; you will obtain your wish soon enough, if it is only well enough. If you have any of the Decads, which many godly persons are expecting from you every fair, al-ready prepared, I would have you dedicate them to the duke of Northumberland. He is exceedingly partial to you, and is a diligent promoter of the glory of God. I left master Mar-tyr on the 20th of this February, at Oxford, sick of a fever. May the Lord be with him, and restore him to health! His wife departed to the Lord on the 16th of this month. My wife and all my family salute your excellence. Salute your wife in my name and theirs; we wish your sons and daughters every happiness. Salute the Mayor, masters Bibliander,

7—2

Gualter, and Pellican, with their wives, and master Butler
and his wife.   London.   Feb. 28, 1553.

Your ever most devoted,

JOHN HOOPER, bishop of
Worcester and Gloucester.

LETTER XLIV.

BISHOP HOOPER TO HENRY BULLINGER.

Dated from prison[1], *Sept.* 3, 1553.

GREETING. You have been accustomed, my very dear
gossip, heavily to complain of me, and very properly, for
having so seldom written to you. But I have now written
you many letters during the past year, without having received a single one in reply. I know that you are not unacquainted with the state of our kingdom. Our king has been
removed from us by reason of our sins, to the very great peril
of our church. His sister Mary has succeeded, whom I pray
God always to aid by his Holy Spirit, that she may reign
and govern in all respects to the glory of his name. The altars
are again set up throughout the kingdom; private masses are
frequently celebrated in many quarters; the true worship of
God, true invocation, the right use of the sacraments, are all
done away with; divine things are trodden under foot, and
human things have the pre-eminence. May God be present
with his church, for the sake of his only Son Jesus Christ!
All godly preachers are placed in the greatest danger: those
who have not yet known by experience the filthiness of a
prison, are hourly looking for it. Meanwhile they are all of
them forbidden to preach by public authority. The enemies
of the gospel are appointed in their places, and proclaim to
the people from the pulpit human doctrines instead of divine
truths. We now place our confidence in God alone, and earnestly entreat him to comfort and strengthen us to endure any
sufferings whatever for the glory of his name. In haste, from

[1 Hooper was committed unto the Fleet from Richmond, Sept. 1,
1553. Letters of the Martyrs, p. 97, Ed. 1844.]

10423

prison, at London. Sept. 3, 1553. Salute your very dear wife, masters Bibliander, Pellican, and Gualter, with their wives, and all the other godly brethren ; likewise my country-man master Butler with his wife.

Yours wholly,

JOHN HOOPER, bishop of
Worcester and Gloucester.

LETTER XLV.

BISHOP HOOPER TO JOHN A LASCO.

Dated from prison, *Nov.* 25, 1553.

THERE is no need for me to commend this noble person to your excellency in many words ; for I think that he is known both to yourself and all the other godly persons who have lately left England. I only request that he may not be deprived of your good offices, should he have any occasion for them. You will learn from him every thing concerning myself, and also the present condition of the church. It is indeed a wretched and miserable one. May the Lord mercifully look upon us with complacency, and weaken the power of our adversaries ! They are becoming more furious and insolent every day. But he, who now seems to us to sleep, will at length make his appearance, and cast down his enemies. Should the Father of mercy grant this favour to us in this life, his holy name be praised ; if otherwise, his will be done. He himself commands us to die for the glory of his name. May he grant what he commands, and then command things yet more painful, if it seemeth him good ! I am now writing in haste and by stealth from prison, being now kept in more close and severe confinement[2] than when your excellency left us. But, by God's help, I am prepared, both to endure these things, and the yet more painful trials that are about to come. Salute my old and godly friend,

[2 For an account of bishop Hooper's harsh treatment from Babington, the warden of the Fleet, see Foxe, Acts and Mon. VI. 647 ; Strype, Mem. III. i. 284, and Letters of the Martyrs, p. 96.]

master Martin, the noble personage Utenhovius, and all the rest of our brethren; and I entreat you to commend both myself and my fellow-prisoners in Christ Jesus to our Almighty Father which is in heaven, that by means of our death his glory may shine forth more and more upon this most polluted world.   From prison, Nov. 25, 1553.

Your excellency's much remembered before God,

JOHN HOOPER, bishop of Gloucester.

LETTER XLVI.

BISHOP HOOPER TO HENRY BULLINGER.

Dated from prison, *May* 23, 1554.

HEALTH.   It is now, my most honoured gossip, the ninth month since I have endured the filthiness[1] of a prison.   Meanwhile, however, I have sent you many letters by the hands of godly persons, to the end that by their means I might excite your reverence, with all the other learned ministers of your church, to shew yourselves kindly affectioned and merciful to those wretched and unfortunate individuals who have fled from hence for the sake of the christian religion. I wrote very briefly, as I was able, because I was not allowed, neither am I at present, to write as I wish ; and I write by stealth, which, as you know, is the miserable condition of those in prison.   Yet, as far as I know, you have not sent me even the shortest answer in return. I am much distressed at this ; for, if I am not mistaken, you are aware how greatly I esteem you.   I have always looked upon you as a most revered father and master.   Of all those who are attached to you, you have never found any one dearer than myself ;

[1 "Having nothing appointed to me for my bed, but a little pad of straw, a rotten covering, with a tick and a few feathers therein, the chamber being vile and stinking, until, by God's means, good people sent me bedding to lie in: of the one side of which prison is the sink and filth of all the house, and on the other side the town ditch; so that the stench of the house hath infected me with divers diseases." Hooper's report of his imprisonment, in the Letters of the Martyrs, p. 97.]

nor have I, to say the truth, ever met with a more sincere friend. Those who have brought you letters from me, since the death of our most godly king until the present time, were very dear friends and brethren; but the bearer of this is master James Haddon, not only a friend and very dear brother in Christ, but one whom I have always esteemed on every account, by reason of his singular erudition and virtue. And I do not think that I have ever been acquainted with any one in England, who is endued either with more sincere piety towards God, or more removed from all desire of those perishing objects which foolish mortals admire. I commend him most earnestly to your good offices. Salute your very dear wife in my name, your children, and all your family, masters Gualter and Pellican, and all the ministers of your church, master Lavater the mayor, and your whole city. I would write more openly, if I dared; but I have often been deceived by my friends. From prison, May 23, 1554.

In a short time, unless the Lord should restrain the tyranny of our enemies, I shall go in the blood of Christ to heaven.

As heretofore and at all times, your most attached,

JOHN HOOPER.

LETTER XLVII.

BISHOP HOOPER TO HENRY BULLINGER.
Dated from Prison, *May* 29, 1554.

MUCH health. I hope, my very dear gossip, that you have received my former letters, which I have hitherto written from prison, to be delivered to you by those godly men who have gone over from hence to you. As in those letters I entreated your accustomed kindness towards my fellow-countrymen, so by this I entreat the same on behalf of the bearer, my friend Guido, my most faithful associate in the labours of the gospel. I have had no one with me who is so devoted to the flock of Christ, or who has undergone continual labours with greater equanimity: I commend him, from whom you will learn all the circumstances of my present condition, to your kindness, and to all the godly members of your church, as the companion of all my labours in the vineyard of Christ. I would write in his favour to the other godly men, who are now, like yourselves, soldiers of Christ, but the keeper of the prison will not allow me to do so. It is with difficulty that I have been able to write thus briefly from prison, whence you may understand that my life is in very great danger. Aid me in your prayers to God. I am not unmindful of you. I salute the lady your wife, all your family, and all the rest whom you know. From prison, May 29th, 1554.

Yours, as I ought to be, most lovingly,

JOHN HOOPER.

LETTER XLVIII.

BISHOP HOOPER TO HENRY BULLINGER.

Dated from prison, *Dec.* 11, 1554.

GRACE and peace from the Lord! Your letter[1], my beloved brother, dated at Zurich on the tenth of October, I received on the eleventh of December. It was very delightful to me, because it was full of comfort. I readily perceived therein your ancient feelings of love and affection towards me, and am most thankful to you that in these most dangerous times you have not forgotten me. I have always entertained an especial love for you on account of your pre-eminent good qualities, and the excellent gifts of God in you. And if, as you write, you have not received any letters from me for a whole year, this has not been occasioned by my not having written, but by my having confided my letters to careless and dishonest persons. Nor have I received all that you have sent to me, but they have been either lost by the carelessness of the postman, or intercepted by the malice of the evil-disposed. The same thing has happened both to the letters and the book of master Theodore: for I never

[1 The letter here referred to is printed in Foxe, Acts and Mon. VI. 675, and Coverdale's Letters of the Martyrs, p. 126, Ed. 1844.]

heard of [his book respecting] our Lord's sermon on the mount, which he sent me, till some days after the death of our most holy king Edward; and then [I saw it] on the borders of Wales, in the library of a certain godly man whom I had appointed dean over some churches there.   But what you have now written, I will take care shall be sent to all my brethren and fellow-prisoners for their perusal.

I congratulate you all upon the safety and stedfastness of your church, and I pray to God for his Son Jesus Christ's sake evermore to fortify and defend it against the tyranny of antichrist.   In this country the wound which he received is entirely healed, and he is once more regarded as the head of the church, who is not even a member of the church of Christ.   You will learn from others both my own situation and the state of public affairs.   We are still involved in the greatest dangers, as we have been for almost the last eighteen months.   The enemies of the gospel are every day giving us more and more annoyance; we are imprisoned apart from each other, and treated with every degree of ignominy.   They are daily threatening us with death, which we are quite indifferent about; in Christ Jesus we boldly despise the sword and the flames.   We know in whom we have believed, and we are sure that we shall lay down our lives in a good cause.   Meanwhile aid us with your prayers, that he who hath begun a good work in us will perform it even unto the end.   We are the Lord's; let him do what seemeth good in his eyes.

I entreat you to comfort occasionally by your letters that most exemplary and godly woman, my wife, and exhort her to bring up our children carefully, Rachel your little goddaughter, an exceedingly well-disposed girl, and my son Daniel, and piously to educate them in the knowledge and fear of God.   I moreover send your reverence two little books for your perusal, consideration, and correction, if they contain any thing not agreeable to the word of God.   I have entitled the one, *An Hyperaspismus touching the true doctrine and use of the Lord's Supper;* and I have dedicated it to the parliament of England, that we may publicly reply to our adversaries in the court of parliament.   The title of the other is, *A Tractate upon discerning and avoiding false religion.*   And I beg that you will cause them to be printed as soon as possible. Both the books[1] are approved by all the godly and learned in this country. I have moreover written many other letters to the bishops, that they should bring forward the books in parliament; and I wish these also to be printed, that all may perceive how unfairly and unjustly we are dealt with. But I need not write to you at length upon this subject; you will understand my wishes from the books and letters themselves. And if your friend Froschover should be prevented from printing them by more important engagements, I wish he would send them to Basle to master Oporinus, who prints very correctly, and sends out all his publications in a superior manner. I know he will do this, if only the books are sent to him with a recommendation from you, and which I earnestly entreat you to supply. There is no occasion for you to fear for me, as though the enemies of the gospel would rage more fiercely and with greater cruelty on account of these books. I have a most faithful guardian and defender of my salvation in our heavenly Father through Jesus Christ, to whom I have wholly committed myself. To his faithfulness and protection I commend myself: if he shall prolong my days, may he cause it to be for the glory of his name; but if he wills that my short and evil life should be ended, I can say with equal complacency, His will be done! I am writing by stealth, and therefore my letter to your excellence is shorter and more confused [than I could wish]; take it, I pray you, in good part. In haste, from prison, Dec. 11, 1554.

Salute for me dutifully your excellent wife and all your family at home and elsewhere; and all others, as you know.

Your excellence's most affectionate,

as I ought to be,

JOHN HOOPER.

[1 Neither of these books appears to have been printed. Search has been made for the manuscript copies here mentioned, but without success. The epistle dedicatory to the latter is given in Strype, Mem. III. i. 283. ii. 267. Bale mentions among Hooper's works written in Latin from prison, *Pro doctrina cœnæ Dominicæ Liber*, and *De pseudo-doctrina fugienda*, Lib. I. and quotes the commencing sentence of each of them. Bale, Script. Illustr. Basil, 1559.]

LETTER XLIX.

ANNE HOOPER TO HENRY BULLINGER.

Dated at LONDON, *April* 3, [1551.]

I HAVE received your letter, most christian sir, in which, as in a glass, I perceive how greatly you are interested for us. But though I acknowledge myself quite incapable of returning you the thanks I ought for your especial friendship towards us, I will not cease from offering them; and I heartily pray God and the Father of our Lord Jesus Christ, that he may abundantly recompense you, as I am unable to do so myself. I will not acquaint you with the reason of master Hooper's imprisonment[2], until I have communicated to him your letter, which at present is quite out of my power; for he went down to his see as soon as he was discharged. I doubt not but that he will satisfy your desire as soon as he is informed of it; and this seems to me far more convenient, than for me to make the attempt without consulting him. But as you inquire how my daughter Rachel is going on, I consider it my duty to give you some information concerning her. First then, you must know that she is well acquainted with English, and that she has learned by heart within these three months the form of giving thanks, the ten commandments, the Lord's prayer, the apostles' creed, together with the first and second psalms of David. And now, as she knows almost all her letters, she is instructed in the catechism. If I could write in German, I should more frequently take pen in hand. But if your son should happen to come to England, I shall have a better opportunity both of writing, and also in some measure of repaying your paternal affection for us, and which I value more than the richest treasures of gold or silver. I have no news to communicate respecting Ireland, except that the French king is reported to have prepared a fleet for the purpose of invading and taking possession of it, but his design was discovered by the activity of some faithful Frenchman.

[2 Hooper was committed to the Fleet for objecting to the prescribed vestments, (see p. 91) by order of the privy council, Jan. 27, 1551. He was consecrated at Lambeth on the 8th of March. See Soames, Hist. Ref. III. 566; Burnet, III. 305.]

I send you a small gold coin, in which the effigy of the king of England is very well expressed, as a return for the token you sent to Rachel, for which she thanks you in her childish prattle, and sends her best love. I entreat you to recommend master Hooper to be more moderate in his labour: for he preaches four, or at least three times every day; and I am afraid lest these overabundant exertions should occasion a premature decay, by which very many souls now hungering after the word of God, and whose hunger is well known from the frequent anxiety to hear him, will be deprived both of their teacher and his doctrine. We are much disturbed by the apprehension of riots; for there is great danger of them very shortly by reason of the dearness of provisions and other things, although there is great plenty of wheat and other grain: but on whom the blame is to be laid you know better than I do. I have forwarded your letter to master Hooper, and will take care to send you his reply. Farewell. Salute master Bibliander and his wife, masters Gualter and Pellican and their wives, master Zuinglius and his wife, to whom also I send a golden coin stamped with the king's effigy. London, April 3, [1551].

Your most dutiful,

ANNE DE TSERCLAS, now HOOPER.

My maid Joanna salutes you, as does her husband, the servant of the French church. When you write to master Hooper or myself, take care that your letters are carefully sealed; for there are certain busy-bodies who are in the habit of opening and reading them, if by any means they can do it.

LETTER L.

ANNE HOOPER TO HENRY BULLINGER.

Dated at GLOUCESTER, Oct. 27, 1551[1].

GREETING. When the bearer of this was with us, there were two reasons which prevented my answering your letter;

[1 This letter was probably sent together with that of bishop Hooper's of the same date, given above, p. 95.]

the one, because I am unable to express my sentiments in German; the other, because I was overwhelmed by so many and urgent engagements that scarce any leisure was allowed me. Yet the regard I bear you drew me aside a little while from my employments, and compelled me altogether to put them off to another time. At length then I have prepared myself with much satisfaction for a diligent though hasty correspondence, that by this effort I might, in some measure at least, gratify your mind with my most insignificant letter. For I love, and esteem, and reverence you most especially, and I return you my best thanks for having condescended to write me a most elegant and kind letter, though I have hitherto been very negligent and remiss in writing. But the receipt of your letter divested me of all sloth, though indeed at this time my engagements will not admit of its indulgence: everything however that I intended to write to you I have turned over to this Mercury; and I pray you to give him credit for what he may tell you, as time forbids my entering more into the subject. I justly lament your absence, who have stood forth as my most excellent friend, nay, rather I may say, my patron; and who have so obliged me by your favours, that were I even to pledge my life, much less my property, I should be unable to return your kindness. Wherefore since my life and property are not sufficient to repay my obligations, I must still remain in debt. Oh! I wish that the distance of place did not separate us at so long an interval, that we might enjoy the same intimacy as heretofore. But I hope that you will shortly visit England, which if you will accomplish, I shall then consider myself most fortunate in being again permitted to enjoy your long wished for society. I pray you, my father, to salute your wife, my mother, affectionately in my name, as also all my other friends. Gloucester, Oct. 27, 1551. Farewell.

Rachel, thank God, is in excellent health, and salutes you and your wife, and begs your blessing, and prays that in your blessing God may deign to bless her also.

Ever your entire and obliged friend,

ANNE HOOPER.

LETTER LI.

ANNE HOOPER TO HENRY BULLINGER.

Dated at FRANKFORT, *April* 20, 1554.

MUCH health.   I recognised, my venerable friend, in the letter you lately wrote me, your wonted kindness : you shew yourself so anxious about me, that I could not expect more even if you were my father.   And indeed that letter was doubly acceptable, both because I perceived that I was not neglected by you, and also, because God had at that time visited me with a calamity in which I was forced not only to lament the common condition of the church at large, but also my own individual affliction.   My woman's mind being battered with these two engines, what wonder if it seemed immediately about to give way ?   But the Spirit of the Lord was with me, and raised up his ministers to give me comfort; among whom you were one, by whose letter I was especially refreshed.   May the Lord Jesus repay you with his blessing ! For after I had received and read it over, I began by God's assistance to bear myself up against such a weight of calamity ; and I am hitherto supporting myself, as far as I am able, by the word of God, often reading over again your letter, to add spurs to this dull flesh.   You will perform an act therefore worthy of your kindness, if you will continue in this manner, by more frequent letters, to uphold one whom you have in some degree already raised up.

I thank you for expressing your wish that I were with you yonder, nor is there any other place I should prefer.   But since the Lord, by my husband's bidding and the advice of my friends, has at length driven me from England, and conducted me safe to Antwerp, I availed myself of an opportunity of accompanying a party every way suitable, and joined my female relative at Frankfort, where now, by the mercy of God, the senate has granted liberty to the foreign church for their whole ecclesiastical ministry both of the word and sacraments. On this account I shall prefer remaining here in my own hired house, until I see how the Lord shall deal with my husband, concerning whom, as I have not yet received any intelligence, I am not a little anxious.   But yet I know that he is under God's care; and I therefore acquiesce in the providence of my God: and although this burden of widowhood is very painful, yet I comfort myself as far as I am able by prayer and the word of God.   I entreat you for Christ's sake, to aid me both with your prayers and correspondence.   Salute, I pray you, most dutifully, my very dear gossip your wife, with all your family.   I salute masters Bibliander, Pellican, Gualter, Sebastian the schoolmaster, and all the brethren.   I pray Almighty God continually to afford you an increase of his Spirit.   Farewell, my much esteemed and revered friend in Christ.   Frankfort, April 20, the day after the opening of the church of the white virgins to us, when master Valerandus Pollanus, the husband of my relative, and the chief pastor of the church, preached a sermon, and baptized his young son in the Rhine.   May God grant to this church a due increase, and worthy of his name!   Do you pray for it.   The pastor himself, my kinsman, earnestly entreated me to salute you in his name, and to commend his ministry to your prayers and those of your colleagues. Again farewell in Christ.   1554.

Your god-daughter Rachel salutes you and your wife. Daniel is still in England, and I shall send a certain most respectable matron, who has hitherto been living with me, to bring him hither.   I commend my honoured husband to your prayers.

Your very loving friend,

ANNE HOOPER.

LETTER LII.

ANNE HOOPER TO HENRY BULLINGER.

Dated at FRANKFORT, *Sept.* 22, 1554.

GREETING.   Your letter, my loving friend, was very gratifying to me, and I thank you for continuing to be so anxious about me.   I thank you too very much for your anxiety about master Hooper.   By the grace of God he bears every thing, even his threatened death, with constancy and fortitude. Your letter I know will be very acceptable to him, as he has already told me more than once. I entreat you for Christ's sake, deny him not this comfort. If I receive your letter, I will easily take care that it shall be delivered. For hitherto, by the goodness of God, he has always been allowed to write to me, and to receive my letters: only take care that your letters are delivered at Strasburgh, either to master Burcher, or to master John Garner, the minister of the French church. I have been hitherto tolerably well, and bear this calamity as firmly as I can. The Lord will aid and succour my weakness. I have need of the prayers and sweet consolations of my good friends: wherefore I earnestly entreat you not to neglect me. As to news, there is not any that I know of but what you may learn from the merchants who return to you from this place. Salute, I entreat you, in my name my excellent gossip, your most honourable wife, masters Gualter, Bibliander, Pellican, and their wives. Master Cechelles salutes you, as does Valerandus Pollanus, who also sends you this little book, from which you may know the constitution and general order of our little church: in which should there be any thing which you think requires correction, you will exceedingly oblige him by letting him know ; and I entreat you to do so, for Christ's sake. I commend myself and my children to your piety and most devout prayers. Farewell. Frankfort, Sept. 22, 1554.

Your very loving gossip,

ANNE HOOPER.

LETTER LIII.

ANNE HOOPER TO HENRY BULLINGER.
Dated at FRANKFORT, *Nov.* 12, 1554.

I RETURN you everlasting thanks, very dear and honoured friend, for your delightful letter, which has afforded me much comfort. I acknowledge, and experience in myself, and perceive also in many others, what the Lord Christ foretold; and I often soothe my mind, when wounded by anxiety, with the sweet reflection, that our God is faithful. I earnestly entreat you therefore, not to cease pleading for me with the Lord in your prayers, and by a letter from time to time to arouse my spirit, which, to say the truth, I very often feel to be all but dead through grief. And I now require the aid of all godly persons, although I am never entirely forsaken of the Lord, who sometimes refreshes me with the anticipation of a better life. But you yourself know how suitable to a diseased mind is the conversation of a sincere friend. I trust in the Lord, that the letter which you are writing to my dear husband, will afford him no less consolation than the one to myself; and in his name I thank you for that service. He is indeed worthy of the kind attention of all godly persons. I wish indeed I may some time have it in my power worthily to repay your kindness; my very readiness to do so would shew that I am not wanting in gratitude. But you know me well.

There is no news much worth your notice. For there has not been of a long time any certain intelligence from England; except that those persons who arrived from thence on the 10th instant, assert that a meeting of parliament had taken place respecting the coronation of the Spaniard; and that the hand of an individual[1] had been burnt off, because he refused to hear mass, and chose rather to be brought to the stake; also that some godly persons had lately been thrown into prison for the sake of religion. If this be the case, I am more than commonly anxious about my husband. May the Lord Jesus preserve us both! The lesser assembly of the states of Germany commenced here on the fourteenth of October; but this has no concern with religion, about which they have not yet said a single word. They are labouring for the tranquillity of Germany, that it may be safe from the attacks of the marquis of Brandenburgh. I cannot say what is proposed respecting the French (king), for I have not heard. I wish the people of Germany would not so rashly trust in foreign princes who are of a

[1 This, probably, was Thomas Jenkins, a weaver of Shoreditch; for an account of whose martyrdom see Foxe, VI. 717. Ed. 1838.]

different religion to themselves : but you will hear more from the very respectable man who will deliver this letter.

I salute my very dear gossip your wife, and all friends. My Daniel and Rachel also salute you. Masters Valerandus Pollanus and Secelles, whom you desired me to salute, salute you in return. The peace of our Lord Jesus Christ be with you! I commend myself to your prayers. Frankfort, Nov. 12, 1554.

Your very loving gossip and sister in Christ,

ANNE HOOPER.

LETTER LIV[1].

ANNE HOOPER TO HENRY BULLINGER.
Dated at FRANKFORT, *April* 11, 1555.

MUCH health. When I received, most loving gossip, the book of my dear husband, I desired, as he bade me by his letter, that it should be published before this fair. For which reason I sent it to master Peter Martyr, that he might get it done at Strasburgh. He excused himself on account of the doctrine of the eucharist, which is not received there. It might be printed here by permission of the senate; but it is better that you should first of all revise the book, and procure it to be printed yonder. But as I am well aware that his memory is most precious to you, I do not doubt but that you will be equally ready to oblige him in this matter, as if he were now alive: indeed, he is alive with all the holy martyrs, and with his Christ the head of the martyrs ; and I am dead here till God shall again unite me to him. I thank you for your most godly letter. I certainly stand much in need of such consolations, and of your prayers. I pray you therefore by the holy friendship of the most holy martyr my husband, of whom being now deprived I consider this life to be death, do not forsake me. I am not one who is able to return your kindness; but you will do an acceptable service to God, who especially commends widows to your protection.

[1 The original Latin of this letter will be found in the Appendix.]

I and my Rachel return our thanks for the elegant new
year's gift you sent us.   Salute your excellent wife, my very
dear gossip, and all friends.   Farewell.   Frankfort, April 11,
1555.

Your very loving gossip and sister in Christ,

ANNE HOOPER.

Your [god-daughter] Rachel sends you an English coin,
on which are the effigies of Ahab and Jezebel[2].

LETTER LV.

JOHN PONET TO HENRY BULLINGER.

Dated at STRASBURGH, *April* 14, 1556.

MANY thanks, most excellent master Bullinger, are due
from us exiles to our Lord God, for having placed over his
church in this calamitous age such a teacher as yourself.
For we perceive you to be one who is willing to afford every
consolation, and who is able to afford very much, to the
afflicted servants of Christ yonder.   But how greatly your
kind offices towards them have bound the rest of the English
to you, I had rather imagine than express, lest, in attempting to declare your acts of kindness towards them, extensive as
they have been, I should seem either to obscure their great-
ness by recounting them, or, by treating of them too lightly,
to diminish their importance.   But in speaking of myself,
namely, an exile, and weighed down with various crosses from
the Lord, I can neither refrain from speaking of the great
consolation you have afforded me, nor can I adequately express my thanks.   Master Burcher, and others, have often told
me of your friendly greetings.   My friend Cheke also has
repeated to me your salutations in your letters to him, and so
likewise has Sampson in his; in which I have perused from
your pen many things most gratifying to me.   For I have
perceived therein your distress and vehement sorrow of

[2 The English money of this period bore the effigies of king Philip
and queen Mary.]

mind for the universal flock of Christ. I have perceived also, at the same time, a signal manifestation of your benevolence and regard towards me. The Lord God, I acknowledge, has taken from me all that I had, which indeed was most ample. But why should he not? He who gave has taken away. But what? worldly, earthly, perishable things; while he is intending, I hope, yea, I do not doubt, to bestow upon me things heavenly and imperishable. What is exile? A thing which, provided you have wherewithal to subsist, is painful only in imagination. I know that it is the scourge of the Lord; but with what mildness and fatherly affection he deals with me, I can readily learn even from this, that he has afforded me for my comforters Bullinger, Melancthon, Martyr, and other most shining lights of his church. Happy was the widow of Sarepta in experiencing the mercy of God, and the consolation imparted by Elijah; wretched and most unworthy were those lepers who rejected Christ their only comfort. But since it has seemed good to my God to raise up in you such an Elijah as can support me in my affliction; I write these things to you, not so much to express my thanks for your so great and truly christian care bestowed upon me, (although those are especially due to you from me,) as to acquaint you at the same time that I have both derived the greatest pleasure from those letters of yours to your friends respecting me, and that I acknowledge myself exceedingly indebted to you for them.

My friend Cheke bade me, on his departure for Antwerp, to salute you in his name: he told me also, that he had heard that Ignatius, in Greek, had been sent over to some printer at Zurich to be printed; if this be the case, will you allow me to trouble you so far as to procure me a transcript of that passage from the epistle to the Philadelphians respecting the marriage of Paul and the other apostles? I have now a controversy about this matter with a most impudent papist[1]. I am ashamed to say more about this request; but you must know that I am of necessity compelled to make it, for I have no other means of obtaining what I wish. But as often as I consider the character that Bullinger bears in the general opinion, my mind tells me before-hand that this little trouble

[1 For an account of this controversy with Dr Thomas Martin, see Strype, Mem. II. ii. 54, and III. i. 524, &c.]

will not be displeasing to you. Excuse, I pray you, this liberty. Excuse also my hasty pen. Farewell, and count me, I pray you, in the number of your friends. Strasburgh, April 14, 1556.

Yours wholly,

JOHN PONET, *Anglus,*

formerly bishop of Winchester.

LETTER LVI.

JOHN PONET TO HENRY BULLINGER.

Dated at [STRASBURGH, *June*, 1556.][2]

Do not, I pray you, most excellent master Bullinger, take it ill that I have not sooner replied to your last letter. The long delay of master Martyr, who wished to be the bearer of my letter, has been the cause. His departure from hence to you is a proof of the exceeding favour of God to your church. I wish my affairs had been so circumstanced as to allow of my accompanying him; as much indeed for the sake of hearing him as yourself. I return you my best thanks for having procured the transcript of that passage of Ignatius by master Gessner. The name of that individual is of so much authority with me, that the very paper, which from your testimony I know to have been written upon by his hand, I lay up among my choicest treasures: for I am willingly superstitious in preserving the memorials of such men. Nothing affords me greater pleasure than to hear from your letter, that you will take care that our friendship confirmed in Christ shall be a durable one; for I seem thereby to be altogether united to you. I wish that what you wrote to me concerning sir John Cheke[3] may not prove prophetic. I doubt not but that he will seal his testimony to the gospel

[2 A note annexed to this letter, in Bullinger's hand, states this to have been Ponet's last letter to him, and adds, that he died at Strasburgh, in August 1556.]

[3 For an account of Cheke's recantation and subsequent repentance and death, see Strype, Cheke, 113, 130.]

with his blood. What will not Pharaoh attempt against Israel, especially on his return from exile? I acknowledge myself very much indebted both to yourself and your church, on the behalf of the Englishman, master Parkhurst. My services, although my power is altogether nothing, yet such as they are, are entirely at your command, if I can be of use to you in any thing. Salute, I pray you, in my name master Gessner, to whom I certainly would have written, had not my modesty overcome my courage. But if I am wrong in this respect, I pray you forgive me. But I hope that he will shortly take care that Ignatius be printed in Greek. May our great and good God long preserve you both in safety to his church!

Yours wholly,

JOHN PONET, *Winton.*

LETTER LVII.

MARIA PONET TO PETER MARTYR.
Dated at STRASBURGH, *July* 15, 1557.

IT is not from any fault of mine, most accomplished sir, that you have been so long without your books. My dear husband has died and left me a wretched widow, and entirely unacquainted with these things: he left also I know not how many or what kind of books, all of which, as I thought they belonged to me, I sold to that excellent person, and my very good friend, master Cook; which when I had done, master Jewel informed me by letter, that some of them belonged to your excellency, and that you were making inquiry after them. As soon as I understood this to be the case, I addressed myself with all diligence, and frequently too, to master Cook, that I might be permitted to re-purchase, at whatever cost, those books of yours, which I had before sold him by mistake for my own. But from some cause or other I could not obtain my request. Since therefore I was exceedingly anxious to restore you your books, and could find no other way of doing so, I have purchased new ones at the booksellers, which I have destined for your reverence, and caused to be forwarded to you by my worthy friend John Abel.   For although I am but a poor widow, I had rather die than do an injury to any one, or than not pay every one their due, as far as lies in my power.   It truly grieves me very much, that I have put off this business till the present time : but your kindness will excuse me, for I should have accomplished it sooner, if I could any where have met with the books on sale before.   Farewell, very learned and dear sir : I request you too of your kindness not to forget me in your prayers, and I will always pray for you.   Strasburgh, July 15, 1557.

Your reverence's most devoted,

MARIA PONET.

LETTER LVIII.

RICHARD COX TO HENRY BULLINGER.
Dated at the Palace, WESTMINSTER, *Oct.* 22, 1549 [1].

THERE are many things, my very dear friend in Christ, which ought justly to inspire me with veneration for yourself; namely, your singular erudition and piety, so renowned throughout all Christendom.   Many and splendid are the monuments of your talent, which have everywhere most clearly set forth the glory of God.   These things however, important as they are, being of general interest, are not so likely to affect individuals : but the instance of your kindness with which you have lately favoured me, has more intimately and powerfully impressed my mind ; I mean, your having done me the honour of presenting me with your most learned letter, and jewel of a book.   For there shine therein the jewels, not of earth, but heaven ; not those which attract the sight, but which wonderfully delight the mind.   I thank you therefore most heartily, and I implore the

[1 See the letter of John ab Ulmis, dated Oct. 20, 1549, in a subsequent part of this volume.]

great and good God very long to preserve both yourself and those like you, as the most solid pillars of his church. Farewell. From the king's palace at Westminster, Oct. 22, 1540.

Your most devoted,

RICHARD COX.

LETTER LIX.

RICHARD COX TO HENRY BULLINGER.

Dated at LONDON, *Nov.* 1, 1550.

I seem very much indebted, very dear brother in Christ, to the divine goodness, for having requited my short and barren letter with such an exuberant and copious treasure of your writings. This is the manner of the Lord our God, who is wont to bestow all things in rich abundance upon those who diligently seek him. You have followed his example, and, in imitation of his fruitful fields, which return more than they receive, you have repaid my letter with abundant interest.

Your letter ought, on these accounts, to be most gratifying to me; first, because it is full of all kindness and affection towards me, and a most certain evidence of it; secondly, because it exhibits a heart glowing with all the ardour of piety and divine love; lastly, because it declares that not only the queen dowager, but likewise others of the more pious nobility of this kingdom, regard their Bullinger with so much love and affection. Your little work presented to the queen dowager was received by her most kindly, and read with the greatest interest and attention. Nothing can be more gratifying to her than studious labours executed by godly men. I return you my best thanks for having again favoured me with another present, and that not so much a paper one, as one that breathes heavenly ambrosia on every side. Moreover you have no reason to fear any exception being taken to your books, as long as the divine mercy shall preserve to us our king; in whom, believe me, there already shines forth an incredible measure of learning, with a zeal for religion, and a judgment all but mature.

I have carefully saluted in your own words the most reverend the archbishop of Canterbury, the earl of Warwick, and the marquis of Dorset, all of whom desired me to salute you most courteously in return. We are anxiously expecting those other works which you promised shortly to publish, that you may never cease to deserve well of us, and receive a most abundant recompence, not from us, but from him in whose service you are especially enlisted. Farewell.

After I had written the above, my letter being long detained either through my own negligence, or by reason of the infrequency of the post, it was reported to me that certain other of your works had been published; which diligence of yours I congratulate both on your account and our own. Again farewell, my very dear brother in Christ. London, Nov. 1, 1550.

Your much attached,
RICHARD COX.

LETTER LX[1].

RICHARD COX TO HENRY BULLINGER.
Dated at WESTMINSTER, *May* 5, 1551.

YOUR having deigned, most esteemed brother in Christ, to honour and distinguish me with such abundant favours, has added very considerably to my former obligations to you. You have requited my laconic and barren letter with almost an entire volume, and that too a most learned one, and most gratifying to me in the perusal. You proceed, moreover, to make me happy with a double present, namely, the treatise of master Calvin concerning that most christian concord established between you in the matter of the eucharist[2], and the fifth Decade of your sermons, which John ab Ulmis brought me yesterday night. For these presents I return

[1 The original of this letter is given in Strype, Mem. II. i. 532.]

[2 This refers to the Consensus Tigurinus in 1549, when Calvin came to an agreement with Bullinger and other divines of Zurich respecting the doctrine of the Lord's supper.]

you the best thanks in my power. I am exceedingly delighted with them both. Oh that the most merciful God would grant, some time or other, that in treating of the holy supper the universal church of Christ would aim at the same mark of truth!

In reading your books, especially when any passage shall occur which may peculiarly affect me by its piety, I will not cease to bear you in my remembrance, and to importune God in my prayers, that he may very long preserve you to his church, and more and more endue you with his holy Spirit. And when in so candid and christian a manner you remind me of my duty, and so seriously excite and so solemnly engage me to the right performance of my office; I con-sider this as done by the most holy Spirit of the Lord, that I may not be inactive or negligent in his work. For I daily feel how supine we are in the Lord's business, and how dili-gent and earnest in our own.

Moreover, I embrace your sound and wholesome counsel respecting the reformation of the church of God, with the greater readiness, inasmuch as you so entirely coincide with me in that belief which a merciful God has given me in these things. For I am of opinion that all things in the church should be pure, simple, and removed as far as possible from the elements and pomps of this world. But in this our church what can I do, who am so deficient both in learning and authority? I can only endeavour to persuade our bishops to be of the same mind and opinion with my-self, and in the mean time commit to God the care and conduct of his own work.

You are most worthy, my Bullinger, of receiving the greatest favours, since you so gratefully accept those which are either of no value, or at least, of very little importance. Those two youths, who resided some time with me, are from their piety, and ardent desire of learning, worthy of the favour and good-will of pious persons. The other two, who have lately arrived, and whom you so greatly recommended to me, I will treat, were it only for your sake, with the greatest kindness in my power. I will not fail to salute in your name those two noble personages, and your great ad-mirers. May the Lord Jesus very long preserve you in safety, and give you both strength and courage for the restoration of his church! Farewell. Westminster, May 5, 1551.

Your much attached and
very loving brother in Christ,
RICHARD COX.

LETTER LXI.

RICHARD COX TO HENRY BULLINGER.
[Dated at WINDSOR, *Oct.* 5, 1552.]

ALTHOUGH I have nothing of any consequence at this time to write to you, very dear brother in Christ, yet I am loth to dismiss our friend John [ab Ulmis] altogether without a letter from me; and he himself would be much grieved at my doing so. As to what concerns the true religion, blessed be the Lord God, a ray of whose glory is wonderfully shining upon us from day to day, we have now for the second time altered the administration of the public prayers and even of the sacraments themselves, and have framed them according to the rule of God's word; but the severe institutions of christian discipline we most utterly abominate. We would be sons, and heirs also, but we tremble at the rod. Do pray stir us up, and our nobility too, by the Spirit which is given to you, to a regard for discipline; without which, I grieve to say it, the kingdom will be taken away from us, and given to a nation bringing forth the fruit thereof.

But there is one thing, my Bullinger, respecting which I most anxiously desire to be thoroughly instructed. I read in the place where you treat of the Lord's supper, in your fifth Decade[1], these words: "Since it is not a public or general assembly when four or five communicate with a sick person, those who affirm that the supper may be administered to the sick at home, if others also receive it at the same time, say nothing to the purpose." What if, when the congregation is

[1 See Fiftie godlie and learned Sermons, divided into five Decades, conteyning the chiefe and principall pointes of Christian religion, written in three severall tomes or sections, by Henrie Bullinger, &c. London, 1577. Tom. III. p. 1080.]

duly called together, three, four, or five only, out of many hundreds, are willing to receive the sacrament of the eucharist, all the rest refusing to do so, is it not allowable for them to receive it either in the presence of the others, or after they have left the church? Why then should a sick person be deprived of this benefit? I much wish for fuller information upon this point, as soon as you shall have leisure to afford it. May the Lord Jesus very long preserve you to us in safety, to the glory of Christ and the edification of his church! Windsor in England, Oct. 5, 1552.

Your brother in Christ,
RICHARD COX.

LETTER LXII.

OWEN OGLETHORPE TO HENRY BULLINGER.

Dated at Magdalene College, OXFORD, *Oct.* 30, [1548].

GRACE and comfort of the Holy Ghost! Your illustrious reputation and singular learning, most accomplished sir, have for many years past excited in my mind a great regard for you; so that it has for a long time been my most earnest desire that a fitting opportunity might sometime be afforded me, if not of personal communication with you, at least of addressing you by letter, that a mutual regard might be established between us. And this ardent desire of mine was in a measure accomplished, when about ten years since Nicolas Partridge, a person most dear to me upon many accounts, being overtaken with sickness on his way into Italy, was entertained by you at your house, and having recovered his health by means of your liberality, on his return to England together with your friend Rodolph[1], was the bearer of a letter to me from you; which as I preserve by me no less willingly than carefully as a signal token of your regard to me, so I most earnestly embrace and reverence your courtesy, who, easily excelling as you do all persons in learning, have nevertheless condescended to write to an individual

[1 Rodolph Gualter accompanied Nicolas Partridge of Lenham, Kent, on his return to England from Zurich in 1537.]

like myself, and, as you have most politely said, to court my friendship. And availing myself at that time of the favourable opportunity of writing, I sent your excellency by that same attendant of yours my unpolished letter, with the intention of writing more frequently, had a suitable means of communication been afforded me. But I am now once more addressing your reverence in this letter with the greater freedom, because John ab Ulmis, a young man of good hopes, has lately brought me a salutation from you, with the expression of your desire (as he informed me) in your letter to him, that John Rodolph Stumphius, a youth no less amiable than studious, who has most courteously offered me his services, might not return to you without a letter from me. I willingly commend him to you; and if you will assist him in his studies, according to your exceeding kindness, there is no doubt but that he will some time or other be of great benefit to the state. Farewell, most illustrious sir, and may the Lord Jesus long preserve you, and prosper your studies! Oxford, from Magdalene College, Oct. 30.

Your excellency's most attached,

OWEN OGLETHORPE.

LETTER LXIII.

ROBERT HORN TO JOHN WOLFIUS.

Dated at FRANKFORT, *Feb.* 2, 1556.

SINCE, my dearest Wolfius, nothing is more becoming a christian man, than to have a mind full of love towards all, and feelings of compassion and kindness towards those who are miserable exiles for the sake of the true religion, (feelings which all the English who heretofore sojourned at Zurich ought to recognise in yourself, and which I myself experienced beyond the rest;) so nothing is more unbecoming him who professes even the least regard to what is right, than to shew himself unmindful of, or ungrateful for, a benefit received. The slightest possible suspicion of such conduct I earnestly desire may be removed from me as far as possible. And I have therefore thought it better to let you know this by a letter, however brief, than by my silence to afford you any occasion of suspecting evil of me. Receive then this short letter, as a testimony of a mind ready and prepared to return your kindness, had not fortune denied me the ability corresponding to the readiness of my inclination. My dear brother Richard [Chambers] salutes you, and acknowledges himself bound to you by an equal obligation with myself. Salute, I pray you, in our name our very dear friends in Christ, masters Pellican, Gualter, Bibliander, Simler, Zuinglius, Lavater, Haller, Frisius, John ab Ulmis, and both the elder and younger Froschover. And especially salute most affectionately in my name one who deserves so well of me, Peter Stainer, with his most amiable wife : nor would I desire to pass over our landlady, who, as she wrote word to master Richard, sold, by your assistance, the two beds for fourteen florins, and I know not what other articles besides ; which amount we desire to be transmitted by Froschover, or some other confidential person, to Frankfort at the next fair, together with a small portmanteau which we also left to be forwarded by your kindness, and that of John ab Ulmis. Farewell, most excellent sir. Frankfort, Feb. 2, 1556.

Yours wholly, in Christ,

ROBERT HORN.

P.S. Out of the money which our landlady has in charge, please to give her one florin for her trouble, and send the balance to us.

LETTER LXIV.

ROBERT HORN AND RICHARD CHAMBERS TO THE SENATE OF ZURICH.

Dated at [FRANKFORT,] *Feb.* 3, 1556.

HOSPITALITY indeed is always commendable in every one; and in you, most grave and potent lords, it has been truly admirable : for that those whom nature, or rather God, has rendered brave and powerful in war, for the purpose, as it should seem, of fighting the Lord's battles,—that you, I say, should become so compassionate, as to be the entertainers of

the humble, wandering, dispersed and wretched members of
the church, cannot indeed be passed over without great ad-
miration ; and chiefly for this reason, inasmuch as not having
been disturbed in your own persons by any storms of misfortune and calamity, your not having hitherto been under any
necessity of requiring assistance, your not having had recourse
to any one for support, in a word, your not having been in
the way of experiencing the benevolence of others in this
respect, proves that this your hospitable feeling cannot arise
from the desire to return a kindness, or from your having
been subjected to the like calamities yourselves.   Many persons indeed are led by the feelings of commiseration to relieve
those who have suffered the like misfortunes with themselves;
and all persons, those at least who have any regard to prin-
ciple, consider themselves so obliged, as it were, by the law of
requital, as that, having been in circumstances of trouble and
distress themselves, and having therein experienced the liberality of others, they are unwilling, through an instinctive
sense of natural justice, to refuse to persons labouring under
the like afflictions that assistance, which the more fortunate
are always able to afford to those in need without any detri-
ment to themselves.

I will not, however, any longer praise you, but rather
acknowledge in you the efficacy of the word, or the power
of God in his word, which was mighty in you also who
believed unto salvation.   "The voice of the Lord is powerful,
the voice of the Lord is full of majesty," as the Psalmist
says; and it has certainly the power of renewing and
transforming us into other men.   That frequent exclamation
of master Zuinglius has also reached my ears, where he is
wont to affirm, speaking from experience, that evangelical
doctrine (though it has done much beside), yet, if it had
effected nothing else, has however produced this advantage,
that by the preaching of it men are rendered much more
civilized in their manners, and altogether much more humane
in their feelings.   If that most excellent man, so worthy of
everlasting and pious remembrance, were now living, I should
address him in the same language that formerly in the gospel
the citizens of Samaria addressed to the woman of that city,
"Now we believe, not because of thy saying, for we have
heard and know ourselves ;" yea, we have experienced, we
have felt it.   For with what entire liberty, as far as our re-

ligion was concerned, did we exercise freedom of conscience among you! how exempted were we from all tributary exactions, which you might justly have demanded for the public necessities even from your own citizens! Nay, how favoured were we by the liberality of your townsmen as well as your own! Why should I mention the advice, the consolations of your ministers; the lamentations of the citizens sympathising with us on our condition; the gratuitous services of the apothecaries and physicians? So that we were evidently not regarded and considered by you as guests, but as citizens, and, if possible, yet more. What pains you took to examine into our wants, our deficiencies, that out of your plenty and abundance you might provide for their supply! Lastly, how did you spontaneously offer us, on our departure, in case we should have occasion to return, the same kindness, the same quiet habitations, the same liberty of permission to reside among you; so that you have, as it were, your gates always open to ourselves and our countrymen! Truly this your affection towards us was more than paternal. We never indeed experienced in our own country greater compassion, kindness, and munificence; so that we all of us regarded almost as a proverb the saying, "It is good to be here." We should never have suffered ourselves to be torn from you, had we not been invited, and almost compelled as it were, by the two importunate letters of our countrymen, to relieve the extreme necessity of the now almost ruined church of our exiles at Frankfort[1]. Forgive us therefore that we could no longer be *onerous* to those to whom we desire to do *honour*.

And since we can in no way gratify you more than by a grateful commemoration of the benefits we have received from you, we will not cease, in returning thanks for them, to have a continual remembrance of you in our petitions to God, that since we ourselves are unable to repay or discharge our debt, he may repay and discharge it [for us] in his Christ. Moreover, taking fresh occasion from our late experience of your hospitality, we earnestly desire that you should be en-

[1] Horn was "in the election" to succeed Whitehead in the pastoral office at Frankfort, where he "entered the churche the first off Marche, Anno Domini 1556, &c." See a Brieff discours aboute the troubles begonne at Franckfort in Germany, Anno Domini 1554, aboute the Booke off common prayer and ceremonies, &c. p. lxii. London reprint, 1845.]

treated and prevailed upon, that, in case any reason of importance should arise to drive us from our present abode, we may still meet with some place among you sufficient for our necessities. In the mean while may the eternal Lord God, the Father of our Lord Jesus Christ, the giver of the Holy Ghost, bless you with all spiritual benediction, make you fearers of God, and feared and dreaded by your enemies; may he furnish you, as the constant patrons of gospel truth, with unflinching boldness, courage, and power, to the edification of his whole church, and the glory and power of his holy name! Amen. Feb. 3, 1556.

Your most attached,

ROBERT HORN, *Anglus.*

RICHARD CHAMBERS, *Anglus.*

LETTER LXV.

ROBERT HORN AND RICHARD CHAMBERS TO HENRY BULLINGER.

Dated *Feb.* 3, 1556.

THOUGH I had long since intended to write to your reverence, I have been prevented by continued and almost endless engagements, as you know is usual with persons who are constantly changing their place of abode: but thus it has pleased God to try us, and the necessity of our church required this very thing, that we, who of late enjoyed among you the most entire liberty, together with no small degree of literary repose, are now on the contrary, through the magnitude of our affairs, scarcely able to obtain leisure for writing a single letter. We will not therefore entertain a doubt but that you will kindly bear with this our tardiness in writing, when you have considered the extent of our necessities, and understood the affection, love, and esteem of our hearts towards you according to our power. And since we have no other method of expressing it, we think it better to do so late than never by a letter addressed to yourself. But if we should here attempt to enumerate all the benefits you have conferred upon us, it would probably be too disagreeable to yourself, who prefer rather to be active in doing good, than to have the reputation of it; and it would be also too troublesome a task for ourselves. For how much should we have to record of your counsel, sympathy, and protection! You it was, who conciliated to us the good-will of your townsmen, and who procured the munificence of the government to be extended towards us. Nor did you content yourself merely with obtaining for us the good offices both of your family and your country; but in addition to this, by letters to those at a distance, you occasioned the liberality of other and unknown individuals to be poured out upon us from all quarters. By your writings also you sought to reach even those our friends at home, by whose kindness we have been supported; and this, that you might not be be-hind-hand in exciting them to so godly a purpose, and in aid-ing us that we should not be deprived of their assistance. It is indeed far more easy for us to relate these benefits than in any measure to requite them. We therefore commend you and your ministry to God, who will repay you in that day.

Meanwhile we entreat you to do us this kindness, namely, to take upon yourself the charge of returning, to the whole senate, more suitable and abundant acknowledgments than such as we could include in our scanty and short epistle; and (forasmuch as we cannot look forward to so long and continued a peace as to effect any change in our condition, before a free permission is granted us to return into our country,) most earnestly to entreat them in our behalf, that if there should, by any possibility, arise such a change, as to expel us from our present abode, we may nevertheless once more freely return to, and obtain a quiet sojourn among you. But we have no fear, either concerning yourself or those ex-cellent men, but that you will grant us this favour. In the meantime salute in the name of us all your most amiable wife, and at the same time all the ministers of the word among you, our reverend masters Pellican, Bibliander, Gualter, Lavater, Simler, Zuinglius, Haller, Frisius, John ab Ulmis, Stumphius, and others, as your occupations will allow. We think master Gessner, whose kind offices to us were innumerable, must by no means be passed over; neither must the two Froschovers and their wives, whose extreme kindness to-

wards us demands rather our letters than our salutations : we
have at this time however contented ourselves with the latter,
because on account of so many engagements we are unable to
write more.   The grace of our Lord Jesus Christ be with
you all !   Amen.   Feb. 3, 1556.

Your very affectionate,

ROBERT HORN,

RICHARD CHAMBERS, } Angli.

LETTER LXVI.

ROBERT HORN AND RICHARD CHAMBERS TO
HENRY BULLINGER.

Dated at [FRANKFORT,] Sept. 19, 1556.

GRACE and peace from God our Father and our Lord
Jesus Christ !

We have received, most excellent master Bullinger, your
letter, in which we easily perceive how much you esteem
us, and that you are not forgetful of us.   Not indeed
that we should have had any doubt upon this point, if
you had not written to us at all.   But now, on the perusal
of this most delightful letter that you have sent to us,
we consider it as most evident, that your regard, fear, and
solicitude extends not only to ourselves, but to the whole of
our country ; by which feelings we hope you will be more
effectually stirred up to offer also more fervent prayers to
God on our behalf, for the reformation of our church, respecting which we certainly conceive better hopes, in that you, and
other men of God like you, are earnest in your prayers for
this very thing ; whose supplications, for the sake of Jesus
Christ our only mediator, cannot be in vain, but acceptable to
God, as being sprinkled with the blood of Christ, and inspired
(as it were) with the breathings of the Holy Spirit.   We
acknowledge your good offices, your labours, your exertions ;
and we pray the Lord to direct, establish, and confirm all
things for the good of the church, the honour of God, and
your own comfort.

The much esteemed master a Lasco still remains at

9—2

Frankfort, in daily expectation of a summons to bring him back into his own country. We communicated to him your letter. As to the matter of Brentius, we only pray that the Lord may compose the dissensions of the church, and multiply its peace. Nor are there every day wanting those, who, desirous of novelty, by their novel errors impugn the truth. It is indeed wonderful with how much loquacity, with what proud bombastic philosophy, certainly not " scientific demonstrations" (as he calls them,) but with the swelling blasts of Pelagius, and vain conceits of human wisdom, a certain Justus Velsius[1] has filled the schools, conceded to us by the kindness of the magistracy who preside over this state, with doctrines opposed to the eternal predestination of God. We send you his conceits : his blasphemies against God, his railings and invectives against master Calvin, (and indeed they are quite severe enough,) we would rather omit mention of than defile our paper with such foul abuse.

We expect no good news from England : all things seem to be growing worse and worse. So great is the number of the martyrs, who in their cheerful profession of the word of God are most cruelly dragged to the flames and to torments, that those godly men who, on former occasions, made it their business to inquire into this matter, are now unable to ascertain either the number or the names of the sufferers. Nor can the ferocity of the queen, and of Bonner the pseudo-bishop of London, and of the other papists, restrain itself, satiated with domestic blood, without moreover crossing the sea, and raging so furiously, that no godly person can now remain at Antwerp in security and free from danger. Sir [John] Cheke[2] and Sir Peter

[1 For an account of Justus Velsius and his opinions, see Strype, Grindal, 135.]

[2 Sir John Cheke, in the spring of 1556, on his return from Brussels towards Antwerp, was, with Sir Peter Carew his companion, by king Philip's secret commandment, suddenly apprehended in the way by the provost marshal, bound, and thrown into a cart, with his legs, arms, and body tied to it, and so conveyed on shipboard, brought a prisoner into England, and clapped up, as some great malefactor, in the Tower of London; and at length was forced to acknowledge and subscribe to the popish doctrines, and recant publicly his former good profession of the gospel, there being no other way to save himself from burning. He fell into exceeding melancholy and trouble of mind,

Carew[3], both taken by treachery, and carried before the queen, were thrown into prison, but are now, it is said, set at liberty, or are shortly to be so. But, alas! it is stated, (yet we hope the report is untrue,) that most iniquitous conditions of their restoration to, and enjoyment of, liberty, have been proposed to and accepted by them both. However it be, we may learn this, that it is vain to place our confidence in man.

Charles, not yet enough broken by disease, and his sister[4], together with his son Philip, being about to visit England, I know not for what reason, are recalled while on their very journey. Neither the nobility nor the people will patiently endure the arrival of these princes, nor do they in the mean time dissemble their impatience in this respect; notwithstanding that the queen with some of the nobles of her party are using all their influence and endeavours to aggrandize Philip with the hereditary right of government, the royal crown, and other distinctions; and this, with consent of parliament, as they call it. In Suffolk, they are proclaiming the lady Elizabeth queen, and they associate lord Courteney[5] as her supporter; by which bold attempt has been occasioned the execution of at least sixty or eighty persons by an ignominious death on the charge of treason. Respecting the number, however, nothing is known for certain. It is more certain, that on this account not only the lady Elizabeth, but also the lord Courteney[6], are brought into suspicion of treason, and in no small peril of their lives: but may God change all things for the better! Thus much concerning the affairs of our country.

Still, however, not yet satisfied with these things, we are keeping secret a thing which is rather to be de-

and in great repentances ended his miserable life within less than a year after. See Strype, Mem. III. i. 515; Cheke, 106, &c. Soames' Hist. Ref. IV. 565.]

[3 Sir Peter Carew had fled abroad on account of having been concerned in Wyatt's rebellion. He was sent to the Tower at the same time with Sir John Cheke. See Strype, Mem. III. ii. 7.]

[4 Mary, queen of Hungary and governess of the Low Countries.]

[5 The real lord Courteney, earl of Devon, was personated by a young man of the name of Cleobury, who was afterwards executed at Bury in Suffolk. Lingard's Hist. of England, v. 112. 4to Edition.]

[6 Lord Courteney died of an ague at Padua a few months after the discovery of the plot here mentioned.]

sired than expected. We will however communicate it to you. We are in fact desirous of a conference about the affairs of religion; but we are not yet able to affirm for certain whether it will take place. Should there occur any thing of the kind, we are in hopes that master Calvin will come back again, and that he will have both yourself and other learned men as his companions not only of his journey, but of his labours in this business. May the eternal Lord God grant this through Christ, that you may, some time or other, being assembled in the fear of God, (with Christ presiding in your council,) set forth at length a pure confession without any stain of error, to the confusion of the adversaries, the peace of the church, and the glory of God; to whose protection we commend you, your wife, family, and all your friends. Farewell. Sept. 19, 1556.

Your reverence's most devoted,

ROBERT HORN, and

RICHARD CHAMBERS.

LETTER LXVII.

JAMES PILKINGTON TO RODOLPH GUALTER.

Dated at GENEVA, *April 7*, 1556.

COME, Lord Jesus, come quickly! Health and peace in Christ Jesus!

Since Paul in all his epistles is so earnest in the salutation of those brethren, whom he perceived to love Christ in sincerity, though many persons think lightly, or rather not at all, of this duty, because it consists only in a few bare words; yet for my part, most illustrious sir, induced by so weighty an example, I can by no means consider it as of no importance. This being the case, whom can we English salute with greater reason than you, our good masters at Zurich, by whom we have been regarded as brethren? and to whom else can I

especially, whom you have so liberally entertained far beyond
my other friends, wish grace and life in my frequent and
affectionate letters, rather than to yourself? Your prudence
knows how to estimate things according to the intention of
the giver, and not according to the value of the gift; and
you are able likewise so to compare the power of shewing
kindness with the opportunities of doing so, as not so much
to regard what each may have given: but if you could have
been enriched by kind words, I should long since have made
you happy; for I am unable to gratify you in any other way.

You will be much surprised at my departure from you, and
not indeed without reason, for I was surprised at it myself;
but when I had considered with myself what a people we are,
and what we proverbially say of ourselves, I then ceased to
wonder. For we commonly say of ourselves, that the English
will never let well alone. Allow us, therefore, to be Englishmen, that, when we have learned wisdom to our cost, we may
perceive the constant evil of being inconstant. I do not say
this because we have been in need of any thing, or suffered
any ill-treatment, but that you may know that we had
learned by experience the happiness of living at Zurich;
and though we have met with many persons who are willing
to do us a service, we have found but few who have shewn
us the same kind attention as yourselves. And though it
is a great alleviation of sorrow for those who are afflicted
to pour out their griefs into the bosom of a faithful friend,
who may be able by wholesome counsel and soothing words
to relieve their distress, and who will entreat the Lord for
them with earnest prayers; I had rather that you should
commune with yourself upon the unhappy aspect of our
church, (both that portion of it which is oppressed by wolves
at home, as well as that which is dispersed abroad,) than that
I should attempt to relate what cannot be described. You
have formerly acted a part in this tragedy yourselves, but
the Lord has granted you a happy issue: we are now brought
upon the stage, that, being humbled by adversity, we may
discover him, whom in our prosperity we did not acknowledge
as we ought, to be a kind and merciful father.

Let this my letter, I pray you, salute as affectionately as
possible that common father of the afflicted, master Bullinger,
to whom, as he so richly deserves, I wish every happiness; and

since the Lord has made you witnesses of my affliction, go
on, as you have begun, to love me, to help me by your
counsel, and entreat the Lord for me in your prayers, that I
may again be restored to you, when it shall seem him good.
I thank also master Gessner for all his exertions on my behalf, and for the letter full of good advice, which I lately
received from him; for by his means, next to the Lord who
worketh all things, the pains in my stomach are daily so
decreasing, that I cherish good hopes of regaining my former
health.   I have not yet tried any of the remedies which he
last prescribed; but should I be compelled to adopt them, I
will write to him that he may know their effects.   I commend
to you master Parkhurst and his wife, my friends Spenser and
Frensham, and would especially desire to be commended to
the venerable Pellican, the most learned Bibliander, masters
Wolfius, John ab Ulmis, and all the other ministers.   If I
can do any thing for you, I am at your service.   May the
Lord keep you pure from this world unto his day!   Amen.
Farewell.   Geneva, 7 April, 1556.

Yours, as you so well deserve,

JAMES PILKINGTON.

LETTER LXVIII.

JAMES PILKINGTON TO HENRY BULLINGER.

Dated at CEVENNES, *June 27, 1556.*

COME, Lord Jesus, quickly!   Since nothing is more foreign to a human being than inhumanity, and humanity adorns
a human being more especially from the connection between
its name and nature; that you may not with reason think me
inhuman because I, whom you have often treated with so
much humanity, have not written to you, your humanity has
induced me to address you by my letter.   For since the
Lord always abhors the ungrateful, who do not acknowledge
benefits received, and the ungrateful are odious to mankind
themselves; lest I should fall into that fault of my own accord
which I had always condemned in others, my duty has

required, your dignity demanded, and both together have impelled me to write, that in words at least I might acknowledge an obligation, which in deed I am unable adequately to discharge. May you live then, I pray, with all your friends, long and happily; and for the hospitality with which you have so kindly received all the exiles, and with the agreeable recollection of which I delight myself, may the Lord, according to his kindness, for ever bless you. Continue, moreover, as you have begun, and do honour to yourself and all your friends by your kindness to the exiles: for the Lord is pleased by such offerings, he has them in everlasting remembrance, and can never forget your beneficence towards his proscribed people. But though your numerous noble actions are quoted by many with much grateful acknowledgment, there is not any thing in which they really rejoice more, than in that you are endeavouring to draw over to you Peter Martyr[1]. Many persons remark how unbefitting it is, and especially in these times, that the mouth of such a man should be stopped; and many persons are promising themselves great things concerning him, when they perceive how great an accession he will be to the cause of truth in your most free city. And though it is agreeable and almost necessary to our exiles, that all we English should meet together in the same church, and by our united complaints and ardent prayers importune, supplicate, entreat the Lord on behalf of our ruined church; yet both my inclination leads me to return to you as soon as I hear that he has arrived, and a light occasion will bring me. Whatever you may wish to know respecting me, the good bearer of this letter is willing and able to give you faithful intelligence in every respect. Salute for me my dear master Gualter, with the rest of your fellow-ministers, and especially master Gessner, through whose means, by the blessing of God, I am still living, and daily somewhat improving in health. May the Lord Jesus continue to preserve you and your church, and in his mercy restore our fallen one! Amen. Cevennes. 27th June, 1556.

Yours most deservedly,

J. PILKINGTON, *Anglus*.

[1 Peter Martyr was invited to Zurich by the magistrates of that city in 1556.]

LETTER LXIX.

EARL OF BEDFORD TO HENRY BULLINGER.

Dated at VENICE, *April* 26, [1557.]

MY singular regard for you, and the constant esteem I have ever entertained towards you for the sake of religion, as well as your incredible kindness, experienced by me in many ways when I was at Zurich, have occasioned me, most learned Bullinger, to give this young man this letter to you, as a most assured token of my affection towards you, and as it were a sealed evidence, which I was anxious to afford, of my continued love to you. And herein I thank you in such wise for your kindness, that I promise to repay it, if I ever have it in my power to oblige you in any respect. And I would have you regard this as said by me, not as men do, who now-a-days make a certain outward shew of words, and a mere parade of serving you, and this, rather that they may seem to be what they assert themselves, than be such in reality; but rather that you may persuade yourself, that it proceeds from a mind altogether sincere and entirely devoted to yourself. Wherefore, should I ever have it in my power to do you any service, (I am aware how trifling it will be,) yet, trifling as it is, it shall be altogether yours. But enough of this, and perhaps too much; especially since it is my intention, should not other circumstances intervene to call me elsewhere, to visit you on my return to England, when I shall confirm in person what I can only express now by bare words.

The young man who bears this letter, has informed me of the death of Conrad Pellican[1], (of whom I make honourable mention;) which when I heard, I grieved exceedingly as I ought to do, not so much for his sake as for that of the whole church. For he has most gloriously finished his course in labours, watchings, constant studies, and encouragement of learned men; and at length, by dying as he lived, he is translated to a better life in heaven. But the church will long regret a man who was every way so perfect; so that while I rejoice on his account, I cannot but grieve most

[1 Conrad Pellican died Sept. 14, 1556.]

exceedingly for her sake.   But your presence, as I hope and
wish, will easily mitigate the occasion of this sorrow; and
may Almighty God in his mercy long preserve you safe to
his church and to all good men!   Venice, April 26, [1557].

Your most attached,

F. BEDFORD.

P. S.   Diligently salute, I pray you, my dear friends
masters Gessner and Gualter.

LETTER LXX.

SIR ANTONY COOK TO PETER MARTYR.
Dated at STRASBURGH, *Jan.* 20, 1558.

UNLESS our friendship, my worthy sir, had been too
firmly established to be affected by any light matter, I should
probably have been charged with neglect for not having
hitherto replied to the most gratifying and courteous letter
you sent me by master ————[2]; by the admonition of
which, however, I am the more reminded of my duty, and
by the repeated perusal of it, from time to time, I console
myself in this winter of our calamity.   But I well know
your candour, and silence does not always imply forgetfulness.
For what the comic writer asserts with respect to asking
advice, that shame forbids it in one quarter, dignity in another, the same may also take place in respect to letter-writing.
For if I were not ashamed to write to you as often as I
desire to address you, to hear you, to enjoy your society, not
a day would be without its letter.   Besides, since (as you
state) more painful and severe trials are daily arising to us,
it not only distresses our minds to relate them, but even to
think about them.   Such an one is that which we have lately
heard concerning Calais[3], that the town is either taken by the

[2 The name is illegible in the original MS.]
[3 The duke of Guise encamped before Calais on Jan. 1, 1558, and
four days after, it was surrendered by lord Wentworth the governor,
after it had been in the possession of the English above 200 years.
See Stowe, 632.   Godwin Ann. 331.]

French, or in the greatest danger.   Should we have lost it, I do not choose to conjecture, though it is not difficult to foresee, what mischiefs will ensue, and which, if we would only have been quiet, might so easily have been avoided.   But alas! for our carelessness, or (shall I say?) our blindness; who, though we have treacherously forsaken the Lord, are yet without fear of the punishment due to our wickedness, and denounced against us by the voice of God.

I wish it were in my power to converse with you at large upon these and other matters, that in the abundance of my grief and tears your learned and godly discourse might afford me comfort.   Frequently indeed have I intended to come and see you, and I may probably pass a month with you during this next Lent.   But do not mention a word of this to any one; for I am not yet sufficiently able to form my plans, and if I should undertake this journey, it will be known to very few persons beforehand.   I pray our Lord Jesus to be pleased to shew compassion upon England, in many ways so afflicted, and to aid his troubled church according to the working of that mighty power, whereby he is able to subdue all things to himself.   May God long preserve you in safety to all godly persons!   Strasburgh, Jan. 20, 1558.

Yours wholly,

ANTONY COOK.

LETTER LXXI.

SIR JOHN CHEKE TO HENRY BULLINGER.
Dated at GREENWICH, *June* 7, 1553.

WILL you then, my Bullinger, strive to be received into my friendship, which I ought rather to have offered, and not wait till it was solicited?   But that which is to be commended in you, I think is blameable in me; for those persons who cultivate real friendships, resemble good husbandmen, and those who receive them, good land.   I therefore, being anticipated by yourself, and also more tardy in cultivating friendships, have the inferior position: for in proportion as the

husbandman is superior to the soil he cultivates, in that same
proportion am I excelled by yourself.   To bestow a benefit
is a virtuous act, to recompense it is a duty; and it is far
more blessed to confer a favour than to receive one, yea
indeed, than either to be grateful for it, to remember it, or to
requite it.   But as your learning, your zeal for true religion,
and your published works are universally known, and the
affection which I had long since conceived for you had nowise
shewn itself; you must still bear in mind, that even if my
regard had been unknown to you, I have notwithstanding been
for a long time your admirer.

The books which you have written to the king's
majesty, have been as acceptable to him as they deserved
to be.   A large portion of them I delivered to him myself,
and am able therefore to inform you how kindly and
courteously he received them, and how greatly he esteems
them; and I can offer you my congratulations upon the
subject.   But since the king's majesty, debilitated by long
illness, is scarcely yet restored to health, I cannot venture
to make you any promise of obtaining a letter from him to
yourself.   But should a longer life be allowed him, (and I
hope that he may very long enjoy it,) I prophesy indeed, that,
with the Lord's blessing, he will prove such a king, as neither
to yield to Josiah in the maintenance of true religion, nor to
Solomon in the management of the state, nor to David in the
encouragement of godliness.   And whatever may be effected
by nature or grace, or rather by God the source of both,
whose providence is not even contained within the limits of the
universe, it is probable that he will not only contribute very
greatly to the preservation of the church, but also that he
will distinguish learned men by every kind of encouragement.
He has long since given evidence of these things, and has
accomplished at this early period of his life more numerous
and important objects, than others have been able to do when
their age was more settled and matured.   He has repealed
the act of the six articles; he has removed images from the
churches; he has overthrown idolatry; he has abolished the
mass, and destroyed almost every kind of superstition.   He
has put forth by his authority an excellent form of common
prayer; he has published good and pious homilies to lessen
the ignorance of uneducated ministers.   He has invited the

most learned men to teach at the universities, and has done many other things of the same kind, every one of which would be considered as a great action in other men, but as nothing in him, by reason of the magnitude of what he has accomplished. Besides this, he has lately recommended to the schools by his authority the catechism of John[1], bishop of Winchester, and has published the articles of the synod at London, which if you will compare with those of Trent, you will understand how the spirit of the one exceeds that of the other. Why should I say more? I send you the book itself as a token of my regard, and believe me yours in Christ. Fare thee well. Greenwich, June 7, 1553. 7 Ed. VI.

Yours in the Lord,
JOHN CHEKE.

Salute, I pray you, masters Rodolph Gualter, and Conrad Gessner, to whom I am shortly about to write[2].

LETTER LXXII[3].

SIR JOHN CHEKE TO JOHN CALVIN.
Dated at Strasburgh, *Oct.* 20, 1555.

At one and the same instant I have been informed of the arrival of master de Sancto Andrea and of his departure. I am anxious, however, to address a few words to you. As far as I can perceive, I shall pass the winter in this place, enjoying in this my exile the society of my old friends, from whose kindly intercourse I shall not willingly withdraw myself. I rejoice that the Lord has delivered you not only from the

[1 This catechism set forth by bishop Ponet, with the articles appended, is printed in the volume of Liturgies, &c. of Edward VI. published by the Parker Society.]

[2 A note added to this letter in Bullinger's hand, states it to have been Sir John Cheke's last letter to him a little before the death of the king, and his subsequent imprisonment. He was committed to the Tower as a traitor, July the 28th, together with the duke of Suffolk. See above, p. 132. n. 2.]

[3 The original of this letter is preserved at Geneva.]

violent illness with which you were afflicted, but also from a calamity[4] which would have been utterly fatal both to your church and state. Though these events are now of long standing, yet they are new to me, who now hear of them for the first time. I therefore heartily thank God for having afforded these extraordinary and remarkable manifestations of his providence to others, that he may call forth their faith and veneration of himself. Nothing is more effectual in bringing over the minds of our enemies to entertain correct thoughts respecting God, than when godly persons are defended by his protection against the snares and machinations of the wicked.

And I pray that in this general confusion and overthrow the Lord may afford some aid and assistance to wretched England, wherein there are very many manifestations of his most heavy displeasure, and but very few of his goodness and mercy. For good men, and, what is yet more distressing, those who take the lead in learning and authority, by whose counsels and prudence many and important measures have been effected in the church, are not only brought in danger of their lives, but are actually under condemnation, and are daily expecting a death, which though desirable to themselves, will yet be lamentable and disastrous to the church. These ought by their example and constancy not only to give encouragement to those of the present age, but to afford an eminent example to future generations. Among whom, Cranmer, Ridley, and Latimer, the bishops of Canterbury, London, and formerly of Worcester, having firmly and boldly persevered in the christian doctrine they had embraced, and not allowing themselves to be led away from it by the terror of punishment, death, and the flames, are now condemned, and degraded, as they call it; and are either, I understand, already burned[5], or are shortly to experience the power of the flames and the cruelty of their tyrants. It is most painful and distressing to us to be deprived of those, whom, if God should be pleased to effect any alteration of affairs in our wretched and now greatly ruined England, we should not be able, or at least should hardly be able, to dispense with.

[4 This may refer to the conspiracy formed against the ministers of Geneva in 1555.]

[5 Ridley and Latimer were burned at the stake Oct. 16, 1555, and Cranmer on the 21st of March following.]

But why should I mention these things to you, who are well aware that this example of constancy and fortitude will tend to strengthen the universal church, scattered as it is far and wide, and that the living cannot be so useful by their teaching, as the dead can by their example? But I must confess, and, humanly speaking, I am confirmed in my opinion, that what Paul said respecting his own life, I think may be applied to them, if this divine chastisement were to have a respite and cessation in England, and to bring us away from ungodly worship to true Christianity[1]. But what must we expect from God in this slaughter of godly men? It may be that our people, like the Amorites, must fill up the measure of their impiety, that the more heavy severity of divine justice may be exercised upon them. But whatever be the Lord's purpose, whom I ought to obey and not prescribe to, I know and believe that he will effect it in such a way as that all things may tend to the good of his elect, whose support and protection he undertakes. So that I feel less anxious about whatever may happen, and think it my duty so to judge of the Lord's purpose, as to consider it replete with wisdom and goodness, and that it neither can, nor ought to be, either amended or found fault with, by our opinions or powers.

You see how, when I am writing to a friend, I write every thing that comes into my mind. But while you are wearied by my prolixity, pardon my freedom, who am less careful in writing to those who love me, as not fearing reproof where the offence is rather worthy of pardon than censure. May the Lord preserve you for yourself, and for me, and his church! Salute, I pray you, master Stafford, and his wife and family, and also his host of St Jerome's with whom he sojourns; and your friend the marquis, if he has yet returned to you, Normandy, masters Budæus, Parr, and your brother. Strasburgh, Oct. 20, 1555.

Your most devoted,

JOHN CHEKE.

[1 The meaning of this and some other passages in this letter is difficult to be made out, from the circumstance of some words being rendered illegible by the binding of the MS.—The allusion seems to be to Phil. i.]

LETTER LXXIII.

SIR JOHN CHEKE TO HENRY BULLINGER.

Dated at STRASBURGH, *March* 12, 1556.

OUR people frequently converse respecting the kindness not of yourself alone, but also that of men of all classes, and of your whole commonwealth, towards the English who came to reside among you by reason of the change of religion in their own country. I consider this not kindness merely, but hospitality, to be especially acceptable to God, and approved of men; and that it will never perish from the memory of any of our countrymen. As to me, should I ever have it in my power to render any service to yourself, or your godly friends, or your commonwealth, I pledge myself to be so ready to perform it, as that the anxiety of a grateful mind and the desire of returning an obligation may evidently appear. I ought also upon other grounds to shew both to yourself, and to masters Bibliander and Bernardine, as much respect as is due to learned, pious, and friendly persons, who have deserved well of the church of Christ. This your hospitality, therefore, is not only praise-worthy in itself, but is yet more so by comparison with the ill-treatment of others. For I suppose you are not ignorant, that those parties who maintain the body of Christ to be every where[2] can nowise endure the members of Christ to be any where, and have harassed them with all kinds of cruelty and atrocity, in order that with the absurdity of the opinions they have imbibed they may also join a savageness of disposition, and a brutal ferocity towards the meek children of God. But if the truth of opinions is to be judged of by their fruits, and there is as wide a difference between men's sentiments as there is in the christian life, truly they ought to have been long since convinced, and to have given up so stubborn an opinion. But of the stupidity of these parties at another time. May God enlighten their blinded mind with the light of his Spirit, and bring them out from this thick darkness of error to a better perception of the truth, and a more harmonious consent of feelings.

[2 This refers to the Ubiquitarian controversy. See Zurich Letters, first series, p. 92, n. 1, and second series, p. 245, n. 6.]

I hear that Ignatius has been sent to you to be translated and printed, a measure which I suppose has been adopted for certain reasons. I had seen the book at Augsburgh, and had copied out some passages where the name of the mass was mentioned, and where he speaks of the wives of the apostles[1]. I request you, my Bullinger, and implore you again and again, to take care that the Greek be printed together with the translation. For it is of very great importance to scholars to read the author himself in his own language, and especially where grave and controverted matters are to be considered. I never read a translation without requiring the author himself as an interpreter of it. And I wish this had been done, not only in this author, but in all others, and in Procopius. It would have removed suspicion in regard to many passages, which appear to have been introduced by the translator, where the meaning of certain Hebrew and Latin words is discussed by a Greek unacquainted with those languages. But now translations are so obtruded upon us, to the depreciation of the authors themselves, that there must of necessity arise that inconvenience which the papists object to us in the eucharist, namely, that we use the antitypes instead of the prototypes. Wherefore, if you will take care that good authors, when put in print, shall either be printed with the translations, as master Gesner has properly done in Stobæus and others; or even separately, if that should be thought more expedient, lest the translations only should be cried up, and the authors themselves perish; you will confer many and important benefits both on the present and succeeding generation.

You see with what familiarity I address you: forgive me, I was only intending to salute you, and to thank you for your kindness towards our people; but when Ignatius and the other authors of whom we are deprived came into my mind, I could not but commend to you the cause of those authors, and entreat you, as it were, in their name not to suffer them to speak only through interpreters, when they might readily

[1 The following passages, from the *interpolated* Epistles of Ignatius, seem to be referred to: Οὐκ ἐξόν ἐστι χωρὶς τοῦ ἐπισκόπου οὔτε βαπτίζειν οὔτε προσφέρειν οὔτε θυσίαν προσκομίζειν οὔτε δοχὴν ἐπιτελεῖν, where the last words in the Latin translation are, *neque missas celebrare*. Ad Smyrn. p. 197. Ed. Voss. Lond. 1680. ὡς Πέτρου καὶ Παύλου καὶ τῶν ἄλλων ἀποστόλων, τῶν γάμοις προσομιλησάντων. Ad Philadelph. p. 178.]

be seen and heard by many in their own language, and be rescued from the danger of destruction which usually attends the Greek writers.   Should there be any thing in which I can be of use to you, pray command me : and I beg you to say the same from me to masters Bibliander and Bernardine. I wish an opportunity were afforded me of performing these my promises.   Salute, I pray you, the good old man, master Pellican, masters Rodolph Gualter, Conrad Gesner, and especially your wife.   May the Lord preserve you!   Strasburgh. March 12, 1556.

Your friend and brother in Christ,

JOHN CHEKE[2].

LETTER LXXIV[3].

SIR RICHARD MORISON TO JOHN CALVIN.

Dated at STRASBURGH, *April* 17, 1555.

IF Cheke has sinned against your kindness, so I cannot but confess, most learned Calvin, that I have now for many months acted in the same manner.   He can aggravate my fault, but can nowise acquit me, nor I him, from the charge of neglect.   Nay, there is rather reason to fear that you should withdraw the hospitality you have so kindly afforded to the English.   Is it for this that you have given up to us your house, and become a mere tenant in your own home, that in so many months from that time you should receive from me not a single atom of gratitude ?   I am writing to the marquis ; and if there is nothing in that quarter to clear me in your eyes, I know with whom I have to do, and had rather acknowledge my fault, than offer you a new injury while I in vain attempt to palliate the old one.   And yet you must know that I have written to him nothing but what is true, namely, that I and mine are at this very time exposed to the greatest danger, and that there are not wanting those who wish me either to

[2 A note in the Simler collection states this to have been sir John Cheke's last letter before his capture, respecting which see above, p. 132, n. 2.]

[3 The original of this letter is preserved at Geneva.]

return home, or, like an outcast, to pass the life of an exile in a foreign country. And as I am not wanting in friends, who make other promises, so I am afraid that my bitter enemies will do more to injure me, than my lukewarm friends will do towards the restoration of my affairs. As to what is going on at home, since every one knows it, I suppose that you cannot be ignorant. This our friend Luke will easily tell you all that I know. I must tell you in the last place, that I had rather requite your deeds by corresponding deeds on my part, than seem to wish to recompense your exceeding kindness by a verbal acknowledgement. Luke will tell you the rest. Farewell, most courteous Calvin, and forgive me, I know not whether to say my silence, or my tedious letter. Strasburgh, April 17, 1555.

Yours heartily,

RICHARD MORISON.

LETTER LXXV.

SIR RICHARD MORISON TO HENRY BULLINGER.
Dated at STRASBURGH, *Aug.* 23, 1555.

I HAD been informed, most learned Bullinger, before the arrival of your letter, that it had been decreed, both by the authority of the chief magistrate, and the order of the senate, that no foreigners newly come should be admitted within your city: not indeed that foreigners are not most kindly received by you, and when received, treated with the greatest hospitality. But the necessity of this enactment has been solely occasioned by the influx among you at this time of Italians from Lugarno being so great, as hardly to leave room in your city for any new guest. When these things were related to me, as my friend Bernardine had not then written an answer to our friends here, the winter too threatening a true German frost, I considered it to be my next best plan, not to decline the house voluntarily offered here, and which by reason of the garden adjoining is very convenient. For it seemed to be quite time to procure wood, and hay, and other things necessary either for the support of a family, or for guarding against the cold : for among the people of Strasburgh, when the cold regulates the price of wood, scarcely an ounce is offered for sale; and when it is sold, you would scarcely be able to procure it at the most exorbitant price.   I would ask you therefore, again and again, that if I have been at all to blame in this matter, you would pardon me for having caused you to wait upon the most illustrious chief magistrate to no purpose; unless I knew for certain that you would easily pardon me both this and far greater faults: although what is not done at this time can easily be arranged at the beginning of spring, should not our affairs induce us to return to England.   Do you, meanwhile, only let the chief magistrate understand, as regards myself, that I have not changed my purpose through any want of decision, but that I was of great necessity compelled to put it off to another time.   This, indeed, is some part of the inconvenience, which men who are compelled to undergo a voluntary exile are wont to suffer, that when they desire above all things to arrange their affairs with some degree of certainty, they are seldom or never rightly able to effect this.   Unforeseen events are so apt to disarrange all our purposes and designs with the greatest ease.

This anti-Paul[1], Paul of the apostasy, the servant of the devil, this antichrist newly created at Rome, thinks it but a very small plunder that is offered to him, that he is again permitted in England to tyrannise over our consciences, unless the revenues be restored to the monasteries, that is, the pigsties; the patrimony, as he calls it, of the souls which are now serving in the filth of purgatory.   Our ambassadors, who went to Rome for the purpose of bringing back the wolf upon the sheep of Christ, are now with the emperor, and bring us these demands of the chief pontiff : God grant that he may urge them in every possible way!   Perhaps those who have suffered the gospel of Christ, that is, the sceptre by which Christ both governs his kingdom and extends its borders, to be taken from them by threats, will not allow

[1 Cardinal Caraffa was elected pope, May 23, 1555, and took the name of Paul IV. He published his bull Rescissio Alienationum, in which he annulled without exception all alienations of the old ecclesiastical possessions.   See Ranke's Hist. of the Popes.]

their revenues, the life and blood of mankind, to be taken away, even by force.   At all events, that will come to pass which Almighty God knows to be best for his people.   If Socrates was accustomed to make no definite request from the gods, shall it be a great thing for us to depend altogether upon the good pleasure of God our Father?   Since he is our Father, he cannot for ever be angry with his children.   Nay rather, when he has an assurance of our improvement, he will then certainly think of punishing both his enemies, and ours for his sake.   Saul sought to destroy David, but did no more than attempt so great a crime.   Among us, how many living members of Christ are thrown into the flames!   Saul, who was his own murderer, saw his three sons slain in one day; and shall Winchester always live?   Shall he live to increase, and not to lay aside his boldness?   God liveth, and is no less a hater of wickedness now than he has ever been heretofore.   But I must conclude.   Farewell, excellent Bullinger, and love me.   Strasburgh, Aug. 23, 1555.

Yours as you so well deserve,

RICHARD MORISON.

LETTER LXXVI[1].

THOMAS LEVER TO ROGER ASCHAM.

Without place or date.

YOUR friends, masters Nevinson, Alen, Butts[2], the king's physician, and Redman[3], have departed this life since I last wrote to you.   Dr Bill[4], the master of our college, has by his

[1 The original of this letter is preserved at Geneva.   The writer's name is not mentioned; but it appears, from internal evidence, to have been written by Lever in 1552.]

[2 See above, p. 37, note 6.]

[3 Dr John Redman was originally of St John's college, but was appointed master of Trinity in 1546.   An account of his opinions, confirmatory of the statement made in this letter, is given in Strype, Cheke, 67; Mem. II. i. 527, &c.   He died in November, 1551.]

[4 A grant of the mastership of Trinity college to Wm. Bill, D.D., for life, void by the death of John Redman, was dated in November, 1551.]

majesty's favour succeeded Redman in Trinity college, and
I have succeeded Bill in St John's college[5]. Dr Redman
died of consumption after a long illness, in constant expectation of death, and in continual discourse respecting God and
true religion, as one who ardently desired to be delivered
from the prison of this body, and to be with Christ.

I will communicate to you, my Ascham, a part of the
communication[6] which John Yong (who, as you heard at
Cambridge last year, was the most violent opponent of Bucer[7]
in the public schools) received in person from the mouth of Dr
Redman immediately before his death. First, Redman was
requested, as Yong himself informed me, by himself and the
other learned men standing by, to deliver his opinion upon
certain points of religion ; whereupon he forthwith undertook to answer as in the presence of God his judge, according
to his real sentiments, upon any subject that they might
think proper to propose. Being asked what he thought of
the see of Rome, he answered, that it was a sink of wickedness, whence was derived the stream of filthiness which had
burst forth like a torrent upon the church of God. Being
asked his opinion respecting purgatory, he said that there was
not any such purgatory as the one imagined by the schoolmen ; but that when Christ shall come, surrounded by fire,
all who meet him will be purified, as I believe, said he, myself, and as many of the ancient doctors are of opinion.
Being questioned respecting the mass, he said, that those who
regard the mass as a sacrifice for the dead, are opposed to
Christ himself, and to the benefit of his death. As to the pro-
position concerning justification by faith only, he declared it to
be a delightful doctrine, and certainly full of comfort, provided
it were understood of a true and living faith; and that no
works were deserving of eternal life, not even works of grace
in the person justified. When he was asked his opinion respecting transubstantiation, he replied that he had for the last

[5 Thomas Lever was appointed master of St John's, by royal
mandate, in November, 1551, and ejected in 1553.]

[6 For a full account of the communication between Dr Redman,
on his death-bed, Yong, and others, together with a letter from
Yong to sir John Cheke on the same subject, see Foxe, Acts and
Mon. VI. 267—274.]

[7 For an account of the controversy between Yong and Bucer,
see Zurich Letters, second series, p. 18, and Strype, Mem. II. i. 327.]

twelve years directed all his studies and attention to that subject, and had remarked that the writings of Tertullian, Irenæus, and Origen were openly opposed to that doctrine, and that it was neither maintained nor delivered in other ancient writers : and when he had long and vainly expected to find some certain and undoubted statement upon that subject in the writings of the schoolmen, he discovered in them nothing whatever sound and solid, but only deceit and gross error.   With respect to the presence, he said (as Yong related the conversation), that Christ was really and corporally present in the sacrament : but when he was asked whether that was the body of Christ, which we see the priest lift up, he affirmed, that the body of Christ was now incapable of being lifted up or let down by any human hands; and it is, he added, a very corrupt custom to carry about the sacrament to be adored.   He affirmed also that the wicked do not receive the body of Christ, but the sacrament of it.   He earnestly exhorted Yong diligently to read the bible itself, and to beware of the doctrine of men.   He added, moreover, that it was an excellent book[1] which the most reverend archbishop of Canterbury had lately written upon the eucharist, and he recommended Yong to read it with much attention. Yong told me himself, "As heretofore," saith he, "I myself would have encountered death with willingness and alacrity, in defence of transubstantiation, and that too more readily than in defence of the doctrine of the incarnation of Christ himself; so it shall be my endeavour for the future that all my studies and opinions may rest upon a more solid foundation than that common agreement of individuals, which they have erroneously denominated the church."

I hope, my Ascham, that not Yong only, but many persons will be led away from the doctrine of men to the true religion of Christ, by means of this divine discourse of Redman just before his death.

[1 The original edition of Cranmer's Defence of the true and catholic doctrine of the Sacrament was published in 1550; his answer to Gardiner, in 1551.]

LETTER LXXVII.

THOMAS LEVER TO HENRY BULLINGER.

Dated at GENEVA, *April* 11, [1554].

MUCH health in Christ Jesus.   On the first night of our journey we arrived at Lentzburg, when father Gervase, having read your letter to him, seemed to me to pour out upon us, as though we were his dearest friends, the admirable benevolence of a pious mind.   For he brought us in the evening from the public inn, and took us to the delightful quiet of his own house; and early the next morning he accompanied us for two hours on our way, and so exactly pointed out to us the description of the road, and the names of godly persons (in our route), that profiting by their advice, and by the marks previously pointed out to us, we arrived at Berne without any difficulty.   We were there informed that Musculus, Haller, and other learned men were exceedingly well disposed, and, in consequence of your letter to Haller, were ready to afford us any assistance: for many of them being assembled in the same house invited us to a good supper.   Haller too, in addition to supplying us liberally with a gratuitous lodging for three days, took us every day to whatever we wished to see or hear.   At Lausanne also Beza[2] and Viret proved both by word and deed, that we were recommended and made welcome in consequence of your letter to them.   At last, however, on the seventh of April, we reached Geneva, where, in the absence of Calvin, to whom I stated that you had given me a letter, we were immediately received as guests by a pious and worthy man, who is expecting Calvin to return within these few days.   I perceive, therefore, and acknowledge, that your fatherly care for me not only provided for myself and my companion a most delightful lodging in your own house, but has also procured for us in other places and with other persons favour and kindness far beyond our expectation.   And for this cause, which next to God I attribute to yourself, I have long since begun to consider myself not so much a traveller exiled

[2 Beza was appointed professor of Greek at Lausanne in 1549, and continued in that office ten years.]

from my country, as a fellow-citizen of the saints now sojourning in the household of God.

I now therefore feel no anxiety respecting myself, but an
almost incurable solicitude for those whom I suspect to be
overwhelmed by most grievous perils at home. For a certain
Englishman, passing through Berne, wrote to his countrymen
at Geneva, that the Bernese government had been informed
by a letter sent to them from the court of the king of France,
that the queen of England had been slain by a mob, exasperated by her perfidious cruelty. Another person, however,
who left London on the 13th of March, has to-day informed
me that no priests were executed in the rebellion raised by
Wyatt, and that very few were put to death after his apprehension. He said that only the duke of Suffolk[1] and his
daughter lady Jane, with her husband, were beheaded, and
that they all continued stedfast in the profession of the true
religion. He affirmed too, that he had heard it for a certain
fact, that Cranmer[2], archbishop of Canterbury, Ridley, bishop
of London, Latimer, a very celebrated preacher, and [sir
James] Hales[3], a pious lawyer, had all been removed together
from London to Oxford, to be burnt at the stake, after
having been condemned for heresy by the doctors of that
university. From all these circumstances I can only conclude,
that either, if the queen is alive, there is a most grievous
persecution of the church; or if a turbulent mob have the
upper hand, the kingly government in England will be irre-
coverably lost. But the hardness of my heart, which ever
prevents my melting into tears, either of commiseration for
these calamities, or of repentance for my own misdoings, is
often wont to disturb my mind, to blunt my temper, and to
confuse my memory. Wherefore I pray you, my father, in the
bowels of Jesus Christ, to invoke with me my heavenly Father
in my behalf, that regarding our miseries, the merits of Christ,
and his own mercies, he may pardon me my neglect and
wickedness, take away my hardness of heart, and bestow upon
me the Spirit of repentance and sanctification. Give, I pray

[1 The duke of Suffolk was executed on the 23rd of February.]
[2 Cranmer, Ridley, and Latimer, were sent down to Oxford about
the 10th of April.]
[3 A full account of Judge Hales is given in Foxe, Acts and Mon.
VI. 710.]

you, from myself and Hugo my companion, our salutations and very many thanks to your wife and all your family. And I again request you to salute in my name the venerable old men, Pellican and Bibliander, and the other learned and pious men, Gualter, Gesner, Lewis [Lavater], Zuingler and Zuinglius. May Christ long preserve you for the benefit of his church! Farewell. Geneva, April 11.

Your son,

THOMAS LEVER.

LETTER LXXVIII.

THOMAS LEVER TO HENRY BULLINGER.
Dated at GENEVA, *April* 23, [1554].

MUCH health in Christ. As I told you before, so I now also acknowledge myself very much indebted to your fatherly foresight, through which, by means of your letter, I received from many persons to whom I was unknown the greatest kindness on my travels. No fresh tidings have reached me from England, except the contradiction of those rumours by which it was stated here for some days that the queen had been murdered. For she is still alive, persevering and increasing in wickedness.

I hear that some Englishmen have come to you at Zurich, together with that very godly man, Richard Chambers[4]: I am sorry that they have reached you sooner than my letter could reach them. For Richard Chambers is the person who has actively devoted himself and all his property to provide for the safety of the ministers during this persecution; and, though my journey ought to have diminished his labours, yet the vain expectation of a letter from me has increased both his toil and anxiety. But Christ, through whom all things work

---

[4 Richard Chambers is represented by Strype as a great friend of learning and favourer of the oppressed. He allowed Jewel 6*l.* a-year for the purchase of books in divinity. He was one of the exiles at Frankfort, and was agent with Grindal to the Strasburgh exiles to treat about the English service-book. Strype, Mem. III. i. 225. Grindal, 14.]

together for good to them that love God, will turn this also to the honour of God, and the comfort of those who seek the glory of Christ with all their heart. I hope therefore that the opportunity now afforded you by God of manifesting your kindness towards true Christians, faithful ministers, and wretched exiles, will not prove unacceptable, and that the contemplation of your church worshipping God with such holiness and purity will not be without benefit to them. Take care, I pray you, that the letter addressed to the above-named Richard Chambers, Englishman, may speedily be delivered to him. Forget me not, I entreat you, in your prayers to God. Master Calvin, like many others, was more favourably disposed towards me for your sake; whence you may understand that you are now much indebted to many for my sake. I will always do what alone is in my power, namely, entreat God long to preserve you for the benefit of his church. Farewell. Geneva, April 23.

Your most devoted son in Christ,

THOMAS LEVER.

LETTER LXXIX.

THOMAS LEVER TO HENRY BULLINGER.

Dated at GENEVA, *June* 28, [1554].

MUCH health in Christ Jesus. The fatherly benevolence and kindness which you have manifested towards me since my arrival in these parts, as an exile from my native land for the sake of religion, has mitigated my distress at leaving my country, and enabled me with cheerfulness to bear the cross of Christ. It has also been of great service to others of my countrymen; and I cannot doubt of its continuance towards us, because I seem to myself to perceive, not our merits, but your kindness, in your continual favours conferred upon us. When indeed I received a little book and letter from you not long since, in both which I may daily hear, by the perusal of them, the words and voice of my most esteemed father in Christ; I considered it as an admonition and encouragement to me, to proceed and advance with the diligence of a son in the path of your paternal piety and instruction. And in truth that book seems, not only to myself, but to very many other pious and learned persons, to be worthy of being translated into many languages. Peter Tonvillanus, the bearer of this letter, has translated it into French, and left it here to be printed, as he was called from this place to advance the cause of the gospel in Poland. And since in my familiar intercourse with him I have found him to be a learned, godly, and honourable man, I have willingly entrusted him with this letter to you, by which he hopes likewise to become better acquainted with you, and on a more intimate footing. Your kindness towards all persons of this character will not allow him to be disappointed of his hope. Should my friend Spenser not return, master John ab Ulmis will, I hope, take care that your annotations on the lesser prophets, or any other that you may have entrusted him with for me, may be copied out. For as I desire nothing more fervently than such writings of yours, I earnestly requested master John ab Ulmis, by letter, to lend me his assistance in this matter; with which request I hope he will faithfully comply.

We have had of late no news from England, except that persecution still continues, or rather increases. May God have pity upon us, and sending power from above may he put forth such labourers into his harvest, who may thrust out the foxes from his vineyard, England!

Salute, I pray you, in my name, your wife and the rest of your family, to all of whom I always wish the choicest blessings in Christ. May the Lord long preserve you to us and to the church of Christ! Farewell. Geneva, June 28.

Your most devoted son in Christ,

THOMAS LEVER.

LETTER LXXX.

THOMAS LEVER TO HENRY BULLINGER.
Dated at GENEVA, *Jan.* 17, [1555].

MUCH health in Christ Jesus. For that true fatherly affection and beneficence, which you have manifested both towards the other Englishmen who are in exile for the cause of religion, and also to myself, as though I were your own son, I cannot sufficiently return due and adequate thanks; but as far as is in our power, we will earnestly and prayerfully entreat God for yourself, for the church committed to your charge, for your family, and for all your friends. May God grant that we may sometime prove by our actions, that we have learned from you to treat with affection, and courtesy, and benevolence, those who are wandering about for the cause of Christ!

Since you have conducted yourself as a father to me, receive, I pray you, from me as from your son an account of my manner of living and of my studies. I am residing here free and unfettered by any public employment. I attend all the sermons and lectures of Calvin, and some of those of other persons, and have hitherto employed the remainder of my time in the publication of a little book[1] in our vernacular English; it is now in the press, and, God willing, will shortly be sent to England. After I shall have sent forth this book, I have determined to bestow as much time and attention as I can upon the study of the prophets. I should certainly proceed in that study with greater alacrity and advantage, if I were able sometimes by any means to consult you. Wherefore, my reverend father, who have never refused me any thing hitherto, I pray you now to impart to my friend, master Spenser, some of your writings which may conduce to the understanding of the prophets, and which are not yet printed; so that he may get them copied out for me, in the same manner as he is now procuring me what you are writing upon the Revelation of St John.

I have not at this time any thing new or important to write to you about: whatever reports there may be, you may, if you choose, hear more easily from the relation of this messenger, than from my letter. For he is a pious and worthy man, by name Richard Harvel; and having left England, his country, for the sake of religion and learning, he is anxious

[1 Entitled, " The right way from danger of sin and vengeance in this wicked world unto godly wealth and salvation in Christ." Written at Geneva, and published in the time of queen Mary; afterwards reprinted in London 1571, 1575. Tanner, Bibl. p. 479; Herbert's Ames, II. 976.]

to see and converse with you.   Such has been my intimacy with him here at Geneva, as to make me wish that this recommendation of mine may be of use to him.

Salute, I pray you, your very dear wife, as my own mother, and that worthy matron who ministered to us English, like the mother of a family, when we were all together under the same roof.   May God long preserve you to us for the benefit of the church of Christ!   Farewell.   Geneva, Jan. 17.

Your attached in Christ,

THOMAS LEVER.

LETTER LXXXI.

THOMAS LEVER TO HENRY BULLINGER.
Dated at FRANKFORT, *Feb.* 12, [1555].

EVERLASTING health in Christ Jesus! As I always found in you, when I was at Zurich, godly counsel, learning, and example, to my exceeding comfort and advantage, so now, most revered father in Christ, I hope that I shall obtain the benefit of your pious prayers for the edification of the church of Christ of the English at Frankfort.   And as many others of my countrymen regard you as their patron, so do I acknowledge you to have been a father to myself, as I hope and desire that you will continue to be.   And since I perceive that I am destitute of all power and opportunity of returning my obligations, I write this, that you may understand me to be neither unmindful nor ungrateful.

There is no certain intelligence from England; but I have heard from uncertain rumours, that the queen has never been pregnant, and that the council, which they call the parliament, was suddenly dissolved; and this, because the king not only rejected, but treated with contempt, three petitions preferred by the magistrates; one of which was, that he should restore the true religion, the second, that he should make peace with France, and the third, that he should not admit into his councils any one born out of England.   I understand that more persons are seeking comfort from empty reports than from true repentance. Do not think it a trouble to salute my mother your wife in my name, together with the rest of your family, to all of whom I shall ever wish every blessing. May the Lord Jesus long preserve you for the welfare of his church! Farewell. Frankfort, Feb. 12.

Your most devoted son in Christ,

THOMAS LEVER.

LETTER LXXXII.

THOMAS LEVER TO HENRY BULLINGER.
Dated at STRASBURGH, *Jan.* 4, [1556].

MUCH health in Christ Jesus! While I was so engaged at Geneva, both in my private studies, and in hearing the discourses of the preachers in the public congregation, as that nothing at that time seemed to be more desirable both for my own individual improvement and the edifying of the church; some of my fellow-countrymen, who were banished from England on account of religion, and had settled at Wesel, sent a letter to me, wherein it was stated that by the majority of their votes, and the common and united consent of them all, in a free election, I had been chosen as their pastor. They therefore earnestly entreated me by letter, and implored me in Christ, that I would neither decline the charge which God (in answer to their prayers, and overruling their votes) had imposed upon me, nor delay my journey to them, who were anxiously expecting me. For since their late pastor had already left them of his own accord, and the magistrates had forbidden them the use of the sacraments, they hoped to be enabled by my arrival both to have a minister, and re-obtain the permission of the magistrates for the free use of the sacraments, or at least that they should receive some useful and necessary counsel. Having therefore perused their letter to this effect, and with prayer to God, after consulting master Calvin and my pious and learned brother-ministers of the church of England, I am now on my road from Geneva to Wesel; entertaining such a view both of their state and condition, and of my own slender abilities, as that I am persuaded that I ought neither to undertake the office of their minister, nor yet to refuse any diligence or labour of instructing them.   For the ministerial office neither seems to myself, nor to others whom I have consulted, to be capable of being exercised either with or among those to whom the ministry of the sacraments is forbidden: and indeed I do not as yet find in myself those qualities which the word of God declares should exist in a minister.   Whatever gifts of God I may discover in myself, I shall never refuse, by God's help, to impart all of them freely and diligently to my brethren in Christ at their request.   In accordance therefore with your fatherly goodwill towards me (which I have so often experienced from our first acquaintance unto this present moment) I entreat you, my reverend father, in the bowels of Christ, to continue always mindful of me in your prayers to God; and sometimes too by your letters to me to advise and instruct me, as your son, how I may better learn to serve Christ and his church with humility, alacrity, and fidelity.   And as I have no means of repaying you, I will diligently endeavour in my daily prayers to obtain for you and yours every blessing from God.

I pray you likewise to salute in my name masters Peter Martyr, Bernardine Ochinus, Gualter, and the other ministers of your church; to all of whom, for your kindness to myself and to my countrymen, I acknowledge myself your debtor to the utmost extent of my power.   Salute too, I pray you, from me in the Lord your wife and all your family, and lastly, that worthy matron who attended upon us English, or rather, supported us in the same house.   May God long preserve you to the edifying of the church of Christ, and the overthrow of the kingdom of antichrist!   Farewell.   Strasburgh, on my journey, Jan. 4.

Yours faithfully in Christ,

THOMAS LEVER.

LETTER LXXXIII.

THOMAS LEVER TO HENRY BULLINGER.

Dated at BERNE, *May* 12, [1556].

MUCH health in Christ Jesus, with my warmest thanks for your constant fatherly kindness and good-will towards me. And though you have often bestowed many favours upon me, yet nothing could have ever happened to me more acceptably, or agreeably, than that by my reliance on your advice, and by making use of your letter, I have at length met with an asylum where my very dear countrymen and brethren in Christ, who are exiled from their country for their avowed and faithful profession of Christ, may by reason of the same profession be kindly and willingly received. For master Haller, upon the receipt of your letter, so advocated our cause, first, with many of the senators of Berne collectively and individually, and at last in a full assembly in the senate itself, that there is now permitted us the liberty of sojourning in any part of the Bernese territory. And master Haller requires or rather recommends us, that after we have examined a number of localities, we should return to Berne to make known to them what place within their territory will best suit us, that we may receive from the magistrates of Berne themselves especial letters of commendation to the mayor and inhabitants of that place. With regard too to the free use of the word of God, and of the sacraments, and also with respect to the manufacture of English cloth, when the subject was mentioned, the Bernese seemed candidly to acknowledge, that this was the very art which they wished us to exercise among them, and that there would be no difficulty in our obtaining permission from them. I am expecting therefore to-day a general letter from the magistrates of that state to all who are under their authority; on the receipt of which I have resolved to set out to-morrow on a journey to the English at Basle, that I may consult together with them upon the hastening all the rest who are still loitering on their road towards Basle, and upon surveying the district around Berne, with the view of discovering and providing the most suitable place of residence. I pray you therefore and beseech you in Christ, that, as you have hitherto done, so you will always continue (whenever God may give you an opportunity) to pour out abundantly upon me your paternal kindness. I should wish indeed to have placed myself with my friends under your wings, had it been possible, in the territory of Zurich. But not what I will, but what our heavenly Father willeth, will be done : to him be all honour and glory, and to us mercy and salvation in Christ Jesus! Do not, I pray you, be displeased at my asking you to salute your wife as my own mother, and all the rest of your family as most dear to me in Christ in domestic love. I do not so much ask, as I wish and hope, that you will always be ready to give me advice upon such matters as you think may tend to the glory of God, and to the comfort and edification of me and mine in Christ Jesus. Farewell. Berne, May 12.

Let us pray for each other.

Your son faithfully in Christ Jesus,

THOMAS LEVER.

LETTER LXXXIV.

THOMAS LEVER TO RODOLPH GUALTER.

Dated at BASLE, *May 27*, 1556.

JESUS Christ God with us! Much health in Christ Jesus. Your great kindness, and the very prudent advice you gave me in your house at Zurich, was an exceeding comfort to me ; and your letter to master Steiger for the magistrates and senate of Berne has been of great service to our cause. That you may not be wanting in an opportunity of persevering in your godly commiseration and diligent attention to us, behold! we are daily coming into greater difficulties and tribulations. For we English, after our banishment from England, our removal from Wesel[1], and wanderings over

[1 At Wesel the English were under some trouble; and the senate were about to command them to depart thence, because of their different sentiments from the Augustan confession in some points. Strype, Cranmer, 507.]

almost all Germany, have suffered a repulse in Basle[1], and
are at length compelled to have recourse to the hospitality
of the people of Berne.   For the councillors of king Ferdinand, who are at Emsen, will not allow any Englishmen,
who are exiles for the sake of religion, liberty of passage
through that territory of Ferdinand which lies between Strasburgh and Basle.   Whence you may easily perceive the
length, fatigue, expense, difficulty and danger of our journey,
and how greatly we are in need of protection, advice, liberality and assistance.   Remember us, therefore, I entreat
you, in your prayers to God, and in your correspondence
and conversation with such individuals as you may know to
be both able and willing to aid us in the cause of Christ.
Farewell.   Salute, I pray you, master Parkhurst and his
wife. The bearer is in haste. Again farewell. Basle, May 27.

Yours faithfully in Christ,

THOMAS LEVER.

[1 The following account of this repulse is given by John Young,
in a letter to Bullinger, dated May 17, 1557. "Measures had been
taken by the brethren for receiving the English exiles, before I had
returned from Constance ; but they suffered a repulse from our magistrates, to the great sorrow and lamentation of the brethren, and of all
godly persons.   On my return, by the advice of the brethren, I again
endeavoured to obtain from the senate that a residence might at least
be afforded to those who were already on their journey ; for that it
would be a most cruel procedure, and an offence to all christian
people, to cast them out.   But this appeal also was made in vain ; for
they would not allow them any greater indulgence than what is
granted to the veriest mob that flock into the town, namely, the
liberty of using the public houses.   Alas! my brother, how blind and
impious must those persons be, who so rashly, so irreligiously, to say
no more, repel from themselves and their families, to the great scandal
of the churches of God, so great a blessing offered them from the
Lord !   Which indeed as it has now returned to the people of Berne,
we congratulate both them and the exiles, as much as we justly deplore
our own misfortunes.   Pray God for us ; for unless he support us in
our distresses, I perceive that entire destruction will ensue."]

LETTER LXXXV.

THOMAS LEVER TO HENRY BULLINGER.

Dated at ARAU, *Sept.* 18, [1556].

JESUS Christ God with us! Much health in Christ Jesus. I have lately received two letters from your reverence, and your truly useful and delightful book for the use of the English church in this place. We plainly perceive therein your true fatherly affection towards us, and must candidly acknowledge, that while we promise you as much as will ever be in our power, we are utterly unable adequately to return our thanks. And as it is a father's nature to rejoice when he beholds his children profiting by his instruction and kindness, and eagerly and successfully making progress towards piety and happiness; so shall it be our earnest endeavour both to derive this advantage from your writings, and to afford you the happiness of observing our improvement.

And now to discourse with you somewhat familiarly respecting myself, I would have you assured that your advice with respect to not contending about things indifferent was exceedingly gratifying to me. For I had previously come to the same determination myself, and, being now supported by your authority, shall persevere with much greater firmness and alacrity in taking care to avoid offences and useless controversies; so that every thing may be more easily and effectually accommodated to the peace, and concord, and edification of the church. For when I sent my friend master Richard Burcher to Berne, to consult master John Haller with respect to the use of ceremonies here in our church, I pointed out the reasons which induced me to wish that leavened bread might be used in the administration of the Lord's supper; but in the mean time I was unwilling either to prefer any petition to the government, or to act in all respects as I was empowered to do, but only in reference to such things as seemed in his judgment both lawful and expedient. And indeed he wrote back the very same advice that I received from you in your letter; so that I shall readily follow your suggestion not on this subject only, but also upon any thing else which with your wonted piety and discretion you may recommend or advise to be done or to be abstained from : and I pray you to write me word at the very first moment you have to spare, what you think I ought to do.　If a man wishes to marry the sister of his deceased wife, or if he has already done so, ought he to retain her or send her away? I request also that you will peruse this little book upon the church discipline of the English at Geneva, and let me know your candid opinion of it.　You see how boldly, relying upon your clemency and kindness, I address your reverence, whom I know to be always engaged in numerous and important affairs.　You must therefore defer compliance with my request until a suitable opportunity of leisure shall occur.　All the English who are here most cordially salute your reverence in Christ, and we all of us beg to offer our best acknowledgments for your letter and the book.

Salute, I pray you, in my name, the ministers of your church and all your family, for all of whom I shall always remember to pray to God, and for you especially, that you may enjoy long life, and ability to adorn the church of Christ, to the confusion of antichrist, and to our comfort.　Farewell. Arau, Sept. 18.

Your most devoted in Christ,

THOMAS LEVER.

LETTER LXXXVI.

THOMAS LEVER TO RODOLPH GUALTER.

Dated at ARAU, *Aug.* 11, 1557.

JESUS Christ God with us! Much health in Christ Jesus.　After a long and wearisome tossing about[1] I at

[1] On the English congregation leaving Wesel, they passed by Frankfort, and "perceiving the contention to be among them so boiling hot, that it ran over on both sides, and yet no fire quenched, many had small pleasure to tarry there, but went to Basle and other places; while M. Lever made suit to the lords of Berne for a church within their dominions, whose letters he obtained with great favour to

length seem to myself to have arrived with some of my friends at Arau, as at a harbour of refuge. For we have explored the whole Bernese territory, both in Germany and Savoy, and found in each country one place especially, namely, Arau in Germany, or rather in Switzerland, and Vevay in Savoy, that was both able and willing to afford a comfortable home to the English exiles for the sake of religion. And in these two towns we found the inhabitants favourable to us beyond all expectation. But the people of Arau[2], by reason of their confined situation, are unable at present to supply and accommodate us with more than seven houses. And the people of Vevay, though in a short time they will be able and willing to receive the whole twenty-five families, are yet a great way off, and difficult of access. Wherefore we have judged it far better and more practicable, that some few persons here in this neighbourhood, commencing with a small number, should gradually advance from small beginnings, and daily increase by fresh additions, than that all of them should

all their subjects for the friendly entertainment of the British nation. These letters obtained, M. Lever, M. Boyes, M. Wilford, M. Pownall, and T. Upcher, came to Geneva to have the advice of that church, what was best to be done touching the erection of a new church. They of Geneva gave God thanks for that it had pleased him so to incline the hearts of the lords of Berne towards them, and gave encouragement that they should not let slip so good an occasion. Passing through many parts of the lords of Berne's dominions in Savoy and Switzerland, they found such favour in all places where they came, as verily may be to the great condemnation of all such Englishmen as use the godly stranger so uncourteously. M. Lever and the company at length chose Arau for their resting-place, where the congregation lived together in godly quietness among themselves, with great favour of the people among whom for a time they were planted." Brief discourse of the troubles begun at Frankfort. p. 185. reprint, 1845.]

[2 A letter from Young to Bullinger, dated Basle, Aug. 5, 1557, states that "a large portion of the English are remaining here. The rest will go to Arau, unless more eligible terms are offered them at Vevay. I went up to Arau with them last week, and easily obtained leave of residence for them among the citizens themselves, but we could not meet with suitable houses and apartments for more than seven families. The church of St Ursula is appropriated to them, and licence to engage in the manufacture of wool, in spite of the opposition of some of the more wealthy of the inhabitants. God be praised !"]

contend at once with great expense, and labour, and peril, for the attainment of their object. As many persons therefore as the seven houses which Arau supplies us with can contain, are now established there with their wives and children. The remainder, wishing rather to join us here than to remove as far as Vevay, are lingering in other places, hoping and desiring an opportunity of coming hither. And thus we English, driven from our country by popery, and from Wesel by Lutheranism, are now, most of us, by our mutual wishes, counsels, and assistance, tending to one spot, where it is still permitted us freely, sincerely, and openly to acknowledge and worship Christ. And we shall all at length come together to such a place, if God see fit : if otherwise, his will, and not ours, be done! But certainly, whatever may happen to us in future, we shall all acknowledge ourselves exceedingly indebted to master Bullinger and yourself, by means of whose advice and commendatory letters I found and obtained for our countrymen from the people of Berne far more and better accommodation than I could have previously believed. Wherefore I entreat you both to continue to assist me by your letters, counsels, and admonitions, that I may retain and improve the favour, kindness, and all other comforts necessary for the gathering together, and consolation, and edifying of those, who, having quitted their country for the cause of Christ, are still looking out for a place where they may best be able to worship God in sincerity, and by mutual kind offices to supply each other with the necessary means of subsistence. Salute, I pray you, in my name, with many thanks, masters Henry Bullinger, P. Martyr, B. Ochinus, and the other godly men; also master Parkhurst and his wife. Farewell.

Yours faithfully in Christ,

THOMAS LEVER.

LETTER LXXXVII.

THOMAS LEVER AND OTHERS TO HENRY BULLINGER.

Dated at ARAU, *Oct.* 5, 1557.

GRACE and peace in Christ Jesus. While others are
wont to dedicate their writings to princes and great men,
with the view either to popularity or reward, you alone, most
illustrious sir, have made choice of us poor exiles to whom to
address your midnight studies and lucubrations, to commend
us in your discourses, and to render our condition (miserable as
regards this world, but glorious if we regard him to whom we
have consecrated ourselves, namely, Christ crucified,) memorable to all posterity. Your motives for having thus acted
we can admire as well as account for. For we are almost
all of us unknown to you, and have no means of returning
the obligation. But herein appears your zeal for the Lord's
household, in that you not only diligently feed the flock over
which the Lord has placed you, and instruct all other churches
by your learned commentaries; but also this our exile, in
which we are deserted by our friends, laughed to scorn by
many, spurned by others, assailed by reproaches and revilings
by the most, you alleviate by your learned discourses, that we
may not sink under the pressure of these evils; and, like a
good shepherd, you tend, strengthen, and cheer us all in our
dispersion. We accept therefore your princely gift, and embrace it with the feeling we ought; and in return send you
what alone we can do, namely, our thanks, our affectionate
regard, and a frequent mention of you our master in our
prayers. For your divine and honour-giving present, which
no time shall ever bury in oblivion, receive this perishable
paper filled with lasting thanks; and as often as we shall
take your book into our hands, so often shall we seem to
ourselves to hear you preaching, or rather the Lord himself
revealing his mysteries to us by your ministry.

Farewell, very dear father and much esteemed master in
Christ, and always regard us poor exiles with the love you
are wont to do: for by your kindness is it that we this day
experience, (nor are we alone in this feeling,) how true that

is, which so many histories bear witness to, that the Swiss have been at all times remarkable for hospitality. Continue therefore to edify the church of the Lord by your unwearied labours and studies, to commend us to your countrymen, and to let pass no opportunity of befriending the distressed. May the Lord Jesus long preserve you for the good of his church! Amen. Arau. Oct. 5, 1557.

The exiled congregation of the English at Arau, most devoted to you in the Lord, has commissioned the following persons to subscribe their names in the name of all the rest:

THOMAS LEVER,
RICHARD LANGHERN[1],
ROBERT POWNALL,
WALTER KELLY,
JOHN PRETIE,
THOMAS TURPIN,
THOMAS ATTYN[2].

LETTER LXXXVIII.

THOMAS SAMPSON TO JOHN CALVIN.

Dated at STRASBURGH, *Feb.* 23, 1555.

I DO not cease from doing here, as I did at Lausanne, that is, I am expecting a reply from your kindness. And indeed I am more anxiously expecting it, in proportion as I perceive the flame is lighted up with increased vehemence amongst us English. For a strong controversy has arisen, while some desire the book of reformation of the church of England to be set aside altogether, others only deem some things in it objectionable, such as kneeling at the Lord's supper, the linen surplice, and other matters of this kind; but the rest of it, namely, the prayers, scripture lessons, and the form of the administration of baptism and the Lord's supper they wish to be retained. Some contend for

[1 Richard Langhern, Robert Pownall, Walter Kelly, and Thomas Turpin, afterwards received ordination from bishop Grindal, in 1560.]
[2 Probably an error for *Allyn*, but it is thus in the MS.]

retaining the form, both because the archbishop of Canterbury defends the doctrine as sound, and also because the opposite party can assign no just reason why the form should be
changed. They exclaim on the other hand, that the sole object
of these persons is the establishment of ceremonies. You see,
most excellent Calvin, how Satan is permitted both at home
and abroad to rage against the English. May God have
compassion upon us! and I entreat you by Christ our common Saviour, to give your best consideration to these disturbances of ours, and shew me how we may best remedy
this present evil. I well know how much weight the authority of your letters will have with both parties in the settle-
ment of this dispute.

I have few things, and those far from pleasant, to tell
you about the affairs of England. On the dissolution[3] of
parliament the bishop of Winchester summoned before him
all those who were in prison in London for the word of the
Lord, in number eighty[4], and he urged them by promises,
rewards, and threatenings, to sign their recantation. All
persevered most stedfastly, these two only excepted, Barlow[5],
formerly bishop of Bath and Wells, and Cardmaker[6], archdeacon, I believe, of the same church: for these submitted
to him. Five of them, after a few days, were again brought
to trial, condemned as heretics, and, as we say, delivered up
to the secular authority to be burned. Whether the execution
has taken place, I know not; but all the English are of
opinion that they will most assuredly suffer. Their names
are Hooper, Rogers, Taylor, Bradford, Saunders; all of them
formerly celebrated as ministers of the word. The three
bishops are still alive, and it is thought that a conference will
be held between them and Pole. Philip has not got possession
of the crown. The bishops are authorised to seize at pleasure
upon all suspected of heresy. You see, excellent sir, the

[3 This parliament was dissolved on Wednesday, Jan. 16, 1555. See
Foxe, Acts and Mon. vi. 584, last edition.]

[4 The preachers were summoned to the bishop's house at St Mary
Overy's, on Tuesday, Jan. 22. Foxe, vi. 587.]

[5 Bishop Barlow got free, and escaped into Germany, where he
"did by exile constantly bear witness to the truth of Christ's gospel."
Strype, Mem. iii. i. 431. Foxe, vii. 78.]

[6 John Cardmaker, prebendary of Wells, was burned in Smithfield,
May 30, 1555. See Foxe and Strype as above, and Soames, iv. 416.]

state of England; I commend it to your prayers and those of your church. Farewell, and write to me in return. In haste. Strasburgh, Feb. 23, 1555.

Yours,

THOMAS SAMPSON.

LETTER LXXXIX.

THOMAS SAMPSON TO HENRY BULLINGER.

Dated at STRASBURGH, *Aug.* 6, 1555.

GREETING. There are two motives which now induce me to write; one, that I may not be so neglectful of my duty, as, after having received from you so many friendly salutations in the letters of others, not to salute you, most learned sir, in return. I both express and desire for you, and that from my heart, eternal blessings. The other reason is, because I wished to make use of your name, under which I might transmit to master Chambers these letters and the parcel which I send along with them. If I have taken too great a liberty in this respect, your courtesy towards the English has given me this licence. But I know that you will undertake this trouble with the same kindness that you are always wont to exhibit towards the English who are in exile for Christ's sake. Merciful indeed and faithful is our God, who, though we have left our natural parents, does not withdraw from us parental kindness. I wish I could sometimes seriously bear this in mind, and both shew myself not wholly ungrateful to God, and in some measure also grateful to yourself and those patrons who are like-minded with you. And because, as I hope, my brethren at Zurich far excel me in this respect, so I am bold more freely to interest you in their affairs than in any private business of my own. Farewell. Master Martyr, who is in good health, salutes you. You will hear the English news, which is but little, from master Chambers. Once more farewell, my father and most revered master. Strasburgh, Aug. 6, 1555.

Yours,

THOMAS SAMPSON.

LETTER XC.

THOMAS SAMPSON TO HENRY BULLINGER.
Dated at STRASBURGH, *April 6*, 1556.

I HAVE received your letter, most reverend sir, in which you state that you have received a packet of letters from me. I am glad that those letters were so faithfully delivered. The kind messages which you sent to the English, I distributed, and especially to our bishop. [Sir Richard] Morison was already dead. Sir J. Cheke has left this place. I have thus acquainted you with these things as my duty required. Dr Cranmer was burned at Oxford on the 21st of March. A certain absurd recantation[1], forged by the papists, began to be spread abroad during his life-time, as if he had made that recantation: but the authors of it themselves recalled it while he was yet living, and he firmly and vehemently

[1 See Soames's Hist. Reform. IV. 515, for a full account of the recantations attributed to Cranmer; also Todd, Life of Cranmer, II. 476. Sampson seems to refer to the fifth of the papers afterwards published by Bonner as a part of "All the submyssions and recantations of Thomas Cranmer, &c.," printed by Cawood, 1556. Dr Todd says: " To these artifices Cranmer yielded, and to the words on the 'little leaf of paper,' which they brought, subscribed, as it should seem, in their presence. 'This recantation,' says Foxe, 'was not so soon conceived, but the doctors and prelates without delay caused the same to be imprinted and set abroad in all men's hands. Whereunto, for better credit, first was added the name of Thomas Cranmer with a solemn subscription; then followed the witnesses, Henry Sydall and John de Villa Garcina.' The privy council were displeased at the hasty publication of this paper, and the two printers of it were commanded to deliver all the copies to be burned." See also Foxe, VIII. 82, and Burnet, III. 375. Soames, p. 525, notices and answers Dr Lingard's theory, that the paper thus printed alone, by Rydall and Copeland, was destroyed as an infringement on Cawood's copyright, and thinks it was suppressed lest it should be disavowed by the prisoner or his friends. It is to be noticed also, that the continuator of Fabian's Chronicles, speaking of the burning of the archbishop in 1556, says, " after he had recanted his *supposed* recantation." The original words of Sampson in the letter here translated are, " Recantatio quædam absurda et a papistis conficta cæpit eo vivente spargi, quasi ille eam palinodiam cecinisset; sed auctores ipsi eam, eo vivo, revocarunt, et ille fortiter reclamabat vivens pernegabatque." They are worthy of notice in connexion with the circumstances already recited. The whole of the " submyssions and recantations," as printed by Cawood in a pamphlet of six leaves (see Herbert's Ames, II. 794), are reprinted by Dr Jenkyns in his Remains of Cranmer, IV. App. p. 393.]

denied it. The enemies of God are plotting dreadful and most cruel schemes against England. May Almighty God turn away his anger from us! Mary declares that her husband Philip shall be crowned in spite of every one. She is so bold as to say this, even contrary to the advice of her council. She is making great preparations both of money and arms. You see whither these things tend; entreat therefore the Lord for us.

As to what I had written in my last letter respecting the "Antichrist" of master Gualter, the matter now stands thus: while I was preparing to translate it into our language, I was informed that some other Englishman had not only undertaken the same task, but had also completed it. I think therefore that it is now either in the press, or already printed. Satan is here trying in many ways to disturb the peace of the churches; nor does he stir up only the turbulent Westphalians and those who are like them, but he is scattering his seed also among us exiles. The French church at Frankfort is now suffering under this disease: for there is a great contention between the pastor and some of his flock, if indeed they are true sheep. Do you, excellent father, since these devices of Satan cannot escape your notice, oppose your prayers against his subtle attacks. I wish we did this with the earnestness that the occasion demands.

I ask but one thing more. When I was at Zurich, it was permitted me (such was your singular kindness towards me) to hear and learn from you by conversation and conference those things in which I had need of advice and instruction. You will do me the greatest kindness if you will allow me, since I am now absent, to experience the same favour by correspondence. I promise you that I will not be too troublesome, neither will I expect from you such speedy replies, as not to be willing always to wait patiently for the immense pressure of your engagements. I dare not however make the experiment before I have obtained your consent, lest I should be a hindrance to one who is so diligently labouring in the Lord's vineyard. May the Lord, whose servant you are, and in whose affairs you are engaged, preserve you long in life and health to his church! In haste. Strasburgh, April 6, 1556.

Yours,

THOMAS SAMPSON.

LETTER XCI.

THOMAS SAMPSON TO HENRY BULLINGER.

Without place or date[1].

GREETING. Although, most learned sir, you have no
time to waste upon reading my trifles, yet since the letters
which I have received from our brethren at Frankfort must
be wrapped in paper, I should wish even the blank paper to
salute you for me, as my duty requires. Your sermon has
long been circulated in English, and, as I am informed, is by
no means unacceptable to the English. The afflicted flock of
Christ is still suffering the misery of persecution; for on the
27th of January there were seven[2] burned at London, and
on the same day five[3] at Canterbury. This is the power of
darkness. Heath, archbishop of York, obtains the office of
chancellor[4]; White of Lincoln is now made bishop of Winchester[5]: our languishing Penelope[6] is waiting the return of
her Ulysses, who is celebrating bacchanalian orgies at Antwerp
on account of his happy attainment of the dukedom. Uncertain tidings are reported about a truce between Philip and
the king of France; but most disgusting accounts are given
of their dancing, nightly buffooneries, and ravishing of virgins,
to which things he has now entirely given himself up at
Antwerp. God will at length appear as an avenging judge:
to him do you stretch forth your suppliant hands, even to
weariness, as Moses did, on behalf of England.

[1 This letter seems, from internal evidence, to have been written
from Strasburgh, and probably in June or July, 1556.]

[2 These were, Thomas Whittle, priest; Bartlett Green, gentleman;
John Tudson, artificer; John Went, artificer; Thomas Brown; Isabel
Foster, wife; Joan Warne, alias Lashford, maid; in 1556. See Foxe,
Acts and Mon. VII. 715, &c., and Strype, Mem. III. i. 470.]

[3 These were, John Lomas, Ann Albright, Joan Catmer, Agnes
Snoth, and Joan Sole. See Foxe, VII. 750, &c. who says the martyrdom took place Jan. 31st.]

[4 He was appointed Jan. 1. 1556. Strype, Mem. III. i. 469.]

[5 This appointment took place, April 15. Strype, Mem. III. i. 487.]

[6 One Mr Kemp came from king Philip about the 19th or 20th of
June, with the news that he had deferred his coming for two months
longer; whereat the queen was much cast down, and for several days
after Kemp's coming she was not in case to hear any suitors. See
Strype, Mem. III. i. 495.]

Farewell, most excellent father. Salute, I pray you, that excellent man, and great patron of the English, master Gualter. May Almighty God requite you all! I am now employed upon his "Antichrist," that the English may see an epitome of that book saluting the pope in English. Again, farewell; live most happily in Christ.

Yours,

THOMAS SAMPSON.

Should master Gualter have any thing else, which, inserted in [my translation of] his work on antichrist, may be a means of improving it, he will do a service most acceptable to myself and profitable to the church, if he will please to send it me. If not, I shall publish his Antichrist, by God's blessing, just as it is, only a little abridged. Now, for the third time, farewell. In haste.

LETTER XCII.

THOMAS SAMPSON TO HENRY BULLINGER.
Dated at LAUSANNE, *Aug.* 12, 1556.

GREETING. The letter, most excellent Bullinger, that you gave me to be delivered to master Haller, has been of considerable service to me. For when I came to Berne, and found none of my friends there, he arranged matters for me most admirably, not only by entertaining me with the greatest hospitality as his guest, but most diligently procuring me a fellow-traveller to accompany me to Lausanne. And all this he has done, because you had made mention of me in your letter to him. I have therefore to express my thanks to you for having so kindly designed to commend me to so kind a friend; and I entreat you to convey to him my thanks for the courtesy he manifested towards me. I acknowledge myself indeed most exceedingly obliged to you both. May our great and good God long preserve you as an useful minister of his church! Salute, I pray you, in my name, my most obliging host, master John James Wickius. Farewell. In haste. Lausanne, Aug. 12, 1556.

Yours in Christ,

THOMAS SAMPSON.

LETTER XCIII.

THOMAS SAMPSON TO HENRY BULLINGER.

Dated at LAUSANNE, *Sept.* 13, 1556.

I WROTE to you, my excellent Bullinger, as soon as I had arrived at Lausanne, but am in doubt whether you ever received my letter; so that I think it well now to repeat what I had also written before, namely, that I am by no means unmindful of my duty towards you, and that I both know and acknowledge myself to be on many accounts much indebted to you. This acknowledgment is due both to your kindness, and to that of Haller, afforded me for your sake. Enrol me therefore, most reverend father, among the number of your friends. Oh! how much am I indebted to Almighty God, who has so provided for me the privilege of possessing such patrons, while my beloved England is in such miserable bondage. I have received from doctor P. Martyr the following account of her servitude,—that Philip is now arrived in London, where he was received with the general applause of the people. Thomas a Becket is publicly set up as a saint[1]. Inquiry is made after all those who refuse to go to mass. Some Friars minor have arrived, and are residing at Winchester. So far concerning public calamities. Respecting those of individuals, he adds, that judge Hales threw himself into the river[2], and so was miserably drowned: such is the punishment of his apostasy. But to return to England: you see how she is compelled to be in bondage to the Spaniards, the worst of all nations, pretended saints, most degraded children of antichrist, and of the worst kind of idolatry. But it is not only this bondage that is to be lamented, and to which we are involuntarily subject; but that also by which we are willing slaves to our impenitence. This slavery it is that so miserably oppresses us; this it is that keeps us in bondage within the stone walls of our hearts, and compels us to be in slave-like

[1 The image of Thomas a Becket was set up in stone in 1555 over the gate of Mercer's chapel. Strype, Mem. III. i. 333.]

[2 See Strype, who says "it was a shallow pond, near his own house, which is shewn to this day." Mem. III. i. 276. A long account of judge Hales is also given in Foxe, Acts and Mon. VI. 710, &c.]

subjection to most filthy swine ; yea, it almost turns us into
swine and dogs ourselves, and yet there is in us no desire of
returning to our Father : and albeit this is the only way for
our recovery, to obtain from our offended Father reconciliation
for Christ's sake, with tears; this only way we disregard,
although we are desirous of being thought over careful in
every thing else.   Hence proceeds apostasy, hence despond-
ency, or desperate recklessness in impiety.

I am complaining to you of these things, my excellent
friend, that you may the more earnestly entreat God on our
behalf, in proportion to our own neglect; and also, that I may
be allowed more freely to beseech you, if you have leisure,
to give some exhortation and advice to the English, (among
whom your influence is very great,) by which they may be
instructed how best to conduct themselves at this critical period.
If you will do this in Latin, there will be those who will
translate your discourse into English. Master Bucer, of pious
memory, published a congratulatory epistle[1] to the English,
when England first received the gospel : and let Bullinger
publish something now, by which the godly may be comforted,
and the wicked admonished.   Should I seem too urgent in
this request, I am ready to bear the charge of importunity,
provided only you will confer this benefit upon our church.
I call it a benefit, because I am most fully persuaded that
very many of our people will hence be led to a solid repentance.   And as soon as the Lord shall have found this to
be the case among us, he will then shew himself a compassionate Father, and will freely restore to us both the gospel
and our country likewise ; and how great a blessing this will
be, any godly person may easily determine. Come then, my
excellent Bullinger, if your other engagements, so useful to
the church, will allow you leisure, come, and direct your
attention to what you consider will most profit our afflicted
church.   May our eternal God, and the Father of our Lord
Jesus Christ, evermore guide you by his Spirit into all truth !

Your most devoted,

THOMAS SAMPSON.

[1 This was published in 1548, and entitled, Gratulatio Buceri ad
ecclesiam Anglicanam de religionis Christi restitutione. Strype, Mem.
II. i. 229.]

Salute, I pray you, in my name, master Gualter, to whom also I commend the care of our church. I know indeed that he has an exceeding regard for her : may he always retain this, and earnestly entreat God on her behalf; and may he also stretch out his hand to her in her state of languishing! Salute also master Wickius my host, and our English friends. Give this letter, I pray you, to one of your boys, to take to my brother. May the Lord Jesus bless you and all yours! If you will do me the favour to reply, master Beza can always forward me your letters.

Lausanne, Sept. 13, 1556.

LETTER XCIV.

THOMAS SAMPSON TO HENRY BULLINGER.

Dated at LAUSANNE, *Oct.* 13, 1556.

GREETING. Such is your favourable inclination towards England, most learned Bullinger, that I can easily persuade myself that your kindness will pay the same attention to what I requested of you in my intercessory letter, as if I had addressed you more fully and frequently upon the same subject. I therefore commend to you my petition for my country England, the state of which is deserving of commiseration in proportion to its wretchedness. Our affairs are indeed getting worse every day. For I have just heard from England, that the earl of Sussex[2] has been sent with some troops into Norfolk and Suffolk, to compel the gospellers to attend mass. What tyranny is this! Do you not think that the truly pious now stand in need of comfort, and the weak of exhortation? Come then, if you have leisure, most excellent father, and address our friends by your letters. Philip has demanded of the council to be inaugurated, that is, as we

[2 Henry Ratcliffe, earl of Sussex, was appointed by queen Mary commander-in-chief of the temporary army raised in the beginning of her reign, and justice of the forests south of Trent. She also entrusted him with the direction of the numerous spies and informers, who were distributed in his counties for the purpose of detecting the protestants. See Lodge's Illustrations, &c. I. 263.]

commonly say, to be crowned king of England; he has also
required ten thousand English troops to be sent to serve under
the emperor in the French war.   Both requests, however,
were denied him.   From hence most deadly evils will arise to
England, unless Almighty God of his great mercy shall avert
them; which that he may do, do you earnestly implore him
for Christ's sake, and make some mention of me, if only at the
end of your prayer.

Yours,

THOMAS SAMPSON.

Lausanne, Oct. 13, 1556.

LETTER XCV.

THOMAS SAMPSON TO HENRY BULLINGER.

Dated at STRASBURGH, *April* 23, 1557.

I HAVE received your letter, my learned friend, together
with the sermon concerning the confession and denial of Christ
our Lord.   But, as I was about the next day to go to Frankfort, I was neither able to answer your letter, nor to satisfy
myself even up to this present time with respect to the object
I had in view.   Having now returned, and obtained some
leisure, I have no other answer to make, save to express my
thanks for your kindness, and this not in my own name only,
but in that of England.   For you have not only performed
a most agreeable service to myself, but a most useful one to
England, unless we stand in the way of our own advantage.
I have already determined with myself to translate that
sermon of yours into our vulgar tongue as soon as possible,
and thus present it to the perusal of Englishmen.   That I did
not undertake to have it printed in Latin, is owing partly to
the terms of my request, in which I only pleaded for the
English; and partly because I was unacquainted with your
wishes on the subject.   I leave the Latin therefore to your
discretion; respecting which, however, if I may be allowed to
give an opinion, I should say that it is very necessary in this
declining age.   However, I will execute as faithfully as I can
what I have willingly taken upon myself.   England owes you

thanks, and, I hope, will pay them.   May God of his mercy
long preserve you in life and health to his church!   Believe
me exceedingly attached to you; for I am yours,

THOMAS SAMPSON.

We all commend to your kindness our brethren, who will
give you every information respecting our affairs.
Strasburgh, Apr. 23, 1557.

LETTER XCVI.

THOMAS SAMPSON TO PETER MARTYR.

Dated at FRANKFORT, *April 8, 1558.*

MUCH greeting.   Though I have had no letter from you
since my reply respecting the Hebrew books, and though nothing has arisen since that time about which it was necessary
to write to you; yet I have now thought it proper to address
you, lest I should seem to be wanting in my duty.   For
the friendship of such a man must not be buried in silence;
and I feel it to be for my advantage to retain your friendship
for me by all possible means.   I am writing therefore, in fact,
from self-love; for my little writing-desk, so empty of all
erudition and knowledge, desires to be replenished with the
crumbs which fall from your table: on which account I have,
God willing, decidedly resolved upon visiting you towards the
end of May, and will then have some conversation with you
respecting my intentions.   Meanwhile I must request (I dare
not say, Peter Martyr to receive me into his house: this is
denied me; yet I should be very glad if that sentence could
any wise be recalled; but if not, I must request) Julius to look
out a lodging for me.   I wish to have a bed-chamber to
myself.   I do not intend staying there beyond three months
at farthest.   Should Julius find any difficulty in meeting with
such a lodging, let him call upon master White in my name,
who was my landlord when I was there last; and if he can
procure a separate bed-chamber at his house, I will willingly
engage it, if I can obtain one no where else.   I requested also
our friend Jewel to receive a parcel from the bearer of this

letter, and take charge of it till I come. You see what trouble I am giving both to you and yours by my proposed visit; but you always pardon my importunity, and therefore I treat you with greater freedom. I will only add, that, should it be convenient, I shall be glad to hear respecting the receipt of the parcel, and also what is done about the lodging; and this before the middle of May, namely, before I leave Strasburgh. I have requested Julius to write; do you also charge him to do so.

We have no news from England, except that the queen is wholly occupied in raising money and troops, it may be, possibly, to make war against herself. However this be, a war is threatened. You have, I suppose, heard of the extinction of the most splendid of all the masses throughout Europe. I was present at its funeral, and saw the emperor crowned[1] without the mass. I have here met with Beza, who obtained from the princes, while they were here, a letter to the French king for the liberation of the prisoners of Christ. What has been done by us besides, I will tell you when we meet. Salute your friend Julius, and all your friends in my name. In haste. Frankfort, Apr. 8, 1558.

Yours,

THOMAS SAMPSON.

Peter Perne has my things, and will send them to you; I will pay the carriage when I come.

LETTER XCVII.

THOMAS SAMPSON TO PETER MARTYR.

Dated at STRASBURGH, *July* 10, 1558.

By the blessing of God I have returned in safety to Strasburgh, and find all my friends well; and I am glad to hear that you are well also. I venerate and embrace that holy and inviolable friendship, which you promise me in the

[1 The college of electors assembled at Frankfort, Feb. 24, 1558, and declared Ferdinand of Austria the lawful successor to Charles V. See Robertson, IV. 267.]

cause of Christ.   Besides, I regard with the greatest delight this most useful kind of study, though I am now, through the fault of certain individuals, compelled to put off till another time that which, for the sake of my studies, I had intended to accomplish immediately after the fair : and that is my journey to you ; at the thought of which, as I often turned it over in my mind, and rejoiced exceedingly, so I am now obliged, not without much regret, both to witness and to desire its postponement.   I shall come however, I hope, shortly : in the mean time, I entreat you for Christ's sake, let there exist between us that inviolable friendship which you promise ; let there always be in you the same mind, the same desire of assisting me in my little studies, and, aided by the divine blessing, I will not neglect the opportunity afforded me.   But I will give you notice of my coming.   Your promise about the Hebrew books is most gratifying ; and I beg that you will act altogether in this matter just as if it were your own concern, and you shall neither find me dissatisfied nor ungrateful. When you have agreed with Perne or others, whom you may think qualified for this business, about the means of obtaining the books, and will let me know, I will send you the money, together with a list of the books that I wish to purchase.   I only add, what you do, do quickly.   Master Heton and his wife salute you.   He hopes to visit you at Zurich before the end of September.   Master Chambers salutes you.   All our friends are well.   My wife and our Joanna salute you.   The people of Frankfort (I mean the English there) are in a perpetual motion, more perverse than useful.   Philip is still in England.   Almost all are making preparation for a war with England.   But your countrymen on their return from the fair will be full of news ; so I will make an end of writing.   Farewell, and live most happy in Christ.   Affectionately salute for me master Bullinger.   Strasburgh, July 10, 1558.

Your most devoted,

THOMAS SAMPSON.

LETTER XCVIII.

CHRISTOPHER HALES TO RODOLPH GUALTER.

Dated at LONDON, *March* 4, [1550.]

ALTHOUGH I promised, most learned Gualter, to write to you from Antwerp, and tell you all the occurrences of so long a journey ; yet, to tell the truth, I was so fatigued with riding, that scarce any part of my body, much less my hand, could perform its office. But now, lest I should seem altogether forgetful of our friendship and mutual promise of correspondence, I write at length, not, as I had intended, from Antwerp, but from London, where I arrived from Calais with greater difficulty and danger than I had met with through the whole of my previous journey. For thus far I had brought all my property in safety, with the exception of a dog, which in the open plain of Brabant, on this side Bruges, refused to follow me any farther : but on our passage over we fell in with a French pirate, (for the truce of fifteen days was on land only, and did not extend to the sea,) by whom our vessel was very near being captured. And had not the tide, as God so willed it, failed the privateer which was in pursuit of us, we should without doubt every one of us have been taken prisoners. But the matter did not end thus. For after we had waited on the shore seven hours in expectation of the flow of the tide, we did not get off without the greatest danger, and some damage to our property. We were compelled, unless we preferred learning French, to run our vessel on shore, sailing and rowing as expeditiously as we could ; in which flight the sailors, as usual in the greatest extremity, that they might more quickly reach the shore, threw overboard whatever first came to hand, without any regard to its value. Among these was my trunk, in which, as you know, were contained my books, and the letters of my excellent friends. I care very little about the destruction of my own property ; but the loss of the letters of those worthy men, to whose kindness I am so deeply indebted, grieves me most exceedingly. But I hope, when they know of my escape, (such is their friendliness and good-will towards me,) that they will not so much regret the loss of their letters, and feel angry with me, as praise the Lord with me, who has delivered me from such great and imminent danger.

Thus much then of myself; I now come to other matters. Throughout my whole journey I could have no suspicion whatever of the emperor being at war, as all things were as quiet as possible; but when I reached home, I heard that a large fleet was in preparation by him, though what he is intending, or in what direction, I have no certain information. This only I know, and I am very glad of it, that no injury can be done you by sea. I found all my friends and property safe and well at home, to my great pleasure and delight. The facts were true which I had related to you concerning my brother; but God, the just judge, and best defender of innocence, delivered him from prison almost at the very time I left you.

Hooper is daily setting forth with all boldness the heavenly doctrine of our heavenly Father : he is to-morrow to preach before the king[1]. The bishop of Rochester, by name Ridley[2], a worthy minister of Christ, succeeds the bishop of London, who is deprived. Another post is allotted to the bishop of Westminster[3], where he will do less mischief. Salute in my name all the brethren in the Lord, and especially that excellent soldier of Christ, and chief minister of your church, master Bullinger, to whom, I pray, make my excuses for having lost his annotations; and request him at the same time to procure me another copy, when I will satisfy the copyist for his trouble. Salute the reverend presbyter, master Pellican, Theodore [Bibliander] learned in the Lord, Otto, Zuinglius, Wolfius, and the witty Frisius, with all the rest; as also each of my fellow-countrymen, whose letters I have lost, which you will mention to them, that they may write them over again. Salute your very dear wife in my name, to whom I would have now sent a small present, if I had any means of forwarding it. When an opportunity is afforded me, I will certainly send it. Meanwhile, I request you, my dear Rodolph, to procure your Apelles to paint for me the following portraits,

[1 This was on Wednesday, March 5, 1550. See above, p. 75, n. 1.]
[2 Ridley was translated to the see of London, in April 1550, by the king's letters patent. Strype, Mem. II. 1, 338. See above, p. 79.]
[3 Bishop Thirlby, who, on the dissolution of the see of Westminster in 1550, was preferred to Norwich. Strype, Cranmer, 129.]

those namely of Zuinglius, Pellican, Theodore, master Bullinger, and yourself, holding books in their hands; of the same size as that oval one of yours which you shewed me, and on wood, not canvass; and I request you to see that four verses, the subject of which I leave to your discretion, be written underneath. Make an agreement with the painter that the colours be good and carefully set off, even though the expense be increased. When finished, let them be packed up in a wooden box, and sent to Burcher, who will pay for them. The sooner they are done, the more acceptable will they be. And if you think the artist can paint a good likeness of Œcolampadius[1], I would have it in addition to the other five. Do not take it ill of me, my worthy host, that I impose upon you this trouble: for did I not love you, and think myself loved by you, I should not do so. If life be granted me, you shall not find me an ungrateful guest. Take care that you be well in the Lord. Send an answer, I pray you, as soon as possible, but take care that the painter put his hand to the work as speedily as he can. I leave the whole matter to your fidelity and discretion. London, March 4.

Your most attached,

CHRISTOPHER HALES.

LETTER XCIX.

CHRISTOPHER HALES TO RODOLPH GUALTER.

Dated at LONDON, *May* 24, 1550.

I HAVE received your letter, my excellent Rodolph, by which I learn with very great regret how little honour there is among men, and how few persons there are in whom any confidence can be placed. But I hope that such is the courtesy of your senate, united with the greatest discretion, that they will endeavour to arrange this whole business, whatever it be, to the glory of God's great name; and I have no doubt

[1 Œcolampadius died Dec. 1, 1531.]

but that the Author of peace will grant them a happy issue. Let us diligently pray in the mean time that he may be pleased to do this as soon as possible. For godliness has no voice in the midst of arms, the truth of which saying we, alas! as you well know, have lately experienced in our grievous intestine discords. And I could wish that others, being warned by our example, would lay aside their arms, and learn to lead a peaceable life in all godliness, a thing we have but lately begun to understand. But now at length, thank God, we are in the enjoyment of great tranquillity : may our good and gracious God grant that we may employ it to his honour, and the benefit of our neighbours! John a Lasco[2] came back to us ten days since, in consequence of things in Poland not turning out according to his godly desires. His king would not grant him an audience, for fear of the bishops. As soon as I have heard from him how your friend Florian is going on, I will let you know in my next letter. Hooper was made bishop of Gloucester two days since, but under godly conditions : for he will not allow himself to be called Rabbi, or my lord, as we are wont to say ; he refuses to receive the tonsure, he refuses to become a pie, and to be consecrated and anointed in the usual way, with many other things, which you shall hear at another time : from this bishoprick he has two thousand crowns per annum. God grant that he may so preside over his flock as to afford a godly example to the other shepherds ; and I would desire you, my Rodolph, and the other learned ministers of that church to labour earnestly in his behalf. Your friend Oglethorpe, as I hear, is imprisoned for superstition, and is about to lose, it is said, the presidency of Magdalene college. The new bishop of London is now employed in his visitation[3], and threatens to eject those who

[2 John a Lasco arrived in England for the first time in September, 1548, upon the invitation of Cranmer, with whom he resided at Lambeth for six months. He returned to Embden in the spring of 1549; but the introduction of the Interim into Friesland accelerated his departure from that country, which he quitted in October, and having resided for some time at Bremen and Hamburgh, he embarked from the last named town, and reached England in the spring of 1550, where on July 24th he was appointed the superintendent of the foreign protestant congregation established in London. See Burnet and Strype.]

[3 For the injunctions given in this visitation see Ridley's works, Parker Society edition, p. 319.]

shall not have come to their senses before his next visitation; and if I know the man, he will be as good as his word.

I wrote to you in my last letter about some portraits; and I now repeat my request, that you will be mindful of me in this matter. Saluto in my name your excellent wife Rachel, to whom I send two candlesticks, and twenty dishes, some of them of pewter, and some of wood. I wish indeed that they had all been silver; for the kindness of you both has deserved that from me and a great deal more. Salute moreover in my name all the ministers of your church, and especially masters Bullinger, Pellican, Theodore [Bibliander], Otto, Wolfius, and Zuinglius, my friend Butler too, and John, if he is over yonder, and your merry friend Frisius, and all the rest. Farewell, master Rodolph, and command my services. London, May 24, 1550.

Your friend and brother in Christ,

CHRISTOPHER HALES.

LETTER C.

CHRISTOPHER HALES TO HENRY BULLINGER.

Dated at LONDON, June 12, [1550.]

I was exceedingly rejoiced, my most excellent Bullinger, at hearing from our worthy friend Abel, that you were alive and well: but when he delivered me your letter, I then knew for a certainty that this was the case; and that you have not yet laid aside from your remembrance our friendship contracted in the intercourse of a few months, which circumstance I am inclined to attribute to your singular kindness. But I wish that an opportunity may sometime be afforded me of being serviceable in any way either to yourself or any of your friends. I would certainly take care that mutual fidelity, faith, and good-will, should nowise be wanting in myself. As to the pictures, I will endeavour that no offence be occasioned by that matter. And not only in this, but also in every thing else, I will defend, as far as lies in my power, the fame and reputation of you all; which I know to be entirely pure from any of those things which can in any way impair the glory and praise of God. I think that my elder brother, John Hales, who was the cause of my quick and sudden departure from you, will come over to you this summer from Augsburg. Should he wish to make use of your most prudent counsel in any matter, let him perceive that my recommendation has been of some use towards the attainment of that object. And any kindness you may shew to him will be much more gratifying and acceptable to me than if you had shewn it to myself: which though it may appear to you a bold assertion, yet such is my love towards him, that when I have said every thing, I seem to myself to have said but little. Farewell, most excellent sir, and believe that I am yours. Salute in my name all the most worthy ministers of your church and school, to whom I wish every happiness in the Lord. Farewell. London, June 12.

Yours heartily,

CHRISTOPHER HALES.

LETTER CI.

CHRISTOPHER HALES TO HENRY BULLINGER.

Dated at LONDON, *Dec.* 10, 1550.

MUCH health, most excellent sir. Your letter has been brought to me, wherein I perceive the candour of your mind, and your more than common kindness towards me. Your candour appears, in that you have borne the loss[1] I occasioned you with so much courtesy and good temper: although I was entirely free from blame, since it arose not from any fault of mine, but from, I know not whether to call it, the wilfulness or bad faith of the sailors. But however it be, you have afforded me no common pleasure by so kindly interpreting the whole matter. Your exceeding kindness appears in this, that you have both sympathised in my misfortune, and so courteously congratulated me on the favourable state of my affairs. What you say, that I have you in my remem-

[1 Namely, of the letters mentioned above, p. 184.]

brance, is indeed true; and not one year only, nor all the years of my future life, will be able to efface that remembrance; as you shall certainly find to be the case, as soon as I shall meet with any opportunity of shewing it.

I have delayed to write respecting the study of medicine at Oxford, and the expenses there, until I could give you a correct statement. I have however learned from a friend, who is resident there, that the university of Oxford is not to be compared with that of Paris or the schools of Italy; but still it is one in which a studious youth may be occupied with great advantage. The same is to be said of Cambridge, but I rather recommend Oxford on account of the greater salubrity of the air. Cambridge, by reason of the neighbouring fen, is much exposed to fever, as I have experienced more frequently than I could wish. With respect to expense, my friend informed me, that thirty French crowns would suffice tolerably well for a year; to which if other ten could be added, a man might expect to live very comfortably. In my time, ten years since, twenty crowns were a sufficient allowance; but in these latter days, when avarice is every where increasing, and charity growing cold, and this by a divine scourge, every thing has become almost twice as dear as it was. And this I attribute to no other cause than our proud and Pharaoh-like rejection of the spiritual food of our souls so liberally and abundantly offered. May God have mercy on us, and give us better minds, that we may at length truly and heartily repent; lest, abusing the singular mercy of God, we should call down upon ourselves a more grievous retribution!

I have written to master Gualter to procure six portraits to be painted for me, which he writes word that he has done; but has retained four of them for two reasons; first, because there is some danger lest a door shall hereafter be opened to idolatry; and next, lest it should be imputed to you as a fault, as though it were done by you from a desire of empty glory. But the case is far otherwise. For I desired to have them on this account, both for an ornament to my library, and that your effigies might be beheld in the picture, as in a mirror, by those who by reason of distance are prevented from beholding you in person. This is not done, excellent sir, with the view of making idols of you; they are desired for the reasons I have mentioned, and not for the sake of honour or veneration. For except myself, who always desire your reputation and honour in all respects unimpaired, there is no one who knows for what reason these pictures are coming to me. I request therefore, most excellent sir, that I may be allowed to obtain from you this favour. Do not, I pray you, shew yourself obdurate in this matter, which is both trifling in itself, and not capable of occasioning injury to any one. Farewell, most accomplished sir. London, Dec. 10, 1550.

Your most devoted,

CHRISTOPHER HALES.

LETTER CII.

CHRISTOPHER HALES TO RODOLPH GUALTER.

Between June 12, 1550, and Jan. 26, 1551.

MUCH health, my excellent Rodolph. I have received two letters from you, by which I clearly understand your affection for me, and that the commission which I too freely imposed upon you, has been executed by you with the greatest fidelity and diligence. And this I do not so much gather from the result itself, as from the favourable disposition of your mind towards me. I know that every thing was most diligently undertaken by you, and rather choose to lay the blame upon my own fate than to entertain the slightest suspicion of any fault on your part; so that there was no occasion for making me any apology. You have indeed admirably discharged your office, and I certainly consider myself undeserving of so much kindness. You must not therefore suppose that I view the matter in any other light than if the whole affair had succeeded according to my wish. I am greatly surprised that Burcher should persist in thinking that portraits can nowise be painted with a safe conscience and a due regard to godliness; since there is not a single letter in the holy scriptures which appears really to sanction that opinion. For, if I understand aright, images were forbidden in the

sacred books for no other reason, than that the people of God
might not be drawn aside from the true worship of one true God
to the vain worship of many false gods.   And if there be no
danger of this, I do not see why pictures may not be painted
and possessed, especially when they are not kept in any place
where there can be the least suspicion of idolatry.   Who
worships the monkey that is placed in your fish-market?
Who worships a cock fixed on the church-steeple, as your
father-in-law actually has, who is so determined an enemy
of idolatry?   Who bows himself before your Charles[1] placed
on the top of the tower?   Who is so senseless, as to worship a painting or picture deposited in the library?   Supposing that there are those who honour them when hung up
in churches and sacred places, which I by no means approve;
yet where is the man so devoid of all religion, godliness,
fear of the most high and Almighty God, and so entirely
forgetful of himself, as to regard with veneration a little portrait reposited in some ordinary place in a museum?

But it is said that times may occur, when there will be
danger lest encouragement be given to idolatry by their means.
Well then, it may in the same manner be argued, that no
image or likeness ought to be made of any thing whatever!
But I am so far from suspecting you of an opinion of this
kind, that I do not suppose it is entertained by any man
upon earth.   Indeed, my worthy friend, if I thought it possible that the worship of idols could be re-established by such
means, believe me, that if I had the pictures, I would tear
them into a thousand pieces with my own hands.

Another reason is next alleged, which if I had considered
a true one, I certainly, my Rodolph, should never have made
this request.   I know your disposition, and that of the rest
of you.   It is impossible that you should ever suppose me
capable of thinking so unfavourably of yourself and of the
other ministers of your church, whom I consider to be as far
removed from all anxiety for display as any persons living.
But you have no occasion to fear what others may think of
you, as there is no one, or at least very few, with the exception of our two selves, who know from what source these pic-

[1 The south tower of the Gross-munster or cathedral at Zurich is
called Charles's tower, from a statue placed there, which is supposed
to be that of Charlemagne.]

tures will be brought to me.   Who lays it to the charge of
the Romans of old, that we have their resemblances engraved
upon numerous medals?   Who blames Luther, Bucer, Philip
[Melancthon], Œcolampadius, and very many others now
living, because their likenesses are every where to be met
with?   This is nothing extraordinary, but a thing of very
frequent occurrence among all nations, for men fond of learning to adorn their studies with the memorials and images of
literary characters; and this I think no one would say is
done with a view to the establishment of idolatry.   These
things are done in general for the sake of ornament, not to
do honour to individuals; so that you need not imagine that
you will ever become the instruments of some impious and
ungodly purpose.

As to your telling me that each of you has retained his
own portrait for himself, I have no right to find fault, since
you seem to have done this under the excitement of godly
zeal.   I know that you are prudent and well-judging men,
and that you have not rashly changed your purpose, which
I certainly wish you had not done without being influenced
and supported by grave reasons; and if they had known me
well, they would not have thought they had any thing to
fear from such a circumstance.   For I am not one who would
have the true worship of God adulterated in any, even the
least, matter; much less would I wish the reintroduction of
gross idolatry, so hateful to the Lord of heaven and earth.

Wherefore I request you, my beloved brother in Christ,
to explain to them these my sentiments on this subject, and
to ask, in my name, permission for me to obtain from their
kindness this single request, namely, that the remaining four
portraits may be sent me.   And if you cannot obtain this,
(though I hope otherwise,) I at least beg and indeed insist
upon this, that your Zeuxis shall be paid at my expense.
For I by no means consider it fair, that those worthy men
should pay the penalty of my offence, if offence it be: I
have been in fault, and I must bear the blame.   In the
next place, I entreat you, my worthy friend, that should I
not be able to obtain all the portraits, I may at least obtain
the two others, namely, that of Theodore, which you tell me
was taken without his knowledge, and as it were by stealth,
and also your own; for I am well assured that you are of

quite the contrary opinion, unless you have lately very much changed it, or else you would never have had the portraits taken of your wife and little girl. I am now dealing with you upon what you have set your own seal to, as they say; see what reply you have to make. But I know that not only yourself, but that the most excellent master Bullinger is of the same way of thinking, and this too from your own statement. For you tell me that the portrait of Œcolampadius is taken from the copy which he has in his possession; which if he had considered to be unlawful, I am sure that a man of so much piety and godliness would never have allowed so impious an act. But enough of this. Excuse me if I have dwelt somewhat too long upon the subject.

And now respecting the expenses and studies at Oxford; I have been more diligent in my inquiry, because the youth was a connexion of yours, and the son of that excellent man, the senator Cellarius. You must know then, that I have ascertained from an Oxford friend, who has himself tried it, that medicine is so studied there, as that a man may devote himself to literature with great advantage. In the next place, that the expense of living is such, as that thirty crowns a year will be amply sufficient; but if ten more be added, there will be no deficiency of means for every proper purpose. And if I may interpose my opinion, I would rather that such allowance should be provided, as that there should be ten pounds too much, rather than one too little. Should he come hither, I shall most willingly shew him every kindness for your sake. Lastly, with respect to the pewter and the cloth, I cannot send them at present, but, God willing, you shall certainly receive them at the next Frankfort fair. Christopher Froschover is now at Oxford; I have received a letter from him, but have not yet chanced to see him. Your Zurich courtesy will not allow me to refuse any service that he may require. I hear that your wife is in the family-way; wish her from me a happy delivery. Take care of your health, Rodolph, my very dear brother in the Lord. Salute from me all our godly brethren sojourning among you. Though Butler is named last, let him know that he has not the last place in my friendship. Salute him therefore, and his wife, when you have an opportunity. Although the church of God be oppressed, it cannot be destroyed. Our godly bishops are planning, for the second time, a more complete reformation of our church. God grant that all things may turn out to the glory of his name! Amen, Amen. Farewell, my beloved Rodolph.

Yours heartily,
C. HALES.

LETTER CIII.

CHRISTOPHER HALES TO RODOLPH GUALTER.

Dated at LONDON, *Jan.* 26, 1551.

MUCH health, most excellent Rodolph. You desired me, in your last letter, to send you some of the pewter ware of this country, and some cloth suited for hose. This commission I have executed as faithfully and diligently as I could, and I hope that it will meet your approval. I have delivered the articles to our friend Richard Hilles, who has promised to take care that they shall be handed over to Froschover at Frankfort at the next fair. And that you may know more certainly what you are to receive from him, you must know that I have inclosed in the package six dishes of a larger size, and as many smaller, to which I have added six saucers. There are also twelve plates, which, if I am not mistaken, are of the kind you wished for. They cost six and twenty shillings and seven pence of our money: if this price appear to you too great, I assure you, that not only ware of this kind, but also every thing else, is twice as dear as usual. As to the cloth, I purchased it for seven shillings of our money, which, at the present rate of exchange, amounts to one French crown and two batzen. As you gave me no positive direction in your letter, I have sent as much cloth as will make one pair of hose. Should I understand that this expensive kind of cloth meets your approbation, I can easily contrive for you to have at any time as much as you may require.

And now as to the pictures and the labour of the artist. I must again entreat and implore you that, if it be possible, you will let me have them. But if I cannot obtain this, at least let the work of the artist be paid for at my expense.

13—2

For I do not think it right for me to impose such a burden upon those excellent men.   Farewell, my worthy Rodolph, and number me among your friends.   Salute in my name all the worthy ministers of your church, together with your excellent wife and our friend Butler.   Entreat the Lord continually for us in your prayers; for his church was never placed in greater danger.   The affair of the bishop of Winchester[1] is now going on, and he will probably ere long be deprived of his office, together with some other not godly bishops.   May Christ grant, (for the whole cause is his,) that other godly men may be appointed in their stead!   London, Jan. 26, 1551.

Yours heartily,

CHRISTOPHER HALES.

The whole cost of the pewter and cloth together amounts to five French crowns and one or two batzen.

LETTER CIV.

RICHARD HILLES TO HENRY BULLINGER.
Dated [in *August*, 1540.]

PATIENCE, that when you have performed the work of God, you may obtain the promise!   God knows, my most honoured master, how greatly I have always desired to write to you, and how slenderly I am furnished with materials for writing in Latin.   He who dealeth to every man the measure of faith, and gifts according to his will, has bestowed upon me some little knowledge of Latin, but not the ability of expressing myself at all clearly in that language, so that I have never yet ventured to write in Latin to any one.   But as you have so often challenged me with your hortatory and truly comforting letters, and, so to speak, have compelled me to write you something in reply; and especially as I am persuaded that with your wonted courtesy and kindness you will take every thing in good part that will anywise admit of a right

[1 For an account of the proceedings against bishop Gardiner, see Foxe, VI. 64, &c.   Soames, III. 607.]

interpretation; I have now sent you this ill-composed letter, which however I certainly should not have sent at present, had I not previously lost all hope of seeing you this year. I certainly intended to have gone into Switzerland with my wife this present August, chiefly for the sake of paying you a visit; but my brother Butler, who is now busily engaged in courting a widow of Strasburgh, has been away with her relatives the whole of this month; so that unless we choose to travel by ourselves, we are at present obliged to remain here, though I do not expect to have so much leisure time again for a whole year. Do not, I pray you, mention this to any one; but he is at present uncertain whether she will marry any body, and I am afraid she will hardly become his wife, by reason of a disorder under which she has long been suffering, even during her late husband's lifetime. It has often come into my mind to write you the news from England, and the changes that are continually taking place; but I have been prevented by a becoming modesty from persevering in my intention; for I not only write Latin as barbarously and ungrammatically as I speak it, but even the words themselves fail me. Relying, however, upon your wisdom and good nature, by which you know how to be unlearned among the unlearned, that you may unite them to Christ, I send you herewith a summary of those matters respecting the state of our kingdom last year, which I have gathered from the letters of brethren worthy of credit, and which I had intended to communicate to you in person. I only request you to receive in good part what has been written, though in a rude and barbarous style, with a friendly disposition towards you.

As to the state of our commonwealth before the feast of Easter last passed (namely in the year 1540), I hope you have been sufficiently informed by our aforesaid brother Butler. For in my letters to him I described very carefully, as far as my abilities would allow me, all the events that had occurred, and this that he might afterwards communicate them to the learned and godly men yonder, and especially to yourself. I received your letter dated on the sixth of this month, and also the one you had previously forwarded by that Frenchman, at the same time, and heartily thank you for them both; and especially because you thought fit therein to afford me such true and godly consolation from the holy scriptures, and so diligently to exhort me to patience and longsuffering, in which graces I am greatly deficient. In the next place I have received from your letter, by God's blessing, this great benefit, namely, that I have considered and deliberated much more carefully and discreetly than before, what it is to leave one's first love, and how unbecoming it is for a Christian to return to his vomit; and how fearful a thing it is for any one to fall into the hands of the living God! Blessed be God, even the Father of our Lord Jesus Christ, the Father of mercies, and the God of all comfort, who has doubtless oftentimes comforted you in your tribulation and distress, that you may thereby be more able to comfort them which are in any trouble!

Meanwhile however, that you may know the state of my affairs, it is as follows. When I perceived that there was no place left for me in England, unless, as Ustazades[1] replied to the king of Persia, I chose to become a traitor both to God and man; I forthwith left the country, but on the pretext of carrying on my trade in this place. This motive however is known by all my godly acquaintance to be a false one, and also suspected to be such by my ungodly adversaries. But as I have not been indicted for heresy, or summoned before the courts of law, all my property yonder is at present tolerably safe; so that I remit to England at every fair, for the purpose of importing a fresh supply of cloth, the money that I receive both here and at Frankfort. I have mentioned this with the view of making you acquainted with my affairs, lest, in case you should hear any report of my voluntary exile in these parts, the account of my troubles in England should fail of being noticed. Meanwhile, I freely confess to you, (though it would not be safe for me to make the same acknowledgment to every one,) that I have determined not to return thither, unless it should first please God to effect such a change, as that we may serve him there without hinderance, and without being forced to sanction what is evil. My wife, thank God, makes provision for our comfort here quite as well, or indeed better than myself. Although, by God's help,

[1 See Historia Tripartita, Lib. III. cap. ii. p. 325-6. of *Auctores Historiæ Ecclesiasticæ*, Basil. 1533. Also, Pilkington's Works, Park Soc. Ed. p. 637.]

I do not doubt of my perseverance even unto the end, I entreat you to pray the Lord for us, that he which hath begun a good work in us may perform it until the day of Christ. Our brother Butler returned to England after the last Frankfort fair; but so miserable was the state of things in that country, that he did not remain there more than eighteen days.

Furthermore, I entreat you for God's sake not to mention to any one what I am now writing, except to masters Theodore Bibliander, Pellican, Leo Judæ, and other godly and learned men of the same stamp; and above all, let it not be known as coming from any Englishman. And I implore you not to let them read my letter, for fear they should ridicule, as it deserves, my rash and foolish presumption in writing in this unpolished and unconnected manner. I should have given my letter to Butler, if he had been at home, or to some other Englishman in this place, to be put into better Latin, only that I am not willing for them to know (though I do not distrust them) that I have communicated so many things to all of you together; lest probably, when they are writing to England, they may, with a good intention, acquaint some godly person or other, who, without sufficient caution, as frequently happens, will[2]......

I thank you much for the information you give me respecting Falckner; and I request that if there are any other pious and God-fearing men yonder, who are in the habit of purchasing English cloth, you will let me know their names, that, should they at any time wish to obtain some cloth from me upon credit, I may let them have it. For I do not feel disposed to credit any persons with any large sum, except the people of Zurich, and a few, it may be, at Schaffhausen: wherefore, if you will do me this favour, I shall be much obliged. I will pray Christ to requite you in return, for whose sake I know that you love me; just as you hate the ungodly for the devil's sake, and for his image in them, as did the prophet David, and all holy men besides. How well do we learn by daily experience the truth of that verse of Solomon, The righteous abhor the wicked, and those who are in the right way are abominable to the ungodly. Farewell, honoured pastor, most happily in the Lord, and may Christ, the chief

[2 The remainder of this sentence is altogether unintelligible.]

Shepherd, grant you so to fulfil your ministry, that when he shall appear, you may not be ashamed, but have confidence, and obtain the incorruptible crown of glory promised to those who are like you. Amen. My wife dutifully salutes you, and especially your wife. We both of us very much desire to visit you. You have no need to wish for us, for we cannot in any way be of comfort or service to you, but in many ways a hinderance and impediment to your studies. Again farewell in Christ, my very dear master, and do not, I pray you, forget to salute in my name your godly wife, and joint heir with yourself of the kingdom of heaven.

Yours heartily,

R. H.

LETTER CV.[1]

RICHARD HILLES TO HENRY BULLINGER.

Dated at [LONDON, 1541].

BEFORE Whitsuntide three persons were burned in the suburbs of London, in that part of the city belonging to the diocese of Winchester, because they denied transubstantiation, and had not received the sacrament at Easter. And as these things took place in the diocese of Winchester, it was remarked by many persons that these men were brought to the stake by the procurement of the bishop; just as he burned, shortly after, a crazed man of the name of Collins[2]. This man had previously been kept in prison for two or three years, but I do not exactly know for what reason. Once, as he was passing by a crucifix, to which processions had sometimes been made, (principally by the Spanish sailors on their arriving safe in harbour,) he aimed an arrow at the idol, and

[1 This letter is quoted by Burnet, III. 215, &c. "It is writ," he says, (226) "with much good sense and piety, but in very bad Latin;" which indeed in some places renders it very difficult to find out the meaning.]

[2 Collins became insane through the evil conduct of his wife, who deserted him for another. He was burned in 1538. See Foxe, v. 251.]

striking its foot, called out to it to defend itself, and punish him if it were able.   Many persons, however, say that this was not the cause of his imprisonment ; but rather, because he was wont to exclaim against the nobility and great men of the kingdom, and rashly to bring forward against them many passages of holy scripture, especially the prophets, wherein there was any mention made of unrighteous judgments, or the cruel treatment of neighbours and dependents.   Meanwhile, I know this for a fact, that when Lambert was confined with him in the same prison, (that Lambert[3], namely, who was condemned by the king himself for his opinions respecting the eucharist, a short time before Burcher fled from England,) four or five days before he was brought to the stake, this Collins was not so crazy or ignorant but that he was able to bring forward and apply very expeditiously and aptly on Lambert's behalf, against the bishops and other ungodly persons who appeared against him before the royal tribunal[4], various passages from the New Testament, and from the Psalms, such as these, " Blessed are they which are persecuted for righteousness' sake, &c."   " The Lord knoweth the days of the upright, and their inheritance shall be for ever."   [Ps. xxxvii. 18.]   " The wicked shall not dwell with thee, neither shall the unrighteous stand in thy sight."   " Thou hatest all workers of iniquity, thou shalt destroy all that speak leasing." [Ps. v. 5, &c. vulgate.]   " The Lord abhorreth the bloody and deceitful man ; they shall not live out half their days," &c. [Ps. lv. 23.]   Now to other matters.

Before the feast of John the Baptist it began to be whispered about that the king intended to divorce his queen, Anne, the sister of the duke of Gelderland, though he had married her publicly with great pomp, in the face of the church, on the feast of Epiphany, after last Christmas.   This was first of all whispered by the courtiers, who observed the king to be much taken with another young lady[5] of very

[3 For a full account of the proceedings against John Lambert, see Foxe, v. 181, and Soames, ii. 324.   He was burned in Smithfield in 1538.]

[4 The king determined to hear the cause in person, and Westminster Hall was prepared for the purpose.   Soames, ii. 327.]

[5 This was Catharine, daughter to Lord Edmund Howard, and niece to the duke of Norfolk.]

diminutive stature, whom he now has.   It is a certain fact,
that about the same time many citizens of London saw the
king very frequently in the day-time, and sometimes at midnight, pass over to her on the river Thames in a little boat.
The bishop of Winchester also very often provided feastings
and entertainments for them in his palace; but the citizens
regarded all this not as a sign of divorcing the queen, but of
adultery.   After a few days, Cromwell[1], the king's vicegerent
in causes ecclesiastical (for such was his official designation)
fell from the king's favour, and at the beginning of June was
sent to the Tower of London, from whence he never went
forth till the twenty-eighth of July, when he was beheaded,
together with another nobleman, the lord Hungerford[2], whom
they charged with having attempted to calculate the day
when the king should die.   I know nothing for certain as to
the cause of Cromwell's execution, because he was not brought
for examination before the tribunal, as had always been the
case heretofore with all noblemen, and especially when accused
of treason against the king.   But it was commonly said by
most persons, and with great probability, that the real cause of
his execution was, that he did not support the king, as Winchester and the other courtiers did, in his project of a divorce,
but rather asserted that it would neither be for the king's
honour, nor for the good of the kingdom.   Not long before
the death of Cromwell, the king advanced him, and granted
him large houses and riches, and more public offices, together
with very extensive and lucrative domains; (and in the same
way he also endowed queen Anne, a short time before he
beheaded her.)   But some persons now suspect that this was
all an artifice, to make people conclude that he must have
been a most wicked traitor, and guilty of treason in every
possible way; or else the king would never have executed
one who was so dear to him, as was made manifest by the
presents he had bestowed upon him.   It was from a like
artifice, as some think, that the king conferred upon Crom-

[1 For an account of Cromwell's fall, see Foxe, v. 398, and Soames,
II. 409.]

[2 Walter, lord Hungerford, was accused, among other crimes, of
ordering Sir Hugh Wood, one of his chaplains, and one doctor Maud-
lin, to use conjuring, that they might know how long the king should
live.   See Burnet, I. 580.]

well's son Gregory[3], who was almost a fool, his father's title, and many of his domains, while he was yet living in prison; that he might more readily confess his offences against the king, at the time of execution, and that his majesty might not be provoked to take back the presents and estates that he had bestowed. There are, moreover, other parties who assert, with what truth God knows, that Cromwell was threatened to be burned at the stake, and not to die by the axe, unless at the time of execution he would acknowledge his crimes against the king; and that he then said, "I am altogether a miserable sinner. I have sinned against my good and gracious God, and have offended the king." But what he said respecting the king was carelessly and coldly pronounced by him.

Our sins have doubtless deserved this change in our affairs, because, when God sent forth his word amongst us, it was not regarded by us as the word of God, nor were we sufficiently thankful to its author; but we have been dreaming that it was understood by our own strength and ability, and have constantly ascribed its success to the conduct of some, and the learning of others, while we fancied that God was all the while asleep and inactive. Wherefore the Lord, purposing gradually, but not all at once, to manifest his mercy towards us, as well as his power in the general course of his providence, has taken away, together with purity of doctrine, those individuals also upon whose wisdom we so much depended for support; willing that his providence should herein be shewn forth, by frustrating and destroying our expectations from men, and our boasting that interfered with his glory; and manifesting too his mercy, by permitting these things to be gradually taken away, together with those persons in whom we trusted; and this, that, being so often deceived in our expectations from the creature, we might place all our confidence in him alone, and acknowledge him as the continual agent, as well as the original source, of all grace and goodness. This long-suffering of God, so tempered with instruction, ought to have worked repentance in us, unless we had been a stiff-necked people. But such was the wretchedness of our condition, that we did not consider it was the Lord's teaching: but as soon as he had destroyed the hopes

[3 Gregory Cromwell was summoned to parliament 28th April, 1539, and created, by patent, Baron Cromwell, 18th Dec. 1540. Ob. 1551.]

we had reposed in one individual, we raised up to ourselves
another in whom we placed our confidence; until at last God
has taken them all away from us, and has inflicted upon us
such a want of sincere ministers of the word, that a man may
now travel from the east of England to the west, and from the
north to the south, without being able to discover a single
preacher, who out of a pure heart and faith unfeigned is
seeking the glory of our God. He has taken them all away.
(And here I mean queen Anne, who was beheaded, together
with her brother; also the Lord Cromwell, with Latimer [1] and
the other bishops.) Oh the great wrath and indignation of
God! yea, rather the far greater mass of our sins, by reason
of which the tender severity of God could not but inflict upon
us this punishment! But whither am I wandering? It is as
though a swine should endeavour to instruct Minerva. I will
therefore return to the subject.

At the time when the lord Cromwell was imprisoned, the
king held a public assembly of the nobility, bishops, and certain of the citizens, according to the custom of this country,
and which our people call a parliament; in which were published more than forty-eight new statutes, (and the king intends them to be of perpetual obligation,) of which I here only
mention a few, but not all, of those which concern religion.
The following is the title of one statute, thus set forth by the
king and parliament: A bill [2] for moderating the penalties
inflicted upon priests for incontinence. You have heard, I
know, my honoured master, of the statute that was put forth
among us in the year 1539, against six articles [3] of the christian religion. One clause of it, if you remember, provided that
priests were to put away their wives, upon pain of being condemned as felons, upon the first conviction. But by the same
statute it was allowed priests to commit fornication once or
twice; but if they were detected a third time, they were to

[1 Latimer resigned his bishoprick July 1st, 1539, in consequence
of his opposition to the statute of the Six Articles.]

[2 This bill was brought in on the 16th July, for moderating the
statute of the Six articles in the clauses that related to the marriage of
the priests, or their incontinency with other women. By it the pains
of death were turned to forfeitures of their goods and chattels, and
the rents of their ecclesiastical promotions, to the king. Burnet, I. 453]

[3 These articles are given in Burnet, I. 416; Soames, II. 368;
Foxe, V. 262; Strype, Mem. I. i. 542.]

be hung as they do thieves in this country. Felony has from olden time been punished among us with the gallows, if the thing stolen exceeded the value of six batzen. The king has considered the punishment provided by the statute, namely, that aforesaid, the title of which you have heard, of hanging upon a third conviction, to be too severe, or, as we say, extreme. And it is therefore the king's pleasure for parliament to enact, that priests should for the first offence be punished by fine; then, upon a second conviction, by the loss of one benefice, if the priest should have more than one; and for the third time, by the forfeiture of all their temporal goods, together with all their preferment whatever, and perpetual imprisonment during life. And yet meanwhile it does not appear to the king at all " extreme " still to hang those clergymen who marry, or who retain those wives whom they had married previously to the former statute.

Another bill bears the following title, "An Act to dissolve the king's pretended marriage with the lady Anne of Cleves." I will procure this that you may have it translated into Latin, word for word. And yet, what is pretended shortly after the preamble, that the commonalty of the realm have had many doubts and perplexities respecting that marriage, is altogether false. For not a man would have dared to open his mouth to mention such doubts and perplexities, even if they had existed, which was not the case. What a termination will the godly expect to this bill, which is thus founded upon falsehood! It is false too, what the statute declares, that the nobility and members of parliament petitioned the king to refer the whole matter concerning this marriage to the consideration of his clergy : whereas it is certain, that no nobleman or citizen would have dared to utter a single word about that business, either openly or in secret, until they had perceived that the king's affections were alienated from the lady Anne to that young girl Catharine, the cousin of the duke of Norfolk, whom he married immediately upon Anne's divorce. As to the reply of the archbishop of Canterbury and the other bishops to the king's letter, requiring them to examine and decide upon the case, "that they had found Anne of Cleves was still a maid, and had never been carnally known by the king[4],"

[4 The answer which the council wrote to the English ambassador at Paris was, that the queen herself affirmed that her person had not

this is a likely thing forsooth! Who, judging of the king
by his fruits, would ever believe him to be so chaste a
character? Especially when he was in such a hurry as to
send for her before Christmas, and to have her alone with him
every day in his chamber, and in public, as a queen, during
five or six months. This single pretended fact was, as far as
I can conjecture, that which these five courtiers, the bishops[1],
with their episcopal brethren so gravely considered, and
weighed, and sifted, as you find in their reply above mentioned. Our preachers, in all their sermons, used to pray for
her in these terms, "The most noble queen Anne, the right
lawful wife of our sovereign Henry VIII." &c.

This bill, moreover, gives indemnity to all those persons
who had spoken, or taken any measures, against the king's
marriage with queen Anne. But this was done with a view to
deceive, as though there were any such persons to be pardoned.
Let all England stand forth and produce even a single individual of this stamp, if it can. And those parties who
endeavoured to promote the dissolution of the same marriage,
have no need of a pardon from parliament, since it is most
certain that they would never have made the attempt without
the sanction and approval of the king.

By the authority, too, of the same parliament, the king
has imposed many burdens upon his subjects. For there
was granted him a fifth of all the yearly revenues of the
bishops, and the benefices of the clergy, in addition to the
tenths which he annually receives from them. From the laity,
as well the nobility, as citizens and peasantry, there was
granted him the tenth of all their yearly income, patrimony,
and lands; and from those who have not any patrimony or
yearly revenue, there was granted the king a twentieth of
their monies, goods, cattle, fruit, and all kind of property what-

been touched by king Henry; that a learned convocation had judged
the matter; that the bishops of Durham, Winchester, and Bath, were
known to be great and learned clerks, who would do nothing but upon
just and good grounds; so that all persons ought to be satisfied with
these proceedings, as she herself was; and here the matter ended.
Burnet, III. 223.]

[1 The case was referred by convocation to a committee, consisting
of the two archbishops, the bishops of London, Durham, Winchester,
and Worcester, and six others, doctors of divinity and law. Strype,
Mem. I. i. 558.]

ever. The north of England, however, where the rebellion
took place immediately after the execution of queen Anne,
was now excused these payments by the favour of the king.
Moreover, this business was so artfully managed, that the
archbishop of Canterbury and the other lords spiritual (as
these carnal persons are called) offered the king, of their own
accord, the payment of this money, in the name of all the
clergy, because the king had delivered them from the yoke
and bondage of the Roman pontiff. As though they had
ever been, when subject to the pope, under such a yoke as
they now are; when all their property, and life itself, are at
the king's disposal! In like manner too, the laity made the
king a voluntary grant of this money, which they are bound
by parliament to pay under a heavy penalty. But every
thing is given freely and voluntarily in this country!

In the same parliament, too, the king published a general,
or, so to speak, an universal pardon, by which he forgave the
nobility and others of his subjects all heresies, treasons, felo-
nies, with many other offences against the laws and statutes
of the realm, committed before the first of July, 1540, (with
the exception of such crimes as might fairly be interpreted as
having been committed by word or deed against the royal
person;) and also voluntary homicides, robbing churches, and
many crimes of the like nature. It was however provided
that this act of indemnity was not to extend to the lord
Cromwell; nor to doctor Barnes[2], Thomas Garrard, William
Jerome, three preachers who were then in prison for the
sake of the gospel; nor to the two sons of a certain marquis
(who had been beheaded,) and of the lord Montague[3], the
brother of Pole, an Englishman, a cardinal of Rome. The
name of him [who was beheaded] was marquis of Exeter:
he would have been the heir[4] to the throne, had the king

[2 For a full account of these martyrs, who were burned in Smithfield in July 1540, see Foxe, v. 414—438. Soames, II. 430, &c. See
below, p. 209.]

[3 Dr Lingard observes that our historians are ignorant of the
attainder, and even of the existence of the son of lord Montague. He
is mentioned however in Cardinal Pole's Epistles, II. 197, as well as in
the text. Lingard, IV. 284.]

[4 Henry Courtenay, 17th earl of Devon, and marquis of Exeter,
was son of Catharine, youngest daughter of Edward IV., and con-
sequently first cousin to Henry VIII.]

been without lawful issue. Many other also of the nobility were excepted from this pardon; among whom was the popish bishop of Chichester, and a man of the name of Wilson (who had, on a former occasion, been pardoned by the king, and set at liberty after two years' imprisonment for his support of the pope), together with some other priests, who, as they maintained the supremacy of the pope, would not admit the king's title, wherein he styles himself "supreme head of the church of England." All anabaptists too were excepted, and sacramentaries, as they are called, and all those who do not admit transubstantiation; and those, likewise, who affirm that every kind of death, together with the time and hour of the same, is so certainly appointed, foreordained, and determined, that neither the king can change it by the sword, nor any one prevent it by his own rashness. These are the very words of the statute.

A little before the aforesaid pardon was granted, very many persons, especially the preachers of the gospel, were imprisoned in every part of England; and at London four or five of the principal of them. They made search too after Doctor Crome[1], a man of great gravity and wisdom, (who, together with Latimer, was the first who in our times sowed the pure doctrine of the gospel;) he, when he heard from a certain *Nicodemean* individual that he was denounced, went privately to the palace, and falling on his knees before the king, (after he had first informed him of the cruel treatment of some preachers and citizens at London,) prayed him for God's sake to put a stop to these severities, and of his wisdom and godliness to apply a remedy. The king forthwith gave order, that no further persecution should take place on account of religion, and that those who were then in prison should be set at liberty, upon their friends giving security for their appearance whenever they should be called for. The king, probably, as you have heard, was partly induced to grant this indulgence, in the hope that when these things were once set at rest, and the old errors (as he considered them) forgiven, the people would be more quiet and obedient in future. I am aware, nevertheless, that it is usual for his clemency to bestow pardon upon his subjects in

[1 A full account of Dr Crome is given in Strype, Mem. III. i. 157. Burnet, III. 223.]

this way (some particular crimes, as in the present case, always excepted), after they had allowed him by their liberality (as they have now done) to scrape together a large sum of money ; or when, by authority of parliament, they have entirely released him from the payment of every penny that he had borrowed from them.

Soon after the dissolution of parliament, namely, on the thirtieth of July last year, were executed six of those men who had been excepted from the general pardon. Three of them were popish priests, whose names were Abel, Powell, and Fetherston[2], and who refused to acknowledge the king's new title, and his authority over the clergy. They were dealt with in the usual manner, first hung, then cut down from the gallows while yet alive, then drawn, beheaded, and quartered, and their limbs fixed over the gates of the city ; but the heads, in general, of as many priests or monks as are executed in this city, are fixed on the top of a long pole, and placed upon London bridge, as a terror to others. The remaining three were preachers of the gospel, and of no mean order ; their names were Barnes[3], Gerrard, and Jerome. They were first brought from the Tower of London, and drawn on a sledge through the middle of the city to a place called Smithfield, where they were tied to one stake, and burned at the same place where the others were executed. This place had never been used before, as far as I remember, for the execution of any persons excepting heretics. They remained in the fire without crying out, but were as quiet and patient as though they had felt no pain; and thus they commended their spirits to God the Father by Jesus Christ. I could never ascertain, though I have made diligent inquiry, the true reason why these three gospellers were excepted from the general pardon ; so that I can conjecture none more

[2 For an account of these persons, see Foxe, v. 438. Burnet, I. 477. Soames says that "Powell and Abel were two political pamphleteers, on the queen's side, during the ferment occasioned by Catharine of Aragon's case, who, together with another Romish partizan, named Featherstone, were notorious for their opposition to the royal supremacy." Hist. Ref. II. 439.]

[3 Dr Robert Barnes had been prior of the Austin friars at Cambridge ; Thomas Gerrard (or Garrett) was curate of All-Hallows, in Honey-lane ; and William Jerome was vicar of Stepney. See the authorities quoted above, p. 207, n. 2.]

likely, than that the king, desiring to gratify the clergy and the ignorant and rude mob, together with the obstinate part of his nobility and citizens, appointed these three victims, as he probably considered them, as it were for a holocaust, to appease those parties, or to acquire fresh popularity with them.   I think however, that they would not have had more than one, or at most two of them in the same year, only that the clergy and the greater part of the nobility and commonalty might pay more readily the money granted to his majesty by parliament.   If any one should assert that these three persons were burned on account of their preaching and doctrine, it then appears strange that they were not brought before the judges, and condemned by due course of law, as had always been the practice in such cases before this instance.   Then again, in my opinion, the parliament did not deal justly, if it condemned them for their doctrine.   For I know this for a fact, that from the twelfth of July, 1539, (on which day the bill[1] by which the truth was condemned began to take effect,) until the day when they were apprehended, they never once opened their mouths expressly against that statute, either in their public preaching or private conversation, except when they found that they were with honest and godly men, and sufficiently safe from their enemies.   They were committed to prison in Easter-week of the following year, 1540, even after they had in many things submitted to the king in their sermons at Easter[2].   Thus we see that neither the king nor his parliament could justly condemn them to death for their doctrine, unless they chose to assert that all those opinions, which in the statute aforesaid they condemned as heresy, were not pardoned before that appointed day, the twelfth of July.   And if this were the case, it was then only an artifice and a snare to entangle men, thus to fix and appoint a stated day when the act was to begin to take effect.   I am here more brief, by

[1 Namely, the Act of the Six Articles.]

[2 By certain complaints made to the king of them they were enjoined to preach three sermons the next Easter following, at the Spital; at which sermons, besides other reporters who were thither sent, Stephen Gardiner also was there present, sitting with the mayor, either to bear record of their recantation, or else, as the Pharisees came to Christ, to trip them in their talk, if they had spoken any thing awry. Foxe, v. 420.]

reason of a little book printed in German, concerning the protest of the said Robert Barnes at the stake, where he acknowledged that he did not know for what reason he was brought thither to be burned.   In the week following the burning of these preachers, were executed many others of those who had been excepted from the general pardon.   The reason of their execution is unknown to me ; but it was reported to have been for treason against the king.   However, to confess the truth, people were not so active in inquiry, or in investigating matters, as they were wont to have been, because it is now no novelty among us to see men slain, hung, quartered, or beheaded ; some for trifling expressions, which were explained or interpreted as having been spoken against the king ; others for the pope's supremacy ; some for one thing, and some for another.   The bishop of Chichester, however, and doctor Wilson, such a papist as Eckius[3], were set at large by the king, notwithstanding they had been exempted out of the general pardon.   The crime of treason, as I hear, which they had committed against the king, was the sending some alms to the papist Abel[4], when reduced to the greatest distress from having been long kept in a most filthy prison, and, as the papists here affirm, almost eaten up by vermin.

And now I am about to say somewhat of that learned and godly man, doctor Crome.   At this time (as had always been his practice, whenever any storm arose that seemed to do injury to the truth) feeling the necessity of the case, he preached with more zeal than ordinary, until the approach of Christmas.   And on that day those who were his enemies on account of the gospel, brought together against him some articles which they alleged to be heretical.   Meanwhile the clergy set up their champion Wilson, to oppose the purer doctrine of Crome, and to affirm the falsehood of whatever truths he had preached.   This those wise children of this world did with the greater readiness, that they might have a better handle for accusing Crome (as though it was through his preaching that such a controversy had arisen in the city

[3 John Eckius was professor in the university of Ingoldstadt, where he died in 1543.   He is memorable for his opposition to the reformation, and his controversial writings against Luther, Melancthon, &c.]

[4 See above, p. 209, n. 2.]

of London), and so for bringing him forth to answer for himself either before the king or his council. Which object they effected after a few days. For after Christmas-day they were both of them forbidden to preach, until either the king or his councillors should hear the case and determine it according to their pleasure. After Christmas-day, 1540, (for our people begin to reckon the new year from the feast of the annunciation of Mary), a day having been appointed for the appearance of both parties, namely, Crome and Wilson, the enemies of Crome produced against him, as impious and heretical, nearly thirty passages from his late sermons; the sum of which, as far as I am able to judge, is as follows:

"No works can justify in the same manner as Christ does, nor do they so satisfy as he satisfied by suffering for us. For he is the only oblation, and price of redemption, &c.

"No truth is necessary to be believed or obeyed by us under the penalty of sin or eternal death, unless it be somewhere expressly revealed to us in the holy scriptures, or can truly, piously, and justly be collected and deduced from them.

"To offer masses for the dead is plainly contrary to holy scripture, and is a superstition. And it was first," he says, "introduced into the church by means of a vision, yea, rather a delusion of Satan, in the time of pope Gregory."

"The king himself confesses, with his bishops, in his Institution[1] of a Christian Man, that the masses *scalæ cœli*, ordained by the pope, are altogether unprofitable to the dead. But this is the principal kind of mass for the departed, by reason of the prayers, &c. Wherefore, if these masses profit not, much less do others. Again, if the mass were profitable to the dead, the king and parliament have done wrong in destroying the monasteries, where so many masses were endowed and celebrated for the dead.

[1 The passage referred to is this: "Wherefore it is much necessary that such abuses be clearly put away, which under the name of purgatory hath been advanced; as to make men believe that through the bishop of Rome's pardons souls might clearly be delivered out of purgatory, and all the pains of it; or the masses said at Scala Cœli, or other where, in any place, or before any image, might likewise deliver them from all their pain, and send them straight to heaven; and other like abuses." The Institution of a Christian Man. Lond. 1537. Ed. Oxford, 1825, p. 211.]

" Those who teach men to pray to the saints, if only that they may pray for us in the same way as here we pray for each other, inculcate a practice neither necessary nor useful.

" The church of Christ is the spouse of Christ. But she must certainly be an imperious and pert wife, who should speak and exercise authority above her husband. You call us seditious preachers, and say that we introduce new doctrine; but you speak falsely. For you are the seditious parties, who defend superstition and human traditions, and refuse to obey with us the word of God, and to listen to the voice of Christ.

" Men wonder that we preachers cannot agree together. But this is not to be wondered at. For they teach the commandments of men ; we, on the contrary, those of God alone. And yet, if they would give over preaching their dreams, falsehoods, human traditions, and puerilities, and would preach, as we do, the word of God only, we should forthwith come to an agreement.

" The church of Christ is suffering, and ever will suffer, persecution, as some parties have suffered of late among ourselves. And though the world tried to persuade them, it was by no means able to overcome them.   Neither, I hope, shall you conquer us, notwithstanding your persecution of us. For you would be able to say that you had conquered us, if you could prevail with us to speak as you do. But we should then be liars like yourselves, and chaplains of the devil, as you are."

When the king and his council had received these and other like articles, of which Crome was accused, they allowed him a certain time wherein to answer them. Which when he had done, (as appears from the royal injunction which he was ordered to recite to the people,) his reply was beyond doubt a manifest confirmation of the articles alleged against him ; for he persisted in affirming that they were true and orthodox. The king, however, whether from a secret horror, or fear of the people, (or from the working of God, in I know not what other manner,) were he to condemn to death so eminent a man, who was, as it were, a father in religion, would not deliver him to the flames to be sacrificed as a burnt-offering, like Barnes and the others; but sent him a certain paper, with which he was to comply in all respects, as you shall now hear; for the following is a copy of it:

"The judgment of the king respecting Dr Crome,
on the 18th January, in the year of our Lord 1540.
The king's majesty, having received the answer of Edward
Crome, doctor in divinity, to certain articles about which he
was examined by chosen commissioners appointed by his majesty on that behalf; the king's excellency, too, being advised
that the said doctor Crome was so manifestly persuaded in
his heart, as he confessed in his answer subscribed with his
own hand, and laid before his majesty; the king, out of
his most godly benignity, and accustomed goodness and mercy,
is content for this time to relax the rigour and severity of the
laws which his majesty might justly execute against the said
Crome.   Moreover, his royal majesty, being desirous of
establishing a christian peaceableness and tranquillity among
his subjects, by an uniform agreement in the office of preaching, has determined as follows, &c."

The king then enjoined Dr Crome to preach on a certain
day in Lent, at London, in St Paul's church-yard, (namely,
that of our principal church,) and there recant all the preceding articles.   Then at the end of this royal document there
was added the following, which Crome was to repeat, after
he had read his recantation: "Moreover, his majesty makes
this known to all his subjects, that if the said Crome shall
hereafter be accused of these or the like articles, the severity of the law shall be executed upon him without any
favour."   Against Crome's assertion, that masses did not benefit the dead, it was objected at the trial, that he had preached in that article expressly against the royal statutes, which
enacted that private masses had been properly retained in the
church of England, by reason of the many advantages that
Christians receive from them.   But the statute does not specify
those advantages; so that Crome answered, that he understood them to be, the commemoration of the death of Christ
by the ceremonies of the mass, and also prayers for the living;
especially as the king had abolished so many monasteries.
This evasion did not avail him, for the king enjoined him in
his instructions to read his recantation of that article in these
terms: "Public and private masses are a profitable sacrifice
as well for the living as for the dead.   And although masses
and other prayers and helps profit the departed, yet the king's
majesty and the parliament have piously and justly abolished

the monasteries in his realm." For what reason, it was not added.

You have here the sum of the king's judgment respecting Dr Crome in this matter. Now when the Sunday came, on which he was to recant, he preached a godly discourse, and at the end of it told the people, that he had received a written document from the king's majesty which he was ordered to read to them. And after he had read it, he committed the congregation to God in a short prayer, and so went away : whereas the king certainly intended him to receive that writing as a specimen of the doctrine which he was to follow in his sermon; and also to extol to the skies his wisdom, learning, and mercy, as doctor Barnes and the two others had done, when they preached at Easter, and yet were burned notwithstanding. It certainly was not the king's intention that Crome should read his judgment so carelessly, and then go away as he did : wherefore I am afraid that the clergy will not let him off thus. For immediately after he was forbidden by the king to preach any more, as he had before forbidden Latimer, bishop of Worcester, and Shaxton, bishop of Salisbury ; who by the providence of God, as I think, (and as also is evident from their having been so long preserved by him in this dangerous world,) were delivered from death by the general pardon. Those two bishops were a long time under restraint, because they would never give their sanction to the statute published against the truth in the year 1539, as the other Ecebolian bishops did at once. But how favourable to them the king now is, and how much he appreciates their sound and pure doctrine, is evident even from this, that he has not only prohibited them from preaching, but also from coming within two or three German miles of our two universities, the city of London, or their own dioceses! O atrocious deed, thus to drive away faithful shepherds from their flocks, and intrude ravenous wolves in their stead! God will not, I hope, allow this tyranny much longer. Meanwhile, you perceive how much iniquity abounds among us, and therefore that in many respects charity is growing cold. Farewell in the Lord! May our good and gracious God long preserve you in safety to us, and for the edification and comfort of his church! Amen, Amen.

LETTER CVI.

RICHARD HILLES TO HENRY BULLINGER.

Dated at FRANKFORT, *Sept.* 18, 1541.

GRACE and perseverance in the truth from the Lord, &c. I received, my revered master, three days since, your pious and consolatory letter, dated on the 31st of August; on account of which I consider myself exceedingly indebted to your kindness, for having so condescended to correspond with me, a worm, and not a man, (as the world accounts me,) and also so frequently and in such comforting terms.

Falckner wrote to me for the black and red cloth, which I send you by Conrad Eblie, that it may be for you to fix and determine whether Falckner shall have it upon credit. For he owes me already about a hundred florins, to be paid here at Frankfort at the next fair, besides forty-five which (as he writes me word) Christopher Froschover ought now to pay me, but which I doubt whether I shall ever receive : for he says in reply, that he is willing to pay these same forty-five florins for Falckner, should he have a good sale at the fair, but not otherwise. The black cloth contains fifty-five Frankfort ells; the red fifty and a half. The black cloth is tolerably good and strong, but I had sold all my bêst before Falckner's letter was delivered to me. I inquired after it of the above-named Christopher at the beginning of the fair; but he denied that he had any letters for me, because he hardly knew who I was. I met him afterwards, and he found Falckner's letter for me. The price of forty ells of that cloth is twenty-two florins. I have sent you also another piece, of a better sort, which I have left at this fair, and which contains forty-five ells. Should it seem adviseable to you, I wish Falckner to have this, in case he declines the black. But this cloth bears a higher price, namely, twenty-eight florins for forty ells, reckoning sixteen batzen to a florin. Falckner knows that we are accustomed to receive this value for every florin. I pray you to dispose of whatever cloth he may leave to some one else, and lay out the amount this year for the benefit of the poor, (if you have among you any who are exiles for the gospel's sake). If you decline doing this, by reason of not having among you exiles of this description, (and I admit no other claim,) I then wish you to make over the same sum to master Calvin for the same object. I am thinking moreover of sending you, by the Conrad above-mentioned, a fifth piece of cloth, of another colour, which a great number of my country-men are accustomed to wear. I have much pleasure in making you a present of this, as being the stoutest. If you decline accepting it (which I hope you will not), you shall pay the money for it when I come. The price is thirty-two florins. Both here and at Strasburgh I am beginning to sell some cloth of the same colour, which has hitherto been very little in use.

I cannot, by reason of my engagements, write this letter over again, either in a better or a larger hand. For I am here alone. At Strasburgh likewise I have no domestics, except one female servant. I have left them all but one in England; for I have still an establishment in that country, such as it is. I only brought one servant with me from England, who at that time appeared to every one to be most zealous; and certainly, as long as he lived with me there, he was truly pious: but after he had seen the simpli-city of the religious worship in this country, and especially not having his friends with him, and abundance of provisions and meat in the larder, as with us, he seemed to me very much to wish to return home. When I discovered this, I discharged him, after having given him a letter, by which he might obtain a situation with another master in the same line of business. I previously, however, set before him, as well as I was able, the wickedness of falling away from the truth on any ground of superstition. He left me notwithstanding; but I hope that he still continues to savour of Christ in some measure. He is now living with a certain merchant, who in the time of liberty, three years since, professed the gospel among us after his way. But what indeed am I saying? I scarcely know any one (with the exception of learned teachers,) who had a greater knowledge of religion than our friend Peterson. My late servant requests you to send his letters to Clare: I have inclosed them in my own letter, which in addition to this I have already sent you by Froschover. After he returned home from Strasburgh, from which place he fled with the greatest danger, he could not be compelled by the severest threatenings of his master; but said that things were optional, and indifferent, and I know not what.

By what means or by what persons he has been thus infatuated, I know not; but this I know, that before my departure he voluntarily attended masses for the departed, and now does so on every feast-day through almost the whole autumn, as is the custom here.   His wife indeed had a tolerable fortune; he had with her, as I think, above three or four hundred golden angels of our money.

My wife requests you to be kind enough to ask Falckner to send hither to Strasburgh, as soon as possible, a hundred, or at the least eighty pounds of the best butter.   If he cannot contrive to send so large a vessel to my house, I wish him to send it to my friend, John Burcher, (who lodges either with master Myconius or master Isengrinius,) that he may send it to Basle for me, and I will pay whatever expense he may have incurred.   I gave Christopher Froschover for you an English cheese with this mark +, wrapped in a linen cloth. My wife wished me to send one of the same kind to you and your wife, that you might make trial of our cheese as we do of your butter.   But I would not have you return any thanks for this.   I would not indeed on any account that you should trouble yourself to write your thanks for things of such little value as the trifling presents of my wife.   I will diligently salute brother B. in your name.   I do not understand the other matter about which you wrote.   I shall therefore say nothing about it, lest I should still more cast down the mind of him who is sufficiently cast down already.   Should he happen to be summoned and sent for home, and should refuse to come, he will lose all that he now has.   He is now anxious upon this subject, but more especially because, if that event should take place, it is not likely that he will obtain the lady[1] he wishes to marry; one who is truly pious, but, as I hear, from some constant disorder unsuited to the married state.   Farewell.

Yours,

RICHARD HILLES.

P.S. I am not a citizen of Strasburgh, for fear of losing the privileges I already enjoy in England and Brabant.   The senate of Strasburgh is very well disposed towards me.   I pay them ten florins every year.   I have not taken any oath.

It has happened, honoured sir, that before this my letter

[1 See above, Lett. CIV. p. 197.]

was sealed, Christopher Froschover has paid me the forty-five florins owing to me by Falckner, and which were to be paid at this fair.   He offered also to be answerable for whatever cloth I might choose to send to the aforesaid Falckner : so that there is no occasion for you to keep by you the cloth which I have above stated I would send you by Conrad Eblie; excepting only that black cloth at twenty-eight florins, together with those eight ells of yours, at thirty-two florins, as I above stated.   I request you also to be kind enough to tell Falckner, that it has just come into my mind how often he used to speak to me about the yellow cloth; and that I have therefore sent him thirty-one ells by the aforesaid Conrad, together with thirty-one ells and a half of white cloth, and twenty ells of green.   The price of these is the same as that of the two entire pieces above-mentioned, namely, twenty-two florins for forty Frankfort ells.   I request you, in case he should refuse any of these pieces of cloth, kindly to take them under your care, till I send you word by letter to whom you may deliver them; unless you should happen to know any friend of yours who will take them at the same price, and send me the amount without fail by master Christopher Froschover, at the next Frankfort fair.   For he has given me a bill in Falckner's name for one hundred and three florins and six batzen, which is the exact price of the two entire pieces, with these last half pieces that I mentioned above.   All these cloths, of which I have made mention in this letter, with the exception of your eight ells (which I have not cut from the same cloth that Conrad Eblie bought of me, lest you should perhaps wish to have another ell), are stamped upon their leaden seal with this my mark in the margin (×).

You will receive, together with this letter, the opinion of our friend Capito on original sin.   I have no news from England this fair, except that the king has not yet returned to London from the northern parts of the kingdom; whither he proceeded with one thousand soldiers, after a new fashion, and a great number of tents, after the French fashion, to reduce a rebellious and very superstitious people.   About twenty persons (of whom about twelve had formerly been monks) had endeavoured, five[2] months since, secretly to raise

[2 The northern countries broke out in open rebellion in April, 1541.   Sir John Neville was their leader, but, with several of his accomplices, perished by the hand of the executioner. Soames, ii. 475.]

a new disturbance in those parts : they were beheaded, hung, and drawn, after our custom, the June following, at London and York, which are the two principal cities in the kingdom. The king, before his setting out, beheaded also the mother[1] of our countryman the cardinal, with two[2] others of our oldest nobility. I do not hear that any of the royal race are left, except the nephew of the cardinal[3], and another boy[4], the son of the marquis of Exeter. They are both children, and in prison, and condemned, I know not why, except that it is said that their fathers had sent letters to Rome to the pope, and to their kinsman, the cardinal. The king's son by the third wife is still alive, but I do not speak about him. There is also living a natural son of king Edward, whose daughter Henry VII., the father of our present king, married after the death of Richard the second [third]. But shortly before I left England he was sent from Calais (where he had formerly been the king's lieutenant, and, as you know, too near upon France,) to the Tower of London, the receptacle for such persons, where he was imprisoned by parliament at the same time as lord Cromwell was condemned, and still remains there waiting for the king's pardon. This illegitimate old man, when at Calais, was a most grievous persecutor of the gospel. (Edward left two sons, heirs of his kingdom, under the protection of the aforesaid Richard, their uncle. This Richard privately put to death these two amiable youths, his nephews, and for nearly

[1 Margaret, countess of Salisbury, the mother of Cardinal Pole, had been kept in close confinement in the Tower since 1539, on suspicion of having carried on a secret correspondence with her son, by means of the rector of Warblington, a parish on the Hampshire coast, within a few miles of her seat at Cowdray, in Sussex. She was beheaded on the green within the Tower, on May 27, 1541, on the rising of the new disturbances in Yorkshire. See Soames, ii. 359, 475.]

[2 One of these was lord Leonard Gray, deputy of Ireland, who was beheaded for suffering his nephew, proclaimed an enemy to the state, to make his escape. The other was Thomas Fynes, lord Dacre of the south, for having murdered a poor man who resisted him in an attempt to steal deer. He was hanged on the 25th of June. Soames, ii. 477.]

[3 Cardinal Pole was a younger son of sir Richard Pole, earl Montague, and had several brothers.]

[4 This was Edward Courtenay, who was restored in blood and honours by parliament, Oct. 10, 1553. He died in 1556, s. p., when all his honours became extinct.]

three years held forcible possession of the kingdom.) 'Another of the chief nobility, a most cruel tyrant, not long after, fell from his horse, who was galloping of his own accord; but he never afterwards spoke a word, for he miserably broke his neck.   This was the earl of Essex[5], whose property and lands, with his great manors and riches, Cromwell immediately obtained, but not for any length of time, as I know you have heard before now, if you have received the former letter sent by Froschover[6].

Strasburgh, Sept. 25.   The king has appointed Thomas, archbishop of Canterbury, and the chancellor of the kingdom, (both of whom are now considered as our friends,) to be his deputies in the south of England.   But immediately on the king's departure they burnt at the stake in London, for fear, (as our English gospellers think,) a young man[7] eighteen years of age, on account of his entertaining the Lutheran opinion touching the eucharist.   He did not altogether deny a corporal presence, but asserted, as our Wycliffe[8] did, that the accident of bread did not remain there without the substance.   Again farewell.   The son of that great light of the world, master Zuinglius, is dead here, or rather has fallen asleep; as have also many others, of whom there were the greatest hopes, in the college of Strasburgh.   Once more farewell, and live happily in the fear of the Lord!

[5 Henry Bourchier, earl of Essex, was killed by a fall from his horse in 1539.   Thomas Cromwell was raised to the earldom 17th of April of the same year, and obtained all the property that fell to the crown on the decease of his predecessor, but was beheaded and attainted the year following.   See Soames, II. 402.   Burnet, III. 216.]

[6 See the preceding letter, p. 217.]

[7 This was Richard Mekins, a boy according to all accounts not above fifteen years of age, and both illiterate and very ignorant, who had said somewhat against the corporal presence of Christ's body in the sacrament, and in commendation of Dr Barnes.   See Burnet, I. 481.   Foxe, v. 441.]

[8 "Of all the heresies that have ever grown up in the holy church of God, none is more abominable than that which makes this venerable sacrament an accident without a subject."   Wycliffe's Trialogus, B. IV.]

LETTER CVII.

RICHARD HILLES TO HENRY BULLINGER.

Dated at STRASBURGH, *Nov.* 23, 1541.

THE consolation of the Holy Ghost in your studies, attended as they sometimes are with so much anxiety !

I received, most learned sir, your very gratifying letter on the twentieth of November. For your loving me as a brother (as I have frequently perceived to be the case from your former letters) I return you my warmest thanks. I now repent of having sent Falckner the cloth, because he is annoyed at my having sent him so much. I should not have sent him the black unclipped cloth, of which he complains, had not his letter been delivered to me so late at Frankfort. Nevertheless, I cannot let him have that cloth for eighteen florins; for it cost me more than twenty florins in England. Still, however, as it is now yonder, and especially as the texture is so thick, and the wool coarse, I will be content with twenty florins, if he chooses to keep it. If he does not like to do so, I pray you to receive back the cloth from him, and keep it by you until I write you word about it after next fair, or sooner. For I may probably think fit, if Falckner should decline it, to devote it to another purpose. I did not reckon the fine cloth at more than twenty-eight florins. I sold Falckner some of the same quality, and at the same price, at the last Strasburgh fair. And yet I hardly know what to say about that cloth, as your merchants think it so dear, except that you advise master Falckner to return it to me next Lent, by some carrier of his acquaintance, who will pass through this place on his way to Frankfort. For I have no doubt but that I can sell it here at the same, or perhaps a greater price. If Falckner sends back the cloth, he will very much oblige me by sending at the same time three reams of the best paper that is manufactered by master Froschover. A ream contains twenty quires, and is called in German *ein Riecks.* I am greatly in want of paper of that sort. I have written this letter on a sheet of such paper as I require; but should he have any of a better quality, I wish he would send one or two

reams more, for Miles Coverdale, and the other English
who are here. I will pay Froschover or Falckner for this
paper, God willing, at the next fair. I request, moreover,
master Froschover to pay you yonder on my account fifteen
florins and twelve batzen for half the entire piece of fine
black cloth, intended for the use you know of, (if Falckner
will forward it to me here,) and I will faithfully repay the
amount to Froschover at Frankfort. I am satisfied with
your proposal respecting the other half pieces of cloth,
namely, that Falckner may retain them, on condition that,
if he is able to dispose of them, he shall pay me the money
at the next fair; if not, he is to deliver them afterwards to
some one at Frankfort, whom I will point out to him.

I have sent some maxims to your excellency, not that you
may write back your opinion respecting them, for I cannot
desire such an interruption to your studies on my account; but
I shall be greatly obliged to you, if, when I come, you will
condescend to tell me what you think about them. Salute,
I pray you, my dear brother Falckner, and thank him in
my name for the butter, which has been of great use to my
family this winter. Request him too to remember the paper
above-mentioned. He wishes me to let him know whether
I have yet received your letter from the Frenchman, Von
Homberg. In my last letter, if you remember, I informed
your excellency of my having received it. I purpose sending you by the bearer a quart of fenugreek[1], if he does not
refuse to take it with him. My wife salutes yours, and do
you also salute her in my name. May the God of all might
preserve you from the baneful pestilence, and protect you
under his wing, that his kingdom may be more widely extended by you on earth, and your reward be so much
greater in heaven! Amen.

Yours in the Lord,

RICHARD HILLES.

P. S. I have sent the fenugreek to Basle, to John
Burcher, an Englishman, who lodges at the house of master
Myconius or Isengrinius.

[1 Fenugreek was considered to possess many medicinal qualities:
a decoction of it was recommended for diseases of the chest. John-
son's Gerarde's Herbal, Lond. 1636, p. 1197.]

LETTER CVIII.

RICHARD HILLES TO HENRY BULLINGER.

Dated at STRASBURGH, *May* 10, 1542.

HEALTH and perseverance in the truth of Christ! After I returned home safe from Venice, I received your letter written on the 31st of March, and was affected on the perusal of it with no small delight, that you were engaged about a work so pious and so useful to the church, as to have it in contemplation to publish some books of commentaries upon Matthew. May our great and good God prosper your intention, and give it a happy issue!

Nothing has yet been done with H. Falckner at Frankfort respecting the fine cloth, and there is no reason why he should expect that I either will or can abate him a single batz. If, however, there should be left any of the same quality, I am content that he should send it me here to our fair; and I shall be as willing to receive the remainder of the cloth as the money itself; for I am well aware what kind of cloth it was. I scarcely charged eleven batzen and a kreutzer for a Frankfort ell. And if I had the same cloth here, I could soon sell it by the piece at twelve batzen for a Strasburgh ell. I entreat you, my master, that we no longer defer the appropriation of that money, which I have destined out of the produce of this same cloth for the use of the poor exiles, namely, half the price of the same, or, if you choose, the whole of it. For I have already given master Calvin some money for the like purpose, although I mentioned not a word to him about you or that cloth, and never intend to do. Distribute therefore, what I have desired of my own free-will to be applied to the poor by your instrumentality; whether you choose to retain either the price of half the cloth, or, if need so require, of the whole. For the more I devote to them through you, so much the less do I leave to be applied to the like object by myself. Whatever I do in this matter, I do it voluntarily and cheerfully, and without a murmur. I therefore pray you, that, whether you determine to retain half the sum, if you prefer it, or the whole sum, as I prefer myself, you will let me know by letter at our next fair.   For I desire that, immediately on the receipt of this letter, you receive from H. Falckner thirty-one florins and a half (reckoning sixteen batzen to a florin) on account of that cloth ; so that when Falckner shall come, there may be no occasion for any farther reckoning between him and me respecting it.   Should he object, that he does not choose to purchase the cloth at that price, I pray you in that case to receive from him what is left, and sell it there, if you can, to your friends, or (which I would prefer for fear of interrupting your studies) take care that it may be forwarded by some merchant to me here, and I will in return faithfully send you the amount in money to Zurich.

I am glad that you have commended to me by letter Peter Hurtzel, and especially Andrew Rappenstein ; and if my wife had known as much at the last fair, she would not have required C. Froschover to be surety for them.   I beg however that they will not be offended at what my wife did in this business ; for she had never seen them before, nor, as I remember, had ever heard them commended by me as they deserve.   Those two honest men dealt honourably with me at Frankfort at the preceding fair ; for they owed me at that time about one hundred and thirty-three florins, all of which, save three, they sent me by master Conrad Eblie.   But Henry did not act by me with so much good faith : for he owed me at the last fair (besides the fine cloth above-mentioned) near two hundred florins ; out of which[1] ...... he has only paid forty-six florins and fourteen batzen for a friend of mine at Basle ; and these he paid so long after they were due, that my friend was obliged to send his servant from Strasburgh to Basle, during Lent, with twenty out of those forty-six florins, because Falckner, even in so small a matter, had not performed what he had promised.

My brother Butler, as I hear by letter, sold his whole patrimony in England last Lent ; but he had not then received the whole amount.   And I am in fear for him, lest, when what he has done shall have come to the king's ears by means of his sister's husband, who belongs to the court, he may be forbidden again to leave the kingdom.   Elliot is studying the civil law or, to speak more properly, the laws

[1 A word is here unintelligible in the MS.]

of our realm, in which he has made such proficiency, that he is now holding an office, from whence he derives an annual income of nearly two hundred florins. But Bartholomew Traheron has, with much difficulty, retired from court into the country, where he is about to marry tho daughter of a gentleman who favours godly doctrine; and with this young lady he will have a yearly income, as I hear, of one hundred and twenty florins, for sixty years, out of some estate which is leased to him for that time by his father-in-law for a certain sum. He intends, moreover, to teach grammar, and to keep a school for little boys, in some small town in that district.

Respecting the state of the kingdom at large I have nothing certain to communicate, except what I imagine you must have heard these three months, namely, that the king has beheaded his wife, Catherine Howard, whom he married immediately after his divorce from Anne of Cleves. This Catherine was condemned upon a great suspicion of adultery (as is universally reported by the English) with two gentlemen, who had also intercourse with her before the king married her. The lady Rochford too, tho widow of that nobleman who was capitally punished, as you know, for incest with his sister, queen Anne, was beheaded at the same time. This widow, as they say, was privy to the licentiousness of that Catherine who was lately beheaded: for she used often to sleep with the queen; and when she knew her once to have been a long time absent from her bed-chamber in a private place, at the same time, as they say, that one of those gentlemen who were beheaded was there, she nevertheless refrained from mentioning the circumstance to the king.

The old duchess dowager of Norfolk is also condemned to perpetual imprisonment in the Tower of London, and likewise lord William Howard, a brother of the duke of Norfolk, because they were cognizant of the vicious life of queen Catherine, when the king first fell in love with her, and did not acquaint him with it before that hasty marriage had taken place. One of the parties[1], who was first hanged, and afterwards beheaded and quartered, for adultery with the queen, was one of the king's chamberlains; and two years

[1 This, probably, was Culpepper, who was a gentleman of the privy chamber. See Holinshed, III. 823. Ed. 1808.]

before, or less, had violated the wife of a certain park-keeper in a woody thicket, while, horrid to relate! three or four of his most profligate attendants were holding her at his bidding.   For this act of wickedness he was, notwithstanding, pardoned by the king, after he had been delivered into custody by the villagers on account of this crime, and likewise a murder which he had committed in his resistance to them, when they first endeavoured to apprehend him.   God, who is just, will not always suffer wickedness, either here or elsewhere, to go unpunished.

You cannot, without danger to my affairs, write me anything concerning the christian religion: besides, if you could, I am not worthy of such honour.   I have therefore to return many thanks to your benevolence for your favourable inclination towards me; and I pray you to confer this honour upon some one else, who may be worthy of it.   I received your cheese before sealing this letter, and I am very sorry that you have spent so much money on my account; and most of all, that you are ill of a fever.   But all the works of the Lord are just judgments, who chastiseth those whom he loveth, and scourgeth every son whom he receiveth.   I pray you to accept, as a present from me, those eight ells of cloth, and not to send the money; for I heartily wish you to keep it, and to make use of the cloth, if you please, as a token, such as it is, that I love you in the Lord, and have a real affection for you.   After having read over again this barbarous letter of mine, I was so ashamed of it, that I was almost determined to tear it, and not to write to you at all; and I certainly should have done so, had you not invited me to write to you upon the state of all our affairs.

And now, my most esteemed master, farewell in Christ: for in future I have no intention of writing to you again, except, perhaps, by some amanuensis when necessity obliges me.   My wife salutes you, and your most amiable lady. Deign also to salute your wife in my name.   Once more, farewell in God, who is our portion in the land of the living, and our hope in eternity!   Amen.

Yours, you know who,

RICHARD HILLES.

15—2

LETTER CIX.

RICHARD HILLES TO HENRY BULLINGER.

Dated at STRASBURGH, *Dec.* 18, 1542.

I RECEIVED your books, most esteemed master, together with the letter; and I feel more gratitude for them in my heart than I can express with my pen. And yet, had I known that you were about to present me with those books, I should certainly have bought a copy for myself at Frankfort, and not have said a word to you about them. For why should I lay an additional burden upon your kindness, after the great expense you have already incurred there on my account? I wish, sir, I had consulted you sooner about reading authors and studying histories. For first I read Bernard Justiniani[1] on the affairs of the Venetians, the Tripartite History[2], and the Ecclesiastical History of Eusebius, together with his Evangelical Preparation, and Demonstration. I do not so much regret having read them, only that I now perceive from your letter, that I could have employed the time I spent in perusing them to better purpose.

The Demonstration of Eusebius was rather wearisome to me, because the holy scriptures are every where explained so absurdly, if I may use such an expression, especially with respect to the WORD[3], and against the Jews[4]. He seems,

[1 Bernard Justiniani or Giustiani was nephew of the patriarch of Venice of that name. He went many times to Rome as ambassador from the republic, and died in 1489, leaving several works, the principal of which is, a History of Venice, printed in 1492.]

[2 The Tripartite History is a compilation by Cassiodorus from the Latin translations of the ecclesiastical histories of Socrates, Sozomen, and Theodoret.]

[3 Hilles probably refers to the third chapter of the fourth book of the Evangelical Demonstration of Eusebius, in which he discusses the nature of Christ, the *Logos;* which, he says, God produced from himself, as the sun produces his light, or the flower its scent, &c. The passage is too long to quote.]

[4 The object of the second book of the Evangelical Demonstration is to prove the vocation of the gentiles, and the rejection of the unbelieving Jews.]

moreover, to entertain wrong notions about free-will[5], the marriage of the clergy[6], and the fifth chapter of Matthew. I found some things, however, in that work which pleased me exceedingly; for instance, his opinion respecting the new testament, and about Daniel's seventy weeks[7]. I ran through these books before I came to Zurich; and also Tertullian, whom I found to be such as you had commended him to me. I was not so much displeased with the difficulty of his style, as I was delighted and profited by his remarkable piety, simplicity, and right judgment respecting the eucharist, as well as on many other points. I collected many things from him, (as also from the ecclesiastical histories,) by which I shall be able to stop the mouths of many of my countrymen, who are always telling us, that to the pure all things are pure; that God is a spirit; that he only requires of us our heart, and a mind well imbued with knowledge,—and the like epicurean sentiments.

I happened to light upon that author on sale here in the market, on which occasion (not, as I think, without the providence of God) I bought and read him over. But as he was scarcely known to me by name before, he procured me this advantage, namely, of affording the first handle for my pouring forth my questions to you when I was with you. Not however, thank God, that I am ignorant of what has been observed by many, and as you well know, that the opinions of this writer are frequently to be rejected; and that in other places he must be read with judgment, even in the treatise *De præscriptione Hæreticorum:* as when he says, that one must not dispute with heretics[8], nor must they be

[5 The following passage may perhaps be referred to. Τοῦτον γὰρ ἁπάσῃ ψυχῇ φυσικὸν νόμον βοηθὸν αὐτῇ καὶ σύμμαχον ἐπὶ τῶν πρακτέων ὁ τῶν ὅλων δημιουργὸς ὑπεστήσατο, κ.τ.λ. Præp. Evang. VI. p. 250. Ed. Viger. 1688.]

[6 Μάλιστα δ᾽ οὖν τούτοις (sc. διδασκάλοις καὶ κήρυξι τοῦ τῆς θεοσεβείας λόγου) ἀναγκαίως τὰ νῦν διὰ τὴν περὶ τὰ κρείττω σχολὴν ἢ τῶν γάμων ἀναχώρησις σπουδάζεται, ἅτε περὶ τὴν ἔνθεον καὶ ἄσαρκον παιδοποιΐαν ἀσχολουμένοις, οὐχ ἑνὸς οὐδὲ δυεῖν παίδων, ἀλλ᾽ ἀθρόως μυρίου πλήθους τὴν παιδοτροφίαν, καὶ τὴν κατὰ Θεὸν παίδευσιν, τῆς τε ἄλλης ἀγωγῆς τοῦ βίου τὴν ἐπιμέλειαν ἀναδεδεγμένοις. Dem. Ev. I. p. 32.]

[7 The passages here referred to are in the Dem. Ev. Book I. ch. 5, 6, and Book VIII. ch. 2, but are too long to quote.]

[8 Hunc igitur potissimum gradum obstruimus, non admittendos eos ad ullam de scripturis disputationem. De Præscr. Hær. Cap. XV. p. 207. Ed. Rigalt. 1695 See also cap. xxxvii.]

permitted to have or compare holy scripture with catholics:
likewise, that what the apostles preached ought not otherwise to be proved than by means of the very same churches
which they themselves founded[1], &c.   Although indeed he is
speaking of real heretics, and of the church in his age; whose
doctrine was the same as that of holy scripture, and which
invented nothing of its own to remedy by omission, addition,
or change any contrariety supposed to be discovered in the
scriptures[2].

After I returned from you, I read, first, Cyprian, and
then Lactantius, the reading of which authors I do not altogether regret.   I regard the one as the defender of my
cause, yea, as I think, the cause of God, against the adversaries; and the other I have become acquainted with (as you
told me I should do) not without abundant fruits of godliness.

From the death of queen Anne, who was beheaded, until
my departure, some of my neighbours in London grievously
detracted from my character, because I refused to give a
small piece of money (for the honour of God, as it is commonly said), according to the annual custom of the parish, for
placing large wax candles in the church before the crucifix
and the sepulchre.   They first of all acted kindly with me,
through my parents and friends, (whose opinions they knew
would have great weight with me in this matter,) and brought
forward a custom of I know not how many five hundred
years, when a custom of only one hundred years' continuance
had with them the force of law.   I replied, that I knew of
no custom that could prevail in opposition to Christ, who
saith, that "God is a Spirit, &c." Joh. iv. They immediately
objected, having been taught by the minister of the parish,
"Do you then deny that God is worshipped by external
"observances?"   No.   For Christ, who is not "custom," but
the truth, saith: "Let your light so shine, &c."   And for
this reason I think he added in John iv. [24], "and in
truth."   Which clause I thus explained to them: "In truth,
that is, truly, and according to the word of God; that is to
say, in innocence, piety, mercy, and holiness of life, without

[1 Quid autem prædicaverint, id est, quid illis Christus revelaverit,
et hic præscribam non aliter probari debere, nisi per easdem ecclesias
quas ipsi apostoli condiderunt, ipsi eis prædicando, tam viva (quod
aiunt) voce, quam per epistolas postea.   Ibid. p. 209. cap. xxi.]

[2 The concluding part of this sentence is confused in the original.]

which no one shall see God. But the divine Majesty is by
no means worshipped by external observances, which are
merely invented or devised by men for worship; for he need-
eth not any thing, neither is he pleased with these vain and
corruptible things." Then, after some months' time, when
they began to have some hope of a change of affairs, they
often returned to me with menaces; and threatened that, in
case of my not coming to my senses, they would lay an information against me before the bishop[3] of our diocese. This
they did, as I continued firm in my non-compliance. But the
bishop ordered them to be quiet for a short time, (at least so
it was told me,) and that all things would at last turn out as
they could wish. For he was in expectation that the happy day
would shortly arrive, but he did not live to see it; for being
much harassed by Cromwell and others on a frivolous suspicion of not having aided the king's attempts in abolishing the
pope's supremacy, and the destruction of the monasteries, he
died miserably, being, as it appeared, almost worn out with
grief. But to return to my subject. The year but one before I left England, the public orders[4] of the king were sent
to the bishops and to the principal laity in every parish, that
by reason of the superstition of the common people they were
not to permit any wax candles to be burned or placed before
images in the churches, except only before the crucifix, and
at the festival of Easter before the sepulchre of Christ. The
churchwardens immediately sent for me, and inquired of me
in the church, whether I still continued obstinate in my purpose against the king's majesty's injunctions. I replied that
those orders did not concern me, respecting which they
appeared to me to triumph before they had gained the
victory. For I am neither, I told them, a bishop nor a
churchwarden; nor, supposing I held any office of the kind,
do these orders enjoin me to maintain your lights, but only
not to remove them from the church, which I do not attempt
to do. Moreover, I said, from this letter, coming from the
king, I have great hopes that after no long interval you will

[3 This was probably John Stokesley, who preceded Bonner in the
see of London. He died in 1539.]

[4 These injunctions were issued by Cromwell in 1538, for the
direction of the parochial clergy. They are printed in Burnet, IV. 101.
See also Strype, Mem. I. i. 496, and Soames, Hist. Ref. II. 306.]

not be at liberty to burn those candles of yours any longer, either before the crucifix or at the sepulchre. For the same result is to be expected from this tradition as from other superstitions, when it is manifest to every one, that the same planting is the work of an earthly high-priest, and will be plucked up by our heavenly Father, just as that is, which is now extirpated by the king's commandment. They then dismissed me, saying, "You tell us that you do not attempt to remove the holy lights from our churches, when yet you endeavour by your example to draw, if they dared, all men after you, (especially foolish boys, and young men like yourself;) refusing to do what your own and your wife's parents, grave and prudent persons, and what all your honest neighbours, do not disdain to do." Which is certainly true ; for my mother, as I have just heard, has paid the sum for me for one or two years, that she might appease the fury of the dogs, and that I might not fall into worse peril, as she much feared would be the case.

After this I heard no more about this affair, except that the day after I left London for this place, or at least for Antwerp, [the bishop of] Winchester, who had just been appointed the king's lieutenant in ecclesiastical matters, to whom I had probably been known by name, (for his diocese extends to the middle of London bridge,) being openly about to examine some of my neighbours who were apprehended before my departure, endeavoured to fish out of them something about me. And he said to one of them, in the presence of them all as they were standing in his palace, "And you, you foolish man, for what purpose did you daily receive so many persons into your house, seeing you are a poor and needy mechanic ?" The man replied "There was no such assembly of persons at my house, especially of suspected ones." "What," said the bishop, "you are lame with those who halt," (or he used some proverbial expression of the kind:) "was not Richard Hilles every day at your house, teaching you, and others like you ?" The accused denied this altogether ; and my most bitter enemies, who were men of wealth, were unwilling openly to inform against me of their own accord, in compliance with the last injunction of the king, and to be regarded in the sight of all as guilty of treachery against their neighbours. The bishop too, not perhaps being aware of my absence, made open inquiry respecting me, and said that I should take myself off, and no longer continue to poison his flock.

You now see, my most reverend master, what I meant by saying that Lactantius was the advocate of my cause, and that I was 'glad, or at least did not regret, that I had read him through. I wondered, however, what he meant by his discourse about the pollution of dæmons, and of their intercourse with women[1]; about the virtue of almsgiving[2]; on the passion of anger, which he ascribes even to God himself[3]; on the abstaining from the use of flowers and perfumes, which he calls the allurements of pleasure, and the weapons of the enemy of mankind[4]: also, about the comparing and weighing good works with evil ones[5]; about the life of the just upon earth after the day of judgment, with Christ reigning a thousand years[6]; who, during those years, shall give all nations in

[1 The passage is as follows: Illos (scilicet angelos) cum hominibus commorantes dominator ille terræ fallacissimus consuetudine ipsa paulatim ad vitia pellexit, et mulierum congressibus inquinavit.—Instit. Div. II. 15.]

[2 Quod si mortalis conditio non patitur esse hominem ab omni macula purum, debent ergo largitione perpetua peccata carnis aboleri.—Ibid. VI. 13.]

[3 Quidam putant ne irasci quidem Deum omnino . . . quæ persuasio veritatem atque religionem funditus tollit.—Ibid. II. 18.

Et gratia et ira et miseratio habent in Deo materiam, recteque illis utitur summa illa et singularis potestas ad rerum conservationem.—De Ira Dei. XV.

In some cases, he says, non cohibenda ira, sed etiam, si jacet, excitanda est. Quod autem de homine dicimus, id etiam de Deo, qui hominem similem sui fecit.—Ibid. XVIII.

Ubi ira non fuerit, imperium quoque non erit. Deus autem habet imperium; ergo et iram, qua constat imperium, habeat necesse est.—Ibid. XXIII.]

[4 Illecebræ istæ voluptatum arma sunt illius cujus opus unum est expugnare virtutem.—Div. Instit. VI. 32.]

[5 Judicabuntur ergo qui Deum scierunt, et facinora eorum, id est, mala opera cum bonis collata ponderabuntur; ut si plura et gravia fuerint bona justaque, dentur ad vitam beatam; si autem mala superaverint, condemnentur ad pœnam.—Ibid. VII. 20.]

[6 Ille (scil. Christus) cum deleverit injustitiam judiciumque maximum fecerit, ac justos qui a principio fuerunt ad vitam restauraverit, mille annis inter homines versabitur, eosque justissimo imperio reget.—Ibid. VII. 24.]

bondage to the elect, who nevertheless shall again lie concealed a short time under the earth, through fear of the
prince of the dæmons[1] then unbound, who shall attack them,
and of the multitude of the nations who shall rebel against
them; with other things of the same kind, in his epitome.

Cyprian likewise in many places seems to be too severe;
especially in the 2nd Epistle of the 4th Book, where he treats
of those who come to a late repentance.   He also prates most
wonderfully about the purging of sins by alms-giving[2], and
about the trial of the good by fire[3].   Besides, it may be doubted,
in my judgment at least, whether the various passages about
satisfaction can be so reconciled, as that he may appear to
have a godly and correct notion of the righteousness of Christ,
especially in Book i. Ep. 7, and Book iii. Ep. 14, and on the
merits of the martyrs and righteous, Discourse v.   Moreover,
what he writes about free-will, in the Epistle to Quirinus;
about the same subject, and the primacy of Peter[4]; and on
the meaning of the word water, which every where, with
him, signifies in holy scripture baptism[5]; also respecting the
admixture of the holy cup with water, which he affirms Christ
to have appointed at the supper[6].

[1 Idem (scil. princeps Dæmonum) cum mille anni regni, hoc est
septem millia cœperint terminari, solvetur denuo, et custodia emissus
exibit; atque omnes gentes quæ tunc erunt sub ditione justorum con-
citabit, ut inferant bellum sanctæ civitati; et colligetur ex omni orbe
terræ innumerabilis populus nationum, et obsidebit, et circumdabit
civitatem . . . Populus autem Dei tribus illis diebus sub concavis terræ
occultabitur.—Ibid. vii. 27.]

[2 The following passage may perhaps be referred to among others.
Nec haberet, quid fragilitatis humanæ infirmitas atque imbecillitas
faceret, nisi iterum pietas divina subveniens, justitiæ et misericordiæ
operibus ostensis, viam quandam tuendæ salutis aperiret; ut sordes
postmodum quascunque contrahimus, eleemosynis abluamus.—De
Oper. et Eleemos.   See the second part of the Homily of Alms-deeds,
where Cyprian's doctrine is explained.]

[3 Aliud pro peccatis longo dolore cruciatum emundari, et purgari
diu igne, aliud peccata omnia passione purgasse. Lib. iv. Ep. 2. Erasm.]

[4 See the treatise De Unit. Eccles. pp. 106, &c. Oxon. 1682. with
Fell's notes upon the passage.]

[5 Quotienscunque autem aqua sola in scripturis sanctis nomina-
tur, baptisma prædicatur.   Lib. ii. Ep. 3.]

[6 Calix Domini non est aqua sola, aut vinum solum, nisi utrumque
sibi misceatur.—Ibid. The remaining references in this paragraph are
too long for quotation.]

I determined with myself, as soon as I should have leisure, to read Origen for the sake of his antiquity; but I have now changed my mind, because you have made no mention of him in your letter to me. Wherefore I shall substitute in his place some work of Augustine, or perhaps Jerome upon the prophets, only that this is contrary to your judgment. I once heard master Capito, in a lecture on Isaiah, severely censure him, and say that Jerome was good for nothing except as a rhetorician. I had not believed this before, but he seemed to have his reasons for thus finding fault with him.

If at any time you deign to write to me again, advise me, I pray, as to the best means of retaining in memory what I have once read. Hitherto I have been accustomed to collect into one book the heads of many common-places and sentences; but this is troublesome to me, as I am a very slow writer. Moreover, sir, I want your books on the authority of scripture, on the office of bishops, and on the origin of error; and all of them, if it shall seem good to you, bound together. I pray you also to send at the same time with these books the bible of Leo Judæ[7], if it is yet completed, or as soon after as you may meet with a fit opportunity. But first of all fix the price, and receive it from Henry Falckner, or else I will not on any account receive the books from any one. Lastly, I earnestly entreat you to salute the same H. Falckner and Peter Hurtzel in my name, and tell them, that such is the state of lower Germany, that I scarcely think any English cloth will arrive at Frankfort at the next fair, by reason of the war between the emperor and the duke of Guelderland. Wherefore, I pray both of them to pay the money that they owe me (although it is but a small sum) either to myself, or my wife (in case of my absence), here at Strasburgh; or else to provide for the payment of it through some citizen of Zurich. For I am now in great want of it, especially during Lent, because I have neither cloth nor

[7 Leo Judæ was minister of Zurich, where he undertook the translation of the old Testament, but died June 9th, 1542, before the completion of the work, leaving unfinished Job, the last forty Psalms, Proverbs, Ecclesiastes, Canticles, and the last eight chapters of Ezekiel, which were translated by Theodore Bibliander. The entire work was edited by Conrad Pellican.]

money with me. For all the money which I could scrape together from my friends in every quarter, I have sent to my friends in England to lay out in cloth, and send it to Antwerp, where it now is; and they dare not transmit it into upper Germany on account of the cruel war, which may God soon deign to put an end to, for the sake of Christ our Lord and our hope! Amen.

My wife salutes you most respectfully, and also your most amiable wife, to whom I desire my best thanks for her great favours conferred upon us, when we lived with you in those parts. Either your wife, or the wife of Megander, wrote to my wife about something or other; but really we cannot make out what it is. I therefore request that they will let us know what they wish for, and it shall be diligently attended to at the next fair. I was aware that the black cloth they wanted may be bought here, only that it may be had, every one says, with you at a much cheaper rate.

I commend myself most dutifully to masters Megander, Theodore Bibliander, and Pellican, and pray you to salute their wives in my name. I desire also my most respectful salutations to master Erasmus and his wife. And if, my very dear master, I can serve you in any way whatever, only command me, and you shall find me most ready to do your bidding. But I had not intended, as your reverence knows, to write to you any more, and you know the reason; but on account of your excellent presents I am now compelled to write, and I must entreat you to take in good part my barbarous and vain prattling. But I implore you for the Lord's sake, to promote in your senate, as far as you may be able, the cause of my brother and fellow-countryman, John Burcher[1]; respecting which my brother Butler, who is, as I well know, beloved by and dear to you, has lately written to you from Basle.

I have received no news from England since the Frankfort fair: but then (as I requested Peter Hurtzel to inform you) my friends wrote me word that a war had suddenly arisen between the Scots and our countrymen, and that it was reported to have begun in the northern borders of England and the south of Scotland; whether by the Scots or ourselves,

[1 John Burcher wished to obtain permission from the magistrates of Zurich to export wood for making bows.]

is not certainly known; they so accuse each other and excuse themselves on both sides.   This however is certain, that on account of an inroad made by the Scots, in which some of our men were slain[2], our king threatened that he would shortly declare war with Scotland.   The Scot was not much pleased at hearing this, but sent ambassadors into England for the maintenance of peace.   The king, as our people tell the story, promised peace upon these conditions; namely, that the king of Scotland should, at every parliament, do homage to our king and his successors, as to his superior and a potentate of more exalted rank, (as was formerly done by some of his predecessors;) that he should promise to depose the Roman pontiff with his monks, as soon as might possibly lie in his power; and admit our religion in other respects (which you are well acquainted with) into his country; that he should engage in the next place to make satisfaction to our king for damages sustained in the north, and for the great expenses which he has incurred in fitting out an army by land and a fleet by sea.   For while these matters were in treaty between these sovereigns in August and September, all necessary preparations for war were making on both sides.   The Scotsman briefly refuses almost all these conditions, except the payment of a certain sum of money which he granted to the king of England for renewing the peace, and for the expenses he had incurred.   Then the king, trusting, as I fear, in chariots and horses, and in the multitude of men, rather than in the name of God, sent into Scotland[3] more than a hundred and twenty thousand men, who, as I have just learned from England by a letter of the 30th of November, have again

[2 Sir Walter Lindsay led the van of the Scottish army, commanded in chief by the earl of Huntley, at a place called Haldanrig; where two hundred of the English were killed, and six hundred taken prisoners.]

[3 Lord Erskine and others proceeded to York, where the duke of Norfolk, the lord privy seal, and the bishop of Durham were ordered to treat with them.   The conference was unsuccessful; wherefore the duke advanced to Scotland, which he entered on Oct. 21, with forty thousand men, according to the Scottish historians; but only twenty thousand, according to the English.   As soon as he had passed the Tweed, he was so harassed by the foraging parties of the earl of Huntley, that he thought it adviseable to retreat, and recross the river at Kelso.   See Holinshed, III. 828.]

returned from Scotland. But the reason of their return was so closely confined to the leaders, that it was not generally known among us. Meanwhile, it is here stated by those who exercise their traffic in France, that our people have suffered a loss of fourteen thousand men in Scotland. How true this statement may be, I am at present unable to say, although I suspect something of the kind has taken place. I know that you have already heard almost all these things from our friend John Burcher, for I acquainted him with them as they occurred. But that you may not think that I have consigned your wish to forgetfulness or neglect, I thought it worth while to repeat the same account to you, who deserve so well of me in many respects.

God has lately taken away from me, by two or three debtors who (as I hear from England) have become bankrupts, and by other casualties, about two hundred florins, perhaps so much the sooner because I am not there myself to manage my affairs. But let this be told to a stone wall. Besides, I have promised, within this month, to afford yearly (if God do not take every thing away from me) a certain sum of money to some strangers, who, having been lately banished from their country for Christ's sake, have come hither; so that I cannot now afford you so much for the poor exiles as I would have done most cordially, had you desired me. Nevertheless, cease not, I pray you, to remind me of my duty, and you shall find me ready according to my power. For I know that you will not ask me to aid the poor out of my necessity, but of my abundance. And I know what Paul requires of the rich in 1 Tim. vi. and what Christ requires every where. But the flesh, forgetful of divine and heavenly things, and covetous and tenacious of earthly things, cannot be too often reminded of its duty. Write to me therefore freely, whatever you will, because it may be profitable also to others. And I hope that I shall bear your exhortation and warning as it becomes me to do. Farewell in Christ Jesus, and live happily in God; and love your Richard as you are wont to do.

Yours,

RICHARD HILLES, *Anglus.*

LETTER CX.

RICHARD HILLES TO HENRY BULLINGER.

Dated at FRANKFORT, *March* 24, 1543.

PRAISE to God! I most humbly commend myself to your piety, my revered master. I have lately received your letter by Falckner, in which you apologize for not having been able to answer me at that time as fully, as you say, as I might probably expect. But I must reply in my turn, that I did not require an answer of such length, though really useful and most gratifying to me, lest I should be, as I no doubt was, too troublesome to you. I am exceedingly obliged to you on account of John Burcher, for having served him the more readily, as you say, upon my recommendation of him.

I wrote to John Butler a little after Christmas, respecting the king of Scotland, that he was certainly dead, and that it was reported by some persons at Antwerp that he had died of his wounds. This was not indeed mentioned for certain in my letter, but it is allowed by the Scots themselves, that their king died immediately after some of his nobles[1] had been taken prisoners by the English. From that time I have received no positive intelligence from England, except that our king, without delay, sent those nobles back to Scotland, to intercede with the Scots on his behalf, and to exert themselves to the utmost of their power that the kingdom should be given or offered to him by the Scots. But, as I have just learned from an English nobleman at this place, they obtained hardly any thing from the Scots, but returned back to the king, who was completely disappointed in the result of their endeavour. Others however of our countrymen at Antwerp boasted that the estates of Scotland, upon the entreaties or by the contrivance of these noblemen, had sent into England the Scottish

[1 Namely, the earls of Cassilis and Glencairn, the lords Maxwell, Fleming, Somerville, Oliphant, and Gray, with above two hundred gentlemen. James V. is generally supposed to have died of grief at the event of this expedition, which is to this day called the *Raid of Solway Moss*. His death took place Dec. 14, 1542.]

cardinal [Beaton]. But my English informant above-mentioned told me just the contrary, namely, that the Scots had chosen a new king from among themselves, had implored the aid of the French king, and determined with all their power to drive back our king. I do not hear that the king of England is in alliance with the emperor, or that he has renounced the French alliance; although it is very probable that, should the latter assist the Scots, he will shortly do so. Nevertheless, news is brought me at this fair, that the Scots, who have taken some ships from us, are forbidden by the estates of Scotland to sell their cargo, till they have ascertained the pleasure of our king respecting it. Some artifice may however lie concealed in this matter, for fear that the king of England may adopt stronger means of defence, and sooner prepare for war.

Farewell, and commend me most diligently to your very dear wife, and to all those godly and learned persons with whom I have there, by your means, been made acquainted. May God preserve you, and those like you, and do you pray for me! Amen.—I am now setting off to Nuremberg (whence I shall return, God willing, in about a month) to sell my cloth, which those friends of mine, who manage my concerns at Antwerp, did not dare to send hither this fair, on account of the duke of Juliers[1]. They have therefore sent them to Nuremberg, for the fair now approaching. Again farewell, and live happy! Amen.

Yours,

RICHARD HILLES.

LETTER CXI.

RICHARD HILLES TO HENRY BULLINGER.

Dated at STRASBURGH, *Sept.* 26, 1543.

PRAISE to God! Health in the Lord, my most esteemed master and brother in Christ, our hope. I send herewith to

[1 William, duke of Cleves and Juliers, had at this time some differences with the emperor Charles the fifth, on account of the succession to Guelderland. See above, page 235.]

your piety ten Italian crowns, which I desire to be laid out according to your pleasure, as occasion may offer, upon the poor exiles, (rich however in Christ,) and those especially, if such there be, who are in distress among you.

My wife is expecting shortly, that is, in three weeks, her time of confinement, and earnestly entreats both you and your wife to commend her in your prayers to the Lord, whose strength is made perfect in weakness.

At our last fair I gave the four florins for your books to Henry Falckner, to whom I pray you to commend me, and to tell him, that although he most solemnly promised me that he would take care that I should be paid all the money that he owed me at this Frankfort fair, (amounting to about one hundred and twenty-four crowns,) in golden ducats, yet that I have not received above four from master Christopher, but in other money as usual, which he most honestly paid me. But the case was this. Henry Falckner at first agreed to give me one hundred and seventy-five florins at our Strasburgh fair. He then requested me to extend the time of payment till the Frankfort fair, when he would pay the whole in golden ducats, as appears from his note, written with his own hand. I agreed to this, on condition that he would keep his promise, as a merchant ought to do. He told me that he could get a large profit with those one hundred and seventy-five florins by the purchase of arraas[2] and merchandise of that kind. But I am sustaining this inconvenience from this business, that had I sent those ducats from the Strasburgh fair, together with the rest of the money I then had, fresh cloth would have been bought in England with that money before this time; whereas, too, in this city of Strasburgh I could soon have bought among my friends, with those one hundred and seventy-five florins which Falckner ought to have paid me in ready cash, golden crowns for twenty-three batzen, I was obliged at Frankfort to give a Jew twenty-three batzen and a quarter: so that I lost two florins, besides the interest of the money. But I hope that another time he will perform what he has promised.

I have no leisure to write more, except that our king has within these two months, as I wrote to John Burcher, burnt

[2 It is thus in the MS. Arras is probably intended.]

three[1] godly men in one day.   For in the month of July he married the widow[2] of a certain nobleman, of the name of Latimer ; and he is always wont to celebrate his nuptials by some wickedness of this kind.   Farewell in Christ!

Yours, Rych. H.

[RICHARD HILLES.]

P.S.   I pray you to give, together with these letters addressed to Germans, ten other French crowns and my other letter, to John Burcher.

LETTER CXII.

RICHARD HILLES TO HENRY BULLINGER.

Dated at STRASBURGH, *Nov.* 15, 1543.

HEALTH and peace from Christ our hope!   You must know, reverend sir, that, according to what you told me in your letter of the 13th of October, Henry Falckner wrote to me shortly after, to inquire about the price of my cloth.   I send you my answer to him inclosed in this letter, and request you will kindly explain it to him at your leisure.   You will thereby do me an acceptable service : for, as you are aware, I cannot write Latin sufficiently; and as to German, I am still more ignorant, for I cannot yet master the idiom of your language.   But to return to my subject.   If master Falckner (after you have explained my mind to him from my letter, or procured some one else to do so) should return my cloth to you, I pray you, my master, to take charge of it, and keep it in your house till the arrival of John Burcher, to whom I will write my mind respecting it, as to what he should do

[1 These were Antony Person, Robert Testwood, and Henry Filmer, who were burnt at Windsor, July 27, 1542.   For an account of their trial and martyrdom, see Burnet, I. 523; Soames, I. 538, and Foxe, v. 486.]

[2 Katherine Parr had been formerly married to Neville, Lord Latimer, and was married to Henry VIII., at Hampton Court, July 12, 1542.]

with it.   For in good truth I cannot part with it for a less sum, as times now are, than what I stated to Falckner.   If I were solely intent upon gain, I could make more money by a thousand florins employed upon other wares, especially in this time of war, than I can by two thousand florins laid out upon cloth.   But I always have in mind what the apostle says, 1 Tim. vi. 17, respecting those who desire to be rich in this world.   I was never very anxious about those four florins which I sent you by Falckner from the fair; but I wrote about them, merely to know whether the letter of the young man who is in my house, and which I sent by Falckner at the same time with the money, had been delivered.   That letter treated of some ungodly laws enacted about that time by our parliament: if you have received that letter, it is well.   For this young man, whose name is Francis Warner, has often inquired of me whether it had arrived safe: I replied that I had no doubt of it, because we gave it in charge to Falckner.   My wife heartily wishes for you and your wife every happiness; and says she has no doubt but that God helped her the sooner in her confinement by reason of your good prayers.   On the second of this month she brought forth to the church of Christ a son, who, as the women say, is quite large enough for a mother of tall stature, and whom I immediately named Gershom.   I am in daily expectation of a letter from England, but not of any news.   My wife very affectionately salutes above all others your most godly wife, and says that she wishes, I know not what, but that as she has already so many fine children herself, she would pray for the wife of master Megander, that she also may have a family.   Salute, I pray you, in my name all those learned men among you, to whom the church of Christ is so much indebted; and may our Lord Jesus, the chief Shepherd, recompense them all in that day, and especially yourself! Amen.

Yours,

RICHARD HILLES.

16—2

LETTER CXIII.

RICHARD HILLES TO HENRY BULLINGER.

Dated at STRASBURGH, *Sept.* 26, 1544.

PRAISE to God! Health and peace from the Lord! Your letter, my reverend and very dear friend in Christ, dated in the month of June, I received by Falckner at this our fair; and I offer my warmest thanks for your answer to Cochlæus's[1] book, of which you have made me a present : for I read it in the month of August, and it has confirmed me not a little in the true religion of our Lord and Saviour.   I think myself too exceedingly obliged to your piety for having condescended to exhort me a second time in your last letter by Froschover, that I should so use the world, as not to lose heaven; that I should love the Lord God before and above all things, and not be too much immersed in perishable concerns, business, and money.   I now know that the love of Christ abideth in you, because you keep his commandment, as it becomes a good shepherd.   "If thy brother," saith the Lord, "sin against thee," &c.   Doubt not, beloved master, but that the more you admonish me of my duty, or reprove me for neglect, the more I shall value and love you from my heart.   I confess that I am engaged in various, and perhaps too many, occupations; but, except at the Frankfort fairs, I am seldom absent from home.   And hence it is, that I apply myself to the reading of scripture less frequently than I could wish; because, having no servant, I transact almost all my business myself, especially here in Strasburgh, and I am almost always engaged in correspondence, settling my accounts, and things of the like nature.   Yet last winter, by God's blessing, I read the whole of the holy Bible which you gave me, besides the new Testament, with as much attention as I was able. From this sacred reading, if I have derived no other advantage, I have at least learned this, that when the prophets,

[1 John Cochlæus, the well known antagonist of Luther, was a canon of Breslau, where he died in 1552, aged 72 years.]

according to this your translation, intended to describe a knave or impostor, they called him a merchant[2]. I learn from hence, as you also say, what a dangerous and slippery thing is trade, in which occupation I may fall very soon, and I wish I may not have fallen very frequently. Moreover, from that reading I learned repentance. Do you, my master, aid me by your prayers as well as by your very godly and frequent and seasonable advice, by which you are truly, as you write, performing the part of a friend and brother, and are watching over my welfare: may God reward you for this in that day! Amen.

Furthermore, I received here from my wife, after my return, that book of yours which you lately sent me by Froschover; and as soon as I have any leisure, God willing, I will read it. For it is much commended by those of our countrymen who favour the gospel, as our *Michael*[3] (I mean Miles Coverdale) immediately after my arrival from England in these parts clothed it in an English dress; but I am more pleased with reading it in Latin. For the same book I also return you many thanks; but am sorry that you should be always sending me presents, when I have here nothing worth sending to your kindness in return. My wife also desires her thanks (as I doubt not but that you heard from Falckner) for that old medal representing concord. If there is any news from England, our friend John, the bearer of this letter, will tell it you much better than I can describe it in this most barbarous and, as I fear, incongruous style. The same person will bring you with him, inclosed in this my letter, twelve Italian crowns for the poor exiles. I request you will distribute them, as you may have opportunity, at the beginning of the year; and pray the Lord for me, that he may mercifully regard this little offering, and have mercy on us all. Amen! Deign to salute in my name Theodore, Pellican, Megander, and your other pious and learned men. My wife salutes you and your most amiable wife, whom I also beg you to salute in my name. And may the Lord Jesus, our hope, grant you to make full proof of your ministry even to the end; that when the chief Shepherd shall ap-

[2 See Hosea xii. 7.]
[3 Coverdale was known during his exile by the name of Michael Anglus.]

pear, you may receive a crown of glory that fadeth not
away! Amen.

Yours in the Lord,

RICHARD HILLES.

LETTER CXIV.

RICHARD HILLES TO HENRY BULLINGER.

Dated at STRASBURGH, *April* 15, 1545.

PRAISE to God! Health in our Lord and Saviour Jesus
Christ! Although I never doubted of your love to every
member of Christ, and have often experienced your especial
kindness to myself, you nevertheless do not cease to make it
every day more apparent by your presents; which indeed are
so far most gratifying to me, inasmuch as they are the manifestations of that regard towards me, which it has ever been
my earnest desire that you should entertain: they have however been less acceptable, because I would wish rather to
spare you any expense in this respect, and especially since
I know of no way of returning the obligation; and if I did,
your kindness would not allow me to do so. But of these
things at another time; it seems best now to come to the
chief subject of this letter.

My countryman, John Burcher, has lately informed me
by letter, that he is exceedingly desirous of obtaining the
freedom of your canton; which however, according to the
laudable custom and law of your city, he is prevented from
obtaining, until he can produce a testimonial signed by some
persons worthy of credit, to shew that he was born in lawful
wedlock, and that he has not fled from his country by reason
of any crime against the state; but rather for having embraced the pure and christian doctrine, and freely made a
profession of it. But now, since it would be too great an
expense to send to England for a testimonial of this kind,
and since also John Burcher feels quite confident that the

testimonials of any persons of approved credit and probity,
resident in these quarters, respecting him will be favourably
received by the magistracy of Zurich, (according to the kindness by which they are distinguished;) he has requested me
to obtain for him the testimonials of at least two Englishmen
of sufficiently known reputation and piety.   One of them is
named William Swerder[1], a gentleman, in whom with zeal for
learning are united piety and sobriety of life.   The other I
think is somewhat known to you, both by my commendation,
and also by his own letters sent to you some time since.   He is
called Miles Coverdale, and is truly one who is very dear to
and honourably esteemed by all the ministers of the word,
and other learned men in these parts.   He is the master of
a grammar school at Bergzabern, a town not far from Weis-
semburg, where, by translating in his leisure hours, for the
sake of the more extensive advancement of the kingdom of
Christ, various religious works into our language, partly yours,
and partly those of other learned men, he is of very great
service in promoting the scriptural benefit of those persons in
the lower ranks of life, who are anxious for the truth, and inflamed with zeal and desire of obeying the will of God.   He
is one of those who, after the example of Moses, rather choose
to be banished, and suffer affliction with the people of God,
than with a wounded conscience to enjoy the pleasures of sin
in their native Egypt.   But that I may dismiss this subject in
few words, and reduce it into a narrow compass; since, I say,
this John Burcher has not very long since written to me, and
not only that, but another Englishman also, of approved
character, has borne testimony to the above named William
and Miles, that they can, if they choose, bring sufficient evidence that it was only for the sake of true religion, and for
no other reason, that John was compelled to abandon the
excellent prospects which he had in England before he came
into Switzerland, where, as is not altogether unknown to you,
he has been seeking to maintain himself by manual labour; I
called upon William Swerder, who is now on business at
Strasburgh, to ask him that, as it is well known to him that
John Burcher is a man of spotless character, and suffering, as

[1 William Swerder was at one time master of the ancient hospital
of St Thomas, of Eastbridge, in Canterbury, from which he afterwards
had an annuity of ten pounds out of the rents. Strype, Parker, I. 566.]

I before stated, for the sake of the gospel, he would not refuse to confirm that testimony respecting John with his signature, which you perceive he has done.

But since the same Burcher has likewise entreated me, that in my journey either to or from Frankfort I would procure a similar testimony from Miles Coverdale at Bergzabern, (and indeed a more ample one, as I am told by the bearer of this letter, that he is the best acquainted with him of all the English who are sojourning in Germany,) I could not in any way do this without great inconvenience. For although I will not deny that Bergzabern is not much out of the high road from Strasburgh to Frankfort ; yet, because on that side of the Rhine the journey is not so safe, to those especially who are supposed to have money about them, as through the territory of the Margrave of Baden, I have neglected to procure the testimonial of my brother Miles ; and the less reluctantly, because I hope that you, by reason of your piety and benevolence to the afflicted people of Christ, will so commend to the mayor and most worshipful senate of your city the testimonial which I send with this letter, that they may consider it as sufficient, and receive Burcher into the number of their citizens.

But now, as far as regards my testimony, I must confess that this person was entirely unknown to me before his departure from England ; for the place where he was born is very far distant from my native place, that is to say, by an interval of seven or eight German miles. This report however prevailed there concerning him, among those who are counted gospellers, and it also came to my ears when I was still residing in England, that he had not left the country for any other reason than because he was discovered to maintain the orthodox opinion concerning the eucharist ; but that in other respects he always conducted himself with piety and sobriety, wherever he resided. And indeed as he has never, since he has been personally known to me, given me any reason to think otherwise of him, so, in truth, it has never been my lot to hear from any person any thing in opposition to this character ; although both in England, and also after I came to reside here, I have frequently heard him spoken of, and at times too, when, if there had been any thing to find fault with in him, a fit opportunity offered of doing so. Moreover, I may be allowed to bear this additional testimony respecting him, that I have seen a long letter of his to the lord Cromwell, the king's chief councillor, and one who at that time possessed the greatest authority with the king in England; in which letter he explained the whole cause of his banishment, and how unjustly he was treated by the sanguinary bishops and the ecclesiastical order : from which writing no other suspicion could possibly arise either to myself or any one else, than that he had suffered persecution only for the sake of the gospel, and not for any thing else, either a criminal offence, or the maintenance of any erroneous doctrine. In fact, as I perfectly remember to be the case, the principal, and indeed the only scope of his appeal was to this effect, that since he had been in many ways so unjustly dealt with, as that the impious bishops were within a very little of passing sentence of death upon him, he [Cromwell] would deign to obtain for him, through his influence with the king, that without denying the truth (for that he constantly declared he would not do) permission might be granted to him to return to England in safety from the fury of his enemies. Hence therefore it is easy to conclude (and when I read it, it removed all doubt whatever from my mind), that he would never have employed so much diligence and pains, as it is evident he did, in the composition of that letter, in endeavouring to explain therein to a man placed in such a post of dignity and authority, as Cromwell was at that time, the entire cause of his banishment, if that persecution which he then endured for the profession of the truth, had not been the chief, nay, the only reason of his seeking refuge in your canton.

Wherefore, my very dear master Bullinger, I entreat you by Christ, for whose sake doubtless he is now an exile, not only to aid him in this object of obtaining the freedom of your city, but to shew yourself easy of access and kind to him in whatever other matters he may chance to need your assistance and faithful counsel. And God, who, as you well know, and most truly teach, leaves no act of piety without recompence, will bestow upon you abundant mercy in the world to come. And if in my turn I shall be able to oblige you by a service of this kind towards any of your friends, I hope that you will not find me less willing and ready on my part, as our Lord Jesus Christ knows, who is our life and hope, and in whom I wish you all safety and every happiness, to the glory of his name and the welfare of your neighbours! Amen.

I know of no news from our country, except what the bearer of this letter can inform you of. My wife most dutifully commends herself to you and to your most faithful wife; and she also thanks you for that godly prayer which in your late letter to me you poured forth to God on behalf of our little son Barnabas, and also for the Swiss shoes given to my Gershom.

Salute, I pray you, in my name Theodore Bibliander, Pellican, Gaspar Megander, Erasmus Schmidt, and especially your friend Gualter, and the other learned men who have deserved so well of the church of God. May almighty God very long preserve you all in safety to the glory of his name! Amen.

Yours,

RICHARD HILLES.

LETTER CXV.

RICHARD HILLES TO HENRY BULLINGER.

Dated at STRASBURGH, *Jan.* 28, 1546.

PRAISE to God! Health and peace in the Lord! As it is a long time since I have written to your piety, it is not right for me longer to abstain from writing. And first of all, I am exceedingly obliged to you, sir, for having deigned to send for my perusal, although not as a present, the books you last forwarded to me. But since this is your pleasure, I receive them gratefully, and, the Lord willing, will soon finish reading what yet remains in them to be perused. May God grant that I may be able to read them with great advantage, as you have published them with great labour, to the glory of God's name, and the edification of his church!

Lewis Lavater (I know not through what circumstance) did not remain with master Matthew Zolle, but, as he told me, is now with one master Marbach, whom I understand from your letter, dated in October, not to be one with whom the father of Lewis would like his son to have any intercourse. You mention, as a reason, that Marbach is altogether a Lutheran: but this is no new thing among us, that any preacher should savour of Lutheranism, because almost all the preachers and lecturers here are chiefly imbibing and inculcating Lutheranism: so that either Luther has drawn them over into his error, or else, fascinated by the world, they pretend themselves to be Lutherans. So that if we consider this, there is no occasion for your friend Lewis again to change his lodging; since he will have just such another, if he should lodge with any learned man in this place. And as for myself, sir, there is indeed scarcely any one here, with whom I am acquainted, who takes boarders, with whom I should think him better placed than with master Matthew Zolle. For I have not only heard him well spoken of by Gerard Frisius and others, but also by the scholars who board with him; among whom, however, I have known very few since I came to reside here. I am prepared, and I made him the offer, that if Lewis should desire it of me, I would lay out money on your account for the youth's tabling, either for a quarter or half a year. Yet, as his father is a man of property, I think it will be no loss to him to pay down the sum beforehand to John Burcher, that I may be able to pay for him the same amount here afterwards. For in truth I scarcely ever keep any money by me for a week together, but lay it out forthwith in merchandise. Do not, I pray, be offended at my writing to you with such freedom; for I am only pointing out to your reverence the state of my affairs, as to the employment of money. Meanwhile, however, I will by no means refuse to lay down the sum here, before I receive it from you by John Burcher, although the amount should be three times as much as I think it will be.

If there is any news here, or from England, you will learn it by the letter of a certain countryman of mine who is studying here, whose name is John Hoper, formerly in the court[1] of our king, but now a disciple of Christ, the King of kings, and glowing with zeal and piety, and most attached to your name among those of all other divines. He was

[1 See above, Lett. XXI. p. 33.]

sick at my house, almost unto death; and when, to all appearance he was on the point of departure, he uttered the language and profession of a most godly christian breast respecting the matter of the eucharist, and all the articles of the christian faith, before many by-standers. May the great and good God give him grace to persevere unto the end, that he may be saved! Amen.

When I first read your letter, I was grieved at the death of Megander; but now, when I look upon the condition of this world, and the happiness of those who die in Christ, I begin to praise God for him. Meanwhile, however, may God repair the loss, which, as you write, the church of Zurich suffers by his departure. John Burcher lately wrote me word, that either you or your pious wife had intended to send us a cheese against Christmas. But I am glad you did not, for we have received more gifts and favours from you than we shall ever be able to return. Wherefore be sparing, I pray you, sir, of your presents, and notwithstanding entertain no doubt of our regard towards you. For we love you, as we have been wont to do, in the Lord. My wife salutes you and your wife, as I also do, and likewise the widow, if she is still a widow, of Megander, and especially Pellican, Theodore Bibliander, and your beloved Gualter, as he deserves. Farewell in Christ Jesus our Lord and hope, in whom live happily! Amen.

Yours,

RICHARD HILLES.

P. S. Lewis tells me that he has agreed with master Marbach for board at thirty florins a year. But he has doubtless himself informed you of this by letter long since.

LETTER CXVI.

RICHARD HILLES TO HENRY BULLINGER.

Dated at STRASBURGH, *April* 30, 1546.

PRAISE to God! Health, and the peace of God which passeth all understanding! Your letter, my master, beloved in the Lord, dated on the first of this month, I have to-day received from your friend Lewis, who kept it for me until my return from Frankfort. I cannot altogether acquit myself either of ingratitude or indolence, for not having as yet replied to your letter of February the sixth. For that letter of yours was not, as you write with your accustomed kindness to plead my excuse, of such a nature as to require no answer; for I must confess that it was so full of godly and pious admonitions, and so necessary to me who am employed in so dangerous a calling (if indeed trade can be so called, as the world now conducts it), that if there were nothing else that might seem to require an answer, I ought at least to have returned you long since, on account of that letter, the thanks due to your kindness and christian love. But O unhappy me! who am so overwhelmed with worldly business, as thus to neglect my duty to my father, and spiritual and godly physician. I therefore entreat you, my master, honoured in the Lord, that you will deign to persevere in praying for me (as I collect from all your later letters that you do) to the Lord Jesus Christ, that the thorns of riches may not so pierce me, as to call away my attention from the study of godliness, and meditation upon heavenly things: our life is indeed, as you say, short upon earth, and we die daily. These things I have always before my eyes, whether at leisure or engaged in business, eating and drinking, yea, even in my dreams when I am asleep. May the great and good God grant (and I hope he will grant it the sooner for your prayers), that I may not bear these things in mind, or in a manner desire death, because it is said to put an end to the cares and anxieties of this life, (by which we are continually harassed in heaping up and preserving riches,) rather than because I desire with the apostle to be dissolved and to be with Christ. Thus in me the flesh oftentimes seeketh its own, and not only the glory and life of Christ. But I have not now leisure to write to you upon this subject as fully as I could wish.

You will obtain information, as to the state of England, from the bearer of this letter, more fully and conveniently than I can write it. Meanwhile, however, I would have you to know, that while those are alive who now hold the reins of government and authority, it is not probable that the gospel will be purely and seriously received there. For the king, the leading men, and almost all the bishops of that nation, are altogether intent upon war. They desire to retain the good-will of the emperor by every means in their power, and regard the simplicity of the protestants for the most part as idle folly, and court their friendship (provided only they may not be compelled to admit religion in the first place,) not, as I think, because they love them, but that they may have them partakers in the wars, and in the hatred with which they are regarded by the French. As for an alliance with them, I believe they revolt from it on account of the free confession that they make of the truth. But God, who knows all things, knows whether I am deceived in this opinion, or not. I wish I may be. . Moreover, the bishop of Winchester[1] has very lately republished a book against Bucer, altogether full of bitterness and invective, in which he professes his contempt of him on every account, attacks his learning, and considers yours as the most impious of all. What kind of a book this is, the bearer of this letter can inform you at length ; for he has read it through at my house.

Nothing else, but what you write, is to be expected from those unclean birds now assembled at Trent. May God therefore grant, according to your prayer thereupon, that the antichrist, who is now wounded by the sword of the Spirit of the wrath of God, may be entirely destroyed by the coming of our Lord! Amen.

Meanwhile, I pray you, do not cease to admonish me as you are wont, as frequently as your necessary engagements will admit, and (as you think me to deserve it) to reprove and rebuke me, that by the grace of God I may continue sound in the faith even to the end, and have my confidence stedfast in that glorious and awful advent.

I have not as yet advanced any money for our brother Lewis, but am at all times ready to obey your wishes or those of his father in this matter. Your attached friend, master Hoper, is now in England, but will shortly return to us, God willing, and afterwards to you. Let us pray our

[1 Bishop Gardiner wrote two letters in condemnation of a work of Bucer against the celibacy of the clergy. See Strype, Mem. II. i. 103.]

God to bring him back with success; for he desires, and indeed it is the only object[2] of his present absence from us, to procure, if he can, some money, with which he may be able always to reside either here, or with you, in holiness and with a good conscience, far from the impurity of Babylon. My wife prays for all happiness to your wife, and tells me that she has sent, by master Froschover, I know not what trifle for her acceptance. We both of us thank you as much for the cheese about which you wrote, as if you had really sent it us. Salute, I pray you, masters Bibliander, Pellican, Gualter, and all the rest of you who are very dear to me in the Lord. And I regret, had not God so willed it, that I can no longer send any introductions or recommendations to master Erasmus; for Froschover tells me that he is dead. Farewell in Christ, our only hope, and live always most happy in him! Amen.

Yours,

R. HILLES.

LETTER CXVII.

RICHARD HILLES TO HENRY BULLINGER.

Dated at STRASBURGH, *Jan.* 26, 1547.

PRAISE to God! Health and perseverance in the Lord Jesus Christ, our hope! I now at last reply to your letters dated Oct. 28th and Dec. 4th. And first of all, I owe you infinite thanks, my most esteemed master, for your condescension in presenting me with your Commentaries upon Luke, as you had before presented me with those upon the other evangelists and apostles. I pray almighty God that I may be able continually to meditate upon them, and, as you exhort me, to devote the best part of my life uninterruptedly to the study of godliness and to good works. And I entreat you to pray the Lord for me, that I may do this, and cleave to the Lord, even to the end.

[2 See above, p. 34.]

I told our brother Lavater what you commanded, or at least wished; and I doubt not but that he will always well employ his time here, and be diligent in learning; and my constant exhortation shall not he wanting to that effect. I fear, lest, as you write, the time be at hand, when the Lord will visit our iniquities by a cruel war, and will give us over into the hands of our enemies for correction and punishment. For I hear (though I hope it is not the case) that master de Buiren is now attempting to set up the mass at Frankfort in some of the churches, though in the mean time he permits those who wish to hear the gospel and follow the truth, to do so without hinderance.

There has lately been, as I think John Burcher wrote you word, some change in England, and there will doubtless be one yet greater. For England has now had for some years only one[1] duke, namely, of Norfolk, whom, together with his son, the king committed to prison, for having, as they say, when he was in a declining state, endeavoured to restore the pope's supremacy; and I have lately heard (but I have not yet received a letter from that quarter), that both father and son have been beheaded, and that that spirit of godliness or rather of popery, the bishop of Winchester, has succeeded into their place, I mean the Tower of London. God grant that all these things may be subservient to the glory of his name and the propagation of evangelical doctrine, as many of our friends think it will be! And this may be the case, after God shall have visited the sins of this kingdom. For the new queen and the earl of Hertford, who is the uncle of the prince, the king's son, are well disposed to pious doctrine, and abominate the fond inventions of the papists.

Salute Bibliander, Pellican, Gualter, and the rest who are known to me there, and especially your most pious wife, to whom also my wife desires to be commended.

Farewell, and live always happy!

Yours,

RICHARD HILLES.

[1] This letter was written Jan. 26, 1547. Shortly after the accession of king Edward VI. the earl of Hertford was created duke of Somerset.]

LETTER CXVIII.

RICHARD HILLES TO HENRY BULLINGER.

Dated [at STRASBURGH], *Feb.* 25, 1547.

I HAVE no later news to tell you of, than that it is certain that our king in England died on the twenty-eighth of January[2]; and that on the following Monday his only son was publicly proclaimed[3] king, according to custom, throughout the country; and on last Sunday he was publicly crowned[4]; which they write me word from England is all true. The young king aforesaid is called Edward, the sixth of this name.

About one or two weeks before the death of the afore-mentioned king Henry, he commanded, as some say, by his will, that the duke, who in this country is called the duke of Norfolk, together with his only son, who in England is called the earl of Surrey, should both of them be beheaded[5]. The government of England, according to the king's will, which is also confirmed by the parliament or diet, is placed in the hands of sixteen persons, eight of whom, it is said, are bishops[6], until the young king be grown up[7]. The most

[2] Henry VIII., departed at Westminster on Friday, Jan. 28, about two of the clock in the morning. Strype, Mem. II. i. 18.]

[3] For the ceremonies and circumstances that attended the pro-claiming of the king, see Strype, Mem. II. i. 19.]

[4] King Edward was crowned by archbishop Cranmer on Feb. 20th, being Shrove Sunday. For an account of the form and solemnity attending it, see Strype, Cranmer, 202.]

[5] The earl of Surrey was arraigned at Guildhall on Jan. 13, on a charge of having quartered on his shield the arms of Edward the confessor; and perished on the scaffold six days after. The duke of Norfolk was attainted and condemned; but his execution was pre-vented by the death of the king. He remained, however, a prisoner in the Tower till the accession of queen Mary. See Burnet, I. 554, &c.]

[6] Cranmer, archbishop of Canterbury, and Tonstal, bishop of Durham, were the only prelates nominated in the king's will. A list of his executors is given in Burnet, II. 5; and Strype, Mem. II. i. 19.]

[7] Namely, till he should arrive at eighteen years of age.]

distinguished of them, however, is not a bishop, but the king's uncle, or his mother's brother. He is also appointed lord protector or governor of the king his nephew, and of the whole realm. This said guardian of the king is called the earl of Hertford : he is not very favourable to the priests[1], and a great enemy to the pope of Rome.

Now if I thought that you did not know it already, I would also tell you the news that was sent me on the fifteenth of this month from Erfurt; namely, that the elector of Saxony, after having laid siege to Leipsic[2] for three weeks, with an army of thirty thousand men, composed both of cavalry and infantry, was unable to take the town, although he had bombarded it very severely, and had done much damage to the houses. He was forced to retreat with his army, and is now five miles from Leipsic; at about four miles from which duke Maurice is encamped with his troops, with king Ferdinand and the Margrave of Colbach. But on the duke of Saxony's side are the king of Denmark, and the Saxon towns, Bremen, Hamburgh, Brunswick, with some others, so that both parties are considered equally strong; and if they do not shortly make peace, (as some hope they will,) a battle must ensue. I have likewise received intelligence from Erfurt, that the kings of England and France sent ambassadors to Hamburgh, who have been there together ever since Christmas, with the elector of Saxony, and the diet of the Saxon towns above-mentioned. The king of Denmark has also been with them; but what they have done or determined amongst themselves, time will shew. May Almighty God sometime bless us with a long and lasting peace!

Your servant to command,

RICHARD HILLES.

[1 The nation being then divided between those who loved the old superstition, and those who desired a more complete reformation, the protector set himself at the head of the one, and the lord chancellor at the head of the other party. Burnet, II. 7.]

[2 This siege began on January 13th, and was raised about the end of the month. Nevertheless the town was miserably shattered and defaced by the batteries of great guns that continually played upon it. Sleidan, B. xviii.]

   P.S. Health in the Lord Jesus, our Saviour and hope! I
would have informed you, my revered master, of the most
certain intelligence which I have lately received from England,
by an express letter from myself, unless, as is frequently the
case, I had been so much engaged upon other business.
Meanwhile, however, that you may not be without any information from me, though upon matters which I think you
must have heard from others some days since, I forward to
your reverence this copy of a letter which I lately sent from
Strasburgh[3] to a fellow-countryman of mine now resident at
Basle.   Commend me most affectionately to all your brother
colleagues in the Lord, and to your godly wife, and also to the
wife of John Burcher[4]; and tell her that I have lately received a letter from Cologne, by which I learn that he
arrived there safe with all his wares, with which he happily
set sail for Dort in Holland about ten days since.   Farewell in the Lord.   Dated February 25, 1547, by yours,

R. H.

LETTER CXIX.

RICHARD HILLES TO HENRY BULLINGER.

Dated at STRASBURGH, *May* 19, 1547.

PRAISE to God! Health and peace in the Lord Jesus our
Saviour! I would have you know, my most honoured
master, that I have received your most acceptable letter,
dated two months since; and I owe infinite obligations to
your piety for thus keeping me in your remembrance, and
so constantly exhorting me to an innocent and upright conduct, and the continual study of the holy scriptures. But as I

[3 The original of the preceding letter is written in German, the
postscript alone is in Latin.]
[4 John Burcher was at this time a partner with Hilles as a cloth
merchant.]

17—2

do not perceive any thing in this your letter which of necessity requires an answer, except that I ought to return you my thanks for that German book which I received together with it, and also for your having condescended to write to me concerning what the French king's ambassador required of your townsmen, I have till now deferred my reply. And I pray you not to be displeased at this; for I have scarce leisure to reply forthwith to the letters of all my correspondents without great inconvenience to myself.

They state here as a certain fact, that the duke elector of Saxony has been taken prisoner[1] by the emperor's troops; and the various statements of those who bring this news, are so consistent, that it seems highly probable, and is universally believed to be the case. I have lately, however, received intelligence from Cologne, (but I do not altogether believe it,) that this news was circulated in all quarters by a courier from Hesse, and in Hesse itself; but that the landgrave had discovered that the report was false respecting the capture of the duke, and had in consequence severely punished at Marpurg, as he deserved, the messenger who first spread the report, and who declared himself to have been present at the battle, when the elector was taken prisoner. But in the same letter it was stated that a letter had been written from Erfurt, on the first of May, to an inhabitant of Cologne, by name John Pelmke zum Rynberch, to the following effect:

"As to our own affairs, very dear friend, I have to inform you that the emperor's troops made an unexpected attack, as it were by forced marches, upon the army of the duke of Saxony, on the 24th of April; and that there fell on the duke's side two thousand infantry, and one hundred and fifty cavalry; and that the son of the elector was severely wounded, but escaped with his life. It was also generally reported at that time that the duke himself was slain; but he was found upon the ground unhurt[2], to the great joy of the whole army.

[1 This took place April 24, 1547, at the battle of Muhlberg, for an account of which see Sleidan, B. xviii, and Robertson, Charles V., B. ix.]

[2 This was not the case. Having received a wound in his left cheek, he was taken, and brought to the duke of Alva first, and then to the emperor. Sleidan.]

Moreover, it is stated that on the 25th of April a certain gentleman, named William Thunsern, fell upon the forces of the emperor with some thousand men from Bohemia, and took from them fifteen pieces of artillery, together with some wagons laden with silver, which had before been taken from the troops of the duke of Saxony; and that on the emperor's side there fell five thousand men; so that he himself was forced to retire towards Egra," &c.

But I look upon all these things as fabulous. I have no news from England, except what I wrote to John Burcher about a month since. Farewell, and commend us to all your godly colleagues, and also to your faithful wife.

Yours,

RICHARD HILLES.

LETTER CXX.

RICHARD HILLES TO HENRY BULLINGER.

Dated at STRASBURGH, June 18, 1548.

PRAISE to God! Much health. You must know, my very dear friend and master, that I have at last received a third letter from you since my return from my native land; one too, which, besides many other things contained in it, abounds in holy exhortations to patience and perseverance, and every kind of virtue. I return you for it my warmest thanks, and pray our good and gracious God to enable me to practise what you have so properly recommended.

In the first of the letters above-mentioned, you speak much of Josiah Simler, for whom at his baptism you undertook the office of sponsor. I will most readily do for him, for your sake, what you request. But I do not think it will answer to me to advance him in future any money, which is to be repaid yonder, after our friend John Burcher has left you; nor will there then remain any hope of procuring the bows. If, however, you will receive from his father those fifteen florins which I was to send you for this year, for the purposes you know of, I will hand them over to his son here, and am ready to pay them whenever he thinks fit. Should, however, the young man be in want of money, I will supply him, upon the condition that it shall be remitted hither from you by a trustworthy person.

In your second letter you desire to know the circumstances of the most learned John a Lasco. All that I know about his condition I have learned from a citizen of this place, to whom he wrote last autumn. For he was then at Embden in Friesland, and in good health; but very much grieved and dejected on account of the present state of Germany.

And now to come to your third and last letter. The book which you have sent to the archbishop of Canterbury, I will undertake, shall ere long be safely delivered; but this can hardly be done before our fair in July, except by means of a courier on purpose, which would be very expensive: for I must give five kreutzers for every half-ounce, as far as Antwerp, in addition to the carriage from thence to the archbishop. If it had been brought but an hour sooner, I could have sent it by a native of Antwerp, who was then at my house.

It is most certain, God willing, that I intend to return to England with my wife and children at the next Frankfort autumn fair. I thank you for your friendly prayers, that God may prosper our journey. You desire, moreover, to know by what means, and through what persons you may be able to write to my countrymen during my absence. Our common friend, John Burcher, will most readily forward my letters. For we have agreed to carry on our business in partnership for two or three years, or even longer, should it seem expedient; and on this account he has purchased a convenient residence in this town, which he will begin to occupy as soon as he shall have returned from the next Frankfort fair.

You may also most readily obtain information respecting the affairs of England through master John Hoper[1], as long

[1 It appears by Letter XXV, that Hoper was now resident at Zurich.]

as he shall remain with you. To whom, and to his pious wife, I pray you commend me; as also to that most learned man, master Theodore, master Pellican, doctor Gesner, and the pious widow of Megander, together with your wife. My wife heartily salutes all the above-named, but especially yourself and your wife.

The last news I have received from England is to this effect; namely, that some persons had presumed to marry a second wife while the first was living, but divorced, and even to have two wives at once. This liberty has been prohibited, as it ought to be, by a public proclamation[2] of the king and council. The chancellor too, as they call him, of the kingdom, in a speech delivered in the king's name before the judges[3] of the whole realm, warned them to take serious cognizance of the like offenders. There are also papists who, by their false rumours, endeavour to excite the people against the king and nobles of the realm. Their lies are to the effect that the king is intending to oppress the people by a new and unheard of kind of tax; namely, that when any person marries, he must pay half a crown to the king; and so in like manner for baptizing an infant, or burying the dead; with various lying surmises of the same kind[4]. Against these also he [the chancellor] inveighed most severely, warning the judges to put a stop to these falsehoods as soon as possible, and to punish the authors of these wicked errors.

I received this speech, together with the proclamation, about the end of May, and sent it long since to my friend

[2 This proclamation was dated April 24. The king charged all archbishops and bishops, and others that had spiritual jurisdiction, to proceed against such as had or should hereafter have two wives, or any that should put away his wife and marry another; and to punish such offenders according to the ecclesiastical laws, that others might be afraid to fall into such insolent and unlawful acts. Strype, Memor. II. i. 142.]

[3 The judges and justices of the peace were required by proclamation, dated at Westminster, April 30, to appear before the king's council in the star-chamber, where the lord chancellor Rich gave them a charge. See Strype, Memor. II. i. 143.]

[4 See Strype, Mem. II. i. 141, who says that "hereby many were seduced and brought into such disorder of late, and in some parts in a manner to insurrection and rebellion."]

John Butler, that when he had read them both he might send them to master John Hoper, who might interpret them to you in Latin, as they are printed in English.

Before sealing this letter, I have heard from England that the bishop of Winchester, doctor Edmund Redman[1], and another, named Robinson, have been summoned to London by the king's council, I know not for what reason. All the women and children are sent away from Boulogne; for there is some apprehension that the French are about to attack it. The lord Cobham[2], however, the king of England's deputy at Calais, has written to me within this month, that he does not think it at all probable that the French will feel disposed to contend with us this present year. Besides, our people have a great deal of work upon their hands in Scotland. They have lately taken there a certain town named Haddington[3], distant only about twelve English miles from Edinburgh, and the English are daily fortifying it, as also very many other fortresses in Scotland. I commend you, your wife and children, to our only Saviour and Redeemer. Farewell, and long live happily in the Lord! Amen.

Yours from my heart,

RICHARD HILLES.

[1 Dr John Redman is probably intended; for an account of whom see above, note 1, p. 150. He was concerned in drawing up the first Liturgy of king Edward, as was Thomas Robertson or Robinson, archdeacon of Leicester, also mentioned in the text, and who, as well as Dr Redman, was supposed to be favourably inclined to popery.]

[2 George Brook, lord Cobham, was summoned to parliament in 1529, and died in 1558.]

[3 Haddington was surprised by the English under William lord Grey of Wilton, in April 1548.]

LETTER CXXI.

RICHARD HILLES TO HENRY BULLINGER.
Dated at LONDON, *June* 4, 1549.

PRAISE to God! Much health in the Lord! You are surprised, as you write me word in your last letter, dated March 24th, that I have been able to refrain from writing to you since the day I left Germany, and especially since you have now written me a second letter. But you will receive, you tell me, whatever excuse I may patch up for the discontinuance of our correspondence; if I do not write, that no excuse, however ingenious, will avail with you, &c. I reply, my master and most honoured friend, that I have not written to you all this time, because I have scarcely had leisure, since my return, to arrange and write about such affairs as I was necessarily obliged to complete. For Germany did not very well agree with me, as the air was unfavourable, nay, even most inimical to my constitution, and the mode of living and wine of that country, and especially the stoves in winter, suited me but little better; so that now, since my return to England, especially from the month of February, my strength seems to be so exhausted, as that I have hardly any energy left me. Wherefore, unless God should restore my health, of which there is no sign, I shall from henceforth write to you much less frequently than I have done these two years, and principally, because I am not in the habit of writing Latin (which is a most troublesome business to me) to any but yourself. And I hope you will not take it ill, because you may as readily be informed respecting the state of the realm of England, the war in Scotland, and my own affairs, through masters John Butler and John Burcher, as by letters from myself. In the mean time I admire your truly pious admonitions, and will diligently attend to what you so abundantly bring forward in your letter from holy scripture, as well the examples of the godly, as the threatenings of the Lord against the impious despisers of the divine word; and I will daily implore the great and good God in my prayers, not to lead me into temptation on account of my grievous past sins, but to deliver me from all evil.

I return you many thanks for the two decades of your sermons, which I believe master John Hoper will here present me with in your name. I much wish to send you some good thing from hence in return; but theological books are rarely printed in this country except in our vulgar tongue. When I find any book of this kind worthy of perusal, I will send it to one of my countrymen in Germany for master John Butler, that he may interpret to you the substance of the work in Latin. I have saluted in your name master Bartholomew Traheron; besides which you desired me moreover to exhort him to be faithful to the Lord, and to continue constant in the truth. And he most certainly does so; for he is a truly pious man, and one who fears God. He endeavoured as far as he could, (for he was one of the burgesses in the last parliament,) that there should be no ambiguity in the reformation of the Lord's supper; but it was not in his power to bring over his old fellow-citizens to his views. Therefore, as master John Butler will more fully inform your reverence from my letter, we have an uniform celebration of the Eucharist throughout the whole kingdom, but after the manner of the Nuremberg churches and some of those in Saxony; for they do not yet feel inclined to adopt your rites respecting the administration of the sacraments. Nor do I doubt but that master M. B. [Martin Bucer] and the other learned men from Germany and Italy, (who are here with the most reverend the archbishop of Canterbury, and are lecturing in the universities of this country,) teach, nay, exhort and persuade that there is no occasion for it, and perhaps even, that it is not becoming. Thus our bishops and governors seem, for the present at least, to be acting rightly; while, for the preservation of the public peace, they afford no cause of offence to the Lutherans, pay attention to your very learned German divines, submit their judgment to them, and also retain some popish ceremonies.

I can make no answer to your letter written Nov. 9, 1548, because you therein desire me to let you know, if possible, how the archbishop of Canterbury received your letter and your book. For I have no such familiarity or intercourse with him, or with persons of his rank and authority, as to be acquainted with such matters; and I therefore pray you not to take it ill that I have not, during this whole year, given you any information on the subject. Be kind enough to salute in my name all your fellow-ministers, and especially your wife and all your family. My wife also salutes you much, as likewise your most chaste partner. May the Lord Jesus preserve you for ever! Amen.

Yours,

RICHARD HILLES.

LETTER CXXII.

RICHARD HILLES TO HENRY BULLINGER.
Dated at LONDON, *Nov.* 17, 1549.

PRAISE to God! Much health in the Lord! It is only two days, my honoured master, since I received your most courteous letter, dated August 31, together with a packet of letters for master John Hoper and certain other brethren and friends of yours, which I immediately delivered to those to whom they were directed by you. To write a few words respecting my own letter, I owe in the first place many thanks to your kindness in continuing to exhort me to the duties of religion, and to caution me against the too great cares of this world. And I must confess, that we ought to admonish each other in turn by mutual letters and discourses of this kind. I hear with pleasure of the agreement between you and master John Calvin respecting the sacrament[1], and doubt not but that master Hoper will shortly allow me to read it. I will deliver your salutations to master Bartholomew Traheron and master Bernardine with much pleasure at the earliest opportunity, and will pray them, as you desire, in your name, that although you had not at this time leisure for writing to them, they will not, on that account, omit their office of writing to you. I gave your very kind salutation to my wife, who salutes your piety in return, and most cordially desires your advancement in sacred learning, to the glory of God and the edification of the church. She has been afflicted with severe illness ever since the month of August, so that for a long time we all of us despaired of her life. But the Lord liveth, who bringeth down and raiseth up; and he has

[1 See above, p. 121, note 2.]

now afforded her a little respite, so that we have begun to cherish some hopes of her, that she will shortly be better, and at length be restored to health. To this end I pray you, and all your fellow-ministers and brethren yonder, earnestly to entreat the Lord. She was first afflicted for a long time by a *suffocatio matricis,* and then by fainting fits, which lasted occasionally for a whole week; and lastly, she is severely suffering with a quartan fever up to this very day.

You will, I know, be informed as to the existing state of our kingdom by the letter of our very dear brother, John Burcher. On the whole, we are hoping that Christ may yet remain with us, though but a month since it seemed to many that he was inclined to depart from us, even beyond sea. But the strength of the Lord is perfected in weakness. Salute Pellican, Bibliander, and your other friends with whom I am acquainted, and especially master Butler together with his wife, and your most pious partner. And give, if you please, to master Butler the printed paper inclosed in this letter, that he may read it, and interpret it to you. Farewell. May the Lord Jesus long preserve you to us! Amen.

Yours,

RICHARD HILLES.

LETTER CXXIII.

RICHARD HILLES TO HENRY BULLINGER.

Dated at LONDON, *June 25,* 1550.

PRAISE to God! Much health! This day, my very dear master, I have delivered some letters of yours addressed to master John Hoper; and I doubt not but that, if there is occasion, he will shortly reply to them. I have received the letter which was inclosed in one of John Burcher's, addressed to me in this present month; for I have for a long time occasionally received most of your other letters through Burcher, and have taken care that they should be delivered, as soon as I conveniently could, to the persons to whom they were addressed: and you will always find me most ready to do the like, whenever occasion shall require.

In the month of May last I received your letter, dated March 13th, together with a copy of the third decade, which you therein mention; and I feel exceedingly obliged to your piety for having thought fit thus to bear me in your remembrance. I have not yet read the book itself; but the subjects which you therein promise to treat of, please me very much, and I am especially anxious to read what you have written respecting trade. As I know you rejoice in the prosperity of England, I can assure you, that never before in our time has there been such hope of the advancement of the pure doctrine of the gospel, and of the complete subversion and rooting up of antichristian ceremonies and traditions; so that we are daily expecting some Balaams to preach the truth, and bless the people of God. And it is reported that the bishop of Winchester will shortly be discharged from the Tower of London, where he has been detained for his obstinacy these two or three years, and will publicly assert the pure doctrine of Christ; with what mind, God knows, probably an unwilling one. But, however this may be, we are all of us, who favour the gospel, rejoicing in the mean time, that Christ Jesus will be plainly preached. But of these matters I have lately written more at length to master John Butler, whom I entreat you to salute in my name, together with his pious wife.

As to what relates to your letters to others, or those of others to you, I will most willingly perform what you desire; and I have long since carefully cautioned the aforenamed Burcher respecting them. And I doubt not but that he will willingly do as you desire, provided only that he can receive at Strasburgh the money which he will have to pay for the postage of such letters.

My wife, who by the blessing of God is now recovered from a most severe illness, desires heartily to be commended to you and your most pious wife, and likewise to her, who was formerly the wife of master Megander, and to her other acquaintance yonder. I doubt not but that the Lord, our heavenly Father, hath heard the pious prayers of yourself and others on her behalf; for she was all but expiring on two or three alternate nights in the month of December last, when you wrote to me and others at this place.

You write, that you are deprived of some pleasure, so long

as I do not write to you, and that you are delighted with my letters. Wherefore I now at last answer your letter, though I do not perceive any grounds from whence you could derive such gratification, excepting only that I occasionally write in haste concerning the hope which all godly persons entertain in this country respecting the advancement of the kingdom of God and of Christ.

The reason of your letters having been sometimes so delayed in their delivery, and loitering so long on the road, is, that John Burcher hands them over, as occasion offers, to the seamen at Strasburgh, and also to the wagoners and carriers who convey merchandise by the Rhine to Antwerp. And this he especially does, when the packets of letters are of any great size; otherwise he would be obliged to pay for every ounce weight ten kreutzers to Spires, and not much less to Antwerp and London, if they were sent thither by the post. For at Antwerp the post receives for the conveyance of a sheet of paper to London two stivers of Brabant, besides as much at London; that is, four stivers for a single sheet of paper. But when we give our letters in charge to the merchants, we make them no payment whatever, either at the one place or the other.

Masters Bernardine and Bartholomew Traheron salute you very much in return. And I pray you, my master, to commend me to all yonder who wish me well, namely, to masters Gualter, Bibliander, Pellican, Zuinglius, Lewis Lavater, and the rest. In what state are the affairs of master Hoper, who two months since was nominated by [the king's majesty to the bishoprick of Gloucester, you will doubtless learn from his own letters. He perseveres, by the grace of God, to be a most constant asserter of the gospel; and he preaches every where with the greatest freedom agreeably to your orthodox doctrine in the matter of the eucharist. He exhorts, yea, he persuades all. For our people, as many as sincerely love the truth, have been always inclined to that opinion respecting the eucharist. Your most amiable wife, I pray you, salute for me, in the Lord Jesus, whom I pray evermore to lead us in the way of truth! Amen! Farewell.

Yours from my heart,

R. H. *Anglus.*

LETTER CXXIV.

RICHARD HILLES TO HENRY BULLINGER.

Dated at LONDON, *March* 22, 1551.

PRAISE to God! Much health! I have received to-day,
my most honoured master, together with your letter dated
the twenty-fourth of last February, one from you to the wife
of master John Hoper, to whom I forthwith delivered the
same. As you so much desire me, in the letter aforesaid, to
write you a full statement of his, namely, master John
Hoper's condition, I reply, that I have nothing to make
known to your piety respecting his troubles, beyond what I
wrote on the first of last February to our common friend,
master John Butler, and which I have no doubt but that he
has before now made you acquainted with. But now, thanks
to God! this same master Hoper is discharged from custody,
and restored to his former condition. Previously, however,
he yielded up his opinion and judgment upon certain points
which are here regarded by us as matters of indifference.
And this Lent, habited in the scarlet episcopal gown[1], after he
had been initiated or consecrated after the manner of our
bishops, he preached before the king's majesty; many of the
[bystanders] either approving or condemning his dress, just
as they were guided by their feelings. Master Hoper is
now gone to Gloucester, which is the seat of his bishoprick;
but, as I hear, he will shortly return. I grieve that the
Germans have, in great part, gone over to the council of
Trent. But I think our countrymen, by the grace of God,
are so firm and rooted in the truth, and especially in those
articles which make against the primacy of the bishop of

[1 "His upper garment was a long scarlet chimere down to the
foot, and under that a white linen rochet that covered all his shoulders.
Upon his head he had a geometrical, that is, a four-squared cap, albeit
that his head was round. What cause of shame the strangeness hereof
was that day to that good preacher, every man may easily judge."
Foxe, Acts and Mon. VI. 641.]

Rome, that they will never, at least in our time, give in their adhesion to this same Tridentine council.

In your letter to me of the twentieth of August you relate good news from Italy, that she is beginning to receive the gospel. May God increase in those who live there faith in the Lord Jesus Christ, and may he perfect unto the day of Christ the good work that he has begun in some of them! Amen.

I have to thank you very much for your present of the decades of your sermons. I cannot easily recompense this kindness. But I will certainly requite you in some measure, when opportunity shall offer, both for those three or four decades, as also for the many other books which you have long since presented me with. Salute, I pray you, in my name, your most excellent wife, together with my other friends yonder. My wife salutes you, and all yours, especially your wife. Fare well in the Lord our Saviour Jesus Christ!

Yours,

R. H.

LETTER CXXV.

RICHARD HILLES TO HENRY BULLINGER.

Dated at LONDON, *July* 9, 1553.

PRAISE to God! Much health! Yesterday, my faithful and very dear friend, the lord mayor[1], with some of the aldermen and merchants, citizens of London, were summoned to the king's palace at Greenwich, on the banks of the river Thames, and about a German mile from the city. When they arrived there, in the presence of the king's most honourable

[1 "The 8th of July the lord mayor of London was sent for to the court then at Greenwich, to bring with him six aldermen, as many merchants of the staple, and as many merchants adventurers, unto whom by the council was secretly disclosed the death of K. Edward, and also how he had ordained for the succession of the crown by his letters patent, to the which they were sworn, and charged to keep it secret." Stowe's Annals, p. 1058. King Edward died on the 6th of July.]

councillors, the lord treasurer, the president of the same council, addressed them to this effect, namely, that our very pious and holy king Edward VI. (who has now departed from this world and valley of tears, and, his earthly tabernacle being dissolved, is now, I doubt not, in the enjoyment of his eternal mansion in heaven,) bearing in mind that, mighty sovereign as he was, he was nevertheless subject to death, and the rather, because he had lately been weak and in bad health; studying too, not a little, that this English nation might be ruled and governed after his departure in tranquillity and peace; and considering that both his sisters (of whom the elder, Mary, is ill-disposed to the pure doctrine of the gospel) have been, by certain statutes enacted by authority of parliament in the reign of his father, declared illegitimate, as born of an unlawful marriage; earnestly required his honourable councillors to agree among themselves, in case the Lord should take his majesty from them, to admit, and account for his lawful heir and successor, the son of the lady Frances, now duchess of Suffolk, (provided she have a son during the king's life-time,) who is the daughter of the lady Mary, the aunt of his majesty, and formerly queen of France; and afterwards the lady Jane, a truly learned and pious lady, who has this very year married the lord Guilford, youngest son of the duke of Northumberland, provided the said lady Frances have no lawful male issue during the life-time of king Edward. He stated, moreover, that all the king's honourable councillors, together with nearly all the chief nobility of the realm, had faithfully promised and bound themselves by oath and manual subscription to a writing to the same effect, that they would accomplish and perfect this arrangement, conceived by the king's majesty during his illness. Wherefore they desired the lord mayor and aldermen of London to be in like manner conformable, and to sign this document, which they readily did. So that, though Almighty God, in punishment of our heinous sins, has taken away from us the most holy prince Edward our sovereign, concerning whom all persons who have ever known his majesty state, that they never saw a more excellent or more godly mind in any mortal body; yet we are not altogether without his mercy, since he has now ordained such a successor to so pious a king, under whom we have great hopes (for, praised be the Lord, we do not see any thing to prevent it) that we, her subjects, shall nevertheless be able to live a godly, quiet, and tranquil life, in all peace, virtue, and righteousness; and that the pure word of God will always be sincerely preached in this realm, and the true doctrine of the gospel maintained to the great comfort of all believers who dwell here, which may the Lord Almighty grant! Amen.

When I had written thus far, my honoured friend in the Lord, the 10th of July arrives, when it is publicly proclaimed here, in the name of the aforesaid lady Jane, now queen of England, that the aforesaid king Edward is dead, that the lady Frances aforesaid, the queen's mother, had no son, and therefore, as I understand, that the government of this realm has devolved upon this queen Jane, to which event may our good and gracious God grant his blessing! Amen.

I thank you very much for the little book you presented me with, and which I received together with your letter dated March the 10th, and I pray our good and gracious God, that, as you pray for me in that letter, I may stedfastly persevere in faith and charity, and all good works, the unjust gains and sinful pleasures of this world being trodden under foot. And if I can be of any service to you in forwarding your letters to your friends, I will faithfully and willingly use my best exertions to that effect. You kindly consider it a great service, as I understand from what you have written, that I have caused your letters to be delivered to the parties to whom they were addressed. But I do not consider myself as having any claims upon your acknowledgements for any service that I can render you, much less for one so trifling.

My wife heartily salutes you and your wife, and wishes every happiness to you and to all your children. Salute affectionately in my name master Pellican, and your son-in-law Lewis Lavater; and especially master Theodore Bibliander, and be pleased to tell him that I have delivered his two little books to master Cheke and master Hooper, as in his letter written in March he desired me to do. And I return him my best thanks for having deigned to oblige me by such a present. Salute too, I pray you, my very dear brother in Christ, master Butler, and let him know that I received in the month of June his letter dated May 18th, but have not now time to write an answer; nor indeed is there much occasion for me to

do so, because I wrote very fully respecting all that required
an answer, in my former letter.   Farewell and happily!

Yours wholly,

RICHARD HILLES.

LETTER CXXVI.

JOHN AYLMER TO HENRY BULLINGER.

Dated at [BRADGATE[1]], *May* 29, [1551].

SINCE we are accustomed, most accomplished sir, to regard
any favours conferred upon our friends as extending also to
ourselves, I must consider myself on many accounts exceedingly indebted to your kindness; and first of all, for your
having so studiously and diligently exerted yourself to instruct
the family of our most noble marquis[2] by your very learned
works, and by your excellent advice to retain them in the
true religion.   For, believe me, the letters of that holy man
Bucer, whom when alive we reverenced as a father, and the
remembrance of whom, now that he is no more, we most constantly retain as of a messenger of God; and also your own
letters, which you sent to my most noble patron, were of great
use both to confirm his stedfastness in the religion we had
embraced, and also to rouse and stir up the minds of those
who had begun to be either inactive through length of time,
or fastidious through weariness of the subject in which we
profess an interest, or careless through levity and fickleness
of disposition.   For they always thought it right to submit
to your authority, and to follow your important admonitions.
And as to myself, whenever my lord placed in my hands

[1 Bradgate, near Leicester, was the residence of the Suffolk family.
See Nicholls's Hist. Leicestershire, Vol. III. p. 667.]

[2 Becon thus speaks of Aylmer, in The Jewel of Joy, Parker
Society's Edition, p. 424.   "In Leicestershire I had familiarity only
with one learned man, a countryman of ours [viz. in Norfolk], called
John Aylmer, a master of arts of the university of Cambridge, a
young man singularly well learned both in the Latin and Greek
tongue, teacher to my lord marquis Dorset his children."]

18—2

either Bucer's letters, or your own, (and he always received them from both of you with the greatest satisfaction,) I used to consider myself as highly favoured in being the guardian of such valued treasures.   For as often as I read them over, I seemed to myself to hold converse with the two most precious lights of the church of Christ.   In the next place, the singular regard you entertain towards my pupil[1], compels me to declare my respect for you, if in no other way, at least by letter.   For what favour more useful to herself, or gratifying to the marquis, or acceptable to me, can possibly be afforded her, not only by you, but also by any other person of equal learning and piety, than that she, whom her father loves as a daughter, and whom I look upon with affection as a pupil, may derive such maxims of conduct from your godly breast, as may assist her towards living well and happily? And you are well able to determine, in your wisdom, how useful are the counsels of the aged to guide and direct young persons at her time of life, which is just fourteen.   For at that age, as the comic poet tells us, all people are inclined to follow their own ways, and by the attractiveness of the objects, and the corruption of nature, are more easily carried headlong unto pleasure, which Plato calls the bait of mischief, than induced to follow those studies which are attended with the praise of virtue.   In proportion therefore as the present age teems with many disorders, must more careful and discreet physicians be sought for; that the diligence, and labour, and exertion of excellent men may either remove or correct such evils as are implanted by the corruption of nature, and the infirmity of youth: for as we feed off the too luxuriant crops, and provide bridles for restive horses, so to these tender minds there should neither be wanting the counsel of the aged, nor the authority of men of grave and influential character.   You have acted therefore with much kindness in administering to the improvement of this young lady; and if you will proceed in the same course, you will afford great benefit to herself, and gratification to her father.

Your singular regard for my pupil, as well as the importunity of that excellent and talented youth, John ab Ulmis, has induced me to write thus much to your reverence.   I was indeed afraid to interrupt so learned an individual, and one

[1 Lady Jane Grey.   See Letter IV., p. 4.]

so diligently employed in the vineyard of Christ; but as he pertinaciously urged me, and assured me of your incredible kindness, I have banished all shame and fear from my mind. Receive this, therefore, I pray you, with kindness and complacency; and if I have erred in any way, impute it to my affection for you, and to the importunity of my friend. Farewell, most reverend sir, and pardon this extempore effusion. May God, for the sake of the church, extend your years to those of Nestor!

Your excellence's most devoted,

J. AYLMER.

LETTER CXXVII.

JOHN AYLMER TO HENRY BULLINGER.

Dated at LONDON, *Dec.* 23, [1551].

GRACE and peace in the Lord Jesus Christ our Saviour, and a life of blessedness in him, &c.

I have received, most worthy sir, your letter, abounding not only in affection and kindness, but also in true godliness and piety, wherein you describe me as highly favoured in two respects; both in having such a pupil whom God has thought fit to adorn with so many excellent gifts, and because her family is one that is both well disposed to good learning, and sincerely favourable to religion. In this respect, excellent sir, I agree with you, that for these reasons I may be accounted to have attained such happiness as falls to the lot of man; but I consider myself far more favoured in having formed a friendship with you, and which God, who searcheth all hearts, knows how greatly I value. It has always indeed been my disposition not only to set the highest esteem upon all kinds of learning, but to regard with the greatest affection those who cultivate and profess it. For I well know how brutish this life of ours would be, were not the understanding of mankind cultivated by useful learning and liberal pursuits. And while I have much delight in all these, I am yet ravished by my fondness for theology, and am often lost in admi-

ration of it; so that I give more honour to its professors
than to any other class of mankind soever. For there flows
forth from such persons, as from the purest fountains, all
godliness, knowledge of religion, and innocency of life. All
good men confide in the teaching of such, and approve their
sayings as the most holy oracles of God. Hence faith towards
God is acquired, charity is imparted, hope is increased, and in
fine, all things that appertain to Christianity have their origin.
Since then the Lord has so abundantly heaped his riches
upon you, as that you are in a position not only to inform
your own mind, but to be a teacher and guide in the church
to those who would otherwise err; it is our duty to love and
reverence and look up to you, both for his sake who has been
so gracious to you, and also for your own. For thus does
St Paul exhort us in these words, " Let a man so account of
us, as of the ministers of Christ, and stewards of the mysteries
of God," &c. [1 Cor. iv. 1.]; and in another place, " Let the
elders that rule well be counted worthy of double honour :"
[1 Tim. v. 17.] whence we are taught to pay no less honour
and respect to the ministers of Christ, than to those who,
previously taught of God themselves, treat of, deliver, and
explain, the most sacred mysteries of faith and salvation.

It now remains for me to request that, with the kindness
we have so long experienced, you will instruct my pupil in
your next letter as to what embellishment and adornment of
person is becoming in young women professing godliness. In
treating upon this subject, you may bring forward the example of our king's sister, the princess Elizabeth[1], who goes
clad in every respect as becomes a young maiden; and yet
no one is induced by the example of so illustrious a lady, and
in so much gospel light[2], to lay aside, much less look down

[1 Aylmer, in his Harbour for faithful subjects, speaking of the
princess Elizabeth, says : " I am sure that her maidenly apparel which
she used in king Edward's time made the noblemen's wives and
daughters ashamed to be dressed and painted like peacocks, being
more moved with her most virtuous example, than with all that ever
Paul or Peter wrote touching that matter. Her plainness of dress,"
he continues, "was especially noticed on the occasion of the visit of the
queen dowager of Scotland, Mary of Lorraine, to the court of Edward VI., in October 1551, two months before the date of this letter."]

[2 When lady Jane Grey was urged to wear a costly dress, presented to her by Mary, she replied, " Nay, that were a shame to follow

upon, gold, jewels, and braidings of the hair. They hear preachers declaim against these things, but yet no one amends her life. Moreover, I wish you would prescribe to her the length of time she may properly devote to the study of music. For in this respect also people err beyond measure in this country, while their whole labour is undertaken, and exertions made, for the sake of ostentation. If you will handle these points at some length, there will probably, through your influence, be some accession to the ranks of virtue.

Farewell, most illustrious sir, and may the supremely great and good God grant you a long life! London. From the house of the duke of Suffolk, late marquis [of Dorset]. Dec. 23.

Your reverence's most devoted,

JOHN AYLMER.

LETTER CXXVIII.

JAMES HADDON TO HENRY BULLINGER.

Dated at BRADGATE, near LEICESTER, *May* 29, 1551.

HEARTILY wishing you health from the Lord! Though no correspondence, most illustrious sir, has ever taken place between us, nor have I even seen you in person; yet I seem to myself to be acquainted with you, both from your published writings, and also from your letters to my patron the marquis of Dorset; and especially too, from the conversation and discourse had concerning you with John ab Ulmis, a godly youth, and one much attached to you, who has at length almost compelled me after long delay, and at first almost reluctant, to write somewhat to you. If therefore I have been to blame by this freedom and extemporaneous effusion, and, to speak plainly, this trifling address, I beg you to lay the fault upon him; though I must candidly confess that, from a desire of a more intimate acquaintance with you, I am

my lady Mary, who leaveth God's word, and leave my lady Elizabeth, who followeth God's word." Aylmer, as above.]

in some measure implicated therein myself. May the Lord Jesus evermore bless your ministry, and every way defend and guide you by his Spirit! I hope that you remember me in your prayers to the Lord. Bradgate, near Leicester, May 29, 1551.

Your piety's devoted,

JAMES HADDON.

LETTER CXXIX.

JAMES HADDON TO HENRY BULLINGER.

Dated at LONDON, Dec. 28, 1551.

MUCH health in the Lord! Your letter, I perceive, breathes the same spirit of benevolence that you are universally reported to possess. Wherefore, although at this time no certain intelligence of any great importance presents itself, yet as I have met with a person by whom I can send a letter, I am unwilling to let him depart without one. Your having received my former letter with so much kindness, I consider as an evidence of your regard for me; and you have now given me such encouragement, that if I write nothing of an important or serious character, I will at least write for the sake of establishing the correspondence we have now begun. I conveyed your respects (as you desired me to do) to my patron, who is now duke of Suffolk, in such a way, that he has sent you a letter[1]. You can indeed confer no greater obligation upon his grace than by continuing (as you have once done already) to impart godly instruction to his daughter. For, although she is so brought up, that there is the greatest hope of her advancement in godliness, yet your exhortations afford her encouragement, and at the same time have their due weight with her, either as proceeding from a stranger, or from so eminent a person as yourself. You commend to me John ab Ulmis, with the rest of the Helvetians: I wish I could be of as much use to them as I desire. But

[1 This letter is given above, p. 3.]

though God does not see fit to give me any power in this way
at present, yet they shall always find my labour, diligence,
and zeal ready to serve them, as far as I can, and especially
John ab Ulmis, with whom I am acquainted, and whom I
believe to be a young man of integrity and pure 'morals.
Farewell.   May Christ every way preserve you, and evermore bless your ministry!   Remember me, I pray you, in
your prayers.   London, Dec. 28, 1551.

Your attached,

JAMES HADDON.

LETTER CXXX.

JAMES HADDON TO HENRY BULLINGER.

Dated at RICHMOND, near LONDON, *August*, 1552.

HEALTH in the Lord, most honoured father! While I was
thinking what I should best write to your reverence, in comes
John ab Ulmis, and tells me that it would much gratify you
to be informed either of the progress and establishment of
religion among us, or respecting the management of the household of my patron the duke of Suffolk.   As to religion however,
after the demolition and overthrow of the idols, and the weak-
ening and downfal of idolatry, and after our approach to the
true light of the gospel, by the blessing of God now restored, I
think that you are not ignorant of the path we have entered,
the measures we have adopted, and the order we have maintained for these four years past.   At this moment, however,
it is reported, that the book, called the king's book[2], in which
is contained and explained the manner of divine worship and
the mode of prayer to God, commonly set forth among us,
(and to be used of all persons in public) is about to be amended
in certain places; in what, however, and in how many, doth
not yet appear.   There were certain prayers for the dead[3],
which did not seem very convenient.   Moreover, in the cele-

[2 See Liturgies of Edward VI., Parker Society's Edition.]
[3 See Liturgies, &c., as above, p. 88.]

bration of the Lord's supper there is something either to be altered or entirely expunged. The book too, which is set forth concerning the election and ordination, as they call it, of ministers, seemed to contain some things which were partly absurd, and partly impious. We are in the expectation, by God's help, of their being amended, at least in some measure, if they do not reach the entire perfection they ought and should do, and which, however we may desire it, we cannot perhaps as yet fully hope for. But, thank God, we are in great hopes that ungodly superstition will be entirely abolished.

As to the regulations of the duke's household, you are rather to be entreated of me again and again to point out the method that you think best yourself, than that I should explain to you our family arrangements, of which John ab Ulmis can give you a better account than I can. There is one thing however, respecting which I will lay before you my sentiments and intentions, and on which too I shall request of you your own opinion and advice. You are aware, that in the houses of our men of rank there are practised not only such recreations as refresh both the body and mind after a moderate and godly manner, but such also as occasion sloth, and beget idleness and ungodliness: of this kind are games of cards and dice. The duke has forbidden all his domestics to risk any money upon amusements of this sort; but yet he himself and his most honourable lady with their friends, not only claim permission to play in their private apartment, but also to play for money. As to myself, however, I am of opinion that I can nowise admit it to be allowable for a Christian so to risk his money at any game whatsoever, as to leave off as a winner, with some pecuniary advantage, or else as a loser, to his pecuniary loss. And the matter is frequently discussed in this way. Those who are on their side bring forward for the most part these principal arguments, that they do not wish for another person's money, but that it is the same thing to them whether they win or lose; that the game loses all its interest without a stake, so that its sleepy character, as it were, must be awakened; that no one feels any excitement, unless there be a stake laid down; that in many other things there are superfluous and unnecessary expenses, as in diet, and clothes, &c. Wherefore, in this respect also, we must yield somewhat

to fashion, and not act with so much strictness, or bring every
thing to the test of conscience and of duty, since no one can
live entirely without faults of some kind; with much more to
the same effect.   It is therefore lawful to hazard a small
amount, only the risk must not be excessive.   I tell them, on
the other hand, that I cannot be brought to believe that the
human mind is so equable and indifferent in matters of chance,
as not to regard gain more than loss, or to avoid loss rather
than gain.   Were it not so, gaming would not be a risking of
money, but rather a constant inclination to be generous.   Besides, if any one possesses so even a temper, he will then act
very blameably in endeavouring to destroy this equanimity and
to expose himself to the inconsistency, by introducing a stake,
of incurring the danger of exciting the calm and heretofore
settled and quiet affections (if indeed they can be such, which
I do not believe), whence there forthwith arises the coveting
of another's property, anger, envying, strife, &c.   Let the
game then be cold and lifeless, and (lest it should become
worse) let the act of playing itself, which is, or ought to be,
the chief motive, be a sufficient reward in any kind of game,
and the prize, if it seems fit, be as it were a garland of
praise.   If a person cannot be sufficiently induced and excited by these motives, it cometh of evil, which is an
additional argument.   But the case is different in public
games, which have their certain appointed prizes for the sake
of exercise, and of a contest in other respects laudable and
necessary, and for the good of the state.   As to what may be
superfluous in food or clothing, if one's table be too exquisite
and redundant, and one's dress too gaudy and expensive, or
in any other respect beyond what is necessary, this is a
voluntary superfluity and a self-sought sin.   Besides too,
there is a great difference between money risked without any
necessity, and an expense of this kind, which is in some measure
necessary, because the ends are different.   For clothes and
other ornaments are made and wrought for the very end and
purpose of being used and worn out by some persons or other.
The fault consists only in their being over abundant, and
superfluous beyond what is proper, and when their cost is
disproportioned to the rank of the wearer.   The same judgment must be given too with respect to diet, except only that
its use is more necessary.   But money is intended for use,

and by the sanction of law, as a standard of value for the property of mankind, as Aristotle has admirably shewn both in his Ethics and Politics. Moreover, we must of necessity have some clothing or other : to risk money at play is not necessary, because games are of themselves an exercise without any stakes being produced. And though moderation ought to be observed both in dress and diet, according to the distinctions of rank, yet it is not so in gaming. For it is equally an offence towards God in all persons, inasmuch as by all persons the money might be applied to better and more necessary uses. And because, by reason of our innate corruption, we are always prone to evil, and even when we purpose rightly, unless God assist us by his grace, our very purpose ends in sin; yet, though notwithstanding the greatest possible diligence no one lives without sin, we must not seek after premeditated opportunities of committing sin or of acting wrong, and allow ourselves in them; and it is very inconsistent with christian piety to do so. It is not therefore allowable to risk the smallest sum for the purpose of gain, and in such a way as that loss may hence accrue to any one ; for, however small may be the amount, if it be only a penny, it may be employed to better purposes. And there is no reason why money should be introduced, if not for the sake of covetousness, or at least of gain, since play is play of itself, without a single farthing being played for, &c. In this manner and to this effect the dispute is often carried on.

I am much influenced too by the fact, that I perceive gain of this kind is not approved in any well-ordered form of government. That it is allowed by some of the schoolmen seems to me too trivial, not to say, absurd; though indeed all the sounder writers altogether condemn it, if it is for the sake of lucre, or exceeds the expense of a dinner, or something of the kind, whence no harm can arise, but rather much advantage from the mutual good will and kind feeling which accompanies such entertainments; and when both parties have agreed beforehand as to the expense, so that a stated sum may be laid out. But the expense attendant upon gaming is by no means necessary, and depends upon the mere fickleness of fortune. And you know far better than I can tell you, how much the civil laws forbid things of this kind, and how the right of recovery becomes void. With us, however, a wager won at archery may be recovered by law, and an action may be brought by the winner against the loser, just as in the case of those contracts which are sanctioned both by the civil law, and our common law and acts of parliament.

You now perceive my boldness, in that, for fear of writing nothing at all, I have troubled your reverence with these trifles.   But however, these light matters, and as some may think them, ridiculous, sometimes occasion great and serious mischief by the losses caused and sustained, to say nothing of other evils that have occurred.   Indeed, I always consider them as matters of serious importance. For whatever is wasted in this way, (for I must call it by that term,) however trifling in amount, might nevertheless be applied to far better and more useful purposes. I daily see many evils arise from this practice, and not one advantage. And although these evils are not necessarily connected with the thing itself, because all persons do not thus abuse it; yet I perceive that games of hazard are almost always attended with this mischief, that the shadow follows the substance. And so much for my opinion.

As to my purpose, it is this.   I bear with it for the present, but in such a manner as to reprove it as often as a good opportunity presents itself; but this I do in private, or in conversation with a few, and not by openly preaching against it. Once indeed I publicly denounced it from the pulpit, last Christmas, because at the very time, as you know, when we ought most of all others to sing praises to our most merciful Father, and rejoice in the Lord, people more especially amuse themselves by indulging in mummeries and wickedness of every kind; and rejoice together with the wicked, and are especially serving the devil, in imitation, as it seems, of the ancient *Saturnalia*, as you know better than I do. I am not now speaking of the family in which I reside, for the case is not so with them; and I am quite ignorant how the case is with you, or in other places. But with us, in general, throughout the whole country, (although not separately in the house of every individual,) at this time more especially, and at these holidays[1], we abound in examples of the worst and most abandoned character, and most inconsistent with our profession.

[1 The statute 33 Hen. VIII. c. 9. prohibits to all but gentlemen the games of cards, dice, &c. except in the time of Christmas. See also Latimer's Sermons on the Card, p. 8.   Park. Soc. ed.]

And the evil practice has become so prevalent, that unless
people will make merry (as they call it) at these holidays,
and merry too, in the worst possible way, or one at least of
which they will be ashamed at the season of Lent, as they
say, they not only consider them stupid and unfit for any
thing, but it is almost a part of their religion to act in some
measure in this way; and they fancy that they are merry
after this fashion on account of the birth of our Lord.
This still prevails among the vulgar and the country folk,
who are not yet instructed. In our family, however, there
is nothing of the kind, nor anything so greatly unbecoming,
concerning which I shall say more presently. But I have
described to you the general practice through almost all
England, except in a few particular places; and I explain it
to you more fully, because John [ab Ulmis] told me that you
would be gratified by my doing so. If therefore I seem too
verbose, you must lay the blame upon him, and excuse me.
To proceed therefore. Although the nobility and greater
part of the commonalty (now by the grace of God better instructed) plainly understand that it is not their duty so to
conduct themselves, yet partly from the force of habit, and a
desire not to appear stupid, and not good fellows, as they call it,
but partly and principally, as I think, from their not having yet
so far advanced as to be able perfectly to hate the garment
spotted by the flesh, or to feel as yet the genuine fear of God
implanted in their mind, they have no settled intention, much
less any desire, to conquer and crucify themselves.

But to return from this digression, and explain the reason why I once reproved my flock in my sermon, and what
followed thereupon. It is as follows. When I had openly
reproved the whole thing altogether, and those too, though
in common and general terms, who played for money, I saw
that it was taken in bad part, because in the household of
the duke, my master, the domestics do not play, or at all
events in no wise play for money, so as to be found out. But
since the duke himself and his lady have secretly played with
their friends in their private apartment, they thought it was
my duty merely to have admonished them in private. But
you must hear the reason of my acting as I did. For this
open rebuke was not immediately administered by me at first,
but long after; and in the manner, and with the consideration
and caution that I shall now state. When I had frequently

done this, and, as I perceived, without any effect, although they had nothing to say against it with any shew of reason; and having forewarned them that I would at length sometime or other plainly and openly reprove them, if they should repeat the practice of playing in their apartments, provided they played for money, (for that otherwise I had no fault to find with their playing, as an exercise both of mind and body; but that I could no longer put up with that kind of game, when they played for money, because I saw no sufficient reason adduced by them for that very unnecessary expense,) and having said very much to the same effect, they left off for a time: upon which I was very glad, and began to entertain great hopes.   Afterwards, however, on the Christmas following, when I perceived they were beginning to return to their old habits, I publicly reproved, as opportunity offered, both the thing itself, and those who practised it, but in the way that I have above stated, that is, in general terms, without naming or describing any individual.   Understanding however that offence was taken at this, I was from thenceforth silent, contenting myself with a private and individual reproof, whenever the subject was brought forward in conversation. And so far I put up with and allow the practice, that I do not reprove it publicly and in my sermons.   But since they consider me too strict, and under this pretence choose to be their own interpreters in other matters, contrary to what they have been accustomed; and say, " In this or that point Haddon cannot agree with us, though they are just as much matters of indifference as the play which hardly any one finds fault with but himself;" and they are thus advancing to what is really evil: lest, I say, they should err in that way, and go on by degrees into intolerable evil, I bear with this, as I have above explained, against my will.   I bear with it of compulsion, that I may gain them over in other things of greater importance; I bear with it, just as a man who is holding a wolf by the ears.   But I perceive some good arising from this concession, which in fact is no concession at all, but in some measure a remission of duty, or rather of strictness in the performance of it; because I do not find fault in public, although individually and in conversation I always reprove in the same way as heretofore.   But because they see that I in some measure yield to them, even against my own opinion, and consider that I deal tenderly with this infirmity of theirs, they are willing to hear and attend to me more readily in other respects.

I have now explained, more fully perhaps than is consistent with your engagements, both my own opinion upon this subject, as also my purpose and manner of tolerating it. I request that you will plainly write to me upon this matter, and fully state your own opinion respecting it, and how you think I ought to act : state what you approve, and what you disapprove, as far as it may seem good to you; and give me your advice as to how far you think I may concede in matters of this sort, and to what extent I may connive at them. But do this at your leisure ; for I should be unwilling to interrupt you when occupied in things of greater moment. Unless I judged of you in some measure by myself, (as far as is allowable for so slender a scholar, and one who is but just beginning to learn,) to be a most accomplished and learned man, and one who is perfect in every kind of knowledge, I should not have dared to interrupt you in this way, whom I have scarcely saluted in these three letters. But be this as it may, you are yourself to blame for having wished me to write. I will carry my boldness a little further, and pray you to salute for me that most honoured man master Bibliander, whom I seem to myself to be well acquainted with from his published works. Farewell, ye two lights of the church. May Christ protect you, and by his Spirit aid both you and your ministry! Richmond, near London, August, 1552.

Your attached and most devoted,

JAMES HADDON.

LETTER CXXXI.

JAMES HADDON TO HENRY BULLINGER.
Without place or date. [About *October*, 1552.]

GREETING. I have heretofore written you tolerably long letters; I now send you a short one, and the rather, as you tell me you are in a weak state of health. I shall pass over the formal and almost courtier-like custom of returning you my thanks for having written to me, notwithstanding you were either actually indisposed, or at least a valetudinarian. Your very short letter, most courteous and honoured sir, was, you may be assured, exceedingly gratifying to me, not only because you seem entirely to agree with me, but also for the description of the beginning and progress, and the order now observed among you; all of which things I had a wonderful desire to know. I have conferred with the duke, my master, respecting your friend Schmutz; and he promises, for your sake, to be exceedingly kind to him, and to bestow upon him the same pension as he formerly did on John ab Ulmis. It will be necessary for you some time to recal this to his grace's memory, as I am shortly about to leave his roof, having been summoned by the king's majesty to undertake a certain office[1] in the state, in which, though it is not very lucrative as to my individual benefit and emolument, I purpose to the utmost of my power to promote the gospel. I am telling you this, that when you write about Alexander Schmutz, you may not address the duke as if I were with him, but as though I were absent, as I intend to be. For though I shall not be able to be altogether and entirely separated from his grace, yet I shall be for the most part, as soon as I shall be able to discharge the debt already contracted, and yet to be contracted, for the payment of the first-fruits. But it has pleased God to render his grace so much attached to me, and me too in my turn so devoted and attached to his grace, that I cannot entirely separate from him, but must occasionally visit him. You can however yourself write more fully about Schmutz, or any one of the like sort whom you may wish to recommend to his grace, as supposing that I am not with him; and there is no doubt but that his excellency (such is his kindness towards yourself and those who are like you) will take it in good part. I commend your health and your whole self to God. I would willingly exhort you to preserve it as you can, and as you know you ought. I earnestly pray you to salute master Bibliander in my name. May God be with you by his Spirit, and with your ministry!

Your attached,

JAMES HADDON.

[1 A gift to James Haddon, B.A., of the prebend of Westminster, void by the death of Antony Bellows, LL.D., and master in chancery, was dated in August 1552. He was appointed in October, this year, to the deanery of Exeter. Strype, Mem. II. ii. 272, 274.]

LETTER CXXXII.

JAMES HADDON TO HENRY BULLINGER.

Dated at LONDON, *Nov.* 30, 1553.

I should have to write very much to your reverence, if I could indulge the feelings of my mind. But by reason of the manifold engagements with which I am at present overwhelmed, I can scarcely write to you at all. Indeed all that I have to say could not well be committed to writing, and the bearer John Schmutz will give you far better information in words. Alas! what a severe loss have we sustained! Alas! how true religion is banished! Alas! how justly is the wrath of God stirred up against us! I dare not write more; you must understand the rest. We were not so much in the hope of restoring true religion, as we are now in fear of recalling impious and abominable idolatry. Pour forth your prayers, I entreat you, for me and those like me. A few individuals of this sort are compelled to afford their testimony to real godliness and religion. All our leading men, I mean the bishops and persons of that sort, are overwhelmed by this calamity, and thrown into prison. May God help us! We also are speaking to no purpose, for unless God order it otherwise, it is already determined what is to be done: only that we may profess in whom we believe, and what religion we hold, we accepted an offer made us of encountering our enemies. What will be the result, God knows, and whether this may not be the last letter that I shall be able to write to you. I very much regret that I was unable so fully to provide for your friend Schmutz by means of the duke of Suffolk, as I hoped and expected, had not this event taken place, which I cannot relate without tears. Pardon me therefore, if I do not write more upon the subject. I doubt not but that the order, as it were, of the whole tragedy will be related to you. The duke[1] himself holds to the true God, and I hope by God's help will fully retain his opinions about true religion, in opposition to the devil, whose agents are

[1 The duke of Suffolk was committed to the Tower, Feb. 6, 1554, and beheaded on Tower-hill on the 23rd of the same month.]

striving with all their might to lead his lordship astray : that he may do this more effectually, I commend his lordship to your prayers, and I commend too myself, and those like-minded.   Salute for me, I pray, master Bibliander.   May God be with you by his holy Spirit unto the end, and ever glorify his name by you, as he hath hitherto done! London, Nov. 30, 1553.

Your most attached,

JAMES HADDON[2].

LETTER CXXXIII.

JAMES HADDON TO HENRY BULLINGER.

Dated at STRASBURGH, *July* 9, 1554.

I HAD intended to see your excellence, and deliver to you in person this letter written to you by master Hooper.   But having met with some godly persons and brethren in the Lord, I cannot leave this place at present.   I have thought it there-fore my duty not to retain by me any longer the letter of one who is so much attached to you.   I entrust it to Park-hurst, that brother in the Lord, who is able to give you as much information about our friend Hooper as almost any one else.   For they were most intimately united, as well by dis-position as by vicinity of residence[3].   As for myself, I intend, by God's assistance, to visit some time or other both yourself and the other distinguished men in your church.   Among whom salute, I pray you, for me the reverend father in Christ, master Pellican.   I am now writing to the worthy and excellent Bibliander to the same effect as I have written

[2 Next to this letter, in the Archives, comes a Latin version of the dying speech of the duke of Northumberland. "Joannis nuper ducis Northumbriæ in Anglia, quum ad supplicium productus esset, oratio. Viennæ, ex officina Mich. Zimmermanni. 1553." See Soames, IV. 44.]

[3 Parkhurst was rector of Bishop's Cleeve, near Cheltenham, when Hooper was bishop of Gloucester.]

to you. May God every way be with you, and preserve you
for the benefit of his church! Strasburgh, July 9, 1554.

Your attached,

JAMES HADDON.

LETTER CXXXIV.

JAMES HADDON TO HENRY BULLINGER.

Dated at STRASBURGH, *Aug.* 31, 1554.

MUCH health. I perceive in your letter to me, most
honoured sir, that of which I never doubted, namely, your
grief for the downfall of the church of England, and your
kindness and good-will towards me. Of the former I will
say nothing, lest the wound should break out afresh. Of the
latter, however, I can rather conceive in thought, than express in words, what I ought to say, because I know that
you will not willingly hear it. Passing over these things
therefore, as to your wish that I should inform you respecting
your friend Hooper, whether or not any letter of yours
written to him will be safely conveyed, and delivered into
his hands, I have not yet obtained any certain information
upon this point; nor am I able to do so, for he writes word
that he is now thrust down to the very lowest dungeon, and
that his servant[1] has been taken away from him. Still there
have been, as I hear, many ways and means devised, by
which good men have communication with him, and he in
turn with them. Wherefore I have conferred here with one of
his friends, who has promised to take care that your letter
shall be sent to London, and given in charge to some godly
person who, if he can deliver it safely, will do so; if not, it will
remain in his keeping. You will act therefore as you think
best. But your letter to him will doubtless afford him great
comfort. For this it is that he complains of, respecting many

[1 William Dounton, whom Babington, warden of the Fleet, imprisoned, and stripped him out of his clothes to search for letters.
See Foxe, VI. 648, Letters of the Martyrs, p. 97, and above, p. 102,
n. 1.]

persons, that he cannot hear from them ; and he almost thinks himself deserted by his friends, which (as you yourself know) is the greatest grief to persons in distress, and especially to those who are of a naturally benevolent and well-ordered mind. And the word *well* I refer to teaching in general. For we do not here lay aside our natural feelings, but seek for consolation in adversity elsewhere than from God alone. But to seek it from those more especially, who approach nearest to God, that is, the godly, is not so remote from godliness, (since means are not to be rejected, especially when of a kindred character,) although we ought to depend upon God and his Spirit exclusively. I need say no more to one of your wisdom and piety. Whatever you may determine upon, if you wish for my assistance, you will find me entirely at your service. Farewell very heartily in the Lord. Strasburgh, Aug. 31, 1554.

Your most attached,

JAMES HADDON.

P. S. There is one Banks[2] who has written to you about the lady Jane. He has shewn me your letter in answer to his, from which I infer that he wrote something to you which you did not deem it prudent to publish. It is well that you came to this determination, and I beg of you by no means to make it public, or suffer many persons to copy it. For although he wrote it without my knowledge, yet I know for certain that it will occasion the greatest danger to me, if it be published or appear in his name, because I brought him over from England, and he is with me as my friend. If it were evident that all the statements were certainly true and proved, and that their publication would tend to the glory of God, I would then prepare myself to meet the danger. But I am rather afraid that all the facts are not as described by him, but that he has gathered them from common report, and being himself too in some measure biassed by his zeal. Were the statement published, it would probably do more harm to the truth, and to our cause, than it would do them good ; to say nothing of the certain risk and peril which would hang over others. Nor could the whole account be defended with

[2 See below, Lett. CXLI.]

a sufficiently safe conscience, since, probably, some things have been stated as facts, which may not be found to be such. But as to what regards the lady Jane herself, and what is said in her name, (as for instance, her exhortations to a certain apostate, and her discourse with Feckenham,) I believe, and partly know, that it is true, and did really proceed from herself. It will now be sufficient for me to have pointed out to your prudence, what you have already perceived of yourself, that is, that these things should not be published, and especially the other matters under any circumstances whatever, and I pray you again and again not to allow it. Should it be thought expedient that they should come forth some time hence, this can be done whenever you may think fit; but the present time is most unsuitable for such a measure, even if it were certain that the whole statement is correct. For we have too many matters of fact to make it necessary to collect mere rumours, and those perhaps altogether invented. Our adversaries already partly lay this calumniously to our charge: what will they do if they have sufficient grounds of accusation? Let me soon hear from you, that I may know you have received this, and that I may be assured that the letter neither is nor will be published.

LETTER CXXXV.

JAMES HADDON TO HENRY BULLINGER.

Dated at STRASBURGH, *Dec.* 9, 1554.

MUCH health. As the letters of the absent are a kind of substitute for personal intercourse, I therefore write to you, most honoured and kind sir, with much pleasure; and the rather, because I not only perceive your kindness towards me in your letter to me, but am also informed of your regard for me from the report of others; and not that merely, which you entertain towards all the members of Christ our Saviour, but an especial regard arising from the leaning of your mind towards me, and which, I am told, you manifest

by your frequent inquiries about me.   God be thanked, who
has implanted in you this kind feeling!   I would give you
news from England, if any good tidings were to arrive.
As to bad, there is nothing certainly known at present,
and the bearer of this can inform you of what is reported
better than I can.   In short, every thing seems to be declining, and getting worse and worse.   I could tell you a
great deal about myself and my present condition, but I am
unwilling to trouble your kindness with unnecessary details.
As to that Banks, however, about whom I wrote to you
before, I have an earnest request to make of you on his
behalf.   I have hitherto relieved his necessities out of my
own slender means.   But now, owing to the calamities of the
times and the fury of my enemies, I am stripped of almost
all my property.   And they are so violent against me and
those like me, that God only knows what else will follow.
To his will and providence I resign myself, as to that of a
most kind and merciful Father; and I earnestly implore you
to entreat the same with me and for me, that I may continue
to do so even unto the end.   The reason of this rage of my
adversaries is, I hear, the testimony openly given by me to
the truth in that convocation held at London[1] last year.
But in the mean time they have been seeking with the
greatest possible diligence some other plausible pretext; and
not being able to find one, they at length denounce me as
a heretic on account of my freely declared opinion[2] against
their abominable doctrine of transubstantiation, &c.   I call it
a freely declared opinion, not only because it was freely set
forth by me, but also because that assembly ought to have
been most free, as likewise the opinions which were therein

[1 This convocation was opened Oct. 16th, 1553, by a Latin sermon
by Harpsfield.   For an account of the proceedings, written by Philpot, archdeacon of Winchester, and who bore a principal part therein,
see Foxe, Acts and Mon. VI. 395. Burnet, II. 407. Soames, IV. 103.]

[2 Haddon's argument is thus given in Foxe, VI. 405, and Philpot's writings, Parker Soc. Ed. p. 200.   It was to prove the substance
of bread and wine to remain after the consecration of the eucharist.
The same thing, saith Theodoret, that the bread and wine were before
they were symbols, the same they remain still in nature and substance,
after they are symbols.   But bread and wine they were before;
therefore bread and wine they are after.]

advanced. Concerning which the bearer of this, Chambers[1], my very dear brother in the Lord, can give you fuller information, as well as in what manner our adversaries, filled with the greatest hatred against the truth, acted in entire opposition to what is just and good, and against all laws, human and divine.

But to return to Banks, he will think himself very well dealt with, if he can obtain a situation with some respectable and pious printer, as a reviser or corrector of the press. And he hopes that this may be accomplished by your recommendation. There is no need of commending him to your kindness with many eulogies, or of enlarging upon the ability which he possesses for such an employment. He is well acquainted with Latin, as you can judge for yourself, and not unskilled in Greek; of peaceable disposition, glowing with true religion, and exceedingly devoted to literary pursuits. In my opinion you will confer a benefit upon any one with whom you may be able to place him. And yet, for Banks's sake, I shall consider the favour in some measure conferred upon myself, because, as it appears, I can no longer support him at my expense, as I should wish, unless things turn out otherwise than they seem to be, and really are, at present. I might have written these matters with less plainness, but I did not think it right to do so, but rather to explain nakedly and clearly to your kindness the whole state of the case. May God every way be with you, and preserve you to the glorifying of his name, and the benefit of his church! Strasburgh, Dec. 9, 1554.

Your most attached,

JAMES HADDON.

P.S. I have the greatest regard for that most excellent man, master Bibliander, and for the most honoured father, master Pellican. I request your kindness to salute them both from me.

[1 Chambers and Grindal were sent with a letter from the congregation of Frankfort to that of Strasburgh, Dec. 3.]

LETTER CXXXVI.

JAMES HADDON TO HENRY BULLINGER.
Dated at STRASBURGH, *Jan.* 8, 1555.

GREETING. Your letter, most honoured sir, was most gratifying to me, both on account of the sympathy which you manifest in my misfortunes, and of the regard and truly paternal affection towards me which I now perceive you to entertain.   A fortnight after I had written my last letter to you, one was delivered to me from England, informing me that I have been entirely stripped of all my property, as I before explained to you, but that there was now some hope from other quarters.   I thought it my duty therefore to inform you of this by the very first opportunity, that as you were heretofore distressed on my account, so you may now with me return thanks to God our Father, to whom I doubt not but that you have prayed together with me, and commended me and my cause to him.

I have also to thank you very much on behalf of Banks. For my very dear brother Lever has informed me, that master Sultzer[2] has arranged for me to send Banks to Basle at the Frankfort fair; for he has met with one Parkes, a printer, I believe, with whom he will place Banks.   I would say more, but am suddenly interrupted by the bearer, who will convey this letter early to-morrow morning.   I pray you therefore to take this, as you do every thing of mine, in good part.   For I thought it my duty to send you this by the present opportunity, rather than nothing at all, lest I should occasion you greater concern and anxiety than would become me; because I have not only perceived from your letter, but have gathered from others, the anxious inquiries you had determined to make on behalf of Banks, if this had not succeeded.   May God long preserve you for the benefit of his church and the comfort of many! Strasburgh, Jan. 8, 1555.

Your most attached,

JAMES HADDON.

[2 Simon Sultzer was a divine at Basle.]

LETTER CXXXVII.

JAMES HADDON TO HENRY BULLINGER.

Dated at STRASBURGH, *Jan.* 15, 1555.

GREETING. Most honourable and my very good friend,
I send you herewith certain heads of a discourse held by
him[1] whom the inscription points out. It is possible that he
embraced many more topics at that time, but most likely
they were all to the same effect. I have translated them
from the English, just as they were brought here, word for
word as nearly as I could. Shall we wonder at the unheard
of boldness of the man in inventing, or his singular shame-
lessness in lying, or his subtle and versatile talent, and (so to
speak) most godless mind, for that, having so long stored up
in his remembrance so many slaughters and such heavy
charges of treason, he could cherish and foster them with
such hypocrisy and dissimulation? I think there was never
heard tell of such a turncoat and monster of a man, and pest
of the state, if the book[2] he published many years since in a
quite contrary sense, and written too with such emphasis and
asseveration as that nothing apparently can exceed it, be
compared with his present assertions. But we have justly
deserved portents of this kind, for having almost despised the
godly and those who told us the truth. May God now take
compassion on us, and hear the prayers of his own people, as
in his mercy he is wont to do ; and may he succour our not
only distressed but deplorable, and, as far as human aid is
concerned, desperate condition ! Many signal examples shew
that he has done so; nor do I doubt but that he will again do

[1 On Sunday, Dec. 2, 1554, Gardiner, bishop of Winchester,
preached at Paul's Cross before king Philip and cardinal Pole, upon
Rom. xiii. 11. An account of his sermon is given in Strype, Mem. III.
i. 259, and more fully by Foxe, Acts and Mon. VI. 577, whose statement
is so nearly identical with the Latin heads here referred to, as to
render it unnecessary to retranslate them.]

[2 Haddon refers to Gardiner's book *De vera Obedientia*, published
in 1534, to justify the parliament in giving the king the title of
supreme head of the church. An account of this book is given in
Strype, Mem. I. i. 264. See also Foxe, VII. 594.]

it in his own time. In the mean time, all things are working together for good to his people. He who keepeth Israel will neither slumber nor sleep. And that noble act related by Moses in Exodus, and mentioned by you, and so often recorded in the Judges and Prophets, affords abundant consolation. I will not at this time trespass any longer upon your kindness. I hope that my last letter has been delivered to you ere now, bearing testimony to the good result of your letter to master Sultzer on behalf of Banks, and for which I again thank you in his name. May God every way be with you! Strasburgh, Jan. 15, 1555.

Your most attached,

JAMES HADDON.

P.S. My countryman and friend, Abel the merchant, warmly salutes you. He was with me at the beginning of the winter, and it is from him that I have the copy of the writing which I send you.

LETTER CXXXVIII.

JAMES HADDON TO HENRY BULLINGER.

Dated at STRASBURGH, *April* 24, 1555.

GREETING. Your letter, most honoured sir, testifying your affection and exceeding love towards me, was delivered to me on my return from Frankfort. You tell me that you write to me in all the hurry of business, whereat I partly rejoice, and am partly sorry: for your letter, short as it is, contains singular consolation drawn from the examples of Joshua and Jehoiada; but I am sorry that I was an hinderance to you when so well and so actively employed. For I am aware that the charge of many and most weighty concerns is laid upon you, and that you are almost continually distracted by matters of the greatest importance. I must therefore beg of you not to withdraw yourself in future, even a single moment, on my account from any business whatever, unless when a breathing-time and leisure shall be afforded you. For although, being not now engaged in any public labour or employment, I am able frequently to write to your reverence, the case is not the same with you. Wherefore, although I hear from you most gladly and with the greatest eagerness, yet I shall be content if you do not answer my letters, except at the times and on the terms above stated. On which subject the bearer also will communicate with you by message from me. I have learned also by the information of our friend Chambers the exertions made by your kindness in respect to Banks. He is not yet recovered, but is better. He will always acknowledge himself very greatly indebted to you, and I offer you my best thanks on his behalf. We commit the repayment of this favour to God, who alone can accomplish it effectually, and whom I pray to preserve and direct you for the advantage and benefit of his church. In whom farewell. Strasburgh, April 24, 1555.

Your reverence's most devoted,

JAMES HADDON.

P.S. I have saluted our friend Sampson and the others in your name.

LETTER CXXXIX.

JAMES HADDON TO HENRY BULLINGER.

Dated at STRASBURGH, *Dec.* 7, 1555.

Much health. My very dear friend in Christ, I have been often thinking of writing to you for some months past; but nothing has occurred which seemed worthy of being committed to paper, especially as reports were spread abroad with various degrees of uncertainty. But it is now certain that that bitter scourge[1] of divine justice, the most cruel of all men

[1 Stephen Gardiner, bishop of Winchester. See Foxe, VII. 585. Strype, Mem. III. i. 465, and Philpot's writings, Parker Society's edition, p. 269.]

within our memory, and who most eagerly thirsted for the blood of the saints, has been removed from this life. But though our sins had richly deserved so great an evil, and even a punishment yet more severe, on account of the listlessness and ingratitude which for the most part pervaded our country when the free course of the gospel was allowed us, yet our heavenly Father and Almighty God has manifested his usual kindness and power. That illustrious pair, masters Ridley and Latimer, offered themselves to God a short time before[2], an admirable and noble sacrifice; and their ashes (together with those of others who had gone before them, and who now live in the presence of our Lord and Saviour) have, methinks, called down the judgment of God upon the above-mentioned scourge of heaven. We have no other certain or confirmed intelligence, as far as I am at present aware, worthy of being communicated to you. Besides, I think that you have been made acquainted either previously or more fully from others with the facts I have above stated, though I considered it also my duty to write to you to the same effect; for it seems very long since I had any intercourse with you. Salute for me, I pray you, master Gesner. Please to remember me, and the condition of our country, in your prayers, as I doubt not but you will. May God be with you and your ministry, and preserve you for the benefit of his church! Strasburgh, Dec. 7, 1555.

Yours,

JAMES HADDON.

LETTER CXL.

JAMES HADDON TO HENRY BULLINGER.

Dated at STRASBURGH, *March* 12, 1556.

HEALTH in the Lord. I have written to you before, but I now doubt whether my letter was delivered to you; not

[2 Gardiner died in the next month after the burning of Ridley and Latimer, which took place, Oct. 16, 1555.]

that I wish to interrupt you, occupied as you are in most weighty affairs, much less to draw you away from them for a moment by replying to my letter; nor indeed were the matters upon which I wrote to you of such consequence as to require an answer. They informed you of the tidings which we had then received from England. What I have now to write is much less worth your notice; but I nevertheless send you this letter, because it seems to me a long time since I have corresponded with your reverence, or have heard from yourself. Our friend Burcher, when on his return from you, replied to my inquiries concerning you, that you were not in good health. But as I have not yet received any further account, I very much desire to hear from yourself, how you do. I ask nothing more, and not even this, except at your leisure. There are many reasons why I am anxious to hear of your health. Nor is it to be wondered at that I am exceedingly anxious about you as an individual, since I have discovered your regard for me to be such as it has been declared to be by the report of some of our friends. I doubt not but that these times occasion much grief to yourself, as to all godly persons, and cause many and deep sighs to be breathed forth. But what can you do? He who sitteth in the highest heavens looks down upon lowly things in heaven and earth. He wills his people to be tried, but will not suffer his church to be left altogether destitute; but as that man of sin has already been partly detected by yourself and those like you, so he will at last be destroyed by the breath of the mouth of the Lord. Amen, amen! May the Lord be with you by his Spirit, and preserve you for the good of his church! Strasburgh, March 15, 1556.

Your most devoted,

JAMES HADDON.

P.S. I wish every happiness, according to the will of God, to masters Bibliander, Pellican, and Gesner.

LETTER CXLI.

JOHN BANKS TO HENRY BULLINGER.

Dated at LONDON, *March* 15, 1554.

You will probably be surprised, most excellent sir, at my writing to you in these turbulent times, which I have never done before; and the rather, because I had no personal acquaintance with her[1] [of whom I write], and am about to address you upon those subjects which would occasion the greatest danger to myself, in case my letter should be intercepted before the bearer of it leaves England. But I have not thought this consideration of sufficient consequence to retard my purpose, since it was both godly in itself, and truly deserving of being known by every one, and especially by your reverence, by reason of that kindness and good-will which you entertain towards the very noble family of Grey in this country, and which you have not hesitated to illustrate by your own recorded testimony. But though this family is now overthrown and almost extinct, on account of their saving profession of our Saviour, and the cause of the gospel; yet all godly and truly christian persons have not so much reason to mourn over the ruin of a family so illustrious, as to rejoice that the latest action of her life was terminated in bearing testimony to the name of Jesus; and the rather, because those who rest with Christ the Lord in the kingdom of his Father, will not have to behold with their own eyes the wretched and lamentable overthrow of our nation. It is we, we who are wretched, who are not only hearing every day the name of the Saviour loaded with reproach, but witnessing the most horrible slaughter of those who have endeavoured to promote his glory, and extend his kingdom.

But to return to the Greys, about whom I purposed to commune with you in this letter, both on account of your peculiar regard for them, as evinced by your godly writings; and by reason of my own affection towards those now dead, to whom I diligently endeavoured, during their life-time, to prove my respect.

Jane then, the daughter of the duke, was truly admirable,

[1 Namely, lady Jane Grey.]

not so much by reason of her incredible attainments in literature, by which in the seventeenth year of her age she excelled
all other ladies, as by reason of the remarkable firmness with
which, though a young girl, she surpassed men in maintaining
the cause of Christ; insomuch that she could neither be
defeated by any contrivances which the papists imagined
against her, nor be deceived by any of their artifices, as your
reverence will understand from a discourse of hers which I
now send you.

This conference was held by her with master Feckenham[1],
a clever and crafty papist, upon some controverted points of
our religion, upon which she explained her opinion with much
learning and ingenuity. And that she persevered in this
confession of faith even to the last, is sufficiently evident
from the statement[2] she made a little before her execution.
This I have thought fit to send together with the other,
because they seemed to me worthy of being universally
known. Moreover, it may be seen how her truly admirable
mind was illuminated by the light of God's word, by two
letters, one of which she herself wrote to the lady Catharine[3],
her sister, a most noble virgin, to inspire her with a love of
the sacred writings, and the other to a certain apostate[4], to
bring him back to Christ the Lord. I have taken the pains
to translate both of these letters from our vernacular[5] language into Latin, that your excellence may perceive that the
pains which you have taken to enlighten that family and

[1 See this discourse given in Foxe, VI. 415.]
[2 See Foxe, VI. 424.]
[3 This letter is also given in Foxe, VI. 422. The lady Catherine
was afterwards married to Henry, son of William, earl of Pembroke,
by whom she was divorced. She was committed to the Tower by
queen Elizabeth in 1562, for her clandestine marriage with the earl of
Hertford. See Zurich Letters, first series, p. 103, n. 7.]
[4 This was Thomas Harding, afterwards known as the antagonist
of bishop Jewel. Foxe, who gives the letter, in his first edition,
refrains from naming him, "partly reverencing the worthy learning of
the person, and partly, again, trusting and hoping again of some better
towardness of the party hereafter." See Foxe, VI. 418.]
[5 It is interesting to find that lady Jane Grey wrote to Harding
in English, as some expressions in the Latin version, printed in her
Remains, have given occasion for reflections, which, from this letter of
Banks it appears, rather apply to him as the translator than to her as
the writer.]

incite them to the love of godliness have not been ill bestowed. For I can bear testimony, which, if not very abundant, is at least that of an eye-witness, that the whole family of the Greys, and Jane especially, derived incredible benefit from your writings. She indeed had not only diligently perused, but also committed to memory, almost all the heads of your sixth Decade.

The duke also himself devoted as much time as he could steal from the affairs of the nation, in which he was engaged, to the reading of scripture, and especially to your writings, with the milky eloquence of which he used to say that he was wonderfully delighted. From the reading of which too he derived the greatest benefit, when certain wicked wretches endeavoured to draw him away, while in prison, from the faith and confession of the true Christ. But they were in no wise able to move him; for he confessed the Lord Christ even to his latest breath[6]. And at the time he was led to execution, though the papists brought forward one of the council, a swine out of the herd, who defended the catholic church, the mass, the fathers, and customs established by length of time, yet he would not acknowledge any other atonement than that which was perfected by the death of Christ: by this faith he supported himself, and in this faith he at length ended his life. I would speak of the entire overthrow of religion in England, and the fury of antichrist, only that those who are continually coming over from England to Zurich, that most wealthy mart of all good learning, will make you acquainted with it. It now remains for me earnestly to entreat your reverence again and again to take this my service in good part, and to enrol me among the number of your friends; and to beseech the Lord that our England may at length be delivered from that tyranny of the papists by which she is now oppressed. Farewell, most excellent Bullinger, and continue, as you do, to set forth the kingdom of Christ in your writings! London, March 15, 1554.

[6 This statement is confirmed by the account given in Foxe, Acts and Mon. VI. 545, where Dr Hugh Weston is stated to have attended the duke of Suffolk at his execution.]

LETTER CXLII.

JOHN BANKS TO HENRY BULLINGER.

Dated at STRASBURGH, *Dec.* 9, 1554.

No circumstance has ever afforded me greater pleasure than the condescension of your reverence in not only admitting me among the number of your friends, but in so courteously declaring this by your written letter; in which, whenever I peruse it, as I do very frequently, I seem to observe two things especially worthy of commendation. In the first place your singular kindness appears from this circumstance, that a person like yourself, so justly admired by every one, should condescend, in the midst of so many and important engagements, to write to an obscure individual like myself. Your rare judgment in the next place is shewn by your disapproving of the publication[1] of what possibly may be injurious to many individuals; a circumstance which I had not before considered. I now, however, perceive that our adversaries in England are most mightily disturbed by certain pamphlets, and that they are endeavouring to exclude us from the liberality of those from whom we were expecting the necessary means of subsistence. Nothing indeed now seems to be left for us, but either that we English, who are in exile from our country for the sake of God's word, must support ourselves by the labour of our hands, or else implore the assistance of godly individuals to enable us to continue our studies; whereby, should it please God to restore us to our country, we may be able to refute the doctrines of the papists, and to explain to our people and nation the artifices by which they have been circumvented and deceived by them. The godly men, by whom we have hitherto been aided and supported, are either all of them cast into prison

[1 See above, Letter CXXXIV. p. 293. It seems that together with the preceding letter, Banks had sent to Bullinger the conference of lady Jane Grey with Feckenham, her letters to Harding and to her sister, with a view to their being published, but to which Bullinger made some objections from a fear of injuring the cause of the reformation in England.]

on our account, or, if any are still at liberty, they are so carefully watched by the papists, that they can afford us no assistance without the greatest danger. Whence it is, that we are at this time placed in great difficulty; and it is come to this, that each individual must look out how he can best provide for himself. For my own part, I have no hope of being able to continue in the course of studies I had determined to pursue; for he who has maintained[2] me hitherto, is now reduced to the like straits as the rest of the English, being spoiled of all his property, and (such is the malice of his enemies) without any hope. I speak of master James Haddon, a man who deserved to be rich for his liberality to the poor. Since, therefore, my condition is such, that I am unable, through want of means, to pursue the course of study I had proposed, I would willingly follow that which seems desirable in the next place, and engage in that kind of life which is most nearly allied to literary pursuits; in which object, as I understand your excellence has it in your power greatly to benefit me by your recommendation, relying upon that kindness which you have so manifestly expressed in your letter, I make bold to implore your aid and co-operation. There is a printer in your town, of the name of Froschover, of whose integrity and diligence in his art the bearer of this letter speaks most highly, and has advised me to use my endeavours to induce him by any means to employ me as a corrector and reviser of such books as are printed at his press. Your recommendation, I believe, will go far to effect this object. Wherefore, should your excellence grant me this favour, I shall consider myself to have received an especial benefit, and will use my best endeavours that you may not seem to have recommended an unworthy person. Farewell, most excellent sir, and most esteemed by me in the Lord. Strasburgh, Dec. 9, 1554.

Your piety's most devoted,

JOHN BANKS, *Anglus.*

[2 See Letter CXXXV. p. 295.]

LETTER CXLIII.

JOHN BANKS TO HENRY BULLINGER.

Dated at [STRASBURGH], *Jan.* 9, [1555].

I HAVE perceived by the letter of your reverence, not indeed written *to* me, but to my singular good patron and much esteemed master in Christ, master Haddon[1], *about* me, that you have no less exerted yourself on my behalf, than if I had been your own son, and not a stranger, and only known to you by letter. I cannot therefore express the thanks due to your reverence for the pains you have taken on my behalf. But when I reflect that you were born for this very purpose, to succour the brethren, and to shew yourself a true Christian, namely, one who devotes his talents to the good of all, not only the men of this present age, but of posterity also; I consider you in no respect inferior to the greatest characters, and that in your brotherly affection and incredible diligence you easily excel them all. There are indeed some very learned and truly pious persons, but who will not readily allow themselves to be withdrawn from their studies, even though from such interruption great advantage might arise to their brethren. But you on the contrary, seem to regard nothing as of more importance, than in the midst of your ministerial labours to allow of an interruption in those studies so necessary and beneficial to the church of Christ, and this too for no small interval, for the sake of affording aid to a poor wretch like myself, when placed in circumstances of some difficulty. Most gladly therefore would I express by some grateful attestation, how much I value your good will towards me; but this your more than paternal kindness towards me exceeds all power of expression or even of thought. I will diligently endeavour therefore, and it is all I can do, that you may not seem to have recommended an unworthy person. But as to your excusing yourself to me, who indeed am I, that one like yourself, so justly and universally respected, should think it necessary to excuse yourself in the

[1 See above, Letter CXXXVI. p. 297.]

midst of your important engagements, for not replying to
such an insignificant individual as I am, and who is moreover
so greatly indebted to your kindness, and had rather undergo
any thing than be in any way a hinderance to your studies?
Wherefore I return my best possible thanks to your piety,
and since I can do nothing else, I will always bear your
goodness in mind in my prayers; and I pray our great and
good God, through Christ our Saviour, very long to preserve
you to his church.   January 9, [1555].

Your piety's most devoted,

JOHN BANKS.

LETTER CXLIV.

THOMAS HARDING[2] TO HENRY BULLINGER.
Dated at NEW COLLEGE, OXFORD, Oct. 19, 1551.

IF, as it has been observed of[3] old, friendships have often
been dissolved by neglected intercourse, what is there, most
learned Bullinger, to preclude the hope that the friendship of
good men may be obtained and cemented by their being
addressed with courtesy and respect? and especially when
this is done upon just grounds, and without any suspicion of
flattery or self-interest.

For my own part, a regard to my duty, as well as the
very reasonable request of these young men to be introduced
to your notice, has afforded me a sufficient occasion of writing
to you.   For who can be so insensible to every courteous
feeling, as not to be compelled to write and return you thanks

[2 Thomas Harding was elected fellow of New college in 1536, and
afterwards appointed Hebrew professor by Henry VIII. He became
a papist in the reign of queen Mary, by whom he was preferred to a
prebend of Winchester, and the treasurership of Sarum. He is best
known by his controversy with bishop Jewel; for an account of which,
see the Zurich Letters, first series, Letter LXVII.]

[3 Πολλὰς δὴ φιλίας ἀπροσηγορία διέλυσεν. Arist. Ethic. VIII. 5.]

for those kind offices you did me when I was with you about
the first of May three years since, on my way into Italy,
whither I was then proceeding for the purpose of study? Nor
can I ever forget with what kindness you received me, and
with what liberality you entertained me; not to mention in
the mean time, with what learned and grave discourse you
detained me, who was exceedingly desirous of an interview
with you, for some hours in your house; and, to speak plainly,
satisfied my mind, when, inquiring and hesitating about some
matters, as they appeared to me, of no small importance, you
relieved me entirely from all doubt and perplexity. To this
I must add that other token of no common regard and esteem,
(for such I ought to consider it,) in that you then inquired my
name, just as if I were a person of consequence, and inscribed
it among your papers.

As often indeed as these acts of kindness recur to my
mind, as they do very frequently, I think of what Timotheus[1]
said respecting a supper of Plato, to which he was invited by
him, when he met him the next day, namely, that the suppers
of Plato were not only agreeable for the present moment, but
for the day following. The same thing may be affirmed in a
larger sense respecting your kindness, that it was not only gratifying for the moment, but has now been so for many months,
and will be, I hope, for many years. And indeed, had not
my circumstances ordered it otherwise, and drawn me away at
that time to other places, almost against my will, I should on
no account have suffered myself to have been so soon separated
and disunited from your most learned society, of which I had
then first begun to taste the enjoyment. But as the state of
my affairs has, contrary to my inclination, continually precluded
me from this happiness, it only remained for me to propose
to myself the occasional enjoyment of your society and intercourse by epistolary correspondence. And just as I had
returned to England, and was seeking how to carry this into
effect, and was purposing to write to you, John ab Ulmis,
who was (as he says) formerly your pupil, paid me a most
opportune visit. He prays me to commend these young men
to you by a written letter; which indeed I have promised very
readily, both for his own sake, with whom I have had some

[1 See Cic. Tusc. Disp. v. 35. Athenæus, x. p. 419. Ed. Lugd.
and Ælian, V. H. ii. 18.]

acquaintance, and also for their sakes, as perceiving them to
be such, as for their peculiar modesty, probity, and erudition,
are most entirely deserving of the warmest commendation.
You will not therefore, I entreat you, according to your most
kind disposition, think lightly of this my commendation, but
will receive into your kindness and good-will these youths,
Andrew Croariensis and Stumphius, on their return to you.
I dare assure you in the mean time from their very honourable and gentlemanly conduct, that however great may be
the advantage that may accrue to you from the regard of the
most worthy characters, no less will accrue to you from the
attachment of the persons in question; and that you will
acknowledge them to be young men of tried probity, courtesy,
and honourable feeling, as well as of unvaried good temper.
You will certainly confer upon me the greatest obligation, if
you will so conduct yourself towards them, as to make them
know that this my recommendation has had some weight with
you. Farewell. Oxford, New College, Oct. 19, 1551.

Salute very affectionately from me our friend Butler[2].

LETTER CXLV.

HENRY SIDALL TO HENRY BULLINGER.

Dated at CHRIST CHURCH, OXFORD, *Oct.* 4, [1552].

MUCH health. Last year, most honoured sir, I received
a letter from your excellence in favour of this youth ab Ulmis,
which was on many accounts very gratifying to me, but, if
I must speak the truth, altogether superfluous. For his piety,
integrity, and zeal for learning had already so interested me

[2 John Butler, of a noble family, having travelled about Germany,
and thence into France, and afterwards into Italy, seated himself at
last in Zurich, where he became greatly acquainted with John Wol-
phius, the learned printer, who dedicated to him, in the year 1552, the
second edition of P. Martyr's tract of the sacrament. See Strype,
Mem. I. i. 545.]

in his favour, that I should consider myself to have received
a benefit by having it in my power to confer one upon him.
For any individual, in whom I discover such good qualities,
cannot but be very dear to me, to whatever country he may
belong; for I heartily detest all respect of persons. In this
large college my trifling exertions cannot have been of much
advantage to him; but my mind has at all times been well-
disposed towards him, which I can promise will always be the
case, provided only, which I hope will not take place, he shall
not change his conduct. But since he has now gone back to
you, and is, it seems, somewhat doubtful of returning to
England, I do not see how I can be of any service to him in
future, except perhaps by imploring your clemency to regard
him with greater kindness and affection than hitherto, which
I most ardently entreat your piety to do. For his conduct
in this numerous society of learned men has always been so
amiable and unpolluted, and so obedient to all our statutes
and domestic regulations, that it has most justly earned for
him the greatest commendation from all persons, and a more
than paternal regard from myself. Moreover, his discretion
has always been exceedingly approved by me, inasmuch as
he has so accommodated himself to our habits, that he never
could justly be reproached by any one as a foreigner, but
has deserved universal commendation as one conversant with
our laws and country. I have thought it my duty to acquaint
your excellence in good faith with these matters, lest any
suspicion should arise on your part that he has conducted
himself otherwise in this place than would become a youth of
the most excellent character. I should have written to you at
this time concerning our university of Oxford, and the restoration of religion, and the number of the godly among us,
only that this youth will be able to relate all these things to
you better at your leisure. Your piety may know this for
an undoubted truth, that many among us are exceedingly
united to you in spirit, although personally separated by sea
and land; among whom I wish to be counted the chief. For
although I am far inferior in many other respects, in this
I will yield to no one. Farewell in the Lord. Oxford,
Christ Church, Oct. 4, [1552].

[H. SIDALL.]

LETTER CXLVI.

RALPH SKINNER TO HENRY BULLINGER.

Dated at OXFORD, *Jan 5*, [1550].

HEALTH and peace in the Lord.   John ab Ulmis has frequently requested me long since, most excellent Bullinger, to send you a letter; but latterly he has left no stone unturned to extort from me these few lines, and I must candidly confess that he has not without difficulty induced me to write now.   Not that I entertained any doubt of your kindness, or that the ingenuousness of your disposition has not been well known long since both by your own writings and the report of others; but partly from my having forgotten how to write Latin by reason of long disuse, and partly because I am too modest to presume to trouble, with my unpolished letter, you who are occupied in so many and important affairs of the church.   I readily admit, most learned sir, that I owe you this duty; and I acknowledge also, that I owe you many and great thanks for the honourable mention which you made of me in your letter to my patron, the marquis of Dorset. I have certainly long regarded you with the greatest love and veneration, for the sake of the true religion, and considered myself much indebted to you in the name of all christian people.   But latterly, my Bullinger, you have so bound me to you for my own sake and that of my country, that you cannot in future attach me more.   For you seem to be affected with as it were a father's feeling, and no ordinary regard towards our England.   You have every where publicly eulogised that country in many ways by your excellent lucubrations and most learned writings.   And on this account you have obtained true and just praise with all good and learned men, of whom, thank God, a great number is at this time found among us.   And you may learn from this, that you have not laboured among us in the Lord's vineyard to no purpose; and how much honour and gratitude is owing to our excellent king, and how much we owe to our rulers, who not only are favourers of the truth themselves, but are also good and firm patrons of all who embrace it.   And you have certainly bestowed upon them in these your writings no un-deserved or unworthy commendation. For they justly deserve it, and are to be praised on every account; and we very properly rejoice, whenever it has happened that you have dedicated your lucubrations to men of this character. For an useful stimulus is hence afforded to them in their progress, and encouragement given, that they may not be weary of completing in the best way what they have well begun. And this I hope will very soon be the case. For they have lately assembled a convocation, and appointed certain persons to purify our church from the filth of antichrist, and to abolish those impious laws of the Roman pontiff, by which the spouse of Christ has for so long a time been wretchedly and shamefully defiled; and to substitute new ones, better and more holy, in their place. It will be our duty meanwhile, diligently to implore God our Father and the Lord Jesus Christ, that true, pure, and undefiled religion may at length begin to flourish, not here only, but throughout the whole earth. I have written, excellent Bullinger, at greater length than I at first intended, and yet there remain many things, with which I could wish you to be acquainted, did time suffice for that purpose. But I will defer them for the present. I shall in my next letter possibly impart all my grievances. Mean-while, excellent sir, farewell, and I pray God that he may long preserve you to us for the manifestation of his glory! Oxford, Jan. 5.

Yours heartily,

RALPH SKINNER.

LETTER CXLVII.

JOHN WILLOCK TO HENRY BULLINGER.

Dated at OXFORD, *May* 12, 1552.

HEALTH in Christ. I came over to Oxford on the 11th of May, which as soon as John ab Ulmis knew, he has never ceased asking me, most excellent sir, to send you a letter. I could not therefore refuse him, as he requested what is proper, and rightly reminded me of my duty.   I wrote you a letter soon after Christmas, but know not whether it ever reached you.   I will therefore only at present briefly touch upon the heads of what I then wrote.   First of all, I return ever-lasting thanks for the kindness by which you were induced to make such affectionate mention of me in your dedicatory preface to our prince.   I have ever admired your universally acknowledged learning and erudition; but I now embrace again and again, and most readily recognise, your exceeding kindness and incredible regard to myself.   The prince cer-tainly received that little present of yours with a most grate-ful and well-disposed mind; and you must know that you have not acted more honourably, than usefully and piously; for, as Socrates says, the exhortations of great men are as a whip and spur to happy perseverance in a praiseworthy course of life.   Every night, when we were employed on the Scottish borders, after the book had been received there from John ab Ulmis, with great difficulty on his part, his highness was not satisfied with having a large portion of your book merely read to him, but would have it diligently examined; by which I perceived him, endued as he was with a most excellent disposition, greatly to improve; and indeed he very often expressed himself greatly obliged to you for it.

You will truly learn the state of my affairs from the bearer of this letter.   I had intended at first to have written more, but business and my journey itself necessarily call me elsewhere. I will however add a few things to which you will exceedingly oblige me by sending a reply.   First then, I ask, whether that be a legitimate and true marriage which is contracted without the knowledge or consent of parents; and whether those persons can be said to live piously and lawfully in holy matrimony, who being so married, continue in the same; or whether they may be allowed to separate themselves again at the desire of their parents.   I ask, secondly, whether a woman leaving her own husband, and attaching herself to another during his life-time, may be allowed to marry him after the death of her own husband, to whom during that husband's life-time she had attached herself.   I inquire, thirdly, whether those are to be considered as living piously in holy wedlock, who through fear of death in time of persecution have mutually betrothed themselves without witnesses, but have nevertheless declared before many persons that they were married, and have lived together for the space of twenty years. I entreat you again and again briefly to explain your sentiments upon these points. I have written hastily and in confusion : take it in good part, as I doubt not but that you will do. Farewell, most excellent and very dear master Bullinger, and always commend my ministry in your prayers. Oxford, May 12, 1552.

Your honour's most devoted,

JOHN WILLOCK.

LETTER CXLVIII.

BARTHOLOMEW TRAHERON TO HENRY BULLINGER.

Dated at LONDON, *Feb.* 20, [1540].

I SHOULD indeed be uncourteous, most learned Bullinger, not to address you by letter, who, when I was among you[1], treated me with so much kindness. You can however guess the reason of my not having written last fair. And though the same reason may possibly still exist, I have thought it right to break my silence, lest my delay should seem not so much to arise from the state of the time, as from forgetfulness and neglect. But this, believe me, is not at all agreeable to my disposition. For my mind is by no means insensible to mutual friendship, and I am of all persons least unmindful of any kindness that has been shewn me. I have nothing to relate at present, except that all the monks in this country have lost the appellation, that some of the principal monasteries are turned into schools of studious men, and that three

[1 Bartholomew Traheron was a favourer of the reformation, and had been much persecuted when at Oxford by Dr Loudon, warden of New college, in 1527, or 1528. Strype, Mem. I. i. 581.]

of the most wealthy abbots[2] were led to execution a little
before Christmas, for having joined in a conspiracy to restore
the pope. I must not omit to tell you that the bishop of Winchester preached a very popish sermon, to the great discon-
tent of the people, on the first Sunday in Lent, and that he
was ably answered by Dr Barnes on the following Lord's
day with the most gratifying, and all but universal, applause.
The points which the bishop principally handled I have
related to John Butler, from whom you may learn them.
You will hear other news from other correspondents. The
Lord Audley[3], an excellent man, and in the king's service,
has conceived a great regard for you from my commendation,
and has bidden me not only to salute you respectfully in his
name, but to tell you, that if you send over your son to this
country, he will treat him with the attention due to the
offspring of a very dear and honoured man. I salute much
your mother, wife, brothers, children, and the whole family.
Salute likewise in my name those worthy and excellent men
masters Pellican, [Leo] Judæ, Rhelican[4], and Megander.
Farewell. London, Feb. 20.

[B. TRAHERON.]

LETTER CXLIX.

BARTHOLOMEW TRAHERON TO HENRY BULLINGER.

[Before *Feb*. 18, 1546.]

HEALTH in the Lord. I wrote to you many weeks
since, and gave the letter to our most loving friend, master

[2 These were Richard Whiting of Glastonbury, Hugh Faringdon
of Reading, and John Beach of Colchester. The abbots of Glastonbury and Reading had been found to have aided the northern in-
surgents by large supplies of money and plate. See Soames, II. 278,
and Burnet, I. 384.]

[3 Thomas Audley, lord chancellor, was created baron Audley of
Walden, in 1538. He died in 1544, when the barony became extinct.]

[4 This is probably an error, but it is so in the copy.]

Calvin, who was going to Berne, that it might be forwarded
to you from thence. But as far as I can judge by the letter
which you sent by master Butler's messenger, mine has not
yet reached you; and as I make no doubt but that you
would have made some mention of it, this circumstance annoys
and vexes me not a little. For as the rest of my countrymen have written to you, and as I myself too have addressed
others in your city by letter, you might well charge me with
ingratitude for having neglected you, to whom I owe so
much. Had I really done so, I doubt not but that some time
or other I should have suffered the just vengeance of Jupiter
the protector of strangers. But believe me, I thought of
nothing less, and therefore sent off my letter to you before
my singular good friend and very dear brother, master Butler,
had procured this messenger. But, as I perceive, the matter
turned out unfortunately. It has indeed vexed me most
exceedingly, not that there was any thing in the letter which
I considered worth your reading, but from the fear that I may
possibly be regarded by you as either undervaluing your friendship towards me, or being unmindful of your kindness. And
I hardly know which of these two I should choose the least.
It is a proof of your singular courtesy that you have joined me
in your letter to master Butler. Whence also I have good
hope that you will not unwillingly accept this my vindication,
although I call heaven to witness that I have not in any way
offended against our friendship, unless perhaps this may be
called an offence, that I did not write you another letter
when a regular messenger was at hand; and in this I
acknowledge myself to be somewhat to blame. But who
would have thought that the letter would not reach you
which I gave to master Calvin, and he again to master
Megander? If I ever allow from henceforth any messenger
to come over to you from us without a letter from me, you
are at liberty to esteem me among the number of the ungrateful, or even of those who hate their friends; which however, of
all deeds of wickedness, I would least wish to attach to myself.
For I am, if any one is, so disposed to mutual affection, that
sometimes I do every thing but doat even upon those who wish
no good to myself. At all events, I have such an affection
for all learned men who have deserved well of me, that
nothing affords me more pleasure, or is more deeply rooted

in my mind.   How then can I forget you, whose erudition has always been most delightful and profitable to me, and whose acts of kindness to me are so numerous? There is no reason, therefore, why you should suppose that it arose from forgetfulness of you, that my letter has not yet reached you; but there is a reason why you should make inquiry of master Megander, who has neglected to forward it.   You perceive, I hope, that I am not at all to blame, excepting that I did not write to you twice.   I heartily congratulate you on the accession of a little son, and one too, who was christened on the day of his birth; and I no less rejoice that the very excellent lady, your wife, is delivered from this danger.   We are very anxious to know what Luther and his party are doing about the eucharist.   There is I know not what report here, that the minds of the Bernese are somewhat inclined to Bucer's opinions.   Here, as far as we have been able to judge hitherto, all things are properly set forth.

To yourself, all your children, your excellent wife, grandmother, and Rodolph, I wish all happiness and prosperity, and true joy in Christ.   Farewell, my very dear friend master Bullinger, with all belonging to you.

[B. TRAHERON.]

LETTER CL.

BARTHOLOMEW TRAHERON TO HENRY BULLINGER.

Dated at LONDON, *Aug.* 1, [1548].

WHAT more delightful gratification could possibly be afforded me, than to receive a letter from so great a distance, from one who is on many accounts so dear to me, and whom, by reason of his singular piety and erudition, I can never sufficiently admire?   You have also, my excellent Bullinger, anticipated me in deserving the commendation of courtesy: but as there is perhaps no occasion for me to state the reason of my so long silence, nor indeed can I do so without much pain, I shall let it pass, and express my thanks to you for your most agreeable letter, which has indeed cheered me more than I am able to express. For I am thus led to consider that the pure form of religion is now set forth among you, and that your own exertions in this cause have been such as to render the remembrance of you at all times most delightful to me.

As to our own affairs, and the extent to which we have made progress in matters of religion, I do not think you can be ignorant. You must know that all our countrymen, who are sincerely favourable to the restoration of truth, entertain in all respects like opinions with you; and not only such as are placed at the summit of honour, but those who are ranked in the number of men of learning. I except the archbishop of Canterbury and Latimer, and a very few learned men besides; for from among the nobility I know not one whose opinions are otherwise than what they ought to be. As to Canterbury, he conducts himself in such a way, I know not how, as that the people do not think much of him, and the nobility regard him as lukewarm. In other respects he is a kind and good-natured man. As to Latimer, though he does not clearly understand the true doctrine of the eucharist, he is nevertheless more favourable than either Luther or even Bucer. I am quite sure that he will never be a hinderance to this cause. For, being a man of admirable talent, he sees more clearly into the subject than the others, and is desirous to come into our sentiments, but is slow to decide, and cannot without much difficulty and even timidity renounce an opinion which he has once imbibed. But there is good hope that he will some time or other come over to our side altogether. For he is so far from avoiding any of our friends, that he rather seeks their company, and most anxiously listens to them while discoursing upon this subject, as one who is beyond measure desirous that the whole truth may be laid open to him, and even that he may be thoroughly convinced. But more upon this subject when I have more time.

Salute, I pray you in my name, those excellent and most learned men, masters Theodore Bibliander, the ornament not only of Switzerland, but of all Germany; Gualter, and the rest, together with the most courteous mayor, my host, and your amiable wife. Farewell. London, Aug. 1.

Yours,

BARTHO. TRAHERON.

I have not yet been able to see the young man whom you commended to me, because I was absent from London when he arrived. If I can be of service to him in any way, I shall most readily exert myself for your sake. I hear that he is now at Oxford. Again farewell.

LETTER CLI.

BARTHOLOMEW TRAHERON TO HENRY BULLINGER.

Dated at LONDON, *Sept.* 28, [1548].

How greatly am I indebted to you, most excellent Bullinger, who have thought proper not only to address me in a most courteous letter, but to present me also with your learned and pious lucubrations. I feel myself unable to express by words the pleasure which this your regard to me has afforded. I should most gladly have addressed you by letter long since, but such painful events have occurred among us during this year, and altogether so unheard of, that I could not apply my mind to write; indeed, I scarcely wished to live. I doubt not but that you will have heard the whole history. All things, through the wonderful goodness of God, seem now settled. The religion of Christ, which appeared to be giving way, stands firm; and this we attribute solely to the providence of God. We fear, however, lest Flanders should occasion some disturbance. We have a king who is firm, learned, and pious beyond his age. If there has ever existed a Josiah since the first of that name, this is certainly he. And do you also be pleased to implore our common Father in your public prayers to preserve him to us in safety. Believe me, my Bullinger, a more holy disposition has no where existed in our time. He alone seems to sustain the gospel by his incredible piety, most holy manners, prudence altogether that of an old man, with a firmness at this age altogether unheard of. So great a work of God ought not to

21

be unknown to the godly.   But that you may add yet more
to the praises of God, you must know that Latimer[1] has come
over to our opinion respecting the true doctrine of the eucharist, together with the archbishop of Canterbury[2] and the
other bishops, who heretofore seemed to be Lutherans.   Let
us implore God with our united prayers, to complete a work
so favourably begun; and may he long preserve you and
yours! Salute very much my dear brethren masters Pellican,
Bibliander, and Gualter.   Farewell.   London, Sept. 28.

Yours,

BARTHOLOMEW TRAHERON.

LETTER CLII.

BARTHOLOMEW TRAHERON TO HENRY BULLINGER.

Dated at LONDON, *Dec* 31, 1548.

I CANNOT refrain, my excellent Bullinger, from acquaint-
ing you with circumstances that have lately given us the
greatest pleasure, that you and your fellow-ministers may
participate in our enjoyment.   On the 14th of December, if
I mistake not, a disputation was held at London[3] concerning

[1 "It was but seven years before his burning that he relinquished
that old error," namely, his opinion for a corporal presence, "that is,
about the year 1547, as he confessed to Dr Weston."   Strype, Cranm.
97.]

[2 See above, p. 13, n. 1.   For a full account of Cranmer's sur-
render of the Lutheran tenets, see Jenkyns, Pref. to Cranmer, LXXVI.
LXXVII.]

[3 This seems to be the disputation mentioned in K. Edward's
journal, as given in Burnet, IV. 204.   "A parliament was called, where
an uniform order of prayer was institute, before made by a number of
bishops and learned men gathered together in Windsor.   There was
granted a subsidy, and *there was a notable disputation of the Sacrament
in the parliament house.*"   This parliament sat Nov. 24th—March 15th.
It appears from the journals of both houses, that K. Edward's First
Liturgy was read the first time in the Commons on Wednesday,
Dec. 19 (not 9, as Burnet says, II. 148), and in the Lords on the day
following.   This disputation therefore was probably held to give information to parliament upon the subject to which it referred, and
to teach them how to deal with the new Book of Common Prayer
about to be placed before them by the committee of bishops.]

the eucharist, in the presence of almost all the nobility of England. The argument was sharply contested by the bishops. The archbishop of Canterbury, contrary to general expectation, most openly, firmly, and learnedly maintained your opinion upon this subject. His arguments were as follows. The body of Christ was taken up from us into heaven. Christ has left the world. "Ye have the poor always with you, but me ye have not always," &c. Next followed the bishop of Rochester[4], who handled the subject with so much eloquence, perspicuity, erudition, and power, as to stop the mouth of that most zealous papist, the bishop of Worcester[5]. The truth never obtained a more brilliant victory among us. I perceive that it is all over with Lutheranism, now that those who were considered its principal and almost only supporters, have altogether come over to our side. We are much indebted to the Lord who provides for us also in this particular. I was unwilling, my dear friend, to defraud you of so great a pleasure, and which I pray God you may long enjoy. Cordially salute master Bibliander and the other dear brethren. I heartily wish every blessing to your wife and children. Farewell. Dec. 31, 1548.

[Postscript, added by John ab Ulmis.]

Lo! just as master Traheron was about to send his letter, I happened to come into his room, and can do no otherwise than send you this brief salutation; for, owing to the great impatience of the messenger, I am unable to write more. I will tell you every thing in a few days. In haste. London. The foolish bishops have made a marvellous recantation.

LETTER CLIII.

BARTHOLOMEW TRAHERON TO HENRY BULLINGER.

Dated at OXFORD, *June* 12, 1550.

How greatly am I indebted to you, most excellent Bullinger, who not only condescend to greet me with a letter, couched in the most friendly terms, but also to instruct me by your very learned treatise; while I, for my part, have

[4 Bp. Ridley.]   [5 Bp. Heath.]

21—2

nothing wherewith to repay you, but a heart much attached to you, and which, believe me, I shall retain such as long as I live. And should any thing else at any time be in my power, I will not forget how much I owe you. Do you meanwhile continue to advance the christian religion by your erudite writings; you have all of us in this country favouring and applauding you. If you desire to know the state of our affairs, religion is indeed prospering, but the wickedness of those who profess the gospel is wonderfully on the increase. The people have made no disturbance this year, but there is reason to fear, lest roused partly by their own unquiet temper, and partly by the avarice of the higher orders, they should occasion some confusion, unless the Lord himself should think fit to avert it for the sake of our sovereign, who is making wonderful progress in learning, piety, and judgment. Be pleased to commend to God in your prayers this prince of the greatest hope, who is even now a defender of the christian religion almost to a miracle. For unless God, offended by our sins, should take him away from us before he is grown up to manhood, we doubt not but that England will produce another Constantine, or a character yet more excellent. I entreat you therefore, for Christ's sake, that you supplicate for him every happiness. For, although you are so far distant, even you may hence derive some advantage. For he both loves you, and acknowledges the religion of Christ to be exceedingly well established among you, and would have it ever to remain sound and unimpaired. Farewell, my most honoured brother. Oxford, June 12, 1550.

Yours,

BARTHO. TRAHERON.

LETTER CLIV.

BARTHOLOMEW TRAHERON TO HENRY BULLINGER.

Dated at LONDON, *Sept.* 10, 1552.

You have conferred a great obligation upon me, most learned Bullinger, who have both deigned to address me in

your most delightful letter, and moreover to present me with
one of your productions. For nothing can proceed from you
but what is, and ever will be, most agreeable. It occasions
me, meanwhile, no slight vexation that my circumstances
have not hitherto permitted, and do not yet permit me, to
declare how much I both love you, and acknowledge myself
your debtor. But should my affairs ever take a better turn,
I will certainly endeavour to make you understand, that I
both regard your singular kindness as I ought to do, and that
I bear in mind the especial courtesy which you shewed me
at Zurich. But I am now compelled to ask of you a new
favour, even while I can find nothing wherewith to oblige you
in return. I am exceedingly desirous to know what you and
the other very learned men, who live at Zurich, think respecting the predestination and providence of God. If you ask
the reason, there are certain individuals here who lived
among you some time, and who assert that you lean too
much to Melancthon's views [1]. But the greater number
among us, of whom I own myself to be one, embrace the
opinion of John Calvin as being perspicuous, and most agreeable to holy scripture. And we truly thank God, that that
excellent treatise of the very learned and excellent John
Calvin [2] against Pighius and one Georgius Siculus should
have come forth at the very time when the question began to
be agitated among us. For we confess that he has thrown
much light upon the subject, or rather so handled it, as
that we have never before seen any thing more learned or
more plain. We are anxious however, to know what are
your opinions, to which we justly allow much weight. We
certainly hope that you differ in no respect from his excellent
and most learned opinion. At least you will please to point
out what you approve in that treatise, or think defective, or
reject altogether, if indeed you do reject any part of it,

[1 For a statement of Melancthon's early doctrine, and subsequent
change of views on the subject of predestination, see Scott's Contin.
of Milner, II. 191, 207, &c. See also two letters from Calvin to Melancthon, dated Nov. 28, 1552, and Aug. 27, 1554, in Calv. Ep. Ed.
Genev. 1575, pp. 107, 133.]

[2 Calvin's Treatise, "De Æterna Dei Prædestinatione," is here referred to. It is printed in the eighth volume of his works, Amsterdam,
1667, and in the dedication and commencement is express mention of
its being an answer to Albert Pighius and George Siculus.]

which we shall not easily believe. And now enough of this subject. That worthy young man, John ab Ulmis, who is recalled home by a letter from his family, will better inform you of the situation of our affairs. Religion remains pure. Our most excellent king is in the best health, and makes daily progress in learning and piety. But, as I said, John ab Ulmis will give you a far more full and able account of these things. Farewell, my very dear sir, and love me much. Respectfully salute in my name master mayor my host, together with the other worthy and most learned brethren. London, Sept. 10, 1552.

Yours heartily,

BARTHOLOMEW TRAHERON.

LETTER CLV.

BARTHOLOMEW TRAHERON TO HENRY BULLINGER.

Dated at LONDON, *June* 3, [1553].

I ACKNOWLEDGE, my excellent Bullinger, your especial kindness, who for the sake of satisfying my earnest request have thought it no trouble to write to me so fully and accurately respecting the providence and predestination of God. But though I admire both your exceeding learning and moderation in this writing of yours, nevertheless, to say the truth, I cannot altogether think as you do. For you so state that God permits certain things, that you seem to take away from him the power of acting. We say that God permits many things, when he does not renew men by his Spirit, but gives them up to the dominion of their own lusts. And though God does not himself create in us evil desires, which are born with us; we maintain nevertheless, that he determines the place, the time, and mode [of bringing them into action], so that nothing can happen otherwise than as he has before determined that it should happen. For, as Augustine has it, he ordains even darkness. To be brief, we ascribe all actions to God, but leave to men whatever sin there is in them; which Augustine has, I think, stated in these words: "To sin is in the power of men, but to produce this or that effect by sinning belongs not to them, but to God, who ordains darkness[1]." Again, "God fulfils his own good purposes by the evil purposes of evil men[2]." And to this belongs that saying, that in some wonderful and ineffable manner that does not take place without his will, which is done even against his will.

But I am acting very indiscreetly in reminding you of these things, to whom all the writings of Augustine are so well known. You do not approve of Calvin, when he states that God not only foresaw the fall of the first man, and in him the ruin of his posterity, but that he also at his own pleasure arranged it[3]. And unless we allow this, we shall certainly take away both the providence and the wisdom of God altogether. I do not indeed perceive how this sentence of Solomon contains any thing less than this: "The Lord hath made all things for himself: yea, even the wicked for the day of evil." [Prov. xvi. 4.] And that of Paul: "Of him, and through him, and to him, are all things." [Rom. xi. 36.] I pass over other expressions which the most learned Calvin employs, because they occur every where in the holy scriptures. But I cannot think it either foolish or dangerous to follow that mode of speaking which the Holy Ghost useth. And did it not seem superfluous, I would entreat you again and again, to beware lest any disagreement be occasioned between you by reason of these things. For it will retard the course of the gospel not a little; and unless I am altogether mistaken, you will not be long able to support a cause that is tottering of itself.

If you will send your children hither, they shall be regarded by me as my beloved brothers. I have spoken with my dear friend master Cheke respecting Cœlius Secundus,

[1] Est ergo in malorum potestate peccare: ut autem peccando hoc vel hoc illa malitia faciant, non est in eorum potestate, sed Dei dividentis tenebras et ordinantis eas.—August. Op. Par. 1679-1700. De Prædest. Sanct. cap. xvi. 33. Tom. X. cols. 811, 2.]

[2] Nam Deus quasdam voluntates suas, utique bonas, implet per malorum hominum voluntates malas.—Id. Enchir. de Fid. Spe et Carit. cap. ci. 26. Tom. VI. col. 234.]

[3] See Calvin. Instit. III. xxiii. § 7. In Bullinger's reply to the preceding letter, which is much too long for insertion, after quoting the above passage, he says: "Ego certe sic loqui non ausim, utpote qui existimem gratiæ sinceritatem defendi posse, utcunque non dicamus Deum homines creare in exitium, et in illum finem ipsos deducere aut impellere indurando et excæcando." He adds, "Quis autem inficias ierit, Calvinum magnis a Deo ornatum esse muneribus?"]

who has, I think, informed you by letter either what he has done or is about to do. Farewell, very dear Bullinger, and salute all the brethren in my name, especially my most worthy host the mayor, master Gualter, my countryman master Butler, &c. Once more farewell. London, June 3, 1553.

Your most loving

BARTHOL. TRAHERON.

LETTER CLVI.

BARTHOLOMEW TRAHERON TO JOHN CALVIN.
Without place or date.

I AM now learning by experience, most accomplished Calvin, that whatever men may have proposed or determined, nevertheless every event is dependent upon the will of God; and that it often happens, that what we have purposed to do immediately, is accomplished either not at all, or after a long interval. For whereas I had fully resolved in my mind soon to visit you, it has now so happened that I really cannot tell when I shall be able to do so. For I have received a letter from home of such a nature, that I must go to England forthwith, whether I like it or not. I know not whether any event more painful could have occurred to me, certainly none more disagreeable; for I was desirous of passing at least a year with you, as with one whose society appeared to me most delightful and profitable. But, as I perceive, I must follow where fortune leads me. I pray you therefore, that, though we are far separated in person, we may yet be united in spirit. For you have deserved of me far otherwise than to make it possible for me ever to forget you; and I can no otherwise repay your favours to me than by the faithful remembrance of our friendship, which I shall most diligently and everlastingly retain. As to the rest, with respect to the ten crowns I placed in your hands, I would not ask for them, were I not afraid of wanting money for my journey. But take care that you do not put yourself to any inconvenience. Salute for me the worthy master Farell, with all our other friends by name. Farewell, my dear friend, long and happily!

[BARTHOLOMEW TRAHERON.]

LETTER CLVII[1].

PETER ALEXANDER TO PAUL FAGIUS.

Dated at LAMBETH, *March* 24, 1549.

THAT I have not yet written to you, my dear friend, you must attribute to no other cause but that I considered the letter which I wrote to that illustrious man, master Bucer, as intended also for yourself. But now, since I am commissioned by the most reverend the archbishop to address you in his name, I cannot forbear sending you at least a short letter, to inform you of his exceeding good-will and most favourable inclination towards you and your affairs. That I may not, therefore, detain you by any longer preamble, you must learn in few words the friendly feeling of our most reverend [archbishop], and his singular anxiety for the advancement of all the ministers of Christ. This excellent personage, who is the principal instrument in replacing the church of Christ in this kingdom, and restoring it to its purity, has been informed of your having been dismissed by the senate of your city[2]; and as, from his great anxiety for all godly ministers of the churches, he has taken a very lively interest in you and your affairs, he said it would be a very grievous thing both to you and your family, to be so unexpectedly deprived of a regular means of subsistence. And since these churches of ours are in great want of learned men, and as he supposes that you will not any longer be able to obtain an honourable livelihood in your own country, he desires to see you in this kingdom as soon as possible, and has commissioned me to invite you by this my letter in his name. I pray you, therefore, to come as soon as you possibly can, and cheer the most reverend archbishop, your attached friend, by your very early arrival. There is no doubt, excellent sir, of your obtaining some honourable situation in this country; for I know for certain that you will be appointed to a most distinguished office in the university,

[1 The original of this letter is preserved in the archives of St Thomas at Strasburgh. The letter of Alexander to Bucer of the same date and to the same effect is printed in Buceri Scripta Anglicana.]

[2 Both Fagius and Bucer were forced to leave Germany, upon the business of the Interim. See Burnet II. 140, Strype, Cranm. 281.]

either at Oxford or Cambridge, where you will derive a greater salary from your lectures than you ever received in your own country from your most important duties as a preacher. Do not therefore, I pray you, any longer put off your journey, but come over to us immediately. We have here the most reverend the lord archbishop of Canterbury, the most faithful son of the church, together with the most illustrious prince the lord protector, who, like another Joseph, next in rank to the king, is able to accomplish whatever he will, if only for the sake of Christ and the advancement of his glory. And this he does most admirably, for he is in no wise wanting in his exertions and endeavours for the church of Christ and its faithful members in this kingdom; as whatever we see likely to turn out to the praise of God, and the advantage of the church, he endeavours with all the powers of his mind to effect as speedily as possible. There is, moreover, that aged bishop master Latimer[1], who is most desirous of seeing you both, and who, since he has no little influence with the king, offers you his assistance in every possible way. Come over, therefore, sir, without delay[2]. Salute your wife in my name, together with your [daughter] Charity. Farewell. Dated at Lambeth, March 24, 1549.

Yours, and your host that is to be,

PETER ALEXANDER.

[1 Bishop Latimer was probably at this time nearly seventy years of age. He had for some time taken up his residence at Lambeth with his friend archbishop Cranmer, and refused to dispossess Heath, who had succeeded him in the see of Worcester, which he had resigned in consequence of the "six articles' act." See his sermons, Parker Society's Edition, p. 127.]

[2 Bucer and Fagius arrived safely in England in the end of April, and abode with the archbishop above a quarter of a year, until towards the end of the long vacation, the archbishop intending they should be at Cambridge, when the term should begin, Bucer being nominated professor of divinity, and Fagius of Hebrew. Strype, Cranm. 281. Soames, Hist. Ref. III. 499.]

LETTER CLVIII.

PAUL FAGIUS TO JOHN ULSTETTER.

Dated at CALAIS, *April* 18, 1549.

I GREET you much, my beloved son-in-law. Master Bucer and I quitted Strasburgh on the sixth of April, and having passed through Lorraine, Champagne, Picardy, Flanders and Artois, we arrived at Calais, the frontier city of England, without any difficulty whatever, on the eighteenth of the same month. We were no where better accommodated than in the dominions of the emperor, from whom we were only distant two days' journey. We were most kindly received at Calais by the city authorities, all of whom were most anxiously expecting us: we found also master Peter Alexander, who had been sent thither by the archbishop to await our arrival. Most desirable appointments are in store for us: only may the Lord enable us to accomplish somewhat that may tend to his glory, and the edification of his church, and then all will be well. Do you also, with your wife, my very dear daughter, render hearty thanks to the Lord for having with such fatherly care conducted us through all our enemies; and who we doubt not will mercifully protect us for the time to come. We shall have to remain at Calais for one or two days on account of the high winds. When we have crossed the sea, with Christ our guide, and have arrived in England, I will endeavour to acquaint you with my affairs at the earliest opportunity. Do you also endeavour to let me know, as soon as possible, the situation of your own affairs. Send your letter to Strasburgh to master Conrad Hubert, who will always be able to forward it to me without any difficulty. My son Paul[3] is at Canterbury, and, as master Peter tells me, in good health. I hope to see him on Easter Monday, if not before. Fare you well and happily, my very dear son-in-law[4], with your spouse, my very dear daughter; and salute for me most dutifully all my brethren, especially Erbius and Scriba. In haste, from Calais, April 18, 1549. I hope also my son Timothy is in good health:

[3 See above, Letter XX. p. 32.]

[4 John Ulstetter married Fagius's daughter Sarah, Nov. 11, 1547.]

if he continues to improve his morals, as you have led me to hope, he will in future be not less dear to me than heretofore. Be sure and let me see his letter by the first courier.

Your father-in-law,

PAUL FAGIUS, the elder.

LETTER CLIX.

PAUL FAGIUS TO JOHN ULSTETTER.

Dated at the Palace, LAMBETH, *April* 26, 1549.

MUCH health, my dearest son-in-law. I doubt not but that you are very anxious to learn how and when we arrived in England. You must know therefore, that on the eighteenth of April, under God's guidance, we happily reached Calais the frontier sea-port of England, where we were obliged to remain till the twenty-third of the same month owing to the roughness of the sea. On that day we crossed the channel, and reached London on the twenty-fifth. We thence proceeded by water to Lambeth, the palace of the archbishop of Canterbury, who received us with the greatest kindness. He wishes to send me to the university of Oxford, over which master Peter Martyr presides, for it is the most celebrated; and master Bucer to Cambridge. But we are urgent with his grace not to separate us, but to allow us to remain together for some time, which will be a great comfort to us both. We are however, still ignorant of our destination; for every thing is done by the king's order. May the Lord grant that, wherever we may be, we may approve ourselves unto him; which I request you to implore with us from him by fervent prayer. I cannot at present give you any certain information about English affairs. This however we have observed, that the harvest is plenteous, but the labourers are very few. Let us therefore entreat the Lord to send forth suitable labourers. We found my son Paul at Canterbury in good health. He has become well acquainted with the English language, and has a tolerable understanding of French; so that he now acts as my interpreter. He has so conducted himself, as to gain

the favourable opinion of all good and learned men, which
has cheered me exceedingly. We are still remaining with the
archbishop at Lambeth, in daily expectation of being sent to
the post assigned us. I request you again and again to
acquaint me with the state of your affairs. I hope we may
shortly meet. Farewell, together with my very dear pledges,
Sarah and Timothy. Salute all my brother-ministers most
dutifully from me, especially masters Erbius and Scriba. In
haste, from Lambeth, the palace of the archbishop, April 28,
in the year of salvation 1549.

Your father-in-law,

PAUL FAGIUS, the elder.

Master Bucer, with Negelin[1] and my son Paul desire
their dutiful respects.

LETTER CLX.

PAUL FAGIUS TO CONRAD HUBERT.

Dated at CROYDON, *May* 7, 1549.

MAY the only-begotten Son of God preserve you, your
wife, and all your family unto life eternal, my very dear
brother in the Lord! You will abundantly learn the present
state of our affairs both from the letter of master Bucer, and
the one I wrote to my wife, which I am very anxious for you
to read. On the first of May we removed from Lambeth to
Croydon, where the archbishop generally passes the summer.
On the fifth of the same month we were taken to court, where
access to the king's majesty was granted us immediately after
dinner. I cannot express with what kindness we were received by him, as well as by the lord protector, and others of
the nobility, and how he congratulated us upon our arrival.
This, indeed, exhilarated us beyond measure. Though he is
still very young, and very handsome, he gives for his age

[1 Matthew Negelin, afterwards a minister of Strasburgh, accompanied Bucer and Fagius into England, and was then with them at the
archbishop's house at Lambeth. See Strype, Cranmer, 279.]

such wonderful proofs of his piety, as that the whole kingdom and all godly persons entertain the greatest hopes of him. May our good and gracious God preserve him in safety many years, that he may be able to govern his kingdom long and happily, and at the same time to advance in various ways the kingdom of Christ, which we ought all of us to entreat for him from God with fervent prayers. We hoped that we should very soon have gone to Cambridge, but the plan is altered. For it seemed good to his majesty, the lord protector, and the archbishop, that we should translate the holy scriptures[1] from the original sources into Latin, with some brief explanations of the difficult passages in each chapter, and the addition of summaries and parallel places. All of which they wish afterwards to be translated into English, for the use of the preachers and people. It is certainly a work of much labour ; may God grant us strength!

These things, my excellent brother, I wish briefly to acquaint you with: I pray you communicate them to my wife. Every thing else you will learn from other letters. Farewell, with all your household, and all our brethren in the ministry, especially masters Marbach, Lenglin, Christopher, Martin, and Udalric, and also master Andernach, together with their dear wives. In haste, from the archbishop's house at Croydon, May 7, 1549.

Yours wholly,

PAUL FAGIUS, the elder.

LETTER CLXI.

BERNARDINE OCHINUS[2] TO WOLFGANG MUSCULUS.

Dated at LONDON, *July* 17, 1548.

GREETING. A letter has been brought me from Augsburg, in which are contained sad tidings respecting the state of the

[1 Fagius was to have taken the old testament, and Bucer the new, for their several parts. But their death put an end to the design.]

[2 See first Series, Letter XXIV. p. 58. For a further account of him see Mosheim, Eccles. Hist. cent. xvi. Part ii. chap. ii. § 42.]

church and commonwealth. For I am informed that the impious doctrine set forth by the emperor Charles has been received in many cities of Germany, some of whom influenced by fear, and others by foul superstition, had not courage to resist the ungodly edict. And, indeed, this most heavy chastisement from God, which leads men's minds into a denial of the truth, and into extreme destruction, is much more hurtful and calamitous than an internal and civil war could be to their bodies. But among the other states which have arrived at this wretchedness, is mentioned that of Augsburg[3], which, impelled by the menaces of the emperor, is forced to receive that abominable Interim[4]. They write too respecting yourself, that as you were unable to maintain with integrity and fidelity the office to which you had been called, you had abandoned the city[5], and sought refuge in a place of greater security. When therefore I made mention of your virtue and learning, and present misfortunes, to the most reverend the archbishop of Canterbury, he replied, that if you thought fit to come over into this country, he would provide you with some honourable means of subsistence. I considered that I owed this service to our long friendship; and I recommend and exhort you, by my love for you, not to despise the vocation offered you, in which you will probably be employed with much greater usefulness than, under existing circumstances, in any part of Germany. Farewell. I could not but commend you to him, and point out of what great use you would be, if you would come hither; and he said that he would provide for you and for your family. London, July 17, 1548.

BERNARDINE OCHINUS.

[3 In Augsburg the emperor displaced the magistrates, substituting for them creatures of his own, each of whom was sworn to observe the Interim. See Sleidan, 469, 470.]

[4 Interimendum illud Interim. *Orig.*]

[5 Wolfgang Musculus was minister of the church of Augsburg till 1548, when, on the entry of Charles V. into the city, and the consequent re-establishment of popery, he retired to Berne, where he was elected professor of divinity, and where he died in 1563.]

LETTER CLXII.

BERNARDINE OCHINUS TO WOLFGANG MUSCULUS.

Dated at LONDON, Dec. 23, 1548.

GREETING. I gave your letter to the most reverend the archbishop of Canterbury, having read which, he declared himself exceedingly desirous that you should come hither: he said moreover, that there was but little hope of Upper Germany, and repeated his promise of providing every thing necessary for yourself and family. He has commissioned a certain merchant, by name Richard Hilles, to supply you by his order with the money required for your journey, in case you should come. You will receive, I think, the letter of this merchant together with mine. I will add, that there are in London more than five thousand Germans, to whom you may preach and administer the sacraments; and if you wish to lecture at Cambridge, you will be able to do so. All things, I hope, will be reformed. I have now done my part; may Christ direct you! My wife and daughter are well, and salute you with your wife and children. Farewell, and remember me in Christ. London, Dec. 23, 1548.

BERNARDINE OCHINUS.

LETTER CLXIII.

WOLFGANG MUSCULUS TO HENRY BULLINGER.

Dated at BERNE, March 12, 1549.

(EXTRACT.)

..... BERNARDINE (Ochinus) is inviting me to England by his letters, two of which I have now received dated on the 23rd and 31st December, to this effect: "I have shewn your letter to the most reverend the archbishop of Canterbury, which when he had read, he most decidedly manifested his great desire that you should come to England, and he again confirmed what he had before promised. But as you wrote that you had still some expectation in Germany, he immediately subjoined that such hopes were of a very slender nature; but that as you stated that you had a large family, and feared the expense would be greater than you could afford, he had been speaking to a certain merchant to supply you with every necessary. He will send, I think, a hundred crowns for your journey. Now if you require my sincere opinion, I recommend and exhort you to come. A lectureship will be provided for you at Cambridge; and should not that situation meet your wishes, you might preach publicly in London, where a numerous auditory would not be wanting. For there are more than five thousand Germans[1] here, to whom you would doubtless be most acceptable. I am therefore very desirous that, if you can do so without great inconvenience, you should come over as soon as possible. I have nothing more to write about the archbishop, except that he is daily becoming more favourable to evangelical truth. And though some reports of a contrary character have hitherto prevailed respecting him, he is now really shewing himself to be a most godly person, and that he has nothing more at heart than that Christ should flourish and be triumphant. We are therefore upon the most harmonious and friendly terms."

Thus far he. As to myself, I have no thoughts of this invitation, unless (as I before wrote to Bernardine) there should not be afforded me an opportunity of serving Christ in Germany. I am however very much pleased that the pure form of Christianity is daily more and more prevailing in that kingdom, which will doubtless receive many exiles flying thither for refuge. Wherefore we must unceasingly pray God to put an end at length to that perilous war with Scotland, whence evils of no ordinary kind may arise to that kingdom, unless the mercy of God avert them. Farewell, most illustrious sir. Berne, March 12, 1549.

Yours in the Lord,

W. MUSCULUS.

[1 The king's letters patent to John a Lasco and the German congregation are given in Burnet, IV. 308. They are dated July 24, 1550. Among the ministers is mentioned Ricardus Gallus, of whom see below, p. 339. n. 1.]

LETTER CLXIV.

PETER OF PERUGIA[1] TO HENRY BULLINGER.

Dated at CAMBRIDGE, *Feb.* 10, 1550.

GREETING.   Although I am personally unknown to you, most learned and accomplished Bullinger, this circumstance need not prevent me from addressing you with every feeling of affection and respect, and desiring to gratify you to the utmost of my power.   For I am not so ignorant as not to perceive the extent of those obligations which all those who, like myself, embrace the pure doctrines of the gospel, owe to you and others of the like character, by reason of those admirable exertions and services by which you have again purified the church of Christ itself, which had been miserably defiled by antichrist.   I pray you therefore, most godly Bullinger, to assure yourself of every service from me which a grateful pupil can render to his instructor, and which I would desire to prove to you rather from the active performance of them than from a mere verbal declaration.

The state of England is at this time entirely tranquil, compared with what it was during the last year.   The duke of Somerset, who had been the king's governor, and who was so ignominiously committed to the Tower of London, is now at length delivered by the divine blessing, and most honourably set at liberty.   And although he is deprived of his former office, he will nevertheless be able to live with honour and magnificence upon the revenues that they have left him.   You see therefore the wonderful mercy of God towards his elect : for from the beginning it was the general opinion that he would suffer death; but it has turned out far otherwise.   The gospel in this country is rather extending itself more widely than suffering any change.   Masters Bucer, Bernardine, and Peter Martyr, are most actively labouring in their ministry, and are indeed most useful.

[1 Pietro Bizarro of Perugia is mentioned in a letter of Languet to Sir Philip Sidney, with high commendations of his eloquence, and remarks on the want of wisdom in the English in not "earning the good-will of such a man." See the Correspondence of Sidney and Languet, collected by Rev. Steuart A. Pears, p. 2. He was entertained divers years with the earl of Bedford; and expecting preferment here, failing of it, he departed and lived abroad. Strype, Ann. III. i. 660.]

We have great hopes of a peace with France, although we do not yet know upon what terms it will be effected. May our most gracious God grant that all things may turn out happily: and I earnestly pray him long to preserve yourself, together with masters Pellican, Bibliander, Gualter, Vergerius, and the whole church, to the glory of his name. Master Bucer, who is now at the university of Cambridge, where he is lecturing with the greatest eloquence and godliness upon Paul's Epistle to the Ephesians, most affectionately salutes you and your church. Cambridge, February 10, 1550.

Your most attached and devoted,
PETER of Perugia,

an exile from Italy, his native country, by reason of his confession of the doctrine of the gospel.

LETTER CLXV.

THOMAS NORTON TO JOHN CALVIN.

Dated at LONDON, *Nov.* 13, 1552.

HAVING understood from your letter to master Richard[2], the preacher of the word here in the French church, that you were desirous to know what had become of the children of my late master, the duke of Somerset, the consideration of your kindness affected me with exceeding delight and satisfaction; and I seemed to recognise the kindly feeling of an excellent and truly christian pastor, who do not account as unworthy of your remembrance and regard, in their present fallen state, those individuals who have been cast down from the pinnacle of prosperity on which they had formerly been placed. Wherefore, although it may hardly seem to be within my province to answer for another, yet induced by the request of master Richard, partly because no one can give you

[2 A memorandum written about the end of the 16th century, speaks of Richard Vauville as "a man sound and perfect in christian piety," the minister of a church at London, in which "French was spoken," on the authority of the preface of a work written by Poulain, printed in 1552. See Burns, Hist. of Foreign Protestant Refugees, Lond. 1846, p. 24. Beza says, " Vauville est mort, ministre en l'église Françoise de Frankfort, apres la dissipation d'Angleterre, où il avoit long temps servi heureusement." Hist. Eccles. Anvers, 1580, I. 57. He also bore the name of Richard François.]

22—2

more certain information upon this subject than myself, who
am still attached to them, and partly because, from your most
courteous reply to my last, I perceive that a letter of mine
will not be unacceptable to you, I have thought fit to acquaint
you in writing with their present circumstances.   After God
had taken away from us the duke himself by the hand of the
executioner, because, alarmed for his own life, he was reported
to have plotted the destruction of certain others of the royal
council; it was enacted in the collective assembly of the realm,
(which from a French word we call a parliament, from the
freedom of speech there allowed,) that himself and his sons
by Anne[1] his wife, who cannot be unknown to you, though
you have never seen her, and whom he married upon the
decease of his former wife Catharine[2], should be deprived of
the dukedom, earldom, and barony, as it is called, and also of
any other titles of honour bestowed by reason of services
rendered to the state ; and that they should be reduced to
the lowest rank of nobility.   With respect to their maintenance, the following provision was made.   The eldest
daughter Anne[3], with whom you have corresponded, has been
married nearly three years to the earl of Warwick, son and
heir of the duke of Northumberland, and is happily and
honourably settled.   The other four, Margaret[4], Jane, Maria,
and Catharine, are unmarried, and committed by the council
to the care of their aunt[5], the widow of the lord Cromwell, to
whom four hundred marks are yearly paid by the king for

[1 The duke of Somerset married for his second wife, Anne,
daughter of sir Edward Stanhope of Sudbury, co. Suffolk. She died
in 1587, aged 90.]

[2 This lady was daughter and coheir of sir William Fillol.]

[3 This lady was afterwards married to sir Edward Ampton, knight
of the bath. Strype, Mem. II. ii. 8.]

[4 Margaret was sought in marriage by the lord Strange in 1551,
and with the approval of the king. But that match did not take
effect, and she died unmarried, as did her sisters Catharine and Jane,
the latter of whom it was said the duke secretly endeavoured to
match with the king. Strype, as above.]

[5 Elizabeth, second daughter of sir John Seymour, and sister of
queen Jane Seymour and the duke of Somerset, married successively
sir Anthony Oughtred, and Gregory, lord Cromwell, son of the earl of
Essex.   He died in 1551.   His widow was originally to receive 300
marks, or £50. for each of these four ladies per annum, which salary
was, November 1, increased to 100 marks a year apiece. Strype,
Mem. II. ii. 7.]

their maintenance, according to the act of parliament. Each mark is worth thirteen shillings and fourpence. The youngest daughter, Elizabeth, who is now in her second year, is with her aunt Smith[6], who lost her husband about four months since, and to whom in like manner a hundred marks are yearly assigned for her support. To Edward[7], his son and heir, thirteen years old, and as it were the living image of his father, out of the estates which yielded annually to his father [. . . . .][8] thousand pounds of our money, each of which is equivalent to four golden crowns, as they call them, there is reserved, by the same act of parliament, about two thousand four hundred pounds, more or less. The surplus, with all the personalty, was paid, as is wont, into the exchequer. He, with his two brothers, Henry and Edward[9], the latter five years old, and the other twelve, is with the lord treasurer of England. They are wards of the king, to whom, so long as they are under age, belongs the guardianship of noble orphans, and also the use, enjoyment, and management of their estates. They are liberally educated, and have no other attendants or governors but those to whom they were entrusted by their father in his life-time. Philip Gilgate, a worthy gentleman, is their governor, and I retain my old office of instructing them. But you may perhaps feel uncomfortable at their residing in the house of that individual, the marquis of Winchester[10], of whose religion you may have been

[6] Dorothy, youngest daughter of the above sir John Seymour, married sir Clement Smith, knight, a gentleman of Essex, who died August 26, 1552. In February, 1552, there was a warrant to the exchequer to pay this lady an annuity of 100 marks towards the finding the lady Elizabeth during her abode with her. This Elizabeth afterwards married sir Richard Knightly of Fawsley, and died in 1602.]

[7] A patent was granted in the fifth and sixth years of Edw. VI., to the duke's eldest son, to be restored to as many of the lands as were his mother's, and sold away by the duke without her consent; and that this should be made good to him out of the lands that the heirs begotten of the body of the lady Anne, his second wife, should have. Strype, Mem. II. i. 543.]

[8] Fere millia, MS. Probably a mistake of the copyist for decem.]

[9] Edward, the duke's eldest son by his second marriage, having been dispossessed of all his titles by act of parliament, as above related, continued without estate or title, until created by queen Elizabeth, before her coronation, baron Beauchamp, and earl of Hertford. He died in 1621.]

[10] See his character in Strype, Mem. III. i. 141.]

led, from the reports of others, to entertain a doubt. This doubt, however, I am able to remove. As far as I can perceive, he is a worthy and religious man, nor do I see in what respect he differs from us: so that, even supposing he were to think differently, which I do not believe to be the case, yet as he does not draw us aside, but even goes before us in religion by his own example, there is no danger; and still less so, because their minds are both strengthened by education, and fortified against popery by the presence of us who reside with them. Their mother[1] still remains in the prison, which we call the Tower of London. As she is guarded there with great care, we are ignorant as to what she is doing, or for what offence she is suffering. We hope, however, that she will shortly be set at liberty, because some parties are of opinion that she was not imprisoned for having committed a crime, but to prevent her from committing one; so that when they perceive that the government has no cause for alarm, they will doubtless restore her to her friends. I now think that I have satisfied your inquiries. Wherefore, if I can only obtain this from you, that you will gratify me by writing again, I will cease to give you any further trouble. Farewell. London, Nov. 13.

Your much attached,

THOMAS NORTON.

LETTER CLXVI.

HIEROME MASSARIUS TO HENRY BULLINGER.

Dated at BASLE, *Dec.* 21, 1553.

I was lately at Strasburgh, where I saw and spoke to your son: I inquired after his health, and what company he kept. He frequently visits master Zanchy, from whom I had an excellent account of the youth; and when I took my leave, I told him that I was about to go to Zurich, and that I would convey thither any letters he might have to send.

[1 The duchess of Somerset remained in the Tower during the whole of king Edward's reign. In 1553, £100. was assigned her out of the profits of the late duke's lands, to be paid to the lieutenant of the Tower for her use. And bishop Hoper, formerly the duke's chaplain, was allowed to visit her. Strype, Mem. II. ii. 8.]

He gave me the inclosed, and at the same time requested me, should I meet with a courier at Basle, to forward them by him, as I told him that I intended to go to Berne previously to my visiting Zurich. I therefore send them. I shall leave this place for Berne in about four days, and after staying there two or three days, I shall proceed straight to Zurich, that I may enjoy the delightful society of you all for some little time. But enough of this. Masters Peter Martyr and Zanchy affectionately salute you.

There is no good news from England. We have heard by letter that the most godly archbishop of Canterbury is condemned, first of all to be hung, and then quartered as a traitor[2] to the queen's majesty. All the sons of the duke of Northumberland have also been condemned, and those too of the duke of Suffolk, together with that same Jane who was proclaimed queen; but whether any of them have yet suffered, we do not certainly know. The day before I left Strasburgh, all the baggage of Peter Martyr arrived there by the favour of God, and I hope that he will again obtain a most honourable appointment from the magistrates. He had hired a house, which he was daily supplying with various furniture, in expectation of the aid and calling of the Lord. Public prayers have been had every day for the English church; and it is ascertained that queen Mary[3], the sister of the emperor, is on her way to Calais, whither also that most ungodly Jezebel of England is about to come. It is the general assertion that a marriage has taken place between the king of Spain and Jezebel; and though this was not allowed by the papal laws, it is said that the pope has consented to it upon this condition, that he himself be again recognised as the supreme head of the church in England. We must therefore use diligent prayer on behalf of that miserable and almost ruined church. Farewell, and love me, and salute, I pray you, master Gualter in my name. Basle, December 21, 1553.

Yours heartily,

HIEROME MASSARIUS.

[2 Abp. Cranmer pleaded guilty of high treason on Nov. 13, 1553. The queen, however, pardoned his treason that he might be burned as a heretic, which he was adjudged to be on the 3rd of May following. See Strype, Cranmer, 458. Burnet, III. 341. Soames, IV. 91.]

[3 Queen Mary was the widow of Lewis II., king of Hungary. She was appointed regent of the Low Countries, and died in 1558.]

LETTER CLXVII.

JOHN BYRCHMAN TO HENRY BULLINGER.

Dated *Dec.* 10, 1549.

MOST accomplished master Bullinger, I have received your letter which was very gratifying to me : I should have answered it by my corrector [of the press] whom I sent to master Froschover, if I had received it sooner. If master Froschover needed any exhortation, I could wish for your assistance in printing the English bible : my good friends in England are very importunate, and desirous of its completion. For the emperor had strongly urged upon the English ambassadors the settling a form of religion agreeable to the Interimistic doctrine. But upon due consideration they confirmed by public decrees throughout the kingdom the form established by master Bucer. He had been attacked with very severe illness, but is now recovered, and in the enjoyment of great authority and estimation among the people of London. I have not heard any thing of the Pole, Florian. The maritime cities are urgent with those of Hamburgh, Lubeck, and Luneburgh, respecting an accommodation with the cities of Bremen and Magdeburgh; but nothing will be done, unless they come to an agreement about religion. If your reverence has any thing to tell me about the newly elected pope[1], do not refuse me the information. All persons here seem to be in doubt about him. The emperor has changed his intention, and means to celebrate his birthday at Brussels. He is preparing for a journey into Italy. We are expecting your letter to our archbishop, and also your book, and that of Calvin. Peter Martyr has published in forty-three pages his disputation[2] concerning the sacrament of the eucharist, held at the university of Oxford in England. I would have sent it, had I a messenger who was going to Basle. I have given this letter to master Froschover, that he

[1 Namely, pope Julius III., who was elected Feb. 7, 1550. His predecessor, Paul III., died Nov. 10, 1549.]

[2 For an account of this disputation see Foxe, VI. 298. Strype, Cranmer, 283.]

may arrange the finishing of the bible as soon as possible.
Salute all our friends.

Yours heartily,

JO. BYRCHMAN.

LETTER CLXVIII.

WILLIAM SALKYNS[3] TO HENRY BULLINGER.

Dated at STRASBURGH, *Nov.* 26, [1554.]

HAVING met with so opportune a messenger, most reverend father, to whom I might very conveniently entrust a letter for your reverence, I cannot by any means neglect so favourable an occasion of writing; but will write by him according to my capacity, and detain your prudence, for the time you are reading this, from those matters of far greater importance, in which you are always occupied. And herein I must pray you to excuse my freedom; for I can neither consign to oblivion the extreme kindness with which you entertained me when I was at Zurich, nor anywise refrain from speaking about my master in whose service I now am. The former topic indeed demands a grateful recollection and remembrance, which I hope never to lay aside. And of the latter my duty requires me to say somewhat at this time, and to endeavour now to obtain from your piety, by letter, what I could not so readily accomplish in words when I was with you. For your telling me that from the long intimacy that formerly existed between you and my master, Richard Hilles, you felt inclined to write to him, has very often come into my mind since I left you. For I thus thought with myself; if master Bullinger, who has so much influence, and is so famous for learning, would insert in the letter, which he intends to write to my master, a few words upon fleeing from the abomination of the mass, (by the frequenting of which in England my master is now placing his soul in jeopardy[4],) the result would

[3 William Salkyns was the servant of Richard Hilles.]
[4 It is a curious circumstance that Richard Hilles brings precisely the same charge against one of his servants, above, p. 218.]

be, that either convinced by his argument, or moved by ancient friendship, (which I know has very great weight with him,) he will yield to his exhortation above all others, and consider how he can flee away from such abominable idolatry. I thought too, that your piety would perhaps effect this object without any hint from myself; but on account of my duty and obligation to my master, the love I bear him, and the great anxiety I shall labour under, until I see him extricated and delivered from these defilements, I could not but especially bear the matter in mind, and now, most reverend sir, recall it to your remembrance. To which end I implore and entreat you by Almighty God, that when you write to him, you will not forget this; and I would wish you so to write, that no suspicion may fall upon myself as having persuaded you to do so. But when you have finished what you have to say, I will take care that the letter shall be safely conveyed to him with all diligence. Farewell. May the great and gracious God long preserve your piety to his glory and the good of his church! Strasburgh. From the house of Peter Martyr, Nov. 26, [1554.]

Your most devoted,

WILLIAM SALKYNS,
Servant of master Richard Hilles.

LETTER CLXIX.

WILLIAM SALKYNS TO HENRY BULLINGER.

Dated at STRASBURGH, Dec. 29, 1554.

YOUR two letters, reverend father, written both to my master and to myself, I received, as the saying is, in the very nick of time; for to-morrow, God willing, I purpose to go to Antwerp, whence I will take care that your letters, which otherwise must have been given in charge to some one else, shall be conveniently and safely forwarded. Your letters then were most gratifying to me on two accounts, both by reason of the opportuneness of their arrival, as also of the great and abundant advantage which I certainly hope will be the result. And while I acknowledge this as a singular token of your kindness, so I doubt not but that the great and good God will abundantly recompense you, as it is far beyond my power. But your wishes will be quite satisfied when your letter has answered the end for which you wrote it, and has produced that effect which we both of us so much desired, and which will be salutary to him[1]. In future, however, if you should kindly think fit to write to him, you can send it most conveniently to Christopher Goodman, at the house of master doctor Peter Martyr; and he will take care to forward it, whatever it be, to me at Antwerp. I shall henceforth make use of his assistance, in communicating such news as may occur there, and which it may be desirable for you to know.

Your reverence asks me for news from England: many events have occurred, though of a very painful and distressing character, yet such as the wisdom of God may make use of both for the setting forth of his glory, and the greater consolation of the godly in time to come. Cardinal Pole[2], the legate of antichrist, was some time since received in England, after the popish fashion, with great pomp and solemnity, in the presence of Philip the Anglo-Spanish king, with his queen Mary, at Paul's cross, a most celebrated place in the middle of London; where Gardiner, bishop of Winchester, preached a sermon[3] before a great concourse of people of all ranks, in which with an impudent and shameless forehead he maintained the supremacy of the pope which he had formerly impugned[4], and asked forgiveness (as he said) for his previous error. But when the cardinal addressed the queen, and no human language occurred to him worthy of such a woman, he did not scruple to pervert the holy language of scripture; but addressed the queen on his first interview in the same words

[1 Namely, Richard Hilles. See the preceding letter.]

[2 For an account of the proceedings on cardinal Pole's arrival as legate, and the subsequent submission of England to the pope's authority, see Foxe, VI. 567, &c. Strype, Mem. III. i. 246. Burnet, II. 453. Soames, IV. 256.]

[3 A full account of this sermon is given in Foxe, VI. 577.]

[4 Namely, in his book, De vera Obedientia, published in 1534, to justify the parliament in giving the king the title of supreme head of the church. See Strype, Mem. I. i. 264. Foxe, VI. 139, VII. 594.]

with which the angel saluted the mother of God, and thus the monstrous flatterer begun : " Hail, Mary, full of grace, &c." Shortly after they introduced the primacy of the pope, and proclaimed Pole archbishop of Canterbury, chief primate of England, and introduced him into the senate, or, as we say, the parliament, where the aforesaid bishop of Winchester demanded, with fox-like cunning, the pope's pardon and indulgence for all the peers, who were then disgracefully prostrated at the feet of the cardinal, of which however he said they were wholly undeserving. The queen is said for certain to be pregnant. Philip is not yet crowned, nor is it thought that he will be during this parliament, which will shortly be dissolved, and a new one appointed in due time, in which the papists are in great confidence of obtaining the accomplishment of all that remains for them to wish for. Many individuals are daily committed to prison, and the bishops are still confined in the same place. I have heard from persons worthy of credit, and who have received the information by letter, that the emperor is about to go to Spain, and there wait for the last extremity; but that Philip will come to Flanders, and remain there. This is what I now have to communicate. Should I hear any thing more favourable, I will not fail to let you know. Farewell, most reverend sir, and take in good part this my writing. Strasburgh, Dec. 28.

W. S.

LETTER CLXX.

FRANCIS DRYANDER[1] TO HENRY BULLINGER.
Dated at CAMBRIDGE, *March* 25, 1549.

SHORTLY before I left Strasburgh, I acquainted you with my intended journey. I have not written in the mean while,

[1 Francis Enzinas, known also by the names of Dryander and Duchesne, was born at Burgos about 1515. He became a scholar of Melancthon, and translated the New Testament into Spanish in 1542; for which he was imprisoned, but after fifteen months made his escape, and fled to Calvin at Geneva. He came to England in 1548, to avoid the persecution occasioned by the Interim, and brought with

as I had no opportunity of sending a letter; and I employed
the greatest part of my time in travelling, a thing which was
indeed very irksome to me, till at length, after being long
tossed about, I have fixed my abode in this university, where
I am Greek professor, in which situation I endeavour to
bestow tolerable diligence and fidelity. As I have now
therefore some breathing-time, and an opportunity is afforded
me of sending a letter by persons going to the Frankfort
fair, I have resolved to write to you, that I may renew our
ancient friendship, and give you a motive for writing in
return. I am indeed personally separated from you by a
long distance, but in mind, in studies, in religious opinion, I
am truly most united. For to pass over the religious teaching, in which you excel, I have always ascribed to you the
praise of integrity and faithfulness; and wherever I am, I do
not fail to set them forth, as virtues which I find wanting in
many other nations. But I am of opinion that I am placed
in this corner by the especial counsel of God, that I may be
preserved for some space of time safe from those snares
which tyrants laid for me, even when I was at Basle. But I
am in the hand of God, who can every where preserve his
own; and I ought to render him this obedience, that I may
always be ready to depart from hence, whenever I shall be
summoned by our Captain. With respect to the public state
of this kingdom, you must know, that the parliament is just
ended, in which I understand that, by the common act of
both houses, the lord admiral, the brother of the lord protector, who was said to have been in various ways guilty of
treason, was condemned, and he is also beheaded. I hear also
that a praiseworthy reformation has taken place in matters of
religion: it has not yet seen the light, but its promulgation
is daily expected. It is generally reported that the mass is
abolished, and liberty of marriage allowed to the clergy:
which two I consider to be the principal heads of the entire
reformation, the object of which, as I think, is not to form
an entire body of christian doctrine, and to deliver a fixed
and positive opinion without any ambiguity upon each article,

him letters of commendation from Melancthon to king Edward, and
Cranmer, by whom, as Strype says, (but which seems to be contra-
dicted by this letter,) he was placed at Oxford. See Strype, Cranmer,
580, Mem. II. i. 188.]

but is entirely directed to the right institution of public worship in churches. I hear that there was a great dispute among the bishops about transubstantiation; all which things were managed in secret, like the mysteries of Eleusis, as it would have been impious to communicate such great mysteries to lay-men. I think however that, by a resolution not to be blamed, some puerilities have been still suffered to remain, lest the people should be offended by too great an innovation. These however, trifling as they are, may shortly be amended. But I can say nothing for certain, until I am better informed of the facts. As soon as the act shall be published, I will send it you, if it be in Latin; if not, I will give you an account of every article. You can relate these things to master Hooper, to whom I will now write, if time permit. But I wish he would perform the duty he owes to his country, which is sadly distressed at this time for want of good preachers. And in a calling the most honourable of all others, to lend one's aid to the churches is the duty of a man not only of eminent talent, but of heroic courage; and I think he would do this with dignity. Salute in my name master Pellican and the rest of the brethren, in whose prayers I desire the whole course of my life to be commended to God. Farewell. Cambridge, March 25, 1549.

Yours heartily,

FRANCIS DRYANDER.

LETTER CLXXI.

FRANCIS DRYANDER TO HENRY BULLINGER.

Dated at CAMBRIDGE, *June* 5, 1549.

I WROTE to you lately, before the reformation of the churches was publicly known. A book[1] has now been published, a month or two back, which the English churches received with the greatest satisfaction. A compendium of this book written in Latin I send to master Vadian, on the condition of

[1 Namely, the first book of Common Prayer. See Liturgies of Edward VI. Parker Society's Edit.]

his communicating it to you.   You will see that the summary of doctrine cannot be found fault with, although certain ceremonies are retained in that book which may appear useless, and perhaps hurtful, unless a candid interpretation be put upon them.   But in the cause of religion, which is the most important of all in the whole world, I think that every kind of deception either by ambiguity or trickery of language is altogether unwarrantable.   You will also find something to blame in the matter of the Lord's supper; for the book speaks very obscurely, and however you may try to explain it with candour, you cannot avoid great absurdity.   The reason is, that the bishops could not of a long time agree among themselves respecting this article, and it was a long and earnest dispute among them whether transubstantiation should be established or rejected.   You perceive therefore by this certain proof, that there are no true and solid principles of doctrine in these men, who take a great deal of pains about the most minute and even absurd matters, and neglect those points on which they ought chiefly to have bestowed their attention.   But this is the fate of the church, that the majority overpower the better part; and though many things may be improved, there are nevertheless some causes of offence still remaining.   Meanwhile this reformation must not be counted lightly of; in this kingdom especially, where there existed heretofore in the public formularies of doctrine true popery without the name.   Anabaptists, and other fanatical spirits, are now beginning to shew themselves, and will occasion much trouble to the church; so that we shall ever be in this life under the cross and in a state of most painful disquiet.   Bucer and Paul Fagius have arrived here in safety.   They are at this present time in the palace of the archbishop of Canterbury, and will come hither within two months to give lectures in divinity.   I lately wrote to masters Bibliander and Gesner, whom salute diligently in my name, together with masters Pellican and Frisius.   Farewell.   Cambridge, June 5, 1549.

Yours heartily,

FRANCIS DRYANDER.

LETTER CLXXII.

FRANCIS DRYANDER TO JOACHIM VADIAN.

Dated at CAMBRIDGE, *June* 5, 1549.

GREETING. As no possession in life is more valuable than the friendship of good men, it should be preserved and strengthened with great diligence; and no distance of place ought either to prevent the intercourse and connexion of the good, or to diminish their mutual good-will. For my own part, indeed, most learned Vadian, I retain in mind the most entire and perfect remembrance of you, although you are absent, nor will the most delightful recollection of so dear a friend ever perish from my memory. The same I ask from you, and by the right of kindness and friendship, which you cannot neglect without deserved reproof. You have long since, I suppose, learned the state of things in this country from master Hierome: I now send you the public reformation of religious doctrine which has been effected in this kingdom; in which though you may desire a more judicious and attentive consideration of some important matters, you will nevertheless be tolerably satisfied with the true setting forth of the principal articles of religion. I wish this letter to be communicated also to master Bullinger, that he too may understand, not from general report, but from the truth itself, the alteration that has taken place in England in respect to religion. Should there be any more news, I will send you word. The Germans are allowed to have their own church and preachers in London, where there are said to be four thousand of that nation. Musculus could most ably undertake this ecclesiastical charge, to the great advantage both of himself and of the state. I know what he replied to Bernardine's letter, when he invited him to England in the name of the archbishop of Canterbury; and in my opinion he replied very prudently. But I do not consider that the office of preaching and administration of the sacraments to his fellow countrymen would be attended with any inconvenience. If he feels inclined to a situation of this kind, upon being informed of it I will point out the most eligible way. But I write this for no other reason than because I wish well both to him and to the community. Farewell, with all our godly friends, and let me have from your letters some certain information respecting the state of Switzerland. Cambridge, June 5, 1549.

Yours heartily,
FRANCIS DRYANDER.

LETTER CLXXIII.

FRANCIS DRYANDER TO HENRY BULLINGER.

Dated at BASLE, *Dec.* 3, 1549.

As I hear many reports are here circulated no less painful than groundless, both respecting the realm of England itself, and also our own countrymen, who are professors of learning and religion in that country; I have thought it my duty to deliver you from all anxiety, as I have already done to the people at Basle. It was the persuasion of many persons here, that Bernardine and Bucer had been apprehended together with the lord protector of the kingdom, and that with him the entire form of religion which they had established a short time before, had fallen to the ground. But this is not the fact. I was a spectator of the whole calamity, and not only I saw the external and wretched appearance of the change; but the purposes of the leaders are well known to me, and I will, by God's blessing, acquaint you with them in person, when the times shall be more quiet. I affirm this, meanwhile, of Bernardine and Bucer, that in my opinion they never lived more happily or usefully than at this time. For Bernardine employs his whole time in writing, and this too with a force and rapidity, as he tells me, beyond what he ever did before; and he has a son lately born, in whom he takes great delight. Bucer is created regius professor of divinity, and, as he is now nearly restored to his former health, was to go to Cambridge a day or two after my departure. I say too, that religion is now in a better condition than it was before the imprisonment of the protector. For I have seen a public edict proclaimed by royal authority, and printed, in which is not only confirmed the reformation of which I sent you an account, but it declares that some other matters, yet untouched, shall be reformed according to the tenor of the gospel. This is the truth; and on the fifth of November I was at Lambeth with the archbishop of Canterbury and Bucer, on which day both our public and private affairs were in the same state as I now describe. What has taken place since I know not, nor do I think that either the people of Basle or Zurich can know. For I came as quickly as any one could do, and for no other reason, but that I might publish here this winter what I had written in England, having meanwhile left my family at Cambridge; to whom, by God's blessing, I shall return at the beginning of spring. I wished you to know these things, as being the true state of the case. I would write yet more, if time permitted, or I did not think it better to defer them till my arrival. For I long to see you, whom I have always acknowledged, and in many places openly declared, to be true ministers of God; and to be refreshed with you by the mutual communication of our faith. Salute all the brethren and the church at large in my name. Farewell. Basle, Dec. 3, 1549.

Yours heartily,

FRANCIS DRYANDER.

LETTER CLXXIV.

FRANCIS DRYANDER TO HENRY BULLINGER.

Dated at Strasburgh, *May* 2, 1552.

ALTHOUGH I do not often write to you, I can truly declare that my regard for you is the same as ever. And if I thought there were any occasion, I could prove this by a variety of reasons. For both your eminent virtues and admirable doctrine deserve the perpetual favour of all good men, and teach honourable persons to make a prudent choice of characters whom they may love, and to retain their friendship. And had not these troubles of war kept me at home, it was my intention to have visited you, and to have refreshed my mind, languishing as it is after long continued exertion, by communion with you. But I must remain at my post, and together with the commonwealth encounter the danger that seems to be impending, unless it be by God's mercy averted from us. Since therefore the young Paul Fagius, the son of that most learned man of most honourable memory, is intending to go to Zurich, I determined to write you a short letter, to renew our ancient friendship, and to commend the youth to your friendly notice. He has within these few days arrived from England, in which country he devoted himself to learning; and you may learn from him some particulars respecting the state of that kingdom, which would not perhaps be mentioned in your other correspondence. And since schools here are not very numerous, he intends, by the advice of his friends, to enter himself at your school, to be there instructed in literature and religion. You will provide therefore, with your usual kindness, that he may be placed in some good situation, where he may be able to make much progress both in learning and godliness. He would wish to lodge with master Gualter, who would willingly, I think, afford him room in his house. You will learn from the young man what is going on here; and if God shall grant us some tranquillity, I will either come to you, or write more copiously. Meanwhile, I only say that the prediction which you wrote me at Basle respecting Frisius, has turned out most true. But I was deceived by the appearance of piety which I thought was in the man, since experience has taught me that nothing could be more impious than he was. Salute in my name masters Pellican, Bibliander, Gesner, Lelius, and our other friends. Farewell. Strasburgh, May 2, 1552.

Yours heartily,

FRANCIS DRYANDER.

LETTER CLXXV.

FRANCIS WARNER TO HENRY BULLINGER.

Dated at STRASBURGH, *July* 8, [1543].

GRACE and peace in the Lord! When I heard from master Richard Hilles the great desire that you sometimes feel, most accomplished sir, to be informed of what is going on in foreign parts, and among our English more especially; and when he urged me to acquaint you by letter with the

23—2

disgraceful events that have very lately taken place among
my countrymen; I much hesitated to do so at first, as being
well aware of the rashness of the undertaking in a man like
me, of no learning or talent, presuming to address by letter
you who have long been placed on so high a pinnacle of
learning and popular reputation. But after he had fully assured me of your easy access and courtesy of manners, exhibited
towards persons even of the lowest station and condition of
life; and when you had also yourself (in your last letter to
him, wherein you so kindly salute me) afforded a sufficient
evidence of your kindness; I am at length overpowered, and
impelled both by his request and the state of existing circumstances to take upon myself this office. For the fact itself
seemed to both of us not unworthy of notice, and I considered
it too very greatly to the interest of my countrymen and the
church at large, that you, and those like you, should be
acquainted with it. For inasmuch as, with the Lord's blessing, the most excellent means of protection are afforded to
us by Almighty God against all storms of all times, one of
which is your good opinion, the other, the imploring of
divine aid; the relation of this tragedy may perhaps conduce
in no ordinary degree to our obtaining both of these with
more advantage and effect: inasmuch as when the enemies of
the gospel are pointed out, and the devices, and weapons, and
mode of attack of our adversaries are altogether laid open, it
will be more easy to determine, upon due consideration, how
to oppose them; and we shall also be more ardently excited
to the conflict, when we know that such bitter and shameless
opponents are yet remaining; and again, when we see before
us the recent calamity of the church, we shall be greatly
stirred up to implore from Christ in its behalf, a deliverance
from these evils and anxieties; which may God of his good
pleasure grant to it in due time! Amen.

But now to come to the thing itself: you will receive
herewith inclosed a certain proclamation[1] fixed up in public,
in which the reading of holy scripture is forbidden to men

[1 In the "*Act for the advancement of true religion, and the abolish-
ment of the contrary*," it was provided that every nobleman and gentleman might have the bible read in their houses; and that noble ladies,
and gentlewomen, and merchants, might read it themselves; but no
men or women under those degrees. Strype. Cranm. 142.]

of a certain rank. I had intended to have translated this
decree verbatim into Latin, and have done so, with the omission of some adulatory matter, as far as the thirteenth sec-
tion; but when I had proceeded thus far, I perceived that
for want of time, and by reason of my slowness in matters
of business, I was unable to pursue my design as I had
intended; (for the printed copy did not reach me till Thursday, when I was so engaged in other matters by reason of
the fair, that I had hardly leisure to transcribe it;) so that
I am obliged only to give you the sum and substance of the
remaining sections. It is now your place, with your wonted
courtesy, to take these things in good part; and should there
be any thing unpolished, obscure, or savouring of a solecism,
(as there probably will be,) to excuse it. Farewell. You
are saluted, together with your wife, by master Richard
Hilles and his wife, from whom you will receive a pair of
knives for your wife, which master Henry Falkner will deliver to you. In haste. Strasburgh, July 8, [1543.]

Yours,

FRANCIS WARNER, *Anglus.*

LETTER CLXXVI.

THOMAS KNIGHT TO HENRY BULLINGER.
Dated at VENICE, *Jan.* 23, 1547.

HEALTH in Christ. As I know, reverend and godly
father, that you are not an ordinary acquaintance, but a
most especial friend, of master Richard Hilles the Englishman; I have thought it right, in case the Englishman John
Burcher, an inhabitant of your city, has not yet returned
from his journey to England, to commit to your care this
small portmanteau, that it may reach the aforesaid Richard
with greater safety and dispatch. Should you have paid any
thing for the carriage, John Burcher will repay it upon his
return.

The gospel is daily preached here with greater purity
than in any other places in Italy; and it is ordained by a
decree of the senate, that a sermon shall be preached every
day in the Palazzo maggiore, during the approaching Lent,

a thing that has never been seen since the foundation of the city. The number of the faithful is daily increasing more and more. Your commentaries are daily becoming more esteemed by the Italians; and, were they not so bulky and expensive, no books would meet with a better sale. It will be therefore an act of kindness on your part to continue writing, and to bring forth out of the treasures of your abundance those rare spiritual gifts for that little flock, hungry and thirsting as it is. Should there be any news, you will obtain it from the bearer of this letter. May the Lord, who has chosen you as our pious and faithful pastor, long happily preserve you to us, and grant that we may at length reach together the promised land! Commend me, I earnestly pray you, to Christ, with your other friends. Venice, Jan. 23, 1547.

Your humble son, and servant to command,

THOMAS KNIGHT, *Anglus*, Bookseller.

P.S. You will receive together with this parcel a cask marked with the name of Richard. You will have the kindness to endeavour that it may be forwarded to him by means of some of your friends. You will not receive the jar of figs at this present time, because there was not room for it in the carrier's chest; so I only send you by him a small parcel marked with the two letters R. H.

LETTER CLXXVII.

RICHARD MASTERS TO RODOLPH GUALTER.

Dated at OXFORD, *June* 14, 1551.

THOUGH I have not replied, my dear friend, to your so frequent appeals as well by your friendly letters, as by your repeated salutations, I cannot plead my occupations as an excuse for my not having performed that duty; but you must rather impute it to my being unaccustomed, not to say unskilled in writing, and not to any forgetfulness of you. For I was afraid, unlearned as I am, to intrude upon a man so learned and accomplished as yourself with my unpolished letters. At length, however, I have divested myself of this rustic shamefacedness, as I esteem your sincerity and candour more than I fear my own rudeness of style. You request, and from your kindness towards me readily obtain, that I should inform you of my state and condition. You must know then that, after the lapse of a year or two from your departure hence[1] to your friends at home, a very lucrative benefice was procured for me, which, to speak plainly, because I was not well qualified for the function of a good clergyman, both from my want of sufficient acquaintance with the word of God, and of the duties connected therewith, and also because popery, however it was abolished in name, still flourished among us in reality, I decidedly refused, and resigned into the hands of the patron. Since that time I have devoted myself for ten successive years to the study of medicine, and am now maintaining myself by the practice of it, having become, from a bad divine, a tolerably good physician, like the person mentioned by Augustine, as having become from a bad monk a good divine. But I have not so entirely taken leave of theology, as not to welcome from my heart, value, and delight in, whatever the most godly Bullinger and his like-minded disciple, Gualter, may write.

I had intended to have written to you long ago, but have been unable to do so from having been detained in my native place, and at a distance from Oxford, by a quartan ague of three months continuance; in addition to which, after I had recovered my usual health, my worthy father fell into the like disease, and at length died at the age of sixty[2]. John ab Ulmis, having lately met with an opportuno messenger, at the same time that he informed me of him, has also reminded me of my promise, or rather of my duty; so that I could not allow him to come to you empty, and without a letter, which I doubt not will be gratifying to you, inasmuch as it has proceeded from a heart full of kindness, and which prays for you every happiness. I was eagerly expecting the arrival of your relative, and hoping that from this circumstance some opportunity would arise of doing you a service: but as he is now travelling elsewhere, there is no means by which you can make experiment of my love towards you. Your countrymen are in excellent health, and highly esteemed by all good men for

[1 R. Gualter visited England in 1537.]
[2 A few words are here illegible in the MS.]

their probity of life and conduct : among whom John ab Ulmis, who is as it were their leader, is removed from our society into the king's college, and distinguished by the degree of bachelor in arts ; and, I believe, will shortly take his master's degree, so that he may now be called an incepting master. This individual is a most active defender of the true religion, and a valiant opponent of that which is false; and is not only known to be such in college, but also at court, where he is placed in so honourable a situation by the marquis of Dorset, that it is easier to imagine than express, how greatly he values him for the sake of religion.   But now, as I am called away elsewhere, I must bid you farewell, and pray God long to preserve you in safety to his church.   Oxford, June 14, 1551.

Yours heartily,

MASTERS.

LETTER CLXXVIII.

AUGUSTINE BERNHER[1] TO HENRY BULLINGER.

Dated at BAXTERLEY, *May* 31, 1552.

HEALTH in the Son of God !   Our friend John ab Ulmis being about to return to his native country, earnestly entreats me to write to you; and he is so urgent, that without being considered as regardless of my duty, or as wanting in gratitude, I am altogether unable to refuse compliance.   Your kindness to me, as long as I lived at Zurich with my most revered preceptor, master Wolfius, was exceeding great, and

[1 Augustin Bernher was in the household of bishop Latimer, whose sermons he published with a preface.   He was greatly serviceable to the martyrs in queen Mary's reign, in the letters of whom he is often mentioned.   Robert Glover in his last letter to his wife and children, before his martyrdom, wrote : "As Christ committed his mother to John, so I commit you in this world to the angel of God, Augustine Bernher."   He was instrumental in saving the life of bishop Jewel in the Marian persecution; during which period he, together with Scamler, afterwards bishop of Peterborough, Bentham, afterwards bishop of Lichfield and Coventry, John Rough, a martyr, and some others, acted as pastor of a congregation in London.   In the reign of Elizabeth he obtained a living in the country, called Sutton, [Southam,] and died in peace.   Strype, Mem. III. i. 227, &c. II. 132.]

I am fully sensible of the obligation. But I am now indebted to you more than ever, for your having so diligently and so lovingly commended my sister's son Alexander[2] to some noble personages. I would have you, most learned sir, be entirely persuaded, that without any exception of time or place I shall never cease, as long as I live, my endeavours to promote your interests. I should make this promise more at length, if I thought you could entertain any doubt of my sincerity and gratitude, or if I did not choose to prove it by deeds rather than by a bare assertion. You will fully learn from my friend John my circumstances in life, and the nature of my studies. My master, doctor Latimer, had intended to write to you, but he has to-morrow to undertake a long and arduous journey, so that the excellent old man, and your most loving friend, is unable to send you a letter at this time; but he especially commands me to salute you in his name as honourably and lovingly as possible. Lastly, farewell, and continue your regard for us, namely, Alexander and myself. May God the Father of mercy and loving-kindness faithfully reward you in the last day; and I heartily pray and beseech him long to preserve you in health and safety. Again and again farewell. Dated at Baxterley in England, May 21, 1552.

Your most attached,

AUGUSTINE BERNHER. *Helvetus.*

LETTER CLXXIX.

MATTHEW PARKER AND WALTER HADDON TO THE GUARDIANS OF MARTIN BUCER'S CHILDREN.
Dated at CAMBRIDGE, 1551.

FORASMUCH as master Martin Bucer, of happy memory, when he was dying, committed to our fidelity some particulars of his last will, and appointed us his executors; we, having had due regard to every thing, as far as time and circumstances allowed, have made so much progress in that business, as that we doubt not but that we have satisfied our duties and our consciences. And should your worships desire

[2 This was probably Alexander Schmutz, of whom see Strype, Mem. II. i. 534.]

any farther information upon the case, you will easily ascertain the facts by an inspection of the respective portions into which the property has been divided. But now, since the widow is about to be with you, we have transferred our authority to her; and we have no doubt but that as a mother she will love her children, and that as a wife she will observe inviolate the last will of her husband. We therefore present her to you, together with all the property, and authority to administer the will; that, as we have applied all our diligence to the utmost, yours may follow, and guard this entire will of that worthy and most excellent man, master Bucer, perfect and inviolate in all its parts : this we ourselves have done to the extent of our power, and we feel persuaded that you will do the same. If any other points require a separate consideration, they will appear in the minute accounts which we have made out for this purpose, that, as far as the hurry of Bucer's wife's departure has permitted us, we might leave the whole affair as clear as possible. Farewell, our worthy masters in Christ. In England, Cambridge, A.D. 1551.

Your worships' loving friends,

MATTHEW PARKER,

WALTER HADDON.

THE EXECUTORS' ACCOUNT OF BUCER'S PROPERTY.

The total amount, exclusive of the things not sold or valued, as on the other side, is £380.

Various items[1] *are stated from whence this sum was obtained, as stipend, sale of library, &c. Then two or three small legacies are set against this. The account then proceeds as follows :*

Account of goods which were not sold, but taken home.

Two green carpets. Two long bolsters full of feathers. A red counterpane. All the vessels of tin, weighing xxiv lb. Five brazen pots. A large brass kettle. Eight copper covers. A mortar. Three copper shaving-pots. Two pans of copper. Four upper coverlets, with feathers. Three large, and six smaller pillows. Four bolsters. Five counterpanes, two red, the others green. Two green cloths for covering benches. Twenty-six pairs of sheets. Twenty napkins. Twenty-one towels. Thirty table-cloths. Two black trunks, adapted for journeys. Three long gowns. Two shorter vests, one trimmed with fur. Two pair of hose. Three doublets. A cloke.

[1 The particulars of these sums are not given in the transcript.]

LETTER CLXXX.

THE WIDOW OF BUCER TO ARCHBISHOP CRANMER[2].

[Before *April* 20, 1552.]

I HEARTILY implore for your reverence the grace and favour of God the Father through our Lord Jesus Christ. Although the rank and dignity of your reverence would greatly deter me from writing, yet the exceeding benefits bestowed by your reverence both upon my husband in his life-time, and on myself since his decease, prevent the possibility of my being silent, unless I would be branded with ingratitude. But though I am unable to recount them as they deserve, or worthily to praise them, I nevertheless thank God, and daily implore him on behalf of your reverence, that he who is most rich and most powerful, may regard you with his unexhausted goodness and infinite beneficence. I remember, most reverend prelate, that when I was yet in England, your reverence promised me some document in writing, whereby the gift of his most serene majesty would be confirmed to myself alone, and remain undivided : which indeed seems just and proper, forasmuch as the civil law and statutes allow of the division only of such property as is proved to have been in the possession of the testator previous to his decease ; while that which is given after his death, ought of right to remain entire and inviolate to the party on whom it is bestowed. Since therefore your reverence has promised me this document, and I am in hopes that by its authority and efficacy I may be able to obtain for myself and my little daughter, who very greatly needs it, the donation of his most serene majesty; I beg and implore your reverence to send it me either by Richard Hilles, or in any other way. For if I can procure it, I am in hopes of retaining this donation for mine own use and that of my little girl, which otherwise cannot be effected as being contrary to the laws of our government. But I would not have your reverence suspect that I am seeking this from any motives of avarice, or of envy towards the other heirs, but solely for this reason, that I may be able to aid and supply the slender means and wants of my little girl, who inherits the smallest portion of her father's property, and who has

[2 For Abp. Cranmer's reply to this letter, see above, Letter XVI. and also Letter CCXCIX. in Cranmer's Works, Vol. II. p. 434. Park. Soc. Ed.]

scarcely sufficient to provide her with a decent education and the necessaries of life. For the other children have mostly arrived at such an age, that (to say nothing of their having inherited a far greater patrimony than my little daughter) they may easily gain a livelihood for themselves. Wherefore I again entreat your reverence, that you will take up this cause, and forward me the required document as soon as possible; for which favour, as for all others, you shall always find me grateful, and constantly praying God on your behalf. May the Lord God deign to defend your reverence from all evil, and enrich you with all good things! Amen.

LETTER CLXXXI.

ULRIC CHELIUS AND CONRAD HUBERT TO MATTHEW PARKER AND WALTER HADDON.
Dated at STRASBURGH, *June* 20, 1553.

WE have to inform you, that after the return to us from England of the honourable matron Wibrandis, widow of the late excellent Martin Bucer, a careful account was taken of all the property that he left behind him; after which, according to the municipal law and custom of the state of Strasburgh, a division was made in favour of those parties to whom the inheritance belonged. For which reason both of us having been nominated, I, Ulric Chelius, as guardian to Elizabeth, daughter of the said Martin Bucer, and I, Conrad Hubert, guardian of Nathanael, son of the said Martin Bucer, we acknowledge by this letter to have received that portion which is due to our wards, and to be divided between them by right of inheritance, and that we are therewith well satisfied. Wherefore, reverend sirs, who are appointed executors by Martin Bucer, of happy memory, as far as we are concerned, we release you and others of your trust by this present acquittance, which we have sealed with our seals. Moreover, both of us guardians, together with Windelicius Richelius, the trustee of the widow, most earnestly request your kindness to endeavour, with the same diligence that you have hitherto employed, that the remainder of the debt, which has duly been ascertained by us, may be discharged and forwarded to us at the earliest opportunity: by which you will do us a most acceptable service, and one which shall be requited in due time. Farewell. Strasburgh, June 20, 1553.

LETTER CLXXXII[1].

JULIUS TERENTIANUS TO JOHN [AB ULMIS.]

Dated at STRASBURGH, *Nov.* 20, 1553.

To your very kind letter, my worthy John, which I received on the 18th of September, I now make a brief reply, as I am occupied by various engagements. And first of all, as you desire, I will touch upon the state of England. The most godly Josiah, our earthly hope, died on the 6th of July; of consumption, as the physicians assert; by poison, according to common report, for this is rumoured by the papists for the purpose of exciting a general hatred against Northumberland: nor, to tell the truth, were there wanting many and strong suspicions: but still, if I may say what I think, I believe the papists[2] themselves to have been the authors of so great wickedness; for they have expressed no signs of sorrow, and no inquiry has been made respecting so great a crime. This death, and the other evils which now oppress England, were apparently portended by a dreadful storm, to which I do not remember any equal: it was accompanied by the most extreme darkness, most violent wind, innumerable flashes of lightning, terrible claps of thunder, and an immense body of water, so that our kitchen was entirely flooded. The walnut-tree, planted in the corner at our house, was torn up by the roots, and another tree also was blown down in our garden.

A few days before his death the king made a will at the instigation of Northumberland, by which he disinherited both his sisters, and appointed the lady Frances, wife of the duke of Suffolk, to be his heir. She declined it, and the kingdom was made over to her daughter Jane, who had been married two months before to the lord Guilford, the third son of the duke of Northumberland. Almost the whole of the nobility subscribed to this testament, some of them, as it was after

[1 The original of this letter is printed in Fueslin, Lett. LXXVI.]
[2 Osorius, bishop of Sylva in Portugal, affirmed expressly, in a letter wrote to queen Elizabeth, that king Edward was poisoned in his childhood. But Walter Haddon, who replied to that letter, esteemed this report to be but a fable, raised by idle people, and carried about by such as favoured popery. See Strype, Mem. II. ii. 118.]

wards discovered, with the view of more easily deceiving
Northumberland, by whose advice all these things appeared
to be done, and of concealing the plot they were preparing
in favour of Mary, who is now in possession of the crown:
others added their names from fear of Northumberland, for
you know the character of the man; and some of the better
of them, with the hope of protecting religion, which they perceived would be altogether overthrown, should Mary obtain
the crown; and Northumberland himself excited great expectations that he would favour religion. In addition to this,
the king himself in his will alleged as a reason for disin-
heriting Mary, besides her illegitimacy, the cause of religion.
In fine, he had the assent of almost the whole of the nobility:
Jane is brought down to take possession of the Tower, and on
the same day is proclaimed queen at London, and in the same
week in many parts of the kingdom. Mary, who had most
faithful councillors, by their advice went, as though defence-
less, into Norfolk, where she is received and hailed as queen
with general applause. She forthwith procures herself to be
proclaimed queen in as many places as possible, in all of
which it was stated that the kingdom was being wrested from
her by the treachery of Northumberland; wherefore she
enjoins all her subjects to preserve it to her. Almost the
entire nation rise to her assistance; first of all the people of
Norfolk and Suffolk, and then those of Oxfordshire, Buck-
inghamshire, Berkshire, and Essex. A portion too of the
nobility, who had given in their adhesion to Jane, merely for
the purpose of deceiving her, revolt from her forthwith, and
exert all their energies in behalf of Mary. As to the Lon-
doners, some of them through fear, and others through
treachery, urge upon Northumberland the protection of the
state, and the necessity of seizing upon Mary's person before
her forces can be assembled. He therefore exerts himself
like one whose fortunes are involved in the result, offers
large pay, and engages a soldiery partly unwilling, and
partly treacherous; for they consisted in great measure of
the dependants of those noblemen who secretly espoused the
cause of Mary. Northumberland sets forth, well supplied
with cavalry and artillery, which however were to be turned
against him. Those who remained at London, as though
for the purpose of protecting Jane and retaining the city

in its allegiance, begin forthwith to consult about deserting
her; for which they plausibly allege, partly their fear of the
people, all of whom are flocking to Mary, and partly the
well-being of the kingdom, lest it should suffer from intestine
war. Why should I say more? They immediately proclaim queen Mary, with general applause, and threaten with
death the duke of Suffolk, in case he refuses to leave the
Tower. The good duke yields. They write to Northumberland to dismiss his troops; and being now forsaken by the
people, and betrayed by others, not knowing what to do, with
his soldiers deserting every day, he proclaims queen Mary at
Cambridge, and three days after is carried prisoner in her
name by the earl of Arundel, together with all his sons and
many other noble and influential personages, to London,
where he was received with unbounded abuse on his way
to the Tower.

Thus Jane was queen for only nine days, and those most
turbulent ones. After some days Mary made her entry with
great triumph into the city, to take possession of the Tower;
on entering which she immediately set at liberty the bishop
of Winchester, the duke of Norfolk, lord Courtney, and the
widow of the duke of Somerset. She enrolled the bishop of
Winchester and the duke of Norfolk among her councillors.
The case of Northumberland and the other prisoners was
then brought forward. But after five days the queen removed
to Richmond, during which time Northumberland and two
others[1] were executed. You have heard of the ungodly and
shameful end of Northumberland[2]. The most godly king is
buried; the good archbishop of Canterbury performs the
funeral service at Westminster[3] according to the established

[1] These were sir John Gates, captain of the guards to king Edward, and sir Thomas Palmer, the first accuser of the duke of Somerset. They were executed on Tower Hill, on Tuesday, Aug. 22.
Strype, Mem. III. i. 41. Burnet, III. 335.]

[2] The duke was attended by Heath, bishop of Worcester, whom
he called to bear witness that he was a stedfast believer in the old
religion. See Burnet, II. 376, III. 334.]

[3] Dr Lingard states that it was in compliance with the wish of the
emperor Charles V., who advised her to proceed with temper and
caution, that she suffered the archbishop to proceed according to the
established form at the funeral of her brother. Hist. of England, 4to.
Ed. v. 25.]

form, that is, in English, or in a christian way, with many tears; but before the queen Winchester[1] himself performs the obsequies after the popish fashion. Our preachers, who now perceive the gospel is threatened with imminent destruction, exhort the people to repentance, admonishing them to persevere in sound doctrine. Winchester, in conjunction with other parties who had together meditated the overthrow of the gospel, appoints a most thorough papist, of the name of Bourn[2], as preacher at Paul's cross. A great multitude is assembled to hear what he intends to say. As soon as they hear his blasphemies and falsehoods, they begin to raise a tumult; some of them demanding capital punishment for the man, and others calling out for silence. The lord mayor and some of the aldermen endeavour to quiet the people, but without any effect. Courtney interposes his authority, but is disregarded. Bradford himself comes forth in alarm; but the mob immediately cheer him, and promise silence, because he is a faithful preacher of the word. Some one in the mean time hurls a dagger at that popish preacher, when the mob becomes again excited; and it would have been all over with that wicked knave, had not God by Bradford's instrumentality reserved him to a worse fate. But what thanks do you suppose were given to Bradford for so noble an action?

[1 Within the Tower was a mass of requiem sung for him [Edward VI.] the same day; at which the queen was present, and the bishop of Winchester, with his mitre on, performed it after the old popish form. Strype, Mem. III. i. 31.]

[2 On Sunday, Aug. 13, 1553, Gilbert Bourn, who had been appointed by Bonner a canon of St Paul's, delivered an inflammatory discourse at Paul's cross in praise of Bonner, against the late monarch, and in favour of popery, which so excited the populace that they were ready to drag him out of the pulpit. Bradford, who stood in the pulpit behind him, came forward and addressed the people, and exhorted them to submission and obedience to so good effect, that the multitude, after hailing him with affectionate expression, dispersed quietly. He besought Bradford not to quit him till he was in a situation of safety; and whilst the lord mayor and sheriffs preceded Bourn to the grammar-school house, Bradford and Rogers (another martyr) kept close to him behind, concealing him with their gowns, and thus conducted him safe through the mob. He was afterwards made bishop of Bath and Wells in the room of Wm. Barlow, who had fled on the accession of Mary. See Stevens's Memoirs of Bradford, p. 32. Strype, Mem. III. i. 32.]

Truly such as might have been expected from monsters of this kind. On the next day he was thrown into the Tower, upon no other charge but that, as he could so easily disperse the mob, he must have had some hand in exciting it. Some other preachers are also thrown into the same prison; all preaching is forbidden, and the place is wholly left to papists, who are surrounded by the queen's guard, that they may safely pour forth their poison; and all persons are prohibited[3] from coming near Paul's cross, for fear of raising a fresh disturbance. And because in London there seemed to be some likelihood of a tumult, word was sent by the queen to the lord mayor, that he must either keep the city quiet himself, or that they must look for a guard of soldiers and the deprivation of all their privileges. Then every family, especially of the gospellers, was in great distress. The queen, partly with a view of ascertaining the popular feeling, and partly for the encouragement for her partizans, sets forth a proclamation, in which she declares her adherence to, and protection and support of, popery, and exhorts all persons to conform to it; but nevertheless at that time she would compel no one to embrace it.

The papists, who had been always longing for this most wished for day, dig out as it were from their graves their vestments, chalices, and portasses, and begin mass with all speed. In these things our Oxford folk lead the van; and respecting them I must tell you a little farther. At the proclamation of Jane they displayed nothing but grief. At the proclamation of Mary, even before she was proclaimed at London, and when the event was still doubtful, they gave such demonstrations of joy, as to spare nothing. They first of all made so much noise all the day long with clapping their hands, that it seems still to linger in my ears; they then, even the poorest of them, made voluntary subscriptions, and mutually exhorted each other to maintain the cause of Mary; lastly, at night they had a public festival, and threatened flames, hanging, the gallows and drowning, to all the gospellers.

Master Peter Martyr is forbidden to leave his house; and Sidall[4], a truly excellent man, is ordered to guard against his running away; and thus master Peter has had his own

[3 Part of this sentence is unintelligible in the original.]
[4 See a letter from him to Bullinger, above, p. 311.]

house made a prison of these six weeks. But I, perceiving that the danger was manifest, went to London to seek assistance from my friends. They were now reduced to a very small number, and were so far from being able to assist us, that they were exposed to the greatest peril themselves. Whittingham and I conceive the project of presenting a petition to the queen and council, in which we embrace the entire circumstances of master Peter; how he had been invited over from Strasburgh by the deceased king, and had been recalled by the magistrates of Strasburgh during the last year, but that the king would not give him licence to depart; that the correspondence relative to all these facts was in the royal archives, and that, moreover, many of the council could bear abundant testimony to their truth. We added, that master Peter had committed no offence either against the queen or the laws of the realm; that if his enemies chose to bring any charge against him, he was prepared to meet it; that he now perceived that the queen had no longer occasion for his services, and therefore he petitioned her for a licence to enable him to leave the kingdom. Whittingham and I proceed to Richmond; he presents the petition respecting Peter to the secretary, who, as is customary, lays it on the council table, and bids us wait. On that day nothing was done, we are ordered to come again on the morrow; we are there at the hour appointed, but still nothing is done. We feel at last that we are imposed upon. We agree therefore among ourselves, that Whittingham should return to Oxford and remain with master Peter; for he was now almost entirely by himself, since every one, except only Sidall and master Haddon, had withdrawn from his society. As to me, I remain in London to make what interest I can. At length Whittingham returns after some days: we both of us wait upon [sir John] Mason, who at first declined interposing in so disagreeable a case, and said that he was altogether out of favour; afterwards however he was urgent that master Peter might be allowed to come to London, and plead his cause before the council. He obtains his request, and we have moreover permission to remove all our goods. Master Peter comes to London. He calls upon the archbishop of Canterbury, his ancient and most revered host. Who can express how welcome he was? He had so earnestly wished for his coming, that

he had often importuned the council to that effect, and
offered to give all his property as a security, if they had
any fear of master Peter's running away. When master
Peter arrives, [the archbishop of] Canterbury tells him how
he had caused bills[1] to be posted all over London, in which
he offers to prove that the doctrine, which was received in
the time of Edward the sixth, is sound, agreeable to scripture,
the same with that of the primitive church, and approved
by the authority of the ancient fathers, if only they will
allow Peter Martyr, and one or two others, to be his colleagues. Master Peter commends this act, and says that had
it not been done, he had intended to propose it to him. They
prepare themselves for the disputations. But you should
know, that the popish preachers, when they perceived that
many of our priests were already cast into prison, and that
others had consulted their safety by flight, made a great
boast about disputing with us. But when the placards of the
archbishop were posted up, they began to change their note,
and said that no disputation ought to take place; that they
would abide by the received doctrine; that this was a matter
in which faith, and not reason, was concerned. But those
placards of the archbishop so strengthened the spirits of the
gospellers, that they no longer hesitated to lay down their lives
for the truth; but their enemies were so exasperated by them,
that they instantly brought forward a new charge of treason
against the archbishop, and cited him into court[2], on what
day of September I do not recollect, but I know it happened
on a Thursday. Master Peter then dined with the archbishop,
who after dinner came into his chamber, and informed him
that he himself must of necessity abide a trial; and that it

[1 For the declaration here referred to see Burnet, IV. 331, and
II. 385. He says that the archbishop had drawn up this writing with
a resolution to have made a public use of it; but Scory, who had been
bishop of Chichester, coming to him, he shewed him the paper, and
bid him consider of it. Scory indiscreetly gave copies of it; and one
of these was publicly read in Cheapside, on the 5th of September.
See also Cranmer's works on the Lord's supper, Parker Society Edition, p. 428, where the declaration is printed with the variations of
different copyists.]

[2 On Sept. 13, both Cranmer and Latimer were called before the
council: Latimer was that day committed, and Cranmer was sent to
the Tower the day following. See Burnet, II. 387.]

was certain that he should never see him again: he recommended Martyr to be urgent for his passports, on obtaining which he should depart; but should he fail in obtaining them, he must consult his safety by flight, for that no justice was to be expected from his adversaries. But, O God! who can explore the depth of thy counsels? About five days after the archbishop of Canterbury had been committed to the Tower, a safe conduct, and a most honourable one, was given by the queen to master Peter; who therefore, on the public guarantee, at the persuasion of his other friends, and also bearing in mind the words of the archbishop, commits himself to sea, spreading a report that he was going to Hamburg, when in reality he was proceeding to Antwerp. This he did, to escape the snares of the papists in the dominions of the emperor; and to deceive them more effectually, he wished me to remain some days in London. Meanwhile, after a fortnight's time, having obtained a wind, I set sail towards Antwerp; and on the same day both master Peter and myself arrived at Antwerp in different ships, each of us being ignorant of the other's arrival; which was indeed remarkable, for I thought that he had by this time almost reached Strasburgh. But I think that God intended to relieve us from our mutual anxiety, and moreover, to provide for my expenses. I will not however mention what perils we escaped of the pestilence, of the troops, and of the Rhine; and also what mild weather we had in our journey as far as Strasburgh, whereby any one might conclude that God had certainly recalled us thither. But just as we entered the city, James Sturmius[1], who was waiting for nothing else than the arrival of master Peter, departed this life, and thus we were disappointed of our hope.

But to return to England. During this disturbed state of the kingdom, these persons, namely, lords spiritual, were thrown into the Tower; the archbishops of Canterbury and York, the bishop of London, Latimer, Hooper, Coverdale, and the bishop of Bath. Ponet, bishop of Winchester, and Scory, bishop of Chichester, are also deprived of their bishopricks. The bishops of Ely, Lincoln, and Hereford are removed from parliament; and all the married clergy must

[1 James Sturmius died at Strasburgh, Oct. 30, 1553, after languishing of a fever for two months.]

either relinquish their wives, or be deprived of their benefices. Master Cox is stripped of all his preferment; Marshal has succeeded him at Oxford, and Weston at Westminster. What must we not expect when such men are promoted? Moreover, all the papists, whether bishops or others, are restored. As many as are really godly students at Oxford, have all bidden farewell to that place, and some have already been ejected from our college. The fire of purgatory is now really kindled in England, and the nature of every one's faith is now made manifest. Curtop[2] has wonderfully fallen away; and so has Harding, with numberless others. But the bare mention of this is too painful. The queen was crowned on the twenty-eighth of September[3]. They began parliament on the first[4] of October: transubstantiation was revived; but where is the wonder? no room is left for truth. The deans[5] made a strenuous resistance: their names do not occur to me. Moreover it was enacted in parliament, that on the twentieth of October[6] the popish mass should every where be publicly

[2 James Curtop was a canon of Christ Church, and had been a hearer and friend of Peter Martyr. He recanted in queen Mary's days, and was sworn a witness against Cranmer at his trial. See Strype, Cranm. 285, 536. Respecting Harding, see above, p. 309.]

[3 On the 28th of September, the queen, in order to her coronation, removed from St James's to Whitehall, and from thence to the Tower. The coronation itself took place on Sunday, October 1. For an account of the ceremony see Strype, Mem. III. i. 55. Burnet, III. 390. Soames, IV. 78.]

[4 Parliament was opened Oct. 5. See Strype, Mem. III. i. 57. Burnet, II. 391. Soames, IV. 82.]

[5 Decani, MS. "Among the assembled clergy (in the convocation of 1553) no individuals were present, as it seems, favourable to the Reformation, who were not either deans or archdeacons, dignitaries entitled to seats in the lower house. The members who discovered this feeling were Walter Philips, dean of Rochester; James Haddon, dean of Exeter; John Philpot, archdeacon of Winchester; John Aylmer, archdeacon of Stow; Richard Cheney, archdeacon of Hereford, and another, said to be Thomas Young, precentor of St David's." Soames, Hist. Ref. IV. 103.]

[6 The bill for repealing king Edward's laws about religion was sent from the lords on Oct. 31, and argued six days in the house of commons. It passed Nov. 8, and provided, that from the 20th of December next there should be no other form of divine service but what had been used in the last year of king Henry VIII. Burnet, II. 395.]

restored. On November the fourteenth Jane, formerly queen, together with the archbishop of Canterbury and all the sons[1] of the duke of Northumberland, was arraigned before the judges at Whitehall[2]: you know the place at London. Sentence of death was pronounced upon them all: but a peculiar punishment is intended for the archbishop of Canterbury, namely, hanging, and afterwards the dividing of his body into four parts[3]. But we must expect things yet more atrocious, unless God in his mercy look upon that church, on behalf of which I do not think I have any need to request your prayers; for you know from your own experience, how excellent are the members of Christ in that country. Farewell. Nov. 20, 1553. Strasburgh.

Yours in the Lord,

JULIUS TERENTIANUS.

LETTER CLXXXIII.

MICHAEL RENIGER[4] TO HENRY BULLINGER.

[Without place or date.]

NOTWITHSTANDING, honoured sir, such is the perplexity and pressure of your engagements, that you can scarcely obtain any relaxation from your most important avocations; yet since your kindness and indulgence towards us all is such, that you consider the management and arrangement of our affairs to be a part of your own duty, I have made bold, both from the necessity of the case, and the persuasion of your good-will towards us, to address you by

[1 The lords Guilford and Ambrose Dudley.]

[2 These four individuals were arraigned in Guildhall, on the 13th of November, when they pleaded guilty.]

[3 Cranmer was originally arraigned and condemned for high treason. See above, p. 343, note 2.]

[4 Michael Reniger was on the foundation of Magdalene College, Oxford, whence he was expelled by bishop Gardiner in 1553, and became an exile. He was afterwards made chaplain to queen Elizabeth, and prebendary of Winchester. This letter was probably written at Zurich in 1556.]

letter. And lest it should occasion you any surprise, that
when our houses are so near as almost to be united, I prefer
addressing you through the intervention of a letter, rather
than by a personal conference, you must account for it in
this manner; that I have still about me a kind of foolish
shamefacedness, which shrinks from any discourse and conversation concerning my private affairs; and also, that the
person who is the bearer of this letter is able to explain all
the feelings of my mind just as if I were present myself.
Your kindness will thus briefly understand the whole matter.
Master Burcher, at the persuasion of one of my friends, presented me with twenty florins a year. This assistance I did
not think proper to decline, though I still continued to live
together with the English [exiles;] first, because a necessity
was imposed upon me to receive it: for a certain agreement
and regulation was established among us, that each individual
should exert himself among his relatives and friends to procure for himself such a livelihood and means of support, that
admission might be afforded in their room to the more
indigent English who might be at Strasburgh; on which
account these means of support were not to be rejected by
me, both by reason of the force of that obligation, and from a
regard to others. Added to this, the offer was such, and so
exceedingly liberal, that it was not consistent with my candour or gratitude to refuse it: and in the third place it
affords great assistance to the advancement and convenience
of my studies. In a word, I applied to master Richard
[Hilles,] that, since this allowance was scarcely sufficient for
my maintenance, he would make some addition from the
general fund: he replied, in my opinion reasonably enough,
that the doing so would introduce a most dangerous precedent
to the whole society, and that other persons, from any quarter,
would claim a like addition for themselves. I then asked
him, whether I might be allowed to write to some of my
friends and connexions, who are merchants, respecting their
affording such increase of allowance as might be necessary;
but he thought also that I could not do this without injury
to the society. Being shut out from these means of support,
I had communication with that most friendly man, master
ab Ulmis, by reason of the intimacy which has so long existed between us: the result of which, most accomplished

sir, is, that having tried and explored all possible methods, we have discovered this last resource; for it would savour of too much want of moderation, and intolerable importunity, to expect any increase of allowance from master Burcher, who has, besides, written very doubtfully respecting his own affairs, and that he would continue this pension some time hence, should his circumstances admit. It has occurred to us, that master Vergerius has addressed us with so much affection and sincerity of heart, as to manifest that he was ready not only to do every service in his power to all in general, but also individually to such as may be willing to make trial of his kindness. When we had thought this over together, it occurred to us that we should derive little benefit without the interposition of a letter from you: which I mention on this account, because master ab Ulmis with his usual kindness and good-will towards every one, and especially to myself, is not satisfied with regarding himself as the guardian of my affairs, but is also ready (if only you think it will be of any use) to undergo with me both the trouble of the journey, and the soliciting and management of the business.

The matter now rests with yourself, to whom, as the patron of the miserable men now exiled from England, application has often been made before now, and is now made by myself under like circumstances; and to whom also any thing, whatever it may be, which may procure any alleviation to our misfortunes, is not wont to appear troublesome; that your prudence may ascertain, first, whether it is expedient to try this plan, and in the next place, may aid me, as far as you conveniently can do, with your advice and assistance. This is a short statement. I know how foolish it is to use prolixity with one who is more moved by his own kind feeling and desire to do good than by any private partiality or circumlocution. May the Lord Jesus preserve you to his church, and repay to you out of his riches that kindness with which you daily refresh the bowels of the saints!

Your most attached in Christ,

MICHAEL RENIGER. *Anglus.*

THE

FIFTH ANNUAL REPORT

[FOR THE YEAR 1845.]

OF

The Parker Society,

For the Publication of the Works of the Fathers and Early Writers of the Reformed English Church.

INSTITUTED A.D. MDCCCXL.

The English Reformation.

In One large Volume, 8vo. well bound in extra cloth,
Price Ten Shillings and Sixpence.

THE SECOND EDITION, CHRONOLOGICALLY ARRANGED IN ONE SERIES,

OF

THE ZURICH LETTERS;

OR

THE CORRESPONDENCE OF SEVERAL ENGLISH BISHOPS AND OTHERS, WITH
SOME OF THE HELVETIAN REFORMERS,

DURING THE REIGN OF QUEEN ELIZABETH,

CHIEFLY FROM

THE ARCHIVES OF ZURICH.

TRANSLATED FROM AUTHENTIC COPIES OF THE AUTOGRAPHS, AND EDITED FOR THE
PARKER SOCIETY, BY THE REV. HASTINGS ROBINSON, D.D.

Cambridge:

PRINTED AT THE UNIVERSITY PRESS, FOR THE PARKER SOCIETY.

AND SOLD BY

C. J. STEWART, 11, KING WILLIAM STREET, WEST STRAND; ALSO, BY
PICKERING, DALTON, NISBET, PETHERAM, LONDON; W. CURRY, JUN.
AND CO. DUBLIN; RITCHIE, EDINBURGH; VINCENT, OXFORD; MAC-
MILLAN AND BARCLAY, CAMBRIDGE; ALLOM, YORK; WIGHT AND BAILEY,
CHELTENHAM; GODWIN, BATH; AND ALL OTHER BOOKSELLERS.

☞ This Volume contains the English Translations of both Series of "The Zurich
Letters," excluding a few letters of no interest. Part of a limited impression of the Work
is now offered to the Public, to meet the general demand for it; but the Parker Society will
not again re-print this correspondence. Subscribers to the Parker Society may apply for
copies of this Volume at the Office, 33, Southampton Street, Strand —For them ONLY the
Price will be Seven Shillings.

The Parker Society.

CORRESPONDENCE OF ARCHBISHOP PARKER. The Parker Society being
about to publish a collection of the Letters of Archbishop Parker, it is
earnestly desired that it should be rendered as complete as possible. Any
communication upon the subject, and especially references to letters
of the Archbishop preserved in any public or private repository, or
in any Work not likely to be referred to for such a purpose, will be esteemed
a favor. Communications may be addressed to the Editor, JOHN BRUCE,
Esq., Hyde House, near Stroud, Gloucestershire.

PROCEEDINGS

AT THE FIFTH ANNUAL MEETING OF

𝔗𝔥𝔢 𝔓𝔞𝔯𝔨𝔢𝔯 𝔖𝔬𝔠𝔦𝔢𝔱𝔶,

HELD AT

THE FREEMASONS' TAVERN,

GREAT QUEEN STREET, LINCOLN'S INN FIELDS, LONDON,

ON THURSDAY, THE 14TH OF MAY, 1846.

THE RIGHT HON. LORD ASHLEY, M.P. IN THE CHAIR.

COLLECTS suitable to the occasion were read by the Rev. M. M. PRESTON, Vicar of Cheshunt.

The Report of the Council, and the Statement of the Receipts and Expenditure having been read,

The following Resolutions were moved, seconded, and agreed to.

RESOLVED,

That the Report and Statement of the Receipts and Expenditure, which have been read by the Honorary Librarian and Secretary for General Business, be approved, and that they be received and adopted, and printed for the information of the Members; and also, that the thanks of the Society be given to the President, Treasurer, Council, and Auditors, for their care in preparing the Report and Statement, and their other valuable services during the past year.

RESOLVED,

That the following persons be the Council and Officers for the year ensuing, with power to fill up vacancies :—

THE RIGHT HONOURABLE LORD ASHLEY, M.P.,
was elected President.

SIR WALTER R. FARQUHAR, BART.,
was elected Honorary Treasurer.

GEORGE STOKES, Esq.,
was elected Honorary Librarian.

THE REV. R. G. BAKER.

REV. C. BENSON, Canon of Worcester.

REV. E. BICKERSTETH,

JOHN BRIDGES, Esq.,

JOHN BRUCE, Esq.,

REV. GUY BRYAN,

REV. RICHARD BURGESS

Rev. T. Townson Churton, Fellow of Brasenose College, Oxford.
Hon. William Cowper,
Rev. W. H. Cox, Vice-Principal of St. Mary Hall, Oxford.
Rev. J. W. Cunningham,
Rev. Thomas Dale, Canon Residentiary of St. Paul's.
The Venerable Archdeacon Dealtry,
Rev. W. Goode,
Rev. John Harding,
Rev. Edward Hoare,
Rev. T. H. Horne, Canon of St. Paul's.
Joseph Hoare, Esq.,
Honourable Arthur Kinnaird,
Hon. and Rev. B. W. Noel,
Henry Pownall, Esq.
Rev. Josiah Pratt,
Rev. M. M. Preston,
Rev. Daniel Wilson,

With the Rev. James Scholefield, Regius Professor of Greek in the University of Cambridge,

Were elected as the Council, with power to fill up all vacancies occurring during the year; and

The Hon. Arthur Kinnaird,
Henry Pownall, Esq..
Rev. R. E. Hankinson, and
Francis Lowe, Esq., were elected Auditors.

Resolved,

That the best thanks of the Meeting, and of the whole of the members of the Parker Society, are due to the Right Honourable Lord Ashley, for his invariable attention to the interests of the Institution, and for his kindly presiding on the present occasion, under the pressure of many important public engagements.

Resolved,

That a special vote of thanks is due to George Stokes, Esq., the Honorary Librarian, for his continued zeal and activity on behalf of the Institution, and for his unceasing attention to its interests.

Resolved,

That the thanks of this Meeting be given to the Local Correspondents and other friends of the Society, who have assisted the objects of the Institution during the past year.

THE

FIFTH ANNUAL REPORT

OF

𝕿𝖍𝖊 𝕻𝖆𝖗𝖐𝖊𝖗 𝕾𝖔𝖈𝖎𝖊𝖙𝖞,

INSTITUTED A.D. 1840.

FOR THE PUBLICATION OF

THE WORKS OF THE FATHERS AND EARLY WRITERS OF THE REFORMED ENGLISH CHURCH.

PRESENTED TO THE GENERAL MEETING, MAY THE 14TH, 1846.

" He (*Archbishop Parker*) was a great collector of ancient and modern writings, and took especial care of the safe preservation of them for all succeeding times; as foreseeing, undoubtedly, what use might be made of them by posterity: that, by having recourse to such originals and precedents, the true knowledge of things might the better appear."
" As he was a great patron and promoter of good learning, so he took care of giving encouragement to printing—a great instrument of the increase thereof."
Strype's Life of Archbishop Parker.

THE COUNCIL of the PARKER SOCIETY, in presenting to the members, at the General Meeting, a full Report of the proceedings of the past year, are happy to be able to state that the delivery of the books for the year 1845 has been completed, and the cash account closed. The particulars will be printed in the edition of the Report annexed to the first book for 1846. The amount received was £6966 10s. 11d. and the expenditure £6852 15s. 9d. A balance of £113 15s. 2d. remains, which has been brought forward to the present year.

The volumes for 1845 were five in number. 1. The remaining portion of Bishop Latimer, which contains some interesting letters from the State Paper Office, never before printed. 2. Another volume of letters from the Archives of Zurich, and other repositories in Switzerland, written during the reign of Queen Elizabeth. These are a portion of the documents procured by the Rev. Steuart A. Pears, and supply many chasms in the former series. Upon the value and importance of these communications it is unnecessary to enlarge. 3. and 4. Select Poetry, chiefly devotional, of the reign of Queen Elizabeth. This work was announced in the original prospectus of the Society, but various circumstances prevented it from being given at an earlier period. It is an important publication, shewing how thoroughly the principles of the Reformation imbued the general literature of that age, a fact not apparent in former literary reprints, from which works of a religious nature usually have been omitted. The original intention was to have given only one volume; but the researches of the editor discovered so many authors whose poetry had remained unnoticed, even by bibliographers, that it was found needful to extend the selection, though only giving specimens, to two volumes. The work is also interesting and valuable, by furnishing literal reprints, exhibiting the spelling then usual, thereby shewing how necessary it was to adopt an uniform system of orthography in the other publications of the Society. 5. A portion of the works of Bishop Jewel. This has been called for by the members from the first commencement of the Society, and has never been lost sight of by the Council, who have been unremitting in their endeavours to expedite the publication. Those who are competent to express an opinion, need not to be reminded of the peculiar difficulties to be overcome in properly editing the works of this valuable writer, and the time and application necessary to attain the requisite degree of acquaintance with the numerous authors quoted by him, in some cases existing only in manuscript. The Council have therefore much pleasure in sending forth such an important volume, edited in a manner which they believe will be found satisfactory. If the health of the indefatigable editor be spared, they confidently hope to deliver a further portion in the early part of each of the three next years; and thus they expect to be enabled to publish, what has been in vain desired by the members of our National Church during the last two hundred years—a new and corrected edition of the most important English theological author of the sixteenth century. If the Parker Society completes this publication, its originators and promoters may look with satisfaction on the result of their efforts, even if nothing else were accomplished by their instrumentality.

The Council would briefly allude to the difficulties which must ever attend the editorial proceedings of an effort like that of the Parker Society. Few persons are aware of the very great and peculiar hindrances and difficulties attendant on these labours, and how small was the number of individuals who, at the commencement of the Society, were fully competent to all that is now required in editing such works. Those who possessed the requisite ability and experience were so engaged in other duties, that scarcely any could be found to undertake the work; while, of those few, several have been compelled to relinquish what they had begun, by new appointments of various descriptions engaging all their attention. Each year, however, has added to the number and ability of the editors; while, as in the case of Jewel, more time has been devoted to preparation; so that the Council can now state that their exertions in procuring competent editorial assistance have been far more successful than at first could have been hoped. They have always discharged their trust to the best of their power, and it is hardly necessary to add, that the responsibility for each book must in all cases rest with its editor. They would, however, remark, that in an undertaking of this nature, especially under the peculiar difficulties of this class of writers, the publications should be taken as a whole, when any estimate is formed of the proceedings of the Society. It would be invidious to refer to other proceedings, whether of public bodies or of individual publishers; but the Council feel that it is due to the members, as well as to the editors, and to themselves, to state their full conviction that no similar effort has accomplished so much, and with fewer imperfections. Still they wish that more could have been effected, though they are aware that all literary undertakings will be found imperfect in a greater or less degree, so that objections may easily be raised against any book that ever has been printed.

It may be well here to explain what has been stated respecting the text of the volumes reprinted. The spelling and punctuation have been brought to an uniform standard; but in all other respects they are literal reprints, given as correctly as possible, and, it is believed, far more correctly than is usual in similar publications, with the advantage in many cases of exhibiting a collation of the different editions, and the correction of typographical errors.

As to future proceedings, the Council have learned from experience the impossibility of stating precisely what is to be expected. Another painful instance has occurred in the last year, by the death of an editor who had already devoted some time to the works of Archbishop Whitgift. It is desirable, therefore, only to state, that at the present time fourteen authors are in preparation. Among them is a volume of Archbishop Parker's correspondence, which it is expected will contain many letters that have never been published.

The Council are glad to observe that a continued demand exists for the early publications of the Society, notwithstanding the very large number of 7000 copies actually issued of each book. The two volumes of Zurich Letters in particular have been purchased at high prices when offered for sale, which shews how desirable it was they should be reprinted, to meet the wish of the members, as stated in the last Report, in one volume, and in regular chronological arrangement. This book is now ready, and may be had by subscribers and booksellers for seven shillings, or by the public in general for ten shillings and sixpence. The number printed is limited, and the Council are decidedly of opinion that no other edition should be printed by the Society; nor should any other re-print be undertaken, unless, as in this instance, under very peculiar circumstances, not likely to arise with reference to the books in general.

The researches at the State Paper Office, the Rolls, and some other repositories, both public and private, are in progress, and incur considerable expense; but the results promise fully to justify and repay the proceedings. The Council have much pleasure in reporting the kind willingness with which every application hitherto made by them, for permission to examine such repositories, has been acceded to.

At the commencement of the Society many subscriptions were paid, the names and addresses for which were imperfectly sent, or incorrectly recorded by the booksellers or bankers through whom they were transmitted. Most of these have been traced and the books delivered; but about thirty sets of the publications of the year 1841 remain, the owners of which cannot be found. As nearly five years have now elapsed since these books have been ready, it is considered unnecessary to retain them longer than until the close of the present year. The Council therefore propose, after the first of January next, to place these books in various public libraries destitute of funds for purchase, and that the like course should be adopted with the few sets which may be similarly circumstanced in future years. The books will bear the names in which the subscriptions were paid, and be subject to be reclaimed by the subscribers, or their representatives, if applied for hereafter, and the list of names may be seen at the office.

The Society has more than seven thousand names on its list of subscribers, but many of the subscriptions now due are still unpaid. It is therefore proposed to continue the usual course of subjecting all subscriptions not sent by the first of June, to an additional payment of five shillings, and to allow fresh applicants to have the unclaimed books of 1846, so far as they will go, for the like amount in addition to the original subscription. This proceeding has been approved in former years. It may be well to mention, that several applications for the books of 1844 have lately been made by parties who neglected to pay the subscription of that year, but the books had been previously issued to other applicants, after the notice duly given. And it is requisite now, as in former years, to impress upon the members the importance of paying the subscriptions immediately after the first of January in every year; for the Council cannot otherwise continue to send the volumes to press without considerable and injurious delay. In answer to some inquiries it may here be stated, that the books of the past years now to be obtained at the office, are a few sets of those of 1843 and 1845—with the surplus volumes of the Liturgy of Edward VI. printed for extra applications, and the reprint of the Zurich Letters just completed at the Press. The other back volumes will, however, be found on sale among the booksellers; and in special cases the Secretary will assist the applicant, by pointing out where it is probable they may be obtained.

The objects of the Parker Society have been so fully explained in the Plan and the previous Reports, that nothing need be said respecting them in the present document. The return of twenty-two valuable books for an annual subscription of one pound, paid during five years, also has afforded to the members an assurance of the value and efficiency of the proceedings, so long as adequate support is given.

The main desire of the Parker Society may be briefly summed up in these words of Bishop Jewel: "God give thee the spirit of understanding, that thou mayest be able to judge uprightly: God give thee eyes to see, that thou mayest behold the comfortable and glorious face of God's truth; that thou mayest know the good, and merciful, and perfit will of God; that thou mayest grow into a full perfit man in Christ, and no longer be blown away with every blast of vain doctrine; but mayest be able to know the only, the true, and the living God, and his only-begotten Son, Jesus Christ: To whom both, with the Holy Ghost, be all honour and glory, for ever and ever. Amen."

LAWS OF THE PARKER SOCIETY.

I.—That the Society shall be called THE PARKER SOCIETY, and that its objects shall be—first, the reprinting, without abridgment, alteration, or omission, of the best Works of the Fathers and early Writers of the Reformed English Church, published in the period between the accession of King Edward VI. and the death of Queen Elizabeth; secondly, the printing of such remains of other Writers of the Sixteenth Century as may appear desirable (including, under both classes, some of the early English Translations of the Foreign Reformers); and thirdly, the printing of some manuscripts of the same authors, hitherto unpublished.

II.—That the Society shall consist of such a number of members, being sub-scribers of at least One Pound each annually, as the Council may determine; the subscription to be considered due on the First day of January in each year, in advance, and to be paid on or before such a day as the Council may fix; sufficient notice being given of the day appointed.

III.—That the Management of the Society shall be vested in a President, a Treasurer, and Honorary Librarian, and a Council of twenty-four other subscri-bers, being Members of the Established Church, and of whom not less than six-teen shall be Clergymen. The Council and Officers to be elected annually by the subscribers, at a General Meeting to be held in the month of May; and no per-sons shall then be proposed who are not already members of the Council, or Offi-cers, unless their names shall have been transmitted to the Secretaries on or before the 15th of April in the current year, by nominations in writing, signed by at least five subscribers. And that there be two Secretaries appointed by the Council; also, that the Council have power to fill all vacancies during the year.

IV.—That the accounts of the receipt and expenditure of the Society shall be examined every year, previously to the General Meeting, by four Auditors, two of them selected from the Council, and two appointed by the preceding General Meeting.

V.—That the funds shall be expended in payment of the expenses incurred in producing the works published by the Society, so that every member not in arrear of his or her annual subscription shall receive a copy of every work published by the Society during the year, for each sum of One Pound subscribed, without any charge for the same; and that the number of copies printed in each year, shall be limited to the quantity required for the number actually subscribed for.

VI.—That every member of the Society who shall intimate to the Council a desire to withdraw, or who shall not pay the subscription by the time appointed, shall cease to be a member of the Society; and no member shall, at any time, incur any liability beyond the annual subscription.

VII.—That, after the commencement of the proceedings, no rule shall be made or altered excepting at a General Meeting, and after notice of the same has been communicated to the Members by circulars, or by adver-tisement in two London daily Newspapers, at least fourteen days before the General Meeting.

VIII.—Donations and Legacies will be thankfully received; the amount of which shall be expended by the Council in supplying copies of the publications to clerical, or other public libraries, destitute of funds to purchase the same, and for such other purposes, connected with the objects of the Society, as the Council may determine.

AN ABSTRACT OF THE RECEIPTS AND OF

FOR THE

RECEIVED.	£	s.	d.
Balance brought from 1844 Account	15	12	5
Amount Received for the Subscriptions of Members for the Year 1845, and previous Years	6891	9	9
Amount Received for Subscriptions for future years....	8	0	0
Dividend on Stock..............................	24	10	5
From Exchequer Bill Account for 1845, being Balance of Premium and Interest	9	3	11
Second Donation from Rev. Martin S. Wall	10	0	0

Total £6958 16 6

THE EXPENDITURE OF THE PARKER SOCIETY,
YEAR 1845.

PAID.	£.	s.	d.
Paid for Printing and Paper of the books published by the Society for 1845	3555	1	10
For Binding and Delivery	1618	2	7
For Volumes purchased to complete sets	21	15	6
For Editorial Expenses	631	13	8
For Insurance from Fire	5	12	6
For Books purchased, for the Library, Copy for Printing and use of Editors	119	6	0
For Transcripts, and Examining Libraries and Public Offices	107	11	5
For Printing Plans, Reports and Circulars, and for Advertisements	137	13	6
For Rent of Office, Salary of Secretary, and Wages of Clerks and Porters	487	10	4
For Furniture and Fittings	38	14	4
For Stationery and Account Books	25	16	5
For Incidentals, including postage, carriage, coals, and various petty expenses (deducting re-payment of £7 14s. 5d. from T. Champion)	96	3	3
Balance carried to 1846	113	15	2
Total	£6958	16	6

HENRY POWNALL, } *Auditors.*
FRANCIS LOWE.

THE FOLLOWING NAMES, WITH OTHERS, IN THE WHOLE

SEVEN THOUSAND,

ARE IN THE LIST OF SUBSCRIBERS TO

The Parker Society.

HER MOST GRACIOUS MAJESTY ADELAIDE, QUEEN DOWAGER.
HIS ROYAL HIGHNESS THE PRINCE ALBERT.
HIS MAJESTY THE KING OF PRUSSIA.
HER ROYAL HIGHNESS THE DUCHESS OF KENT.

His Grace the Duke of Devonshire.—His Grace the Duke of Manchester.—His Grace the Duke of Sutherland.—His Grace the Duke of Roxburghe.

The Most Honourable the Marquesses of Bute, Cholmondeley, Conyngham, Downshire, Northampton, Ormonde, and Salisbury.

The Right Honourable the Earls of Cavan, Chichester, Clancarty, De Grey, Essex, Galloway, Howe, Jermyn, Nelson, Rosse, and Spencer.

The Right Honourable and Rev. Lord Wriothesley Russell.

The Right Honourable Lord Viscounts Adare, Alford, Arbuthnott, Campden, De Vesci, Fordwich, Hill, and Lorton.

The Right Honourable the Lords Ashley (President), and Lindsay.

The Right Honourable and Very Reverend Lord Edward Chichester.—The Right Honourable Lord Henry Cholmondeley.—The Right Honourable and Reverend Lords Charles Thynne, John Thynne, Arthur Hervey, and George A. Hill.

The Right Honourable and Right Reverend the Lord Bishop of London.—The Right Reverend the Lords Bishops of Durham, Winchester, Chester, Chichester, Hereford, Lichfield, Lincoln, Llandaff, Peterborough, Ripon, Rochester, Worcester, Oxford, and of Sodor and Man.

The Right Honourable and Right Reverend the Lords Bishops of Clogher and of Meath.—The Honourable and Right Reverend the Lord Bishop of Killaloe and Clonfert.—The Right Reverend the Lords Bishops of Down and Connor, of Ossory and Ferns, and of Cashel and Waterford.

The Right Reverend the Lords Bishops of Calcutta, Bombay, Colombo, Toronto, Guiana, Australia, and of Tasmania.

The Right Reverend the Bishops of Ohio, New Jersey, South Carolina, Virginia, Maryland, Georgia, and of Delaware.

The Right Honourable the Lords Bolton, Calthorpe, Farnham, Littleton, Rayleigh, and Teignmouth.

Her Grace the Duchess of Argyle.—Right Honourable the Countess of Annesley. Right Honourable Viscountess Valentia.—Right Honourable Lady Ward, &c.

The Right Honourable the Lord Chief Justice of Ireland.—The Right Honourable Lord Justice Clerk, Scotland.—The Honourable Mr. Justice Jackson. The Chevalier Bunsen.—The Right Honourable Henry Goulburn, Chancellor of the Exchequer, M.P. for the University of Cambridge.—The Right Honourable W. E. Gladstone, M.P.

The Honourable and Very Reverend the Deans of Norwich, Windsor and Wolverhampton, and Manchester.—The Very Reverend the Deans of Chester, Durham, Gloucester, Peterborough, Salisbury, and Winchester.—The Deans and Chapters of Lichfield, Worcester, &c.

The Right Honourable and Very Reverend the Dean of Raphoe.—The Honourable and Very Reverend the Dean of Clogher.—The Very Reverend the Deans of Cloyne, Connor, Cork, Derry, Cashel, Emly, St. Patrick, Ossory, Kildare, Kilmacduagh, and Limerick.

The Honourable and Worshipful T. W. Law, Chancellor of Bath and Wells. —The Worshipful H. Raikes, Chancellor of Chester; John N. Woodruffe, Chancellor of Cork; E. T. M. Phillips, Chancellor of Gloucester; F. R. Sandys, Chancellor of Ossory; Marsham Argles, Chancellor of Peterborough.

The Venerable Archdeacons Bather, Berners, Bevan, Browne, Buckle, Davys, Dealtry, Hare, Hodson, Hoare, Law, Lyall, Mac Donald, Philpot, Shirley Spooner, C. Thorp, and J. R. Wilberforce.

The Venerable Archdeacons Bell, Beresford, Creery, Digby, Mant, Monsell, Oldfield, Power, Stuart, Verschoyle and St. George.

Reverend Dr. Symons, Warden of Wadham Coll. Oxford, and Vice Chancellor of the University.—Reverend Dr. Phelps, Master of Sidney Sussex Coll. Cambridge, and Vice Chancellor of the University.—Reverend Dr. Graham, Master of Christ Coll. Cambridge.—Reverend Dr. Archdall, Master of Emmanuel Coll. Cambridge.—Reverend Dr. Tatham, Master of St. John's Coll. Cambridge.—Reverend Dr. Plumtre, Master of University Coll. Oxford.—Reverend Dr. Fox, Provost of Queen's Coll. Oxford.—Reverend Dr. Cotton, Provost of Worcester Coll. Oxford.—Reverend Dr. Jeune, Master of Pembroke Coll. Oxford.—Reverend Dr. Thackeray, Provost of King's Coll. Cambridge.—Reverend Dr. Ainslie, Master of Pembroke Hall, Cambridge.—Reverend Dr. French, Master of Jesus Coll. Cambridge.—Joshua King, Esq. D.C.L. President of Queen's Coll. Cambridge.—Reverend Dr. Procter, Master of Catherine Hall, Cambridge.—Reverend Dr. Webb, Master of Clare Hall, Cambridge.—Reverend Dr. Hampden, Principal of St. Mary's Hall, and Regius Professor of Divinity, Oxford.—Reverend Dr. Cramer, Principal of New Inn Hall, Oxford.—Reverend E. Cardwell, Principal of St. Alban's Hall, Oxford.

The Reverend Dr. Sadleir, Provost of Trinity Coll. Dublin.—The Venerable Archdeacon Thorp, Warden of the University of Durham.—The Very Reverend Dr. Lee, Principal of the University of Edinburgh.—Reverend J. Wheeler, President of the University of Vermont, U. S.—Rev. R. P. Buddicom, Principal of St. Bees College.—Reverend Dr. Williamson, Head Master of Westminster School.—Reverend Dr. Tait, Head Master of Rugby School, &c. &c.

LIBRARIES.—The Royal Library, Berlin.—Balliol Coll. Oxford.—Gonville and Caius, Pembroke, and Queen's Coll. Cambridge.—Wadham and Worcester Coll. Oxford.—Trinity Coll. Dublin.—University of Edinburgh.—King's Coll. London.—Advocates' Library, and Library of the Writers to the Signet, Edinburgh.—St. Bees Coll.—Cathedrals of Chester and Cashel.—The London Institution.—The London Library.—The Chetham Library, Manchester; and many other Collegiate, Public, and School Libraries, &c. &c.

THE COUNCIL AND OFFICERS FOR 1845-6.

President.
THE RIGHT HONOURABLE LORD ASHLEY, M.P.

Treasurer.
SIR WALTER R. FARQUHAR, BART.

Council.
REV. R. G. BAKER.—REV. C. BENSON, Canon of Worcester.—REV. E. BICKERSTETH.—JOHN BRIDGES, ESQ.—JOHN BRUCE, ESQ.—REV. GUY BRYAN.—REV. RICHARD BURGESS.—REV. T. TOWNSON CHURTON, Fellow of Brasenose College, Oxford.—HON. WILLIAM COWPER.—REV.W. H. COX, Vice Principal, St. Mary Hall, Oxford.—REV. J. W. CUNNINGHAM.—REV THOMAS DALE, Canon Residentiary of St. Paul's.—VEN. DR. DEALTRY, Archdeacon of Surrey.—REV. W. GOODE.—REV. JOHN HARDING.—REV. EDWARD HOARE. —JOSEPH HOARE, ESQ.—REV. T. H. HORNE, Canon of St. Paul's—HON. ARTHUR KINNAIRD.—HON. and REV. B. W. NOEL.—HENRY POWNALL, ESQ. —REV. JOSIAH PRATT.—REV. M. M. PRESTON.—REV. DANIEL WILSON.

Honorary Librarian.
GEORGE STOKES, ESQ., Cheltenham.

Editorial Secretary.
REV. JAMES SCHOLEFIELD, Regius Professor of Greek in the University of Cambridge

Secretary for General Business.
WILLIAM THOMAS, ESQ. at the Office of the Parker Society, 33, Southampton Street, Strand, London.

Auditors.
HON. A. KINNAIRD, REV. R.E HANKINSON, H.POWNALL, ESQ.& F.LOWE,ESQ.

Bankers.
MESSRS. HERRIES, FARQUHAR, AND Co., No. 16, St. James's Street.

REGULATIONS FOR DELIVERY OF THE WORKS PUBLISHED BY THE SOCIETY.

I.   They will be delivered, free of expense, at the Office, or within three miles of the General Post Office, London.

II.   They will be sent to any place in England beyond the distance of three miles from the General Post Office, by any conveyance a Member may point out.   In this case the parcels will be booked at the expense of the Society, but the carriage must be paid by the Members to whom they are sent.

III. They will be delivered, free of expense, at any place in London which a Member, resident in the country, may name.

IV.   They may remain at the Office of the Society until the Members apply for them, but, in that case, the Society will not be responsible for any damage which may happen from fire, or other accident.

V.   They will be sent to any of the Correspondents, or Agents of the Society, each Member paying the Correspondent or Agent a share of the Carriage of the parcel in which the books were included.   Arrangements are made for the delivery on this plan, in many of the cities and large towns where a sufficient number of members reside; *and it will be esteemed a favour if gentlemen who are willing to further the objects of the Parker Society, by taking charge of the books for the Members in their respective neighbourhoods, will write to the Office on the subject.*

VI.   They will be delivered in Edinburgh and Dublin as in London, and forwarded from thence to Members in other parts of Scotland and Ireland, in the same manner as is mentioned above with respect to England.

A List of the Works

ALREADY PUBLISHED BY THE PARKER SOCIETY.

FOR THE YEAR 1841.

The Works of Bishop Ridley.
The Sermons and other Pieces of Archbishop Sandys.
The Works of Bishop Pilkington.
The Works of Roger Hutchinson.

FOR THE YEAR 1842.

The Examinations and Writings of Archdeacon Philpot.
Christian Prayers and Meditations.
Letters of Bishop Jewell, and others, translated from the Originals in the Archives of Zurich, (1st Series).
The Writings of Archbishop Grindal.
Early Writings of the Rev. T. Becon, Chaplain to Archbishop Cranmer, and Prebendary of Canterbury.

FOR THE YEAR 1843.

Fulke's Defence of the English Translation of the Bible.
Early Writings of Bishop Hooper.
Writings of Archbishop Cranmer on the Lord's Supper.
The Catechism and other pieces of Becon.

FOR THE YEAR 1844.

The Liturgies, Primer and Catechism of the Reign of Edward VI.
Writings of Bishop Coverdale.
Sermons of Bishop Latimer.
The Flower of Godly Prayers, and other Pieces of Becon.

FOR THE YEAR 1845.

Second Series of Letters from the Archives of Zurich.
Writings of Bishop Jewel.
Remains of Bishop Latimer.
Devotional Poetry of the Reign of Queen Elizabeth.

Preparing for publication in the Year 1846, and following Year, as the subscriptions allow, and the volumes can be completed.

A further portion of Bishop Jewel.
Another portion of Bishop Coverdale.
Calfhill's Answer to Martiall's Treatise on the Cross.
Writings of John Bradford.
The Remains of Archbishop Cranmer.
Liturgies and Occasional Services of Queen Elizabeth.
Original Letters relative to the English Reformation.

List of Works

In Royal Octavo.—Becon*—Cranmer*—Jewel*—Whitgift—Parker—Bullinger's Decades—Alley—Whitaker.

In Demy Octavo.—Ridley*—Pilkington*—Philpot*—Fulke*—Nowell—Coverdale*—Curtis—Bale—Tyndale—Fryth—Barnes—Sandys*—Hutchinson*—Grindal* —Hooper* — Latimer* — Bradford — Cooper—Fox— Taverner—Calfhill, and others; Royal Authors, Documents of the Reign of Edward VI.*—Documents relative to the Reign of Queen Mary—Documents of the Reign of Queen Elizabeth—Letters from the Archives of Zurich* (three series)—Letters and Documents from Archbishop Parker's MSS. in C.C. C.C.—Occasional Services of Queen Elizabeth's Reign—The Homilies—Some volumes of Sermons preached before King Edward VI. and Queen Elizabeth, at St. Paul's Cross, in the Universities, and on various occasions —Several volumes of Tracts and small Pieces—Various Letters and Documents— Reformatio Legum Ecclesiasticarum—Queen Elizabeth's Prayer Book—Devotional Poetry of the Sixteenth Century*—Christian Meditations and Prayers, and some other Devotional Manuals.*

It is calculated that the Works above stated may be included in about 18 or 20 volumes royal octavo, and 50 volumes demy, and that the whole may be completed in sixteen years from the commencement. A few pieces of peculiar interest may probably be printed as fac similes. The list, however, is not to be considered as definitely settled. It is not possible to state the order in which the volumes will appear, but each will be complete in itself. The whole series (fully equal to a hundred volumes of demy octavo), when completed, will have cost the original subscribers only about sixteen pounds, paid in as many years, and in proportion for parts of the series.

The Parker Society is also engaged in a complete examination of the State Paper Office, and is under engagement to print the Letters and Documents from that Repository in a separate form, by the express desire of Her Majesty's Government.

The Works of the Authors to whose names this mark (*) is appended, have been already printed, in whole or in part, and delivered to the Subscribers.

All correspondence respecting subscriptions, or the delivery of the Books, is to be addressed to

WILLIAM THOMAS, Esq., *Secretary for General Business,*

To whom all Bank and Post Office Orders are to be made payable,

AT THE OFFICE OF THE PARKER SOCIETY, 33, SOUTHAMPTON STREET, STRAND, LONDON.

Printed at the Milton Press,
corner of Charing Cross Hospital, Strand.